British Politics

FOR

DUMMIES®

British Politics

FOR DUMMIES®

by Julian Knight

A John Wiley and Sons, Ltd, Publication

British Politics For Dummies®

Published by
John Wiley & Sons, Ltd
The Atrium
Southern Gate
Chichester
West Sussex
PO19 8SQ
England

Email (for orders and customer service enquires): cs-books@wiley.co.uk

Visit our Home Page on www.wiley.com

Copyright © 2010 John Wiley & Sons, Ltd, Chichester, West Sussex, England

Published by John Wiley & Sons, Ltd, Chichester, West Sussex

For general information on our other products and services, please contact our Customer Care Department within the US at 877-762-2974, outside the US at 317-572-3993, or fax 317-572-4002.

For technical support, please visit www.wiley.com/techsupport.

Wiley also publishes its books in a variety of electronic formats. Some content that appears in print may not be available in electronic books.

British Library Cataloguing in Publication Data: A catalogue record for this book is available from the British Library

ISBN: 978-0-470-68637-9

Printed and bound in Great Britain by Bell & Bain Ltd, Glasgow

10 9 8 7 6 5 4

WILEY

About the Author

Julian Knight was born in 1972 in Chester. He was educated at the Chester Catholic High School and later Hull University, where he obtained a degree in History.

Julian has been a journalist since 1998 and has written for the *Guardian*, Financial Times Group and many other publications.

From 2002 to 2007 he was the personal finance and consumer affairs reporter for BBC News. Since 2007 he has been the Money and Property editor of the *Independent on Sunday* and has won many industry awards for his journalism. Julian is the author of *The British Citizenship Test For Dummies*, *Wills, Probate & Inheritance Tax For Dummies*, *Retiring Wealthy For Dummies* and *Cricket For Dummies*.

He currently lives in west London with a large mortgage.

Dedication

To Liz Barclay for her love and support over many years and to Rachael Chilvers and the team at Wiley for their patience, energy and enthusiasm.

Publisher's Acknowledgments

We're proud of this book; please send us your comments through our Dummies online registration form located at www.dummies.com/register/.

Some of the people who helped bring this book to market include the following:

Acquisitions, Editorial, and Media Development

Project Editor: Rachael Chilvers

Content Editor: Jo Theedom

Commissioning Editor: Wejdan Ismail

Production Manager: Daniel Mersey

Development Editor: Kathleen Dobie

Copyeditor: Kate O'Leary

Proofreader: David Price

Special Help: Helen Caunce

Cover Photos: © Stephen Bond / Alamy

Cartoons: Ed McLachlan

Composition Services

Project Coordinator: Lynsey Stanford

Layout and Graphics: Nikki Gately, Christine Williams

Proofreaders: Rebecca Denoncour, Melanie Hoffman, Lindsay Littrell, Lauren Mandelbaum

Indexer: Ty Koontz

Contents at a Glance

Introduction *1*

Part 1: The Basics of Politics *5*

Chapter 1: Taking in the Political Universe 7

Chapter 2: Understanding Why Politics and Politicians Are Important 21

Chapter 3: Looking at Participatory Democracy 35

Chapter 4: Examining Political Ideologies 49

Chapter 5: Forming the British Political State 67

Part 11: Elections and Britain's Parties *81*

Chapter 6: Counting the Votes: Differing Electoral Systems 83

Chapter 7: Voting Behaviour and Trends 99

Chapter 8: Homing in on Political Parties 117

Chapter 9: Piling On the Pressure Groups 141

Chapter 10: Scrutinising Politics and the Media 161

Part 111: The Ins and Outs of Parliament *179*

Chapter 11: Examining Britain's Constitution 181

Chapter 12: Britain's Parliamentary Democracy 195

Chapter 13: Gazing at the Summit: The PM and Cabinet 215

Chapter 14: Assessing Ministers and Civil Servants 231

Chapter 15: Taking in the Courts and Judiciary 243

Chapter 16: Laying Bare Local Government and Devolution 255

Chapter 17: Joining the Lawmakers: Becoming a Politician 271

Part 1V: Politics Worldwide *283*

Chapter 18: Understanding Britain's Place in the World 285

Chapter 19: Taking In the International Stage 295

Chapter 20: Expanding Horizons: Europe and the EU 309

Chapter 21: Leading the Free World: US Politics 327

Part V: The Part of Tens 345

Chapter 22: Ten Great Prime Ministers 347

Chapter 23: Ten Major Political Scandals 355

Chapter 24: Ten Political Events that Shaped the Modern World 363

Chapter 25: Ten Political Trends for the Future 371

Index 377

Table of Contents

Introduction *1*

About This Book 1
Foolish Assumptions 1
How This Book Is Organised 2
    Part I: The Basics of Politics 2
    Part II: Elections and Britain's Parties 2
    Part III: The Ins and Outs of Parliament 2
    Part IV: Politics Worldwide 3
    Part V: The Part of Tens 3
Icons Used in This Book 3
Where to Go from Here 4

Part 1: The Basics of Politics *5*

Chapter 1: Taking in the Political Universe 7

Understanding the Difference between Local and National Politics 8
Splitting the Difference: The Devolved Parliament and Assemblies 9
Evolving to Democracy: A Very British Story 9
Assessing the Health of British Democracy 10
Paying Homage to the 'Mother of Parliaments' 12
Introducing the Players in the British Political System 13
    Gazing at the political summit: The central role of
       the prime minister 14
    Declining importance of the MP 15
    Checking the power of the politicians: The judiciary 16
    Mixing in the monarch 17
Coming under Greater Scrutiny: Politics in the Media 17
Britain: Making Its Way in the European Union 18
Looking Further Afield: The UK and the Wider World 19

Chapter 2: Understanding Why Politics and Politicians Are Important 21

Looking at Different Types of Authority 22
Deciphering the Ultimate Purpose of Politics 23
Gauging the Role of Politicians 24
    Making the law 24
    Changing the constitution and the way government works 24
    Ensuring a more controlled state 25
    Galvanising the country in times of crisis 25
    Listening to constituents 26
    Working for the good of the country 26

Tackling the Big Issues: The Current Challenges Facing Politicians.......27
Keeping up living standards – it's the economy, stupid!..............27
Saving the planet..29
Bringing an end to world poverty..31
Fighting terrorism...32
Reckoning with the decline of Western dominance.....................33
Taking Matters into Your Own Hands: Becoming an Activist................33

Chapter 3: Looking at Participatory Democracy..................35

Understanding What Qualifies as a Democracy 35
Starting with Athenian direct democracy..............................37
Getting into representative democracy..................................38
Homing in on British Democracy 39
Putting the monarchy in its place...40
Expanding the franchise 40
Throwing digital democracy into the mix 41
Understanding the Rights that Come with British Citizenship.............43
Evaluating the Pros and Cons of UK Democracy............................44
Looking at the strengths 44
Recognising the weaknesses 45
Being a Citizen..46
Getting involved...46
Gauging voter apathy and the reasons for it.................................47

Chapter 4: Examining Political Ideologies 49

Understanding What an Ideology Is 49
Moderating ideologies: The British way 49
Liberalising the world: The march of the western
    democratic model 50
Focusing on Freedom with Liberalism...51
Joining Together for the Greater Good: Socialism in the UK................53
Focusing on the successes of socialism 54
Rebranding socialism: New Labour.......................................54
Stirring things up: Revolutionary socialism 56
Looking far left: Marxism and communism............................56
Keeping with Tradition: Conservatism 57
Uniting under one nation conservatism 58
Reforming with a small 'r' 58
Changing conservatism: The Thatcher revolution.................59
Examining Alternative Politics...59
Focusing on the far right: Fascism...60
Looking into the darkness: Totalitarian regimes...........................60
Looking to the heavens: Theocracy 61
Pulling everything apart: Anarchism.....................................61
Releasing the bonds: Feminism...62
Saving the planet: Environmentalism.....................................63
Understanding Why the UK Doesn't Do Extremism.........................64

Chapter 5: Forming the British Political State 67

Getting to Grips with the Normans: From Conquest to Magna Carta.....67
Doing the Splits: Church and State Clash..68
Gearing Up for Revolution: Parliament Takes on the King and Wins 69
    Working hand in hand...70
    Chafing under Charles I and enduring Cromwell...........................70
    Reaping the benefits of the Glorious Revolution...........................70
Throwing Political Parties into the Mix...71
Ending the Power of the Lords 72
Expanding the Franchise: Democracy Arrives in Britain 72
    Earning a stake...73
    Recognising the rights of women..74
Switching Parties: The Ebb and Flow of Party Influence 74
    Making a play for power: The Labour Party is born and thrives...74
    Playing musical chairs: Labour and Tories swap power 75
    Leaving out the Lib Dems 76
Concentrating Power in the Hands of the Prime Minister 77
Breaking Up the Union: Scotland and Wales to Go It Alone? 78
Encroaching on Britain's Turf: The European Union................................80

Part II: Elections and Britain's Parties *81*

Chapter 6: Counting the Votes: Differing Electoral Systems 83

Listing the Big UK Elections 83
Coming Up On the Rails: The First-Past-the-Post System.......................85
    Looking at the advantages 87
    Taking in the disadvantages..87
Securing Over 50 Per Cent of the Vote: Majority Electoral Systems.......88
    Laying bare the two-ballot system 89
    Playing the alternative vote system card 89
    Throwing in the supplementary vote system 90
Examining Proportional Representation 90
    Refining PR: Single transferable vote 91
    Varying PR: Candidate list system..91
    Dividing in the D'Hondt method 92
Looking North and West to the Additional Member System 94
Preserving the Status Quo Rather than Rallying for Reform 95

Chapter 7: Voting Behaviour and Trends 99

Looking at Who Can and Can't Vote..100
Understanding Voter Turnout 100
    Declining voter turnout...101
    Declining local democracy 102
    Reversing declining voter turnout...103

Considering What Sways Voters...104
    Taking in the big issues..105
    Throwing personality into the mix: The leadership wild card 106
    Looking at the voters themselves..................................107
Enticing Voters to Vote: Party Strategies 111
    Appealing to the core vote...112
    Broadening party appeal 112
Gazing at Election Campaigning 114
Glancing at the Effects of Media Bias....................................114

Chapter 8: Homing in on Political Parties 117

Understanding Political Parties and How They Operate.......................117
    Recognising the role of the major UK parties 118
    Forming party policy: The approach of Conservative,
        Labour and Lib Dem 118
    Choosing and following the leader – and other senior
        party figures...119
    Whipping up discipline: Keeping party members on
        the same page..121
    Looking at the role of the whips 123
    Living it up at party conferences 125
    Forgoing party to form a national government.............126
Looking at the Benefits of the Party System 127
Witnessing Party Breakdowns...128
Exploring the Tories...129
    Re-inventing the Tories: Cameron's conservatism...........130
    Tapping natural Tory supporters 131
Looking at the Labour Party 131
    Forming the Labour Party..132
    Gauging Labour's followers 132
    Breaking with the unions: Hard to do 133
Taking In the Lib Dems 133
    Understanding the balance of power 134
    Supporting proportional representation 135
    Looking at Lib Dem supporters....................................135
Focusing on the Minor Parties...135
Taking a Look at the Nationalists: SNP and Plaid Cymru 137
Dipping into Northern Irish Politics......................................138

Chapter 9: Piling On the Pressure Groups 141

Taking In the Universe of Pressure Groups 141
    Sorting out sectional pressure groups.........................142
    Seeing to cause-related groups 143
Going Inside, Outside, Up and Down with Pressure Groups.................144
    Differentiating inside and outside..............................145
    Watching the political ups and downs of pressure groups..........146

Looking at How Pressure Groups Exert Influence...............................147
Getting the ear of ministers and civil servants 147
Focusing on backbench MPs...148
Courting public opinion..149
Joining the throng at party conference.......................................150
Taking it to the streets: Direct action 150
Appealing over the heads of politicians 150
Placing Pressure Groups in the System...151
Looking at the downsides of pressure groups............................152
Taking in the plus points of pressure groups 153
Identifying the UK's Big Pressure Groups 153
Business groups...154
Charities...154
Human rights groups...155
Environmental groups...155
Professional groups...155
Trade unions 156
Working on a Bigger Stage: Pressure Groups and the EU 156
Pushing the Intellectual Envelope: Think Tanks 157

Chapter 10: Scrutinising Politics and the Media 161
Exposing the Uneasy Relationship between Politics and the Media 162
Wheeling out the sound bite 162
Media savvy: The role of 'special adviser'..................................163
Reading the UK's Newspapers 165
Waning influence – or not? 165
Taking in the qualities...166
Meeting the mid-markets 168
Checking out the red tops 169
Taking it to the grass roots: Regional newspapers 170
Balancing Act at the BBC..170
Offering News around the Clock..172
Starting up 24-hour TV 172
Breaking the mould: The world of political blogging..................172
Viewing politics at street level: Twittering................................174
Looking at the Media in an Election Campaign................................174
Testing the Temperature: Opinion Polling.......................................176

Part III: The Ins and Outs of Parliament 179

Chapter 11: Examining Britain's Constitution 181
Focusing on Why Countries Need a Constitution.............................181
Exploring Differing Types of Constitution.......................................183
Recording the difference between written and
unwritten constitutions...183
Taking in unitary and federal constitutions 184
Changing the rules: Rigid and flexible constitutions...................185

Celebrating Britain's Constitution..186
  Granting parliamentary sovereignty 187
  Limiting parliamentary sovereignty 188
Quantifying the Success of the UK's Constitution....................189
Moving towards a Written Constitution 190
Crowning the Constitution: The Monarchy...............................191
Stirring Things Up: Republicanism...192

Chapter 12: Britain's Parliamentary Democracy **195**
Honouring the Mother of Parliaments 195
Taking It to the Top: The House of Commons 197
  Looking at the job of MPs 197
  Recognising that the House of Commons holds the power 199
Lording it Up: The Job of Peers 199
  Gauging the independence of the peers 200
  Nominating peers for life 201
Introducing Bills 202
  Explaining government bills 202
  Introducing private members' bills 203
Getting Bills Passed: The Process 205
  Detailing the passage of bills 205
  Talking it over: Debating...206
  Icing the legislative cake: Receiving royal assent.......209
Poring Over the Detail: Parliamentary Committees...................209
  Looking at standing committees....................................210
  Examining select committees..210
Keeping Order: The Role of the Speaker 212
Tying Up the Loose Ends: The Other Parliamentary Players 214

Chapter 13: Gazing at the Summit: The PM and Cabinet.........215**
Going Straight to the Top: The Prime Minister..........................215
  Getting to be the PM..217
  Gauging if the PM is really 'first amongst equals'.......218
  Limiting the power of the PM...218
Concentrating on the Cabinet..220
  Taking in the great offices of state...............................221
  Observing the big beasts of the cabinet jungle............221
  Looking down the political food chain to other
    ministerial posts...222
Assuming Cabinet Responsibilities 224
  Explaining collective cabinet responsibility 224
  Taking in individual responsibility...............................225
Working Behind the Scenes: Cabinet Committees 225
Shaking Up the Cabinet..226
  Falling on their sword: Ministerial resignations 227
  Shifting the seats: Cabinet reshuffles 228

Whispering in the PM's Ear: Special Advisers 229
Turning to the Opposition: The Shadow Cabinet 229

Chapter 14: Assessing Ministers and Civil Servants 231

Examining What Government Departments Do 231
Ranking the Departmental Hierarchy 232
Oiling the Wheels of Government: The Civil Service 234
Becoming a civil servant and doing the job 235
Behaving as a civil servant 236
Climbing the Ranks to the Senior Civil Service 238
Running the day-to-day: The permanent under-
secretary of state 238
Serving as a link: The cabinet secretary 239
Evaluating the Good and Bad Points of the UK Civil Service 240
Reforming the Civil Service 241
Ignoring the Ibbs Report 241
Reducing head count: The Gershon Review 241
Calling the civil service to account 242

Chapter 15: Taking in the Courts and Judiciary 243

Explaining the UK's Three Legal Systems 243
Recognising the Difference between Civil and Criminal Law 244
Committing crimes against the state 244
Suing your neighbours in civil court 245
Examining the Basic Rights of the British Citizen 245
Focusing on the Criminal Courts of England and Wales 246
Starting off in a magistrates court 246
Advancing to a crown court 247
Making your way to the Court of Appeal 248
Hearing Civil Cases in England and Wales 248
Gazing at the civil law process 249
Appealing civil cases 249
Taking in the Scottish Court System 250
Considering the Courts in Northern Ireland 250
Introducing the New UK Supreme Court 251
Looking at the Role of the Judge 251
Glancing at Courts and the Constitution 252
Throwing the European Union into the Mix 253
Fighting the Good Fight: Courts and Civil Liberties 253

Chapter 16: Laying Bare Local Government and Devolution 255

Understanding that All Politics is Local 255
Looking at what local government does 256
Funding local government 257
Taking in the structure of local government in England 258
Heading north: Scottish local government 259

Heading west: Wales and Northern Ireland 259
Reforming local government 260
Granting Power from the Centre – Devolution 261
Focusing on the Scottish parliament..263
Welcoming in the Welsh Assembly 267
Priming the peace process: The Northern Ireland Assembly 268

Chapter 17: Joining the Lawmakers: Becoming a Politician.......271

Becoming Part of the Party System...271
Setting out on the journey: Joining a political party....................272
Moving from party member to candidate..273
Stepping onto the First Rung of the Political Ladder:
Local Elected Office 274
Aiming for a Seat in Parliament 274
Targeting your constituency 276
Preparing for an election 277
Getting to Grips with Life as an MP 279
Climbing the Greasy Pole to the Top Jobs in Government 280

Part 1V: Politics Worldwide *283*

Chapter 18: Understanding Britain's Place in the World 285

Declining Fortunes: From Empire to the Middle Ranks 285
Forging a New Role in Europe...286
Assessing the Special Relationship with the United States 288
Looking Further Afield to the Rise of China...289
Leading the Commonwealth of Nations...290
Ruling the Waves: British Overseas Territories 291
Playing the Role of World Police Officer...292
Sitting at the Top Table: The UN Security Council...............................293

Chapter 19: Taking In the International Stage 295

Starting at the Top: The United Nations..295
Delving into how the UN works..296
Taking in UN agencies 300
Bringing out the Big Guns: The Role of the G8 and the G20.................302
Starting small with the G8..302
Changing times: G8 morphing into G20...303
Looking at the Regional Trading Blocs 304
Factoring in the World Trade Organisation 305
Playing the Power Game: China Taking Over from the United States 306
Providing the Military Might: NATO...307

Chapter 20: Expanding Horizons: Europe and the EU............**309**

Understanding the EU and How it Works.................................309
    Checking the goals of the EU...................................311
    Examining EU institutions.....................................312
    Looking at law-making and the legal system....................315
Forming Relationships Within and Outside the EU......................317
    Looming giant: Russia on the doorstep.........................317
    Testing question: Is Turkey really part of Europe?............318
    Bringing peace to the Balkans.................................319
    Understanding Britain's thorny relationship with the EU.......320
Putting Pen to Paper: Major European Treaties........................321
Holding the Purse Strings: EU Budgets................................323
    Accounting for the Common Agricultural Policy.................323
    Getting a rebate..324

Chapter 21: Leading the Free World: US Politics.............**327**

Understanding US Influence in the Wider World and in the UK..........327
    Being buddies: The US–UK special relationship.................329
    Growing apart? Recent problems with the special
      relationship...330
Looking at the US System of Government...............................331
    Building the Houses of Congress...............................332
    Establishing the presidency...................................333
    Judging disputes: The US Supreme Court........................337
Passing a Bill into Law..339
Throwing Political Parties into the Mix..............................340
    Voting with the Democrats.....................................341
    Siding with the Republicans...................................341
    Rallying the religious right..................................342
    Linking up: UK and US political parties.......................342

Part V: The Part of Tens............................. **345**

Chapter 22: Ten Great Prime Ministers.....................**347**

Our Finest Hour: Winston Churchill (1940–45 and 1951–55).............347
The Welsh Wizard: David Lloyd George (1916–22).......................348
Iron Lady: Margaret Thatcher (1979–1990).............................348
The Trailblazer: Robert Walpole (1721–1742)..........................349
The Great Reformer: Clement Attlee (1945–51).........................350
The First Spin Doctor: Benjamin Disraeli (1868 and 1874–1880)........350
The Grand Old Man: William Gladstone (1868–74, 1880–85,
    1886 and 1892–94)..351

Shaking Things Up: Robert Peel (1834–35 and 1841–46) 351
The Second Master of Spin: Tony Blair (1997–2007) 352
Wiser than His Years: William Pitt the Younger (1783–1801
   and 1804–1806) 353

Chapter 23: Ten Major Political Scandals.......................355

A Very British Sex Scandal: John Profumo...355
From Moats to Maltesers: The MPs' Expenses Scandal 356
Running Out of Control: The Westland Affair 357
Scandal of Mass Destruction: The David Kelly Affair............................358
Roll Up, Roll Up; How Much for This Knighthood? 358
How the Mighty Fall: Jonathan Aitken and Jeffrey Archer 359
Murder Plot? The Jeremy Thorpe Affair...360
The Fall of a President: Watergate 360
More Sordid Scandal Stateside: The Monica Lewinsky Affair................361
Dodgy Property Deal: The Whitewater Affair 361

Chapter 24: Ten Political Events that Shaped the Modern World...363

Hell on Earth: The Second World War...363
Breaking Down the Barriers: Nixon and China 364
Ending Communism in Europe: The Fall of the Berlin Wall 365
Coming Together: The March of the European Union.............................366
Throwback to Another Time: Balkan Wars 367
Long Wait for Freedom: The Release of Nelson Mandela.......................367
Terror from the Skies: 9/11..368
Bringing Down a Dictator: War in Iraq 369
Gazing Over the Brink: The Great Credit Crunch....................................369
Crazy for You: Obama-Mania 370

Chapter 25: Ten Political Trends for the Future 371

Broadening Democracy: Internet Voting..371
Rising Power: Indian Modernisation 372
Loosening the Shackles: Chinese Democracy..372
Securing Natural Resources: Chinese Control of Africa.........................373
Out with the Old: Replacing the Dollar..373
Constructing a Super-State: Expanding the European Union 374
World Going Dry: Shortages of Water...374
Black Gold: Scrambling for Oil 375
Risking Our Future: Global Warming 375
Upping Sticks: Global Population Moves..376

Index **377**

Introduction

Welcome to the fascinating world of British politics. Whether you're a student wanting to boost your chances of getting that A grade or just want the inside track on the big issues that face not just the UK but also the wider world, this is the book for you.

I wrote this book for newcomers and students alike so that you can have a one-stop shop to get to know everything you need to know without feeling overwhelmed or intimidated. I explain how Britain became the modern liberal democracy it is today. Thanks to this book, the next time you hear someone say at a dinner table, on the bus or down the pub that 'politics is all the same', you'll be able to tell them why they're wrong, and why politics and politicians make a fundamental difference to our lives.

About This Book

To make your reading experience a little easier, *British Politics For Dummies* follows certain rules. For example, every time I use a new term or important phrase, I *italicise* and explain it. The key word or term in a bulleted list is in **bold** so that it stands out. Occasionally, you see text in grey boxes. These sidebars are full of what I consider interesting information, but they're not essential to understanding the topic at hand, so you can read them or not as you choose. I explain everything very clearly and try to avoid political gobbledygook.

When reading a discussion of a particular aspect of politics in one chapter, I refer to another chapter when the information there ties into the issue I'm discussing. You can turn immediately to that chapter or just tuck the number away in your memory and decide to read it next.

Foolish Assumptions

Don't feel intimidated if you know nothing about politics. This book will bring you up to speed, fast. Politics can be complex, and even some seasoned commentators have difficulty grasping some aspects. But before long – after reading this book – you're going to be transformed into a nailed-on political expert.

How This Book Is Organised

To make things easier for you, this book is divided into five parts. Each part focuses on an important aspect of the world of politics.

Part I: The Basics of Politics

This part welcomes you into the political jungle. You get to see why politics and politicians are so important and what makes democracy something rather special. I then get all ideological and consider the alternatives to democracy. Finally, I get to Britain and show you how it is that in the first quarter of the 21st century, you're living in a vibrant democracy – the envy of many countries around the world!

Part II: Elections and Britain's Parties

This part covers how the election process works in the UK. I explore the many different electoral systems used in parliamentary, local and European elections in detail – it's number-crunching time! I take a good long look at voting behaviour and consider what influences people to vote for which political parties. I introduce the UK's political parties big and small, as well as cover how the parties organise themselves to get their candidates elected. The increasingly important pressure groups also come under the spotlight, as well as how politicians and the media interact.

Part III: The Ins and Outs of Parliament

This part takes you right to the heart of Britain's ancient democracy. I start with an examination of Britain's unwritten constitution in determining the role of the monarch and contributing to the strengths and weaknesses of the British way of doing politics.

I take a stroll down the corridors of power in parliament itself, uncovering the inner workings of the House of Lords and the House of Commons. I look at who limits the power of parliament and how government policies actually make it into laws we all have to obey, or else! I provide a close look at Britain's most important politician, the prime minister, and how he or she runs the government with the help of the cabinet.

I go into the nitty-gritty of how the civil service actually enforces the laws drawn up by cabinet and passed by parliament. Donning a wig, I take a look at the role of the judiciary, whose job it is to interpret and uphold the law.

Part IV: Politics Worldwide

This part takes you away from the UK into the choppy waters of international politics. First, I examine Britain's 'special relationship' with the US and the ever closer ties being forged with the European Union. From there I look at the major international bodies: the United Nations, with its ultra-powerful Security Council – the closest thing we have to a world government – through to its major economic and development agencies.

I take in the changing face of NATO, then the rising power of China. Back closer to home, I explain the intricacies of the European Union, its constitution and treaties. Finally, I look at arguably the world's only super-power, the United States, and its political parties, constitution and, of course, the globe's number one politician, the US president.

Part V: The Part of Tens

The part without which no *For Dummies* book would be complete, this is packed full of fascinating bits of information that you can store away and draw on whenever you feel like impressing someone with your political knowledge or even sweeping the board at your local pub quiz. This part also gives you some handy inside knowledge on some of the big events that have shaped the political world in which we live.

Icons Used in This Book

To help you navigate through this book, keep an eye out for the icons – the little pictures that sit in the margin. They guide you to particular types of information. The icons in this book mean the following things:

This icon is unique to this book. Every so often I look in depth at a great politician or quirky character from past or present. Politics is full of interesting people!

Politics is chock-full of jargon. Fortunately, this book's mission is to bust it. Whenever you see this icon, you find an explanation of political terms that help you understand just what's going on in the game.

This icon is also unique to this book and you won't see it often. It draws your attention to some of the behind-the-scenes stuff that goes on in the cut and thrust of daily politics. Here's the info the media managers in the big political parties don't want you to know!

Paragraphs with this icon attached contain information that's especially useful to remember.

This icon indicates a technical discussion is under way. You can skip this stuff if you want, because it isn't necessary for an understanding of the basics. If you read it, though, you can boost your political know-how.

Where to Go from Here

Don't be restricted by the order in which the contents of this book appear. This book is designed to be read in several ways. It's a reference book, so you don't have to read the chapters in chronological order, from front to back. Of course, if you want, you can read it cover to cover like a novel – and there are quite a few heroes and heroines in politics. Alternatively, you can pick a topic that you're doing at school or university or you just want to know much more about and read up on it. Or you can just flip through this book, maybe starting with the chapter where I explain the basics of the political game.

But my favourite way of reading this book – and my editor has made sure I've read it a few times now – is to go to Part I outlining the basics of how politics works and then to the sections which interest you or are relevant to your studies. Whatever draws you to politics, *British Politics For Dummies* has something for you.

- ✔ Why is Britain a democracy and not a dictatorship? (Check out Chapter 5.)
- ✔ Who is Black Rod and what on earth does he do? (Turn to Chapter 12.)
- ✔ What does all the jargon mean? What on earth is a spin doctor? (Chapter 10 explains.)
- ✔ What's so important about the United Nations Security Council? (Head to Chapter 19.)

In short, it's up to you how you get to know the world of politics!

Part I
The Basics of
Politics

In this part . . .

This part provides you with an introduction to the world of British politics. If you don't know politics that well or just want to re-familiarise yourself with the basics, this is the part for you.

You get to see what's so special about democracy and why politicians are considered so important. I go through the nitty-gritty of different political ideologies, examining the alternatives to democracy. I also turn back the clock to see how Britain developed from absolute monarchy to a modern, vibrant democracy but with a very British twist!

Chapter 1

Taking in the Political Universe

· ·

In This Chapter

▶ Differentiating local and national politics

▶ Building a very British democracy

▶ Legislating within the parliament

▶ Gauging the strength of the democracy

▶ Scrutinising politicians and the media

▶ Defining Britain's place in the world

· ·

> *Those who are too smart to engage in politics are punished by being governed by those who are dumber.*
>
> Plato, Greek philosopher

*P*lato's quote highlights one – very cynical – way of looking at the wacky (and not so wacky) world of politics. But whatever your view of politics (or for that matter politicians), one thing's for sure: the laws made by politicians have a direct impact on your life.

In this Chapter I take a speed-of-light trip around the political universe through the town hall, the newspaper rooms, Buckingham Palace, the UK Houses of Parliament, to the outer reaches of big international bodies such as the European Union and United Nations.

Time to set out on a political journey of discovery!

Understanding the Difference between Local and National Politics

How many politicians do you think you can name? Five, ten, twenty? Well, there are literally thousands of politicians in the UK and many times that number around the globe. The fact that you and I may only be able to name a handful isn't because we're not very bright; it's because most of the politicians out there have a very low profile in the public eye. They may be big figures in their local community but they don't make any sort of splash on the national stage.

You can divide politicians into local and national ones. Local politicians get to decide what goes on in a particular village, town or city, whereas national politicians have a say in the laws which govern all our lives. Politicians who're elected to the House of Commons and the European Parliament can be said to be national ones as they make laws which apply to the whole country not just to a particular village, town or city.

Here are some of the other key differences between local and national politicians:

- ✔ National politicians receive a salary from the state, whereas local politicians are volunteers with normal lives and everyday jobs.

- ✔ The actions of national politicians are generally covered in the national media, such as national newspapers and television/radio networks, whereas local politicians gain coverage in local newspapers and on local radio and regional television news.

- ✔ The UK is a highly centralised state, which means that the national politicians have lots of power, including the main tax-raising powers, whereas local politicians have to do roughly what the central government says and have much smaller tax-raising powers.

The overwhelming majority of politicians in the UK are local councillors and parish councillors, often elected by a few hundred or thousand voters.

An election for membership of the House of Commons is called a *general election*, a European parliamentary election is called an *election to the European parliament*, and a local council election is called – guess what? – a *local election*.

Usually, voter turnout (the percentage of eligible voters actually going to the polls to vote) is much higher for general elections than for local or European elections. General elections tend to get much greater media coverage and voters are more interested in who wins. (Chapter 7 talks about the other factors influencing voter turnout.)

Splitting the Difference: The Devolved Parliament and Assemblies

The British are noted around the globe for a few things: producing great rock music, drinking too much (but let's not put that one on the tourist brochures!), writing great literature, creating great art and being a world centre for financial services. But ask any foreigner to name a word which sums up Britain and the British, and tradition would come fairly high up the list. Put simply, we're not supposed to do change.

But over the past decade we've gone in for political change in a big way. The Labour government of Tony Blair in 1999 set up the Scottish parliament and Welsh and Northern Ireland assemblies.

The big idea was to move some power away from the government in Westminster and hand it to the peoples – through an elected parliament or assembly – in Scotland, Wales and Northern Ireland. This process was called *devolution* and some say it's the biggest constitutional change in the UK for 100 years.

Why introduce devolution? Well, the Scottish, Welsh and Northern Irish have different identities and traditions and many in these parts of the UK felt that these had been swamped over many hundreds of years by the more populous English.

Every four years the people of Scotland, Wales and Northern Ireland get to elect who they want to sit in their own parliament or assembly; these representatives then make the laws in the policy areas which have been devolved from the UK parliament, for example health care, education or the environment. Plans are afoot to increase the number of powers devolved to the Scottish parliament and Welsh and Northern Ireland assemblies. (For a full rundown of which parliament or assembly does what, check out Chapter 16.)

Why do the Scottish have a parliament, while the Welsh and Northern Irish have an assembly? Well, this situation reflects the number of devolved powers that each institution has. A parliament is considered a more important and august body than an assembly. So the Scottish, who have more devolved powers than the Welsh, thus have a parliament rather than an assembly.

Evolving to Democracy: A Very British Story

Each democratic nation has trod its very own path to the political system it has today. The US democracy was born when rebels beat the British in the American Revolution, while the French democracy can trace its roots back to the deposition and execution of Louis XVI in 1793 and the revolution that followed.

The UK too has had its fair share of strife – the odd bloody civil war – and has even chopped one king's head off (the singularly useless Charles I). But instead of one cataclysmic event such as a war or revolution leading to democracy, the UK has progressed more gradually to the modern liberal democratic society we have today. In fact, the UK is one of only a handful of countries to get rid of its monarch (between 1649 and 1660; see Chapter 5 for more) and then decide to reinstate it.

Put simply, the British prefer political evolution to revolution and the web of government is built up through a combination of laws, traditions and customs. For example, in legal terms the monarchy is hugely important in the British state; in fact, the government itself is there to serve the monarch. However, through custom and tradition the monarch actually plays a very minor role in the government of the country. Much of the power is vested in the hands of the prime minister (PM) and his or her cabinet.

The UK, unlike the US for instance, doesn't have a written constitution. Instead, government is conducted through laws, traditions and customs. This situation is referred to as the UK's *unwritten constitution*, which I discuss in Chapter 11.

An unwritten constitution may sound weak and impracticable but the UK system has stood the test of time. In fact, the UK was one of the few major European countries not to have seen its democracy suppressed by a dictatorship during the twentieth century.

Assessing the Health of British Democracy

Some experts suggest that Britons are becoming less interested in politics and the following evidence does seem to bear that analysis out:

- **Falling voter turnout.** At election time fewer and fewer people are turning out to exercise their democratic right to vote.

- **Falling party membership.** The three nationwide major political parties – Labour, Conservative and Liberal Democrat (and by major I mean these parties always have Members of Parliament elected) – have seen their membership numbers plummet over the past decade. Politicians who stand as party candidates rely on help from party members and now have fewer people to offer it.

However, evidence suggests that people aren't bored with politics in itself; just with politicians and the main political parties. Some say that media training and the whips' control over what MPs say in public have made politicians increasingly bland. Smaller political parties like the Green Party and the UK Independence Party (UKIP) have done better at election time in recent years, however, while pressure groups and trade unions continue to enjoy high levels of membership.

Glancing at the alternatives to democracy

Sitting in a strong democratic country like the UK it's easy to think that democracy is a given around the globe. Surely, everyone must see how well it works and can't live without the freedom of speech and personal liberty that are two hallmarks of democracy.

But much of the population of the world doesn't live in a democratic state. In fact, a large number live under regimes where to be an opponent of the government is to risk liberty and even life and limb.

China, for example, is the world's most populous nation – with roughly one in four people on the planet being Chinese – yet its people live in a one-party state. All the politicians are drawn from just one party, so people can only vote for the candidates representing it. Ostensibly, the party in government in China is communist, which means it's supposed to adhere to communist ideals such as common ownership of property and a society free of class or social divides. However, in reality the Chinese Communist Party promotes individual property ownership and individual wealth creation (two

very western and democratic ideals) as means to improve the national economy. In effect, China now practises communism-lite.

This situation hints at a fundamental truth of political systems around the globe: that nearly all of them, to a greater or lesser degree, have some measure of what we recognise as western democratic ideals, such as free speech and the right to make and spend money without huge interference from the state.

A truly democratic society has to guarantee freedom of the press and the right to protest, as well as hold regular contested elections for government office. The UK, fortunately, ticks all of these boxes and so can be classed as a fully fledged democracy.

Many different forms of government operate around the globe, from communist regimes to western democracies. Religious leaders even run things in some countries, such as Iran – a system called *theocracy*. Check out Chapter 4 for more on different types of government.

In the run up to the invasion of Iraq in 2003, for example, hundreds of thousands of Britons took to the streets in anti-war demonstrations, showing that people do really care about the big global political issues. Likewise, in 2005 before the meeting of the G8 countries (the world's seven biggest economies, plus Russia) held in Gleneagles in Scotland, hundreds of thousands demonstrated in an attempt to persuade political leaders to do more for the poor in the developing world.

The expenses scandal of 2009 was a key factor in undermining public confidence in politics and politicians. A host of MPs were found to have claimed for expenses they shouldn't have and to have worked the system for all they could possibly get. An enormous public furore resulted, which led to scores of MPs deciding to stand down as candidates for the next general election. (Chapter 23 covers this major political scandal and others to boot.)

Some academics suggest that the way to reverse low voter turnout is to make it easier to vote. They probably have a point. At present, electors usually have to attend a polling station in person in order to cast their ballot, and elections are generally held on a work day. Allowing more postal or online ballots would make voting easier and hopefully encourage more people to do so. Making not voting illegal is another possible solution to low turnout. In Australia, for instance, people who don't vote are fined. (Chapter 7 has more on reversing falling voter turnout.)

Paying Homage to the 'Mother of Parliaments'

Standing at the very centre of British democracy is the Houses of Parliament in Westminster, London. This great gothic masterpiece, along with the many government ministries within a short walk, is the fulcrum of British political life. Many of the big government policy decisions and laws which affect all Britons' lives are made in Westminster by the politicians who work there.

The Houses of Parliament are divided into two distinct parts – the House of Commons and the House of Lords. Although they sit in chambers only a few hundred yards apart and have both been in existence for centuries, the Houses are quite different in terms of who gets to sit in them and the powers and responsibilities of those who do so. Table 1-1 is a quick guide to some of the main differences between the two chambers.

Table 1-1	Comparing the Houses of the UK Parliament
House of Commons	*House of Lords*
Members elected by public vote, called a general election.	Members are either appointed by the monarch (on the advice of the prime minister) or have the right to sit as a result of an inherited title.
Laws are proposed, amended and voted down by a majority of members.	A majority of members can vote to amend or oppose legislation but ultimately they can't go against the wishes of the Commons.
Most of the members belong to a particular political party.	Members stay in place for life and tend to be more independent-minded.

The biggest party – in terms of number of seats – in the Commons forms the government, with that party's leader as prime minister.

Within the UK's unwritten constitution, the House of Commons is considered far more important than the House of Lords because most laws start their life there and the government is drawn from members of the biggest party in the Commons. What's more, under the Parliament Act of 1911, the House of Lords can only halt a law which has passed through the Commons for one year, whereas the Commons can kill laws that have passed through the Lords stone dead. Check out Chapter 12 for more on the House of Commons' supremacy in Britain's parliamentary democracy.

When many people in the UK and around the world think of the Houses of Parliament they don't picture great debates and dramatic votes on whether or not a law should be passed. They probably think about some of the traditions of the place, such as splendid set-piece occasions like the monarch's official opening of parliament, the archaic language used by Members of the Lords and Commons when addressing one another and even the tights-wearing and sword-carrying of some of the staff! Chapter 12 lifts the lid on some of the strange goings on and traditions followed in the UK parliament.

Both members of the House of Commons, called *MPs* (short for *Members of Parliament*), and members of the Lords (called *peers*) can introduce new legislation. However, without the support of MPs, peers have zero chance of seeing their legislative proposals become law. MPs have a better chance of getting their policy proposals made into law but only if they belong to the biggest party in the Commons. (See Chapter 12 for more on how the UK's complex legislation process actually works.)

Politicians need civil servants to carry out their policies and the UK has one of the most extensive and highly trained civil services in the world. The civil service has a long history, with members following a well-defined code of ethics which is supposed to guarantee impartiality, integrity and honesty. Check out Chapter 14 for more on the inner workings of the civil service.

Westminster may be the beating heart of UK politics, but thanks to devolution and membership of the European Union (EU), it's no longer quite as important as it once was to the making of laws which actually affect your daily life.

Introducing the Players in the British Political System

Britain's long-standing democracy relies on the nation's politicians, judges and the monarch. Each of these key figures has jobs to do – big and small – in drawing up the laws of the land, running the government of the country, and preserving the freedoms of British citizens and the integrity of our democracy. The effective working of the British political system is based on co-operation between the politicians (elected by you and me), the judges and the monarch.

Here's a run-down of the big hitters in the British political system and what role they play in delivering effective democratic government to some 60 million Britons.

Gazing at the political summit: The central role of the prime minister

One of the major changes in the UK's political landscape over the past couple of centuries has been the concentration of a great deal of power in the hands of one person – the prime minister.

After a general election the leader of the political party with the most members elected to the House of Commons is asked by the monarch to form the government of the country. That party leader becomes prime minister and it's up to him or her to ensure that the country is governed and the policies his or her party told the electors they'd carry out during the general election campaign are actually followed.

In the run-up to a general election every party publishes a *manifesto* – a collection of policy pledges which the leadership of the political party says it will carry out, if elected.

In order to be able to govern, the PM has at his or her disposal lots of powers, such as to:

- ✔ Select politicians to be in charge of government departments. I cover these ministers and their powers in depth in Chapter 13.

- ✔ Draw up a list of potential people for appointment by the monarch to the House of Lords.

- ✔ Chair meetings of the *cabinet*, which comprises the heads of government departments. The cabinet has the say over which legislation is introduced into parliament with the aim of making it into law.

- ✔ Determine when another general election is to be held.

- ✔ Decide whether the country goes to war and, during wartime, tell commanders what to do.

The PM's power derives not only from the office but also from his or her role as the leader of the biggest party in the House of Commons. Party leaders have the power to throw badly behaving politicians out of the party and even to say who should or shouldn't stand for election as a party candidate.

The PM is far and away the most important politician in the country, which means that media attention is centred on what he or she gets up to. Often the PM represents Britain at international conferences and gets to meet up with other world leaders. In fact, some say that the PM has transformed into a president in recent years and is seen by many as effectively the head of state rather than the monarch.

Declining importance of the MP

In politics, when one individual becomes more important it usually means that another has become less so. This state of affairs is certainly true when considering the relative importance of the PM and MPs. As more and more power is concentrated in the hands of the PM, the humble MP finds he or she has less and less influence over what's going on. This change in the balance of power has occurred for a number of reasons, including:

- ✔ **Whipping.** Although it sounds very rude, a whip is actually someone appointed by the party leader to ensure that the party's MPs vote the way the leader wants. Over the past few decades whips have become more important, keeping a tight grip on how individuals vote and even their public utterances.

- ✔ **Public apathy.** In the past, individual MP's speeches were widely reported and even backbench MPs were household names. This is no longer the case, with the press reporting far more of what the PM says or does than individual MPs.

- ✔ **Legislative squeeze.** The UK government is a big old institution and the PM and the cabinet take up the overwhelming majority of parliamentary time for debates and votes on new laws they want to see introduced. As a result, individual MPs are finding it harder than ever to get their own bills made into law.

An MP who isn't also a minister or a member of the opposition shadow cabinet team – in effect, opposition party leaders whose specific job it is to confront an individual minister – is referred to as a *backbench MP*.

Some 646 MPs sit in the House of Commons. Each MP is elected by a vote held in an individual parliamentary constituency. Who wins the seat is decided by the first-past-the-post system, which simply means that the candidate who polls the most votes wins and takes his or her seat in parliament. (Chapter 6 has more on first past the post and the myriad other voting methods used in elections across the UK.)

Some people call for electoral reform as they feel that the current system is unfair. Often those elected as MPs haven't actually polled a majority of votes cast – all they've done is attract the most votes. It's possible under first past the post to win a seat in the House of Commons by getting just one more vote than the candidate finishing second.

Checking the power of the politicians: The judiciary

The UK judiciary is independent. Judges are servants of the monarch and their job is to uphold and interpret the law of the land. The judiciary, through the new UK Supreme Court, provides an important check on the power of government, particularly in the area of civil liberties.

The laws of the land are set by parliament but they don't cover every eventuality, and the judiciary has its powers in interpreting particular laws. The web of hundreds of years of judgements in different cases – called *legal precedent* – in effect sets out what's legal and what isn't. However, legal precedent set by the courts can be washed away by a new law passed by parliament.

Laws made by the UK parliament are called *statute law*, and form the premier law of the land. However, laws passed by the European parliament have equal standing with statute law.

The UK doesn't have one or two legal systems; it actually has three. England and Wales share the same legal system, while Scotland and Northern Ireland each have their own. The patchwork of laws and courts in the UK is highly complex but if you want the inside track, check out Chapter 15.

The UK's three legal systems all operate according to a hierarchical system. This system means that the decision reached by the highest court in the land – now the UK Supreme Court in most cases – is binding on all lower courts and also sets a future legal precedent.

The European Convention on Human Rights was adopted in UK law in the 1998 Human Rights Act. As a result, if someone feels their human rights have been violated they can go to a UK court and have it decide on the matter, rather than go to the European Court of Human Rights in Strasbourg. If that court decides that the individual's human rights have been violated, that violation has to stop!

Mixing in the monarch

The monarchy has been of crucial importance in British history. The first kings of England came to the throne over a thousand years ago and, although their descendants have found their powers reduced, modern monarchs still have their role to play in British life and politics. As head of state, the monarch isn't just a tourist attraction! In the UK's unwritten constitution, the monarch's powers include opening and dissolving parliament, appointing the prime minister, giving consent to bills passed by parliament (without this consent a bill can't become law) and appointing bishops and members of the House of Lords.

While the monarch appears to have a lot of power, in reality it's largely ceremonial. For example, the power to appoint the prime minister sounds great but it's a constitutional convention that the monarch must appoint the leader of the biggest party in the House of Commons. Likewise, the power to appoint members of the House of Lords is curtailed by the fact that the monarch only does so in accordance with the advice of the prime minister.

Under a convention of the UK's unwritten constitution, the monarch must always take the advice of his or her ministers – that is, the elected government.

Most Britons, when asked, support the idea of the monarchy but a substantial minority (usually around a quarter) would prefer it to be abolished. They argue that the monarchy is outdated, elitist and costs too much. However, the UK shows no signs of becoming a republic (a state that doesn't have a monarch) anytime soon; all the main political parties – even the Scottish Nationalists – support the idea of a monarchy.

Coming under Greater Scrutiny: Politics in the Media

You wouldn't guess that there was widespread apathy towards politics in the UK if you turned on the TV, radio or opened up a newspaper. Politics is a major talking point on the airwaves and in the columns of most of the newspapers. In fact, as voter turnout has fallen, the actual coverage of politics has increased, thanks in particular to the advent of 24-hour TV news stations. With so much time to fill, even the slightest piece of political gossip or smallest policy proposal is pored over continuously. Likewise, the private lives of many politicians have been held up to the bright lights of media scrutiny and, as far as some of the general public are concerned, when it comes to politicians, familiarity breeds contempt. (See Chapter 10 for more on politics and the media.)

Despite the march of blogs and the Internet, the newspaper industry is still hugely important in the UK media. What's written in the papers can have quite an influence on the behaviour of politicians. For example, in October 2009 the UK's biggest selling daily newspaper *The Sun* came out in support of the Conservative party and its leader David Cameron – abandoning in the process the Labour government and PM Gordon Brown – and caused quite a stir.

In the UK, each of the national newspapers supports one of the main political parties. For example, the *Daily Mail* and *Daily Telegraph* support the Conservative Party, while the *Daily Mirror* and *Guardian* support the Labour Party. Sometimes, a paper will switch its allegiance; for example, prior to the 1997 general election the *Financial Times* declared its support for Labour but in 2005 they switched back to the Conservatives.

As with everything else in life, the Internet is playing a more important role in politics, particularly in the US but here in the UK too. Politicians are increasingly using social networking sites, Twitter and blogs to get their message across to large numbers of eager readers. Political pundits and the average citizens can bypass the main media outlets and counteract what they see as biased reporting or just say what they want without journalistic scrutiny! (Chapter 10 talks about the burgeoning role of the Internet in politics.)

Britain: Making Its Way in the European Union

Few Britons probably understood just what they were getting into when the UK joined the European Economic Community (now called the European Union, or EU) in 1973.

The EU has metamorphosed from a group of West European nations trying to create a free trade area and improve economic co-operation into what many see as a super state of 27 countries and 500 million people. The EU has its own flag, anthem and parliament. What's more, the laws made by the EU apply in the UK and other member countries. This situation has changed the legal landscape in the UK and means that the government has to always consider whether or not its actions are in accord with European law.

But the EU has been changed by Britain's membership too. It was the British government that pushed for greater powers for the EU parliament within the constitution of the EU (see Chapter 20 for more on this) and for the entry of poorer countries from eastern Europe.

The EU has its own currency – the *euro*. In under a decade the euro has become the second most used currency in the world behind the US dollar.

Many say that EU membership has been a good thing for the UK. For example, the overwhelming majority of UK exports go to member states of the EU. Likewise, Britons are free to travel and work in any EU country of their choosing.

Looking Further Afield: The UK and the Wider World

The EU is crucial to the UK and its trade but it's not the only game in town. The UK has a major advantage in international commerce – the English language. Combined with strong historic ties with former colonies which now form the Commonwealth and the so-called 'special relationship' with the United States, the UK is a major economy and international power.

Looking east, the rise of China and India present huge challenges and opportunities for British government policymakers and business.

On the international stage, the UK is a member of the United Nations, a permanent member of the UN Security Council and the G8 and G20 (G8 is the group of the eight most developed economies and G20 are the G8 nations plus a dozen nations whose economies are developing fast), as well as countless other international organisations.

The UK is one of the five permanent members of the UN Security Council, along with China, France, Russia and the US. This membership gives the UK the right to veto UN resolutions, which are basically international laws. (Chapter 19 covers the work of the UN Security Council.)

The UK isn't just a major economic power; it's also a key member of the North Atlantic Treaty Organisation (NATO), a military body which can deploy well-equipped armed forces nearly anywhere in the world. NATO was originally set up to defend western Europe against the threat of a Soviet invasion in the aftermath of the Second World War.

Chapter 2

Understanding Why Politics and Politicians Are Important

In This Chapter

▶ Explaining different types of authority

▶ Understanding the purpose of politics

▶ Looking at what politicians do

▶ Examining some of the big issues politicians face

▶ Participating in the process as an activist

*M*ost politicians aren't short on ego! They love the sound of their own voice, their name in the papers and their picture on the box. But they do have, at least in part, good reason for their egos because, love them or loathe them, politicians are important. To name but a few of their jobs in a democracy like Britain's: politicians make the laws, negotiate international treaties, and even decide whether to go to war. They're also responsible for meeting the challenges of the major issues – from poverty in the developing world to fighting global warming – which affect not just the UK but the world. Yes, that's a lot of power!

As for politics itself – it's all around you, permeating your life. If you look out of your front window and see a road, it's there because a politician took a political decision that it should be built. Turn on your lights; they work because a politician (perhaps the same one) took a political decision to build a new power plant. And, of course, discussion of politics – political events and political controversies – pops up on your television and radio or in your newspaper all the time.

In this chapter I look at all the reasons why politics and politicians play such an important role in all of our lives.

Looking at Different Types of Authority

I'm going to get all scientific on you for a moment. Not test tubes and lab coats but the wacky world of the political scientist, whose job it is to see patterns in the conduct of politics, from tribes in the darkest, deepest Amazon rainforest to the inner workings of the US president's White House.

One of the big names in political science and philosophy at the start of the 20th century was the German intellectual Max Weber. Weber looked at the world of politics and how politicians – and everyone in authority in the country – gained and held their power. He came up with three types of authority, as follows:

- **Traditional authority.** People choose to obey authority figures because of national traditions and customs. The UK's unwritten constitution is largely based on traditions and customs. For example, the monarch in the UK has many legal powers but through tradition and custom much of this power is actually exercised by the prime minister.

- **Charismatic authority.** A leader has a big personality and qualities which make him or her stand out. This charisma persuades others to follow what the leader says, which in turn gives the leader power. The fascist leaders Hitler and Mussolini are recognised as having drawn much of their power from charisma, although they used it in a destructive way.

- **Legal authority.** People generally respect the law, so a person who gains office through legal means automatically has authority. For instance, in the US, much of the authority of government is outlined in the country's constitution, which is a legal document. Americans respect their nation's constitution and as a result respect those who hold political office by playing by the rules of the constitution. The president, for example, has to win his (there haven't as yet been any female presidents) party's nomination and then win the election to office. This process is what gives the president authority, not charisma or tradition.

No country's political system fits perfectly into just one authority model. The power of the UK prime minister, for instance, can largely be said to rely on a mix of traditional and legal authority – and occasionally, in the case of Winston Churchill during the Second World War, for example – charismatic authority can be thrown into the mix too.

Political scientists draw a distinction between the exercise of authority and coercion. Put simply, *coercion* is when people obey because they're afraid of the consequences of disobedience – dictatorships often rely on a heavy dose of coercion. *Authority* is when people obey because they regard who's telling them what to do as having some legitimacy – traditional, legal, charismatic or a combination. People will even obey when they don't agree with what they're being asked to do. Generally, politicians and political systems relying on authority last a good deal longer than those using coercion.

Deciphering the Ultimate Purpose of Politics

'So, what's the point of politics?' is the sort of question you hear down the pub on a Friday night, normally followed by the statement 'Politicians are all the same!' But understanding why politics exists is a serious question. Political scientists have been busy coming up with their own reasons for why much of the media and our lives are dominated by politics and politicians.

Politics serves to:

- **Resolve conflict.** Some groups in society are simply opposed to one another. People in favour of the better road network and those in favour of protecting the environment and rural landscape are opposed over whether or not to allow more motorways. Now these two groups, although protesting against one another, don't actually come to blows and start killing one another (at least I hope not) because they have access to politicians to press their views. In short, politics helps take some of the heat out of conflicts and provides a forum for the peaceful airing of views.

- **Encourage compromise.** Not everyone agrees about everything. In fact, you put ten people in a room and you're unlikely to get any of them to agree about anything straight away; the only way they'll agree is through compromise. But how do you get people to compromise with one another for the greater good? Politics is the best answer we have to this question. People will accept things happening that they don't agree with because they respect the political process – either its traditions or its legality. It may not seem the case when you see raucous scenes in the House of Commons with political opponents criticising one another, but politics pours oil over troubled waters and encourages compromise.

- **Accommodate different interests.** Politics is an outlet for pressure groups, which I talk about in Chapter 9. Pressure groups are professional bodies which have expertise and policy objectives skewed to one particular area of society. For example, the British Medical Association has a keen interest in how the National Health Service is run. Pressure groups are important in society and their views find expression through politics; they often lobby government ministers hard for changes in the law or the pursuit of a particular policy.

- **Determine who exercises power.** In all societies someone, somewhere has to be in charge. Politics is the means by which the people decide which individual or collection of individuals should govern. In the UK, for instance, roughly 45 million people are registered to vote. These millions elect around 650 Members of Parliament and the party with the biggest grouping of these MPs goes on to form the government of the country. The daily cut and thrust of politics creates an impression in voters' minds regarding which candidate and party they'd like to cast their vote for at the next election.

Gauging the Role of Politicians

Whether or not you love them, loathe them or are just indifferent (and most people seem to be in the latter two camps), politicians are there for good reason. They can have a huge impact on the lives of ordinary individuals and the future of great nations and can even decide if countries go to war or live in peace.

Making the law

The key job of politicians the world over is to make the laws that govern society. These laws can be big and sweeping, encompassing fundamental changes to the way the economy and society are run or they can be small and technical, tinkering with existing laws to make them, hopefully, better.

Politicians may introduce draft laws to be voted upon and speak up for them but the actual writing of the laws is more often than not undertaken by civil servants, who I talk about in Chapter 14. Civil servants are also responsible for seeing that government policy is implemented and that it stays within the law of the land.

Politicians making laws is all very good, but they also need a functioning court system to carry these laws out. In addition, a competent and hopefully honest police force is needed to catch those who break the laws. The UK is fortunate as it's widely seen as possessing a capable judiciary, tested court system and a police force which is noted for its incorruptibility (relative to some other nations).

Changing the constitution and the way government works

Politicians can alter who does what in the government of the country. They do so through changing the constitution. The process of changing the UK's unwritten constitution is a fairly simple matter. All that's needed is for a majority of MPs to vote in favour of a new law changing what a part of government does, and for this law then to be approved by the House of Lords and signed off by the monarch.

The UK's unwritten constitution relies on a combination of written laws and unwritten traditions and customs. It's possible to change the way government works either through changing the law or through a tradition or custom altering over time.

Changing the constitution

The UK constitution can change in a couple of different ways, as the following examples illustrate:

✔ **By custom.** In 1688 the unpopular monarch James II was overthrown. James had brought this situation on himself by ignoring the views of prominent politicians in parliament. After the Glorious Revolution, as James's ouster was called, it became the custom that the monarch could act only on the advice of ministers – that is, the monarch had to do what he or she was told by the leading politicians of the country.

✔ **By law.** Just over two hundred years after James's reign ended, a constitutional crisis arose over a disagreement between the House of Lords and the House of Commons. The Parliament Act of 1911 solved this disagreement by changing the law (and thereby the constitution) so that the House of Lords could only delay rather than vote down laws passed by the House of Commons.

Ensuring a more controlled state

In essence, the politician, particularly in a democracy, has to act as society's conciliator. A politician's job is to listen to the opinions of business, groups of professionals and individuals, and to design government policy that best reflects these views and brings these groups into agreement.

In addition, politicians oversee the civil service. Politicians have the power to hire and fire underperforming civil servants or those who fail to work for the public good. In some countries politicians also control the judiciary and even the religious leaders.

Think of politicians as the string holding the elements of much of government and society together. The leadership of politicians is what prevents different groups in society from coming into conflict.

Galvanising the country in times of crisis

Cometh the hour, cometh the politician. It often falls to politicians to help bring the people of a country together in times of crisis. When an epidemic breaks out, people look to the politicians for leadership and to ensure that the government is 100 per cent focused on providing care for the sick and finding a cure. In 2009, with fears mounting over a worldwide H1N1 flu pandemic, it fell to the Labour government's minister of health – at the time, Alan Johnson – to co-ordinate the response, stockpiling anti-viral drugs and clearing space in emergency wards for the anticipated rush of cases.

Political reputations can be won and lost at times of crisis. In late 1940, with the UK facing defeat at the hands of Germany in the Second World War, the country was inspired by the great speeches and leadership of Prime Minister Winston Churchill. Churchill's reputation as a great leader was cemented forever. At the same time, in contrast, the French leadership crumbled in the face of military defeats at the hands of the Germans. The government disintegrated into factions and a disorganised rabble. This response destroyed the reputations of all the politicians involved. They'd failed the ultimate test of the politician – the crisis!

Listening to constituents

In the UK and many other democracies around the globe, politicians are elected to represent a particular locality. In the UK, even the prime minister is elected to parliament by people living in a locality. For example, Gordon Brown was elected by the voters of Dunfermline, Tony Blair by those of Sedgefield and, before him, PM John Major by those of Huntingdon.

This close interaction between politicians and the public is one of the strengths of the UK political system. All MPs run a weekly surgery where their constituents can come in to see them and discuss their problems. These surgeries are a good way of keeping politicians grounded in ordinary life and mean that the public feel that they have a hotline to those in power. It is one of the key jobs of politicians, in democracies, to represent each and every one of us.

By convention in the UK, the prime minister must be an elected MP rather than an appointed member of the House of Lords. The last time a prime minister was also a lord was over 100 hundred years ago.

Not only MPs represent the interests of constituents; thousands of local councillors across the length and breadth of the country also do so. These councillors are elected by a few thousand voters living in a ward. Their job is to listen to the views of people in their ward and ensure that local services are delivered efficiently. Most of the contact that members of the public have with politicians is with local councillors rather than MPs or government ministers. See Chapter 16 for more on local government in the UK.

Working for the good of the country

Politicians are meant to do what's best for the national interests of their country. At European Union (EU) summit meetings, for example, the British prime minister is meant to stand up for Britain's national interests first. If a new EU law is proposed which may damage Britain's economy or impair the civil liberties of its citizens, the public expects the prime minister and the government as a whole to oppose it tooth and nail.

In fact, along with ensuring the defence of the country, one of the absolute must-do's of government is always to represent national interest.

Tackling the Big Issues: The Current Challenges Facing Politicians

The world can be a dangerous, turbulent place and even countries with a long tradition of political and economic stability – like the UK – still have to face up to major threats. And in an increasingly globalised world, these threats seem more acute than ever; incidents thousands of miles away can suddenly snowball into massive global events.

Of course, it would be nice to light up the Bat signal or call on Superman when problems happen but that's the world of comic books. In the real world, the humble (and not so humble) politicians are the best thing we have for solving crises and ensuring peace and prosperity for as many people as possible.

It's the job of politicians to negotiate with one another and co-ordinate so that government can meet the challenges and defeat the dangers facing the world in the second decade of the 21st century. As well as the day-to-day issues – both big and small – that politicians face, they have to address some big themes too. No single politician is expected to come up with a complete answer to problems on their own, but as a collective politicians have to face up to and deal with the big issues highlighted in the following sections, which dominate the political landscape not just in the UK but around the globe.

All of the issues outlined are of epoch-defining import. Day to day, most politicians deal with far more mundane fare, such as National Health Service waiting list times or whether a weekly or fortnightly refuse collection service is more suitable. However, many of the issues covered in the next sections – such as the economy and protecting the environment – actually influence decisions taken on what may seem less important matters.

Keeping up living standards – it's the economy, stupid!

When he was campaigning for the US presidency in 1992, Bill Clinton's campaign famously posted the slogan, 'It's the economy, stupid!' in campaign headquarters to keep everyone focused on that major talking point.

The economy is an issue in most elections, in most democracies, in most years. Electors like to see their standard of living – which is the money they earn and the goods and services available to them – increase year after year.

Most of the time this scenario is what happens but occasionally the economy goes into recession, jobs are lost and people get poorer.

Understandably, during economic downturns the economy comes to the fore in voters' minds. But even when things only go a little wrong or show signs of potentially going wrong, the economy can race to the top of the list of hot political topics. Normally, governments up for election during a period of poor economic news are beaten by their opponents.

It's seen as the job of politicians to ensure that the right conditions are in place for the economy to grow, but how do they do that? Well, although the government isn't omnipotent as far as the economy goes, it can have quite an influence through the following methods:

- **Setting tax policy.** The government takes a certain percentage of people's earnings and business profits through taxation. By adjusting the amount of money they take in tax, the government can leave people and businesses with more or less money to spend in the shops or invest. Generally, high taxes reduce economic growth while lower taxes increase it.

- **Targeting government spending.** Government spending is hugely important to the economy and accounts for around 40 per cent of the UK's total economic output. By adjusting this spending, either up or down, the government can have a massive influence on economic activity.

- **Deregulation.** Most businesses the world over complain of government red tape. The argument goes – and it's a very solid one – that if you cut this red tape and allow businesses to do what they're good at – doing business and making money – then wider society will benefit and everyone will get richer.

  The flip side to this argument – and, again, it's a solid viewpoint – is that business must be regulated properly to ensure that the pursuit of wealth and profit doesn't damage wider society. For example, although it's expensive, chemical manufacturers should have to dispose of their waste safely; dumping it could cause environmental damage and risk human health.

The government doesn't try to create as much economic growth as it can, as doing so would have all sorts of consequences. For starters, high economic growth often leads to sharp rises in inflation, which can be especially harmful to poorer people. Likewise, a country focused purely on economic growth is likely to be polluted and to poorly protect workers' rights. The government's job – and thus that of politicians – is to balance the concerns of the few with the wider interests of society.

Following on from the credit crunch of 2008 and the subsequent economic recession, the government announced a massive programme of *quantitative easing* – which, in its simplest terms, means the printing of more money as a means of stimulating economic activity. In short, the government was hoping to put more money in the hands of business, government departments and individuals in the hope that they'd spend it on goods and services and thereby ease the recession and return the country to economic growth.

A country is deemed to be in recession if it's suffered two consecutive quarters – six months in total – of negative economic growth; that is, the economy has shrunk in size rather than grown. Whether the economy shrinks or increases in size is measured by the Office of National Statistics. Its job is to collect data on what's going on in the economy and wider UK society in order that politicians can make better-informed decisions.

The current governor of the Bank of England is Mervyn King. King is the UK's number one banker. As governor, King's job is to head up the monetary policy committee, which comprises nine prominent economists and bankers and is responsible for setting the base interest rate. This rate is crucial because all the banks and building societies use it as a base from which to set their own interest rates on loans. The governor, under instruction from the Chancellor of the Exchequer (a politician), also has to decide on how much new money to print and must increasingly oversee the activities of the banking sector as a whole. The governor is appointed by the Chancellor of the Exchequer. The governor is either re-appointed or replaced by the Chancellor every five years. In the City of London – so crucial to the health of the British economy – the governor is the biggest of the big cheeses!

Saving the planet

Superheroes are always being charged with saving the planet but in reality the normally suited and booted and middle-aged politician is the one who takes on the job.

There's little doubt that the industrialisation of the globe, the explosion in the number of cars, and modern air travel have the potential to kill the planet. The globe is warming, the polar ice caps are melting and sea levels are rising. And all this – scientists warn us – is just the start of a process which could have untold consequences for humanity.

As you can imagine, the issue of the environment is one of the biggest if not *the* biggest facing politicians around the globe. However, dramatic environmental change doesn't occur in a short period of time – in 5, 10 or even 20 years. No, we're looking at 50, 100 or even several centuries hence when the environmental doomsday scenarios outlined by scientists are actually likely to come to pass. The problem with developing a long-term strategy to deal with this environmental crisis is that politicians come and go relatively quickly – the longest-serving British PM for the past 100 years was Margaret Thatcher, and she was in Downing Street for just 11 years – and they also have their eye on the next election. It can be difficult for politicians to make unpopular decisions in the short term in order to help ease a problem which is likely to only start having a major impact when they've long departed the political stage, or even after, to put it bluntly, they're dead.

In relation to the environment, politicians are often accused of short-term thinking and policy choices. But in recent years the issue of the environment has steadily moved up the list of subjects that electors are concerned about and with it some politicians have shown an inclination to make the unpopular decisions which may be necessary if humanity is to prosper beyond the 21st century.

The steps politicians take to ease global warming include the following:

- ✔ **Make laws to limit carbon emissions.** Governments have the power to make new laws which cap the amount of harmful CO_2 emissions released by airlines and petrochemical companies, for example. Although laws can be backed up through prosecutions if necessary, at present the UK prefers to use persuasion and financial incentives to try to encourage businesses to emit less CO_2.

- ✔ **Keep a lid on government emissions.** One of the biggest polluters is actually the government itself through the actions of its bureaucracy, military and health service workers. In fact, the government in the UK accounts for some 40 per cent of all economic output. It follows, therefore, that the government can cut a heap of the nation's CO_2 emissions. And it's up to the politicians to make the policy for civil servants to follow to see that this emissions cut happens.

- ✔ **Co-ordinate a global strategy.** Global warming, as the name suggests, is a global problem and it therefore needs – you guessed it – a global solution. Governments get together every so often to discuss how each of them is facing up to the problem. So far many of these climate change conferences, such as the one held in Copenhagen in December 2009, have attracted criticism for being little more than talking shops, and cynics have suggested that many of the promises made are later broken. But ultimately it is only through politicians and governments around the globe coming to agreement, and crucially meeting the terms of those agreements, that global warming is going to be eased.

UK politicians often say that, as a country, the UK can't itself do much about global warming, and they have a point. China, for example, is opening a new coal-fired power station each fortnight, while the UK takes years to decide whether or not it needs to build much more environmentally cleaner nuclear power stations. The UK is home to about 1 per cent of the world's population and is responsible for roughly 2.5 per cent of the emissions linked to global warming. However, the Labour government of Gordon Brown has agreed to cut emissions and it is a key goal of UK diplomats to get other countries to do the same.

Blaming the newly industrialising Chinese or Indians for the recent expansion in harmful CO_2 emissions is easy – and many environmental campaigners do. However, the governments of these two emerging economic super-powers make a simple point when being lectured by Western nations and environmental bodies: they say that all they're trying to do is enjoy the same standard of living as the West has enjoyed for years and that, even now, the Westerners – and particularly Americans – emit more harmful CO_2 per head than the Indians and Chinese combined.

Bringing an end to world poverty

Read any history book and it will tell you that poverty has always been with us. But nowadays politicians around the globe are more aware of the inequities of global poverty. They question the fairness of a situation in which a couple of billion people live in relative luxury – have adequate food, clothing and heat – while another couple of billion are struggling for survival crippled by disease and poverty. Just look at the ultimate indicator of poverty and wealth: in wealthy Japan the average woman can expect to live well into her 80s; in civil strife-torn Zimbabwe the average man can expect to die before he reaches 40. Enough said!

But poverty – like global warming – is one of those giant issues that is well beyond the scope of even the most dynamic of politicians or any single government. It requires a global solution, with many politicians coming together.

However only of late, through campaigns such as Make Poverty History, has the uncertain state of many countries and people in the developing world come to the fore. How poverty is tackled is a matter of some debate but in meetings of the G8 and G20 – the international bodies which bring together the world's biggest economies – the following ways to help the developing world avoid the poverty trap have been identified by politicians:

- ✔ **Forgive debts.** It may seem hard to believe, but some incredibly poor nations, particularly in sub-Saharan Africa, owe huge sums to international banks, foreign governments and the World Bank. In fact, until recently governments across Africa had to repay more in interest each year on loans than they gained through aid from richer countries. In effect, the developing world throughout the 1980s and 1990s was actually handing over more money than it was receiving from the wealthy – normally Western – nations.

  Under PMs Tony Blair and Gordon Brown, the UK government has taken a leading role in trying to persuade other rich nations to forgive African debts in particular. Their argument is that the paying of interest on often decades-old loans was causing these nations to remain poor. Prompted by the UK, many countries around the globe have agreed a timetable for reducing and forgiving debts but some anti-poverty campaigners still say doing so isn't enough.

- ✔ **Target aid.** At present, Western governments such as the UK contribute on average 0.5 to just over 1 per cent of their national income in aid projects for the benefit of the developing world. Now this may not seem enough but when you combine all the monies flowing in from the G8 and G20 member nations it can make quite a tidy pile of cash, which can then be given to the government of the country in need of aid and United Nations agencies to be spent on infrastructure investment in the developing world, such as clean water supplies, better hospitals, schools and transport links. However, some countries have actually reneged to some extent on their aid promises and anti-poverty campaigners say that, long term, more money is needed.

✔ **Promote good governance.** One of the biggest problems facing the developing world is poor governance. Politicians and military leaders are often corrupt, incompetent or a combination of the two. All too often in recent history, particularly in sub-Saharan Africa, government aid money has been spent on weapons or simply embezzled. Some of the abuses by government leaders in these countries are simply shocking, with corrupt politicians siphoning off millions if not hundreds of millions of pounds into their own bank accounts.

Giving a developing world government lots of aid is pointless if it doesn't have the means – through honest civil servants and government officials – to spend the money on the right projects. Trying to ensure proper governance is absolutely key to seeing that a combination of aid and debt forgiveness actually leads to improvements in the standard of living for ordinary people.

Fighting terrorism

If you'd asked a politician from the UK or US to rank the importance of Islamic terrorism on 10 September 2001, they probably wouldn't have put it very high on their list of must-tackle jobs. But on 11 September 2001, following the killing of thousands of US civilians by Islamic extremist terrorists, suddenly terrorism became one of the most important issues facing politicians around the globe.

The 'War on Terror', as it was dubbed by former US president George W. Bush, has been a game-changing event. US and UK foreign policy has been geared towards the elimination of the Islamic terrorist threat, with very mixed results. Invasions of Afghanistan and later Iraq were either wholly or partly justified by the need to bring Islamic terrorists to book. However, both these wars have proved unpopular and a source of disagreement between politicians.

Even nearly a decade on from 9/11, politicians in the UK and elsewhere are still faced with the massive problem of trying to protect their own civilians from an enemy which is well organised and highly secretive. In the UK, in particular, politicians have faced the quandary of trying to curtail domestic-bred Islamic terrorism while simultaneously preserving long-standing civil rights.

One of the biggest arguments in British politics of recent years concerns the right of the police to hold people suspected of terrorist crimes in custody without charge. At one time, former Labour PM Tony Blair wanted the police to be able to hold people on suspicion of terrorist activity for up to 90 days without charge. This proposal provoked outrage from some civil rights bodies and opposition MPs. It was eventually agreed by a vote in parliament to allow 28-day detention but the arguments still rumble on all the same.

Reckoning with the decline of Western dominance

The Western powers such as the US and UK have been the wealthiest, strongest militarily and most economically successful for the past few hundred years. In fact, just over 100 years ago even China looked set to be colonised by white Europeans and India was ruled by the British.

Oh, how times have changed! The economic powerhouses of the 21st century are likely to be China and India, and even America isn't as powerful as it once was (I talk more about this in Chapter 21). How to manage this relative change in the global pecking order peacefully is a key political issue for politicians around the globe.

For example, what role should China – which has a very dodgy human rights record indeed – play in big international bodies such as the G20, World Bank and other UN agencies? Likewise, what about preserving economic stability in a world where massive trade imbalances exist between East and West (in short, the East produces most of the manufactured goods which are bought by the West)?

Taking Matters into Your Own Hands: Becoming an Activist

Okay, politicians are important but they're not the be-all and end-all of politics. Ordinary individuals can and do make a difference not just to the course of political debate but to actual events, and help shape what happens. They do so by being *activists*, which, as the name suggests, means that they take action.

You can be an activist in a variety of ways:

- ✔ **Participate in public demonstrations.** In countries like the UK, groups and individuals are free to protest through peaceful demonstrations, carrying banners and shouting slogans. Protestors aim to get their views across to both politicians and other citizens.

- ✔ **Use the media.** Doing an action, granting an interview or otherwise attracting media coverage are effective ways to publicise your views to a large number of people. Activists that get lots of media coverage can often be successful. (Chapter 10 has more on the media and politics.)

- ✔ **Take part in direct action.** Direct action is normally associated with forms of protest that can be violent at times. The idea is to show the public and politicians that you feel so strongly about an issue that you're willing to take extreme measures. But a less confrontational type of direct action is to actually try to help those that you're calling on politicians to help. For example, a pressure group looking for better rights for asylum seekers will have volunteer lawyers available to help fight their cases in court. This type of direct action is more about giving up your time and energy to the cause to make a difference.

You can rarely make much of a difference as an activist on your own. Instead, you need to form or join a pressure group of like-minded people, which I talk more about in Chapter 9.

In democratic countries like the UK, activists sometimes do see their policy proposals make it into law. But for this to happen, they need to convince the politicians that what they're calling for is the right thing to do and has the support of the wider general public. So, in reality, activists need politicians and do in fact often try to meet MPs and ministers to promote their cause.

Sometimes politics as we know it simply breaks down. Groups of people take to the streets with the aim of toppling the government, which is called a *revolution*. These are incredibly rare in Britain – although violent street protests are far from unknown in dear old Blighty. East Germany probably provides the best example of revolution in recent times. In 1989, people took to the streets fed up with the tyrannical communist regime; their actions led to its collapse and the eventual re-unification of East and West Germany under a democratic government.

Chapter 3

Looking at Participatory Democracy

. . . .

In This Chapter

▶ Qualifying what is meant by democracy

▶ Examining different types of democracy

▶ Laying bare the rights that British citizenship brings

▶ Looking at the strengths and weaknesses of Britain's democracy

▶ Considering growing voter apathy

. . . .

You take it as read that you live in a democracy and most of the people you know from overseas probably live in a democracy as well. But what does the word *democracy* mean and how do you as an individual benefit from living under this system and use it to change the society you live in?

In this chapter, I look at the ins and outs of Britain's unique democracy and how it affects your life.

Understanding What Qualifies as a Democracy

Democracy is a system of government where the people – either the general public, or their elected representatives – basically run the show. It's either the general public or their elected representatives who decide what the government of the country should do. The great nineteenth century US president Abraham Lincoln talked in his famous Gettysburg address about 'government of the people, by the people, for the people', and that's about the best definition of democracy you can find.

Dozens of democratic countries exist across the globe, for example the United States, India, France, Japan and, of course, dear old Blighty. But no two democracies are identical; each has its own twist on the democratic theme.

The US political system, for instance, is two-tiered, with state and federal governments elected in different ways and each part exercising very distinct power. Elections are held for all branches of government, from the president down to the local sheriff. In Britain, on the other hand, until the advent of the Scottish parliament and Welsh and Northern Irish assemblies (see Chapter 16 for more on these) government was centralised, with many of the laws of the land passed by the UK parliament, and electors having the right to change the government in power usually only every four or five years.

Regardless of the approach to democracy a country takes, in order for a nation to be deemed democratic its elections must have some key traits:

✔ They must be held regularly for both local and national government positions.

✔ They must be free and fair so no one is pressured into voting a particular way and ballots are cast anonymously.

✔ The overwhelming majority of the population must be eligible to vote (some groups such as prisoners or the insane may be excluded in some countries).

Holding elections doesn't automatically mean that a country is a democracy. Sometimes, countries which are very far from democracies call themselves democratic merely because they hold elections of some type. But elections to a talking shop (an unproductive, bureaucratic and self-serving organisation) or to a rubber stamp institution for a dictator aren't true democratic elections. Examples of countries which were clearly not democracies but held elections include:

✔ During the Cold War (which ran from 1945–91, with the Soviet Union on one side and Western democracies on the other), East Germany called itself the German Democratic Republic (or GDR). They did so despite being a communist state and having a brutal secret police quelling all opposition to the government. However, the top brass of the GDR believed calling themselves a democracy was legitimate because the party which ran the country had a huge membership and party officials were elected by ballots of party members.

✔ Former Iraqi dictator Saddam Hussein regularly held elections in which he and his cronies were voted into power with an astonishing 99 per cent of the votes cast. Such results aren't the effect of free and fair elections; that the Iraqi people were frightened by years of murderous activity by Hussein's secret police and afraid to vote against his regime is much more likely.

In some fledgling democracies or countries in which elections are being held for the first time ever, it's usual for observers from the United Nations and European Union to be asked in to verify that the election is indeed free and fair.

Starting with Athenian direct democracy

The UK is often referred to as one of the world's oldest democracies, and it is. But long before anyone thought to create a parliament – in fact, about the same time as Britons were discovering that wheels are best if they're round – a flourishing democracy was up and running in the Mediterranean, in Athens to be precise.

The great Greek philosopher Aristotle defined the Athenian democracy of his day as 'rule by the many' or, alternatively, 'rule by the people'. Political scientists call it *Athenian direct democracy*. So what was Athenian direct democracy? Put simply, every Athenian citizen had the right to attend, speak and vote at meetings of the city's assembly to pass laws and decide on the level of taxation.

Ancient Athens is often held up as some sort of democratic Utopia. Some see it as a much purer form of democracy than exists in Britain today, as we only get to vote for candidates at election times, rather than vote on actual bills. Many things weren't quite right about ancient Athenian democracy, however. Citizens could vote but citizenship wasn't conferred on women or slaves, who made up the majority of Athens' population at the time.

The Athenian democracy wasn't that durable either; it was eventually destroyed by invaders. In fact, once the Athenians were invaded, democracy in any form we would recognise today virtually disappeared from the Western world right up until the 1700s and 1800s. But the Athenian model was crucial, as records remained of how it worked, which informed many great political thinkers during the Enlightenment (a period roughly covering the eighteenth century, when scientific endeavour, the arts and political thinking flowered in Europe), who in turn had a key influence on the forming of some of the world's biggest modern democracies. These democracies grew up against a similar cultural and intellectual backdrop, and so influenced each other. Other countries, such as Japan and Germany, suffered cataclysmic events such as defeat in war and the overturning of rulers before they adopted democracy.

If anyone highlights how democratic ideas crossed borders over the past few hundred years it's Thomas Paine. Living in Britain until age 37, his writings calling for greater democracy influenced many in his own country. He then emigrated to America, where he became a leading figure in the American Revolution and the formation of that nation's representative democracy. He wasn't finished there. He was in France during its revolution in the 1790s, where his ideas on democracy were hugely influential too.

Referendums: Direct voting power

Probably the closest thing we have these days to Athenian direct democracy is a referendum. A referendum is a national vote involving all voters on just one key issue. Everyone who wants a say turns up on a specific day at a polling station and casts a vote: yes or no. Once the votes are counted, the government then (usually) follows the course of action that the majority of those who cast their ballot in the referendum want to take.

On parts of the Continent and in America – at a state rather than federal level – referendums are commonplace. But, controversially, in recent years some European governments have held referendums on whether to ratify European Union treaties, only to be told by voters that they don't want ratification to go ahead. The response? In all cases, the governments have waited a little while and then simply put the question to the people again.

Referendums are very rare in Britain. In fact, the last national referendum was held by the Labour government of Harold Wilson back in the 1970s. It asked whether people wanted Britain to remain a part of the European Economic Community (now called the European Union). Roughly two-thirds of votes cast were for the UK to stay in the Community – so it did. More recent referendums have been held in Scotland and Wales, asking people there whether or not they wanted their own parliament or assembly, respectively.

Getting into representative democracy

The Athenian model of direct democracy, with every eligible voter casting a vote himself (and, in Athens, all the voters were male), sort of worked mainly because there were so few citizens to take part. But can you imagine asking the best part of 60 million Britons to turn up 40 or more times a year at the Houses of Parliament to decide on laws and taxes? For one thing, the catering would be a nightmare!

Modern democracies aren't direct like the Athenian model, but are representative instead. In a *representative democracy*, instead of voting directly on laws to be passed, people vote for candidates, and the winning candidates then vote on the laws.

In the UK, people vote for local councillors, Members of Parliament or Members of the European Parliament. In the United States, citizens vote for a president or members of congress, on a state level they vote for governors, members of the state legislature and local mayors, sheriffs and even the local garbage man (the last is a joke but lots of public offices aren't appointed in the US; they're elected). In fact, the Americans have lots of elections, full stop.

Homing in on British Democracy

For most of Britain's history, the nation hasn't been, by modern ways of thinking at least, a democracy. In fact, in early Victorian Britain calling a politician a 'democrat' was often considered a term of abuse. Earlier than that the upper echelons of society, such as the monarchy and landed classes of the realm, were horrified at the idea that common people – that's me and you – could ever be given the vote. We were illiterate and probably smelt; how could our small brains ever cope with the intricacies of political debate? You get the picture. But over time this attitude changed dramatically and nowadays even I – despite the fact that I occasionally still smell – have a vote to elect a representative to the UK and European parliaments and my local council.

Claiming first place in the representative democracy race

Lots of different countries claim they're the first home of representative democracy. But probably the three main contenders are France, the US and Britain.

The French claim lies in what happened during its bloody revolution of 1789. A feudal society and monarchy were overthrown – with lots of cutting off of heads – and replaced by Estates, where the citizens were free to vote for their representatives. The French went from feudal to the most modern of democracies in the bat of an eye. Unfortunately, it ended in tears as, within a few years, Napoleon rose to become dictator and swept away meaningful democratic aspects of the political system.

The United States' claim to be the home of representative democracy holds more water. They had their own revolution – this time against the ruling British – and adopted a constitution guaranteeing citizens' rights and setting out a more fully fledged representative democracy (see Chapter 21 for more on the US political system). Like Athenian direct democracy, however, holes appear in this story too, with large numbers of citizens barred from voting in elections – slavery and segregation of the black minority until the 1960s mean that American democracy has only recently become truly representative of the people's views.

Britain has the oldest system of representative democracy, with elections to the UK parliament held for many centuries before the French and American revolutions. However, although Britain had a parliament which made the laws of the land, the overwhelming majority of people had no say in who sat in that parliament. Right up until the mid-nineteenth century only male landowners could vote at election time. Some still question Britain's democratic credentials because a non-elected body, the House of Lords, has a key role in making laws for the country and most of its members are appointed by the monarch (who follows the advice of the prime minister), although there have been widespread calls to make members of the House of Lords stand for election.

You can find the full lowdown on Britain's path to democracy in Chapter 5 or, for even more detail, *British History For Dummies* (Wiley) is the best place to go. But the next sections talk about some key stages on the road to you and I getting the vote.

Putting the monarchy in its place

If you're reading this, Your Majesty, look away now as this section describes how your ancestors lost top billing. When the Normans invaded in 1066 they brought with them their own knights, lords and a monarch sitting at the top of the tree. The monarch was supposed to have absolute power, meaning anything – and I do mean anything – he or she said, went. If the monarch said Wednesday was 'wear an onion on your head day', everyone would be sporting just that the following week.

This state of affairs continued for some six centuries, but all through that time lords, other powerful landowners and wealthy merchants were wanting to have their say in how things were run, from laws passed to taxes collected. After all, these men were paying taxes, and so expected something in return! Gradually, parliament became the forum through which powerful elites began to voice their grievances against the monarchy. Rather than act as a tool to be controlled by the king or queen of the day, in the sixteenth and seventeenth centuries, it increasingly began to exert its own influence on affairs.

Over time, parliament gained increasing prestige and power. Eventually, after a bloody civil war and quite a bit of political machination, in 1688 – in what is known as the Glorious Revolution – parliament became in effect the supreme law-making body in the land. In future, all monarchs had to bend to the will of parliament and the election of its members became a very big deal.

Britain's transition from monarchy to representative democracy hasn't been without struggle or bloodshed. However, Britain has been more fortunate than a lot of other countries in that its march to democracy has been evolutionary rather than revolutionary. Contrast this situation with Russia, which now at least defines itself as a democracy. Russia has been through a bloody revolution and then 70 years of Communist Party control during which millions of people were put to death for having a different political ideology or simply on twisted whim.

Expanding the franchise

Landowners and wealthy merchants had got one over on the monarch and parliament was now supreme. But parliament was one big club, with only landowners able to vote members in or out. That situation suited the landowners and merchants very much but not the rest of the population – and they, after all, are in the overwhelming majority.

Fighting the good fight: Getting votes for women

Until 1918, the majority gender, women, weren't allowed to vote. If you suggested publicly that women should have the vote in Georgian or early Victorian Britain, there was every chance you could be locked up for being mad! Such was the ingrained prejudice in society and even amongst women themselves.

However, as more and more men got the vote and the country didn't collapse as opponents of expanding the franchise had feared, the idea of votes for women, or *women's suffrage* as it was called, started to take root. Groups of women called *suffragettes* and *suffragists* started to agitate for the vote. Following the crucial role that women played in winning the First World War, the vote was granted, at first only to women over 30 and then ultimately according to the same parameters as men.

As the population and the economy grew, the idea and practice of having so much power concentrated in the hands of so few became unworkable. So during the nineteenth century the *franchise* – the right to vote – expanded, slowly at first and then more quickly. First up, men who rented land were allowed a vote in 1832 (still only one in seven men in 1832 were allowed to vote). In 1867 this was extended to all male householders but still upwards of 40 per cent of men didn't have a vote. This inequality was corrected through further Acts in 1884 and 1918 when all men over age 21 were allowed to vote. The right to vote was extended to women over age 30 in 1918, after the First World War. Not until 1928 were women allowed to vote from age 21, the same as men.

At the start of the nineteenth century less than 10 per cent of the adult population could vote, but by 1900 this had shot up to around 30 per cent.

In the UK, all adults over 18 with some small exceptions – see Chapter 7 for more details – have the right to vote. However, some are calling for this age to be lowered further to 16. They say that 16-year-olds have other legal rights and can pay income tax and national insurance in their own right, so why shouldn't they have a vote. The Labour governments of Tony Blair and Gordon Brown have shown some interest in expanding the franchise but it's not expected to happen anytime soon.

Throwing digital democracy into the mix

Grafting Athenian-style direct democracy (see 'Starting with Athenian direct democracy' earlier in this chapter) onto nineteenth- or twentieth-century British society was obviously impossible. Too many people and too few resources made getting the citizens to make the laws of the land through a never-ending series of ballots unworkable. No one would get anything else done – and just think of the paperwork!

In the twenty-first century, however, we have the Internet and digital technology, which allow us to watch virtually whatever we want and communicate with whomever we want at the flick of a button. It's possible, therefore, even in a country of 60 million, to actually run a direct electronic democracy, or *e-democracy*, with you, me and the postmaster all deciding what laws to introduce and approve – or not.

The Internet also allows everyone much greater access to information. Finding out whole reams of information, in fact enough to make informed choices on complex topics, is possible with a few mouse clicks.

Strong voices argue against e-democracy, making the following points:

- ✔ **Fraud danger.** Whoever controls the electronic method of gathering votes could have the opportunity to rig the ballot without anyone else knowing. This scenario may sound a bit Big Brother but is a concern for civil liberty groups.

- ✔ **Digital divide.** Not everyone is comfortable with or has access to new technology. In fact, for many people Twitter is something the birds do rather than the electronic communication of the minute. If you don't know that much about technology you're less likely to take part in the e-democratic process.

- ✔ **Dumbing down of debate.** No matter how great the resources on the Internet for getting to know about a particular topic before voting on law changes, most people will still simply vote according to a combination of gut instinct, possible prejudice, and what their favourite political party says is right. Who, after all, has the spare time to go through the minutiae of reports and data available on a particular topic to be voted on?

E-democracy is a long way off in Britain because the idea that the elected representatives make the decision on behalf of their constituents has a very strong pull.

The Scottish parliament has an element of direct democracy in that relatively small groups of voters get to vote on contentious issues. These votes don't impact the vote in the parliament directly, but the results of these polls are emailed to Members of the Scottish Parliament (MSPs). The idea is to let the MSPs know how their electors are thinking but the members are free to ignore these snapshot polls.

Understanding the Rights that Come with British Citizenship

Cecil Rhodes, the Victorian colonialist, said that to be born British was to win first prize in the lottery of life. Now that's a fairly big claim, which I'm sure people all over the world would have a few things to say about. Nevertheless being a Brit brings with it certain fundamental rights enshrined in the law of the land. These key rights include:

✔ The right to a fair trial and not to be detained without due legal process.

✔ The right to vote if you're a citizen over age 18 and your name appears on the *electoral register* – the list of people that live in a constituency. All British citizens over age 18 must register as a legal requirement.

✔ The right to the protection of the Human Rights Act.

The Human Rights Act was adopted into British law in 2000. This international agreement enshrines in law many of the rights and liberties already enjoyed by Britons for hundreds of years – the right to free expression, a fair trail, liberty and security, to marry and found a family, and the right to life – this last rather a biggie. Other rights enshrined include freedom of association and assembly and freedom from torture and slavery.

✔ The right to free speech as long as it doesn't libel others or incite violence.

✔ The right to state education and health care.

And these are just the big rights. Lots of little ones exist too, embedded in hundreds of years of laws passed by the UK parliament.

The UK doesn't have a written constitution, unlike the United States, for example. Instead, the judicial system relies on a patchwork of new and old laws passed by parliament and overseen by the courts to protect civil liberties and to ensure fair play in society.

There aren't actually any British citizens; instead we are all subjects of the Crown. However, these days the term *subject* is considered a bit out of date, a throwback to the days when the monarch was all-powerful, so Britons refer to themselves as citizens.

Evaluating the Pros and Cons of UK Democracy

No country and no democracy is perfect; they all have little kinks which mean that some groups of people feel hard done by or find that they're governed by people who have views they don't share or they don't even like!

This is as true of Britain – which has one of the world's most respected democracies – as of any other country. The time has come to look in the national mirror and see what's good and not so good about our system of government.

Looking at the strengths

Now you can puff out your chest with national pride because Britain is one of the most longstanding, stable and successful democracies in the world. In modern times, Britain hasn't succumbed to dictatorships, as has happened in Germany, Italy, Japan and Spain. The rights of the individual and the rule of law are held dear in Britain, as is freedom of speech and of the press.

In fact, only in wartime or when the country has been attacked by terrorists has the state acted to curb some civil liberties. These instances are always scrutinised and sometimes overturned by the courts.

Taking new-fangled citizenship tests

In the recent past, if you wanted to become a British citizen all you had to do was either be born here, marry a Brit or live here long enough to qualify. Handing out citizenship to incomers was always a low-key affair, but that is no longer the case.

Tony Blair's Labour government introduced citizenship tests in 2005 to improve the knowledge of British culture and way of life amongst those who were seeking to become citizens. The test isn't that hard and is multiple choice but it has to be passed or citizenship won't be granted. (If you want to know more about these tests, check out *British Citizenship Test For Dummies*, also written by your humble author and published by Wiley.)

As the icing on the cake, the government also decided to introduce citizenship ceremonies. These are simply gatherings where new citizens swear an oath of allegiance to their new home country and to the Crown.

It's a small world: Westminster Village

Political journalists often refer to something called the Westminster Village, which doesn't mean an actual village called Westminster with its own pub, post office or local shop (although Westminster does have plenty of all three). The term refers more to the community of politicians, civil servants, lobbyists and journalists located in (guess where?) Westminster.

Sometimes *the Westminster Village* is used as a condemnatory phrase meaning that the same politicians, civil servants, lobbyists and journalists get preoccupied with gossip or a political media story that doesn't really impact everyday Britons' lives.

Unlike the United States, Britain doesn't have a written constitution with a clearly defined separation of powers that lets the executive branch, judicial system and legislature know precisely what they're allowed to do or not to do. Instead, the UK relies on laws built up over many hundreds of years to protect liberties and curb the powers of the executive. This system is a patchwork solution that holds the country together well.

Some of the reasons British democracy is held up as an exemplar include:

- ✔ **Flexibility.** The British constitution, because it's unwritten, evolves naturally over time as laws or conventions change. Take, for example, the role of the monarch: he or she is head of state but it's generally agreed that he or she has little involvement in everyday politics.

- ✔ **Strong parties.** The UK's political parties are longstanding and have deep roots in communities and amongst large sections of society. Also none of the main political parties – Labour, Conservative or Liberal Democrat – follow extreme right or left policies. (Chapter 8 has more on the party system.)

- ✔ **Judicial primacy.** Everyone is subject to the law in the UK and everyone is equal under the law. This very important principle means that no matter how politically powerful, rich, well-connected or famous any individual is, he or she has to obey the law. The same goes for organisations. The court system is what holds the invisible strands of Britain's constitution together; Chapter 11 delves into the role of the judiciary.

Recognising the weaknesses

Now, not all is good with Britain (the weather for starters), including its democracy. Some of the common complaints about Britain's democracy include these points:

✔ **Behind the times.** Many say that Britain's approach of adhering to an unwritten constitution is very old-fashioned. In addition, we have a monarch when most nations got rid of theirs a long time ago. The system of electing MPs through the first-past-the-post poll is also longstanding and unique.

MPs are elected through the first-past-the-post system. The candidate who polls the highest number of votes in an individual constituency takes the seat in the House of Commons. The winning candidate doesn't have to get a majority of the votes cast, just the biggest number. Under this system, MPs have the same power and legitimacy whether they win by one vote or by 30,000.

✔ **Not democratic enough.** Voters get to elect their local MP, councillor and Member of the European Parliament, but elections aren't that frequent (MPs stand every four or five years in general). Plus, some important positions, including membership of the House of Lords and the judiciary, aren't elected but appointed.

✔ **Too centred on Westminster.** Most of British government is located within a couple of miles of the Houses of Parliament in Westminster. The Department of Health, the Ministry of Defence and the prime minister's residence, 10 Downing Street, are all within a stone's throw of each other. Critics say that, as a result, politicians are out of touch with the rest of the country and that the concerns of people far away from Westminster aren't given due regard.

This argument is frequently used by the Scottish and Welsh nationalists as a justification for why they should have more power in their parts of the country and even complete independence from the British state.

Being a Citizen

Being a good citizen isn't limited to voting – although that basic obligation is one that many Brits are avoiding these days. But beyond voting, you can be as politically involved as you like.

Getting involved

Participation in politics is much more than simply turning up at a polling station on election day and casting a vote. For many people, politics is a day in, day out interest, something which helps them feel that they're contributing to wider society. Across the country, literally hundreds of thousands of people to a greater or lesser extent are involved in politics, from simply signing a petition to standing for elected office.

Some ways to be politically active include:

✔ Joining a pressure group. (Chapter 9 has more on these.)

✔ Joining a political party and becoming an activist. (Turn to Chapter 8 for information on how the parties work.)

✔ Running for elected office.

✔ Becoming an eminent person in your field and advising civil servants or ministers.

Just about everyone is allowed to run for elected office in the UK. All you have to do is register as a candidate and pay a deposit of £500, which you get back if you win five per cent of the vote. See Chapter 17 for more on being a candidate at election time.

Gauging voter apathy and the reasons for it

In recent British general, local and European elections, an odd thing has been happening: the number of people turning up to cast their vote has been falling, not by just a little but a lot.

After the Second World War around 80 per cent of those eligible to vote in general elections did so and, although this fell back a bit over time, in 1979 still around three-quarters of eligible people participated. During the 1980s voter turnout fell to just over 65 per cent. As the political tables turned and Tony Blair's Labour Party started to win elections comfortably, voter turnout again took a nosedive, this time to below 60 per cent at the 2005 general election.

So why are fewer people voting? Well, for a number of reasons, including in short:

✔ **Disillusionment.** Many members of the public don't trust politicians to keep their constituents' interests at heart.

✔ **The result is known.** Many of the recent UK general elections have been almost a forgone conclusions, so many voters don't bother turning out.

✔ **Party similarity.** The policies of the UK's big political parties are widely seen as substantially the same.

I explore voter apathy in greater detail in Chapter 7.

Voter turnout varies according to the type of election being held. Generally, elections to the UK parliament see the highest turnout as they're seen as the most important. European and local elections are seen as less crucial, so voter turnout is lower; sometimes as few as one in three people eligible to vote do so.

Everyone aged 18 and over has to put their name on the electoral roll – that's the law. However, estimates suggest that as many as six million adults, as a result of chaotic life situations or wanting to keep a low profile, aren't on the electoral roll. The UK population is around 60 million, with around 46 million registered to vote (the lower number accounts for those not on the electoral roll, children and unregistered immigrants).

Lots of proposals are put forward for reversing low voter turnout, including compelling people to vote through legislation, making it easier to vote through online ballots, or allowing more voters to use a postal vote rather than having to turn up at a polling station at a specific time on a specific day.

Chapter 4

Examining Political Ideologies

In This Chapter

▶ Getting to grips with ideologies

▶ Homing in on liberalism

▶ Scrutinising socialism

▶ Keeping the status quo: Conservatism

▶ Looking at alternative ideologies

▶ Avoiding extremes in the UK

*A*t its root politics is all about ideas and the British political system, with its parties, politicians and pressure groups, is no different. Behind the sound bites and the arguments that are the cut and thrust of British political debate lie some very big ideas indeed about how individuals should live their lives and how society is organised.

In this chapter, I give you the lowdown on the big political ideologies that have shaped and continue to influence modern British politics and those of other countries around the globe.

Understanding What an Ideology Is

Put simply, an *ideology* is a single idea or collection of ideas relating to how society, economics and politics should be organised. Ideologies are hugely important as they set out a roadmap for the policies pursued by politicians and they inspire political activists. In fact, politics is dominated by ideology; people enter politics inspired by these ideas and some will literally sacrifice everything for them, both for themselves or others.

Moderating ideologies: The British way

Sometimes the pursuit of an ideology can be used to justify downright cruelty but in modern times in the UK fortunately this hasn't happened. The more revolutionary ideologies don't have many supporters in Britain.

Ideologies are hugely important in all countries and political systems. The major ideologies that hold sway in the UK include:

- ✔ **Conservatism.** The support of national traditions and institutions in order to retain stability and continuity.
- ✔ **Liberalism.** Protecting the rights of the individual from interference from an overbearing state.
- ✔ **Socialism.** A way of organising the economy and society to benefit as many people as possible.

Conservatism, liberalism and socialism are represented through the UK's three main political parties. Working out which ideology goes with which isn't difficult. Socialism is the ideology of the Labour Party, conservatism of the Conservative Party and liberalism of the Liberal Democrats.

Although UK political parties are rooted in ideology, they're also what's termed a *broad church*, meaning they aren't slavish devotees to their ideologies and instead are practical, bending what they do to the prevailing mood of the public.

The ideologies of the main UK political parties are related to the class from which they draw their main support. For example, the Labour Party draws much of its support from the working class. Socialism is the predominant ideology amongst certain sections of the working class. As for the Conservatives, they draw much of their support from the upper and middle classes who have a vested interest in retaining the existing economic and political state of affairs. Liberalism is a bit different. Many of the key ideas underpinning liberalism – such as the importance of individual freedom – are supported by just about everyone in society but many of the people who are the most passionate about it come from those involved in the law or education.

Ideologies are all about 'isms', such as socialism, Marxism or conservatism. The mania for tacking on an 'ism' can sometimes apply to policies pursued by previous prime ministers (PMs) if they happen to have an ideological theme running through them. For example, Conservative PM Margaret Thatcher's policies were referred to as Thatcherism and Labour PM Tony Blair's as Blairism. In fact, if you're a politician and you have an 'ism' named after you, you know you're making a real impact on the political scene of the country.

Liberalising the world: The march of the western democratic model

As recently as the 1940s the overwhelming majority of the world's population lived in undemocratic political systems. Since the end of the Second World War and the demise of communism in Russia and the Eastern bloc in the

1990s, the number of countries worldwide that can be classed as democratic has increased many times over.

What's called western-style democracy, rooted in the ideologies of liberalism, has blossomed so much that for the first time in human history nearly the majority of the world's population now lives in a democracy. The reason democracy has taken off is because the ideology of liberalism that goes hand in glove with it resonates very strongly with people from all corners of the globe.

For example, a free press, the belief in government by consent, and equality under the law can be seen enshrined in the constitutions of many newly democratised states.

Focusing on Freedom with Liberalism

The British are among the most free people on the planet. You're free to say largely what you want, write what you like (as long as it's not *libellous*, in other words a false statement expressed as fact which harms an individual), travel as you see fit and choose who governs you. Add to this the fact that Britons enjoy the protection of a long-standing and deep-rooted legal system and you can easily see why Britain, like America, can be described as the land of the free.

Now these freedoms and individual rights didn't come about overnight; they were built up over centuries. Along with these freedoms grew the ideology of liberalism that runs through much of British politics today.

The main principles of liberalism are:

- ✔ **Popular consent.** Effective government can only work if it operates with the consent of the majority of people in the country.

- ✔ **Equality.** People of every gender and race are equal, which means everyone has the same voting rights and access to justice through the law.

- ✔ **Individual liberty.** Citizens have certain basic rights such as freedom from imprisonment without criminal charges and the right to free speech. Ideally, these rights are enshrined in a written constitution but not always (in the UK, people's rights are guaranteed through a patchwork of laws and customs, see Chapter 11 for more).

- ✔ **Economic freedom.** People should be encouraged to set up businesses, create and retain wealth. Liberals also like to see low taxes.

- ✔ **Small government.** If people are truly to be free it follows that government should keep as much as possible out of their business and personal lives.

Exploring the origins of socialism

Historians and those wacky, laugh-a-minute political scientists often disagree about when socialism as an idea first sprang up in the UK. Some look for its roots way back in the Middle Ages amongst popular uprisings such as the Peasants' Revolt in 1381, when tens of thousands of ordinary Britons took up arms and marched on London demanding better pay and an end to being bossed around by the rich landowners. Others look to the English Civil War of the mid-seventeenth century, when a revolution led to the execution of Charles I and the propagation, through radicals using the printing presses, of all sorts of extraordinary – for back then – ideas such as communal ownership of land and even votes for men who didn't own land. One individual even suggested votes for women but he was promptly locked up for being, according to the authorities, mad!

Whenever socialism was first espoused it was definitely in the UK by Victorian times. During the late eighteenth and throughout the nineteenth century, Britain went through what's called an Industrial Revolution. In short, a small population which mostly worked on the land and lived in the countryside to produce food shifted to become a larger population, most of whom worked in industries such as cotton, coal and steel and lived in large urban centres. This transition was far from easy and the living standards of most of the UK population actually got far worse during the Industrial Revolution as the factory owners got very rich indeed.

The average life expectancy fell for much of the period of the Industrial Revolution. For example, in 1839 in Liverpool, records show that the average man only lived for 19 years – that's 10 years less than Ancient Egypt, 3,000 years earlier. Life in industrialising England was mostly harsh and short.

But workers didn't take this change in their circumstances lying down; they started to agitate for better pay and living conditions. They did this by forming trade unions and within this movement you can see the clearest signs of a socialist ideology developing. Large groups of workers started to talk not just about better pay and conditions but also about how they could change the way in which business was conducted and the country as a whole.

The roots of the liberal ideology date back a long time. The liberal principles of individual liberty and equality were espoused by the seventeenth-century English philosopher John Locke. Liberalism's view of economic freedom and belief in the free market is rooted in the writings of the great economist Adam Smith, who argued in the early nineteenth century for free markets and small government.

The ideology of liberalism is most strongly rooted in the Liberal Democrats, but it also influences the policies of the Labour and Conservative parties. For example, the liberal principles of economic freedom and small government are key components of modern Conservative Party ideology.

Liberalism is a very old ideology and the interpretation of it by politicians has changed over that time. In the nineteenth century, for instance, leading liberal politicians used to argue that only through a free, unfettered market could true liberalism be found. These days, adherents to liberalism tend to focus on the need to protect and extend civil liberties and promote greater democracy and equality in society, even if this actually means bigger government and curtailing the free market.

Many of the UK's most prominent pressure groups share the ideology of liberalism. Take Liberty, for instance (the clue is in the name of course!), led by the prominent campaigner Shami Chakrabarti. The organisation speaks out very loudly when the government does things that it believes damage civil liberties.

Joining Together for the Greater Good: Socialism in the UK

Socialism arose from what was widely seen as massive inequalities brought about by the unbridled capitalism of the Industrial Revolution (see the nearby sidebar, 'Exploring the origins of socialism'). These ideas are the basis of socialism and they still have a very strong pull in British politics today.

Socialists can be summed up as striving for the following:

- An equal share of wealth so that land and industry is owned by the many rather than the few.

- An end to the exploitation of workers by bosses and the promotion of greater sexual equality in society as a whole.

- Making the job of government and communities to help those in most need.

- Raising educational and health standards across the whole population rather than just amongst a privileged few.

- The better organisation of society through rational government planning rather than reliance on capitalism and its market forces.

Socialism is a very big ideology, but what do I mean by big? Well, it has an all-encompassing vision that government should do no less than bring about a fair society and an economy built on the idea of sharing evenly, not on personal wealth and acquisition. Socialism is an alternative – to capitalism – way of organising society.

A fundamental trait of socialism is how it views competition between people. Capitalists see competition as desirable as it means that each individual strives to be the best at acquiring wealth, for example. Socialists, on the other hand, don't like competition as it suppresses the human desire to co-operate. They believe that people and society as a whole achieve more through collective actions rather than by acting alone motivated by personal profit.

Focusing on the successes of socialism

Despite well over a century of socialism in the UK, looking around you today you notice that vast inequality still exists. However, socialists have scored some major successes and have done so through gaining political power through the election of Labour governments during the twentieth century.

Some of the major victories for socialism in the UK include:

- ✔ Recognition of trade unions
- ✔ Setting up of the National Health Service (NHS)
- ✔ Provision of free education for all up to age 18
- ✔ Building of large amounts of social housing and paying of welfare benefits
- ✔ Improvement of pay and conditions for workers

Socialists believe in a *collective worker consciousness.* This term means that people from the same background, working more often than not in industry, believe in the same ideals and hold similar ambitions for how they would like the economy and wider society to be run.

You don't need socialists to be in government in order to see socialism promoted through government policy. If enough people share socialist principles in a democracy, you find that politicians of whatever political party will respond to this and design their policies so as to appeal to these voters. For example, after the Second World War right up until the election of Margaret Thatcher in 1979, all Conservative governments followed policies that may be considered to have socialist ideology behind them, such as closing grammar schools and forming comprehensive schools instead.

Rebranding socialism: New Labour

The ideology of socialism was key to the forming of the Labour Party. In fact, up until recently most Labour Members of Parliament (MPs) would have proudly said that they were socialists and that they wanted British society to be organised along socialist lines.

But times have changed and the ideology of socialism is now less important in the Labour Party. In its efforts to appeal to as wide a group of Britons as possible in order to get into government and thereby gain power, Labour has come to accept some of what capitalism has to offer. This happened most noticeably under the leadership of Neil Kinnock and Tony Blair.

Blair, in particular, believed that the socialist message propounded by Labour didn't take account of how British society had changed in the 1980s and 1990s. The old working class, which had been the bedrock of socialism, had become fragmented and the old industries that had sustained this working class had died away. What replaced the working class was a society focused on more capitalist ideals of individual property ownership and wealth acquisition – particularly under Conservative Prime Minister Margaret Thatcher. (I talk more about the Iron Lady, as she was nicknamed, in the 'Changing conservatism: The Thatcher revolution' section later in this chapter.)

As a result of this change in society, Tony Blair went about reforming the Labour Party and shifting many of its policies away from adherence to socialist ideals to one which accepted capitalism but wanted to shave off its rough edges so as to create a more equal and fair society. Blairism, as this transformation of Labour Party ideology became known, proved very popular as Labour went on to win three general elections on the trot, in 1997, 2001 and 2005. Blair even rebranded the Labour Party, calling it New Labour instead.

Blairism is also often referred to as *the third way*. Put simply, this term means neither strictly capitalist nor socialist. The idea is to create a society in which individuals can become rich through hard work if they wish but that looks after those less fortunate at the same time. Many people who are avowed socialists don't see Blair's third way as a strand of socialist ideology at all.

When Tony Blair became leader in 1994, one of the first things he did was change the constitution of the Labour Party. He got rid of Clause IV of its constitution, which called for the 'common ownership of the means of production, distribution and exchange'. This phrase basically means the government should own the railways, hospitals, industries and even the banks and use them to bring about a society organised along socialist lines. Blair's ditching of Clause IV was a sure sign that Labour was moving away from its socialist roots. On being elected in 1997, Tony Blair famously said: 'We were elected as New Labour and we will govern as New Labour.'

The modern Labour Party follows a watered-down version of socialism, looking to create a more equal society but at the same time allow people the freedom to become wealthy and gain privileges such as private health care or education if they wish.

Stirring things up: Revolutionary socialism

In the UK, socialists generally have tried to achieve their goals through largely peaceful and democratic means such as trade union action and mass support of the Labour Party. For a fair proportion of the last 60 years, in fact, the Labour Party has been the party of government, which means that the socialist ideology has had considerable influence.

However, some socialists believe that this reliance on democratic methods has been a bit of a waste of time, and that what has happened is that the vision offered by socialism has been watered down by Labour politicians looking to garner enough votes to get into government. These people would like to see a revolution overturning some of the UK's political institutions – such as the monarchy and Houses of Parliament – replacing them with a government whose aim is to bring about a socialist society.

Revolutionary socialism has had some appeal in the UK, for example in some parts of the trade unions, and what was called the Militant tendency of the Labour Party in the 1970s and early 1980s. In the main, however, revolutionary socialism hasn't gained much credence in the UK. But outside of the UK, in countries such as Cuba, China and most notably Russia, revolutions have occurred where a variant of socialist ideology called communism has come to the fore.

Looking far left: Marxism and communism

Globally, many people live in what are called Marxist or communist regimes. Marxism and communism are very similar ideologies and are simply an extreme variant of socialism.

Basically Marxists and communists believe that capitalism is unjust and must be swept away – overthrown, if you like. Instead of capitalism, with its reliance on enterprise and business, they believe that everything – such as land and industry – should be owned by the government on behalf of the people. In effect, all individual effort is directed towards producing better living standards for everyone rather than just for themselves.

Communism is a variant of Marxism and is defined as all property being owned by the community as a whole rather than by individuals, with each person working for the common benefit according to his or her skill set. Communists in effect are the political embodiment of Marxist theory. Karl Marx and Friedrich Engels thought up the ideas, while the communists put them into practice in countries like Russia, China and Cuba.

By nature, Marxism and communism are revolutionary socialism, in that adherents believe in bringing about change by direct action and overturning the current political situation through revolution. Generally, Marxists and communists believe that the working class need to be educated about the ways in which capitalists are exploiting them. Then, through this education, the workers will be radicalised and look to start a revolution through direct action.

Marxism gets its name from the great political thinker Karl Marx (1818–83). Marx was German but lived most of his life in England, observing at first hand the Industrial Revolution and the worsening living conditions of many British workers. These observations prompted Marx and his friend and fellow political thinker, Friedrich Engels, to write an analysis of capitalism and suggest that the workers needed to revolt, overturn their current society and build one based on principles of common ownership. Amongst the books published by Marx and Engels are *Das Kapital* and *The Communist Manifesto*.

Generally, British socialists believe in working within the political system to bring about their goals, while Marxists and communists argue that the whole system is corrupt and needs to be brought down and replaced. These days, very few people in Britain hold Marxist and communist views. In fact, membership of the British Communist Party is tiny.

Keeping with Tradition: Conservatism

A strong strand of conservatism is evident in the British psyche, and this is embodied in the Conservative Party – one of the big three UK political parties (which I talk about in depth in Chapter 8).

Conservatives believe in the following:

- ✔ Keeping Britain's political institutions intact
- ✔ Free market capitalism
- ✔ The right of everyone to own property
- ✔ Small government that doesn't interfere in people's lives

Whereas socialists and Marxists would like to see Britain's society radically reshaped or even overturned, Conservatives would like what they see as best about Britain to be retained.

Uniting under one nation conservatism

Conservative ideology may be about small government, free markets and the right to property ownership but it also states that all these 'freedoms' come with responsibilities. For example, people who do well and make money should have to pay a bit of tax so that those who are less fortunate can have welfare, health care and education.

Another tenet of what is called *one nation conservatism* is that, although small government should leave people largely alone to get on with their lives, the idea of the nation state should be a strong, unifying one. In addition, many Conservatives believe that government has a less of a role to play in the economy but more instead in upholding order in society, so Conservatives often campaign for more police and harsher sentencing of criminals.

To a large extent one nation conservatism is quite close to Tony Blair's third way New Labour approach (I talk about this in 'Rebranding socialism: New Labour' earlier in this chapter). One nation Conservatives believe, like Blair, that the rougher edges of capitalism need to be smoothed down – wealth creation is good but with money comes responsibility to your fellow citizens.

Reforming with a small 'r'

Although a large part of Conservative ideology concerns the idea of retaining traditions and the prevailing political situation in a bid to promote harmony within society, this doesn't mean that Conservatives don't ever reform. Conservatives may be opposed to the idea of radicalism and revolution proposed by people following the Marxist or communist ideologies but nevertheless they look to gradualist reforms that take account of Britain's past and its traditions.

Conservatives also say that they like to take a pragmatic approach to society's problems. For example, generally Conservative governments make fewer laws than Labour ones, preferring to let industries self-regulate rather than have regulation imposed by a central government. Take financial regulation in the UK, for instance. The Conservative governments in the 1980s and 1990s relied on banks and insurers to self-regulate how they dealt with customers; however Labour, from 1997 onwards, required banks and insurers to adhere to stricter regulations, although it didn't stop the credit crunch in 2007 and the global recession that followed. If Conservatives do reform, it tends to be with a small 'r'.

Changing conservatism: The Thatcher revolution

Having said that Conservatives reform with a small 'r' in the preceding section, the exception was the prime ministership of Margaret Thatcher between 1979 and 1990. Thatcher, who due to her tough stance on issues gained the nickname the 'Iron Lady', was elected when Britain was in economic and political turmoil. The country was nearly bankrupt and the trade unions had spent the winter striking. Against the odds, Thatcher set about sweeping away many of the policies that had been pursued by Conservative and Labour governments since the end of the Second World War. The main tenets of what became known as Thatcherism were the following:

✔ Reduce the power of the trade unions

✔ Encourage individuals to start their own businesses

✔ Lower taxes and reduce government interference in daily life

✔ Restore national pride through having a strong foreign policy and defence

Boiled down, many of the bullet points of Thatcherism look very close to core Conservative ideology, but Thatcher differed in the speed at which she tried to move the country in a conservative direction. For decades the country had been moving in a more socialist direction and in a few short years she shifted this around. No traditional conservative ideology of gradualism existed in Thatcher's approach. Instead, Thatcher was something of an oxymoron – a revolutionary conservative.

Margaret Thatcher was a highly divisive figure in the country. However she still managed to win three landslide election victories in the 1979, 1983 and 1987 general elections.

Examining Alternative Politics

Think of politics as a mighty river with lots of smaller streams of ideology running into it. Some of these ideologies rise and fall in popularity. They may not find their expression through a particular political party, as socialism has at times through the Labour party, but they're still important because they help form the opinions of millions of Britons as well as wider political debate.

Focusing on the far right: Fascism

Defining what fascism is isn't easy but basically it concerns completely subordinating individual rights and freedoms to the power of the state. In effect, citizens in a fascist state are meant to be utterly patriotic and believe that their nation is top dog; they must be willing to sacrifice whatever is required – even their own lives – in the cause of advancing the power and prestige of that state. Pretty scary, eh? The fascist ideology goes further, too. Fascists believe in a strong military and that conquest of other states can be a good thing.

Fascist ideology is in essence a racist one (its adherents believe in the superiority of their own nation and race; for example, the Nazis despising Jewish people and Mussolini arguing that his country should be able to invade Ethiopia because Italians were superior to Africans). What's more, fascists view democracy as weak and best got rid of, to be replaced by a strong leader able to lead the people.

Fascism is often seen as being at the other end of the political spectrum from Marxism and communism. But they actually share a common theme – that individuality isn't as important as advancement of the working class in the case of Marxism/communism or the unity of the state in the case of fascism. To be frank, if I was drawing up a dinner party guest list I think I'd leave both fascists and Marxist/communists off.

As with Marxism and communism, fascism hasn't gained much popularity in the UK, although the British National Party (BNP) is often dubbed as fascist by its critics due to its extolling of racist and nationalistic policies. (See Chapter 8 for the inside track on the BNP.) In fact, Britain doesn't do extreme politics well at all – which is a relief. A little like the nation's famous weather, British politics tends to be quite temperate and lacks extremes.

Fascism may sound very odd and frankly a bit far-fetched, but back in the 1930s and 1940s over half the population of western Europe lived in fascist states such as Germany, Italy and Spain. Eventually fascist political regimes were defeated by Britain, America and Russia in the Second World War. But prior to this fascism even had some supporters in Britain. The British Union of Fascists led by the charismatic Oswald Mosley, used to organise marches attended by thousands of ordinary Britons.

Looking into the darkness: Totalitarian regimes

When an extremist leader – either from left or right – comes to power, it usually leads to the formation of a totalitarian regime. In short, this means that all power is concentrated in the hands of a leader or group of leaders and these leaders can't be removed by democratic means – an election. They have ultimate power and don't tolerate political opponents.

Totalitarian regimes are often propped up by a strong military and covert police force. Even the laws of the land are either altered or become subservient to the leader or leaders of a totalitarian regime.

Probably the best-known example of totalitarianism was Nazi Germany in the 1930s and 1940s. It was a regime with a fascist ideology and a supreme leader (the Führer, Adolf Hitler). At the same time, in Russia Josef Stalin also headed a totalitarian regime but this followed not a fascist but a communist ideology.

Although Britain doesn't do extremism very well, at times in British history the leadership can be seen as totalitarian. For example, many of the country's monarchs exercised huge power barely checked by legal niceties and they ruled with a strong military and through fear. However, in the past few centuries, with the falling away of the power of the monarchy and the growth in parliamentary democracy, the British people have fortunately avoided falling prey to a totalitarian regime.

Looking to the heavens: Theocracy

Some would say that religion is the ultimate ideology as it maps out a way people should live their lives. Occasionally, religion becomes such a compelling force in society that the government is run according to religious principles by leading adherents to the religion. Those at the top of organised religious structures are also at the top of government and in effect run the show. This type of government is called a *theocracy*.

Probably the most famous modern example of a theocracy in action is the Iranian regime. Iran is effectively run by a group of leading Muslim clerics who dictate policy according to their take on religious texts.

If Britain were a theocracy, logically the leading bishops in the Church of England would be running the government. They don't run the government, however, elected politicians do.

Pulling everything apart: Anarchism

Anarchy in ancient Greek means 'no rule' and anarchists are people who are opposed to all forms of governmental authority. In effect, a true anarchist believes in absolutely nothing except that government should be torn down, which would then allow people to get on with their lives without interference.

Many anarchists are prepared to take what they'd call direct action, which means destroying property and even attacking elected politicians. In the past anarchist groups have carried out violent terrorist acts and most recently mass street protests have been seen at meetings of world leaders.

Anarchism has some major drawbacks in that it is by nature both incoherent and disorganised; therefore the destruction of the governmental system that it wants is nigh on impossible to obtain. How, for instance, can a mob of people with all sorts of different backgrounds and personal agendas achieve anything substantial against an organised government, military and police force.

Anarchist groups have been behind big street protests at meetings of the G8 and G20 groups of world leaders (this is a conference of the leaders of the world's largest nations by economic size; see Chapter 19 for more). These global shindigs have often taken place against a backdrop of street violence caused by the anarchists. Other groups of protestors, including peaceful environmentalists, have complained bitterly that their protest message has been lost in the violence.

Releasing the bonds: Feminism

According to feminists, oppression of women by men runs throughout society – in the workplace, in politics and at home. Feminism itself is an ideology that can often have an influence on politics. It's based around the ambition to establish more rights and legal protection for women and to combat the subjugation of women.

Looking back through history it's not hard to see that feminists have a point. For example, women in the UK didn't get the vote on the same terms as men until 1928, and even today women are paid nearly 30 per cent less on average than men.

Few can doubt that we still live in a sexist society but nonetheless equality between the genders has made great strides. First up was the suffrage movement, which led the successful campaign for votes for women. Then, in the1960s, second-wave feminism emerged, whereby the women's liberation movement agitated for equality at work and in wider society.

Political scientists have split feminists into three distinct groupings:

- ✔ **Liberal feminists** argue that women and men are equal, full stop, and that laws are needed to ensure this equality happens in practice.

- ✔ **Socialist feminists** argue that the oppression of women is a by-product of capitalism. In order to change the lot of women it's necessary to change both the economy and society so that they're based on socialist principles. (I cover socialism in 'Joining Together for the Greater Good: Socialism in the UK' earlier in this chapter.)

> ✔ **Radical feminists** argue that women are in many ways better than men and that if women were in charge aggressive – male – pursuits such as war wouldn't happen.

Many people describe themselves as being feminists without also saying they agree with either liberal, socialist or radical feminism. Although feminism is an ideology, it's also an approach to everyday life, a general belief in equality of the sexes.

Saving the planet: Environmentalism

Very few people now doubt now that the planet's environment is under threat from the side-effects of human activities. Some people respond to this emerging threat by looking to cut down their impact on the environment, for example by taking fewer flights or driving a less polluting car; others go further and adopt an environmental ideology. Put simply, *environmentalism* is about finding a way for people and the planet to co-exist. Environmentalists want an economic and social system based on a sustainable relationship with the planet.

Some key points about environmentalism are:

> ✔ Capitalism is viewed with distrust, as companies are responsible for much pollution and using up the planet's resources.
>
> ✔ Economic growth is regarded as less important than preserving the health of the planet. Being rich is pointless if sea levels are rising and life is endangered.
>
> ✔ Governments are expected to actively try to change individual behaviour towards the environment, ensuring they minimise they damage they cause.

In recent years environmentalism has been on the rise as the true scale of global warming has come into sharper focus.

Environmentalism as an ideology is currently gaining credence in the West, with more and more people becoming concerned about the planet's wellbeing.

In British politics the party seen as representing the environmental ideology most closely is the Green Party, which I talk about in Chapter 8. However, all the big three UK political parties – Labour, Conservative and Liberal Democrats – have placed a greater emphasis on environmentally friendly policies in recent general elections.

Sitting at the top: Monarchy

Unusually for a major modern democracy, Britain is still a monarchy. The institution of monarchy was once based on an ideology called the divine right of kings. This ideology is much older than socialism or conservatism and to be frank is a little strange, so strap yourself in for this one. The divine right of kings was the dominant ideology in Britain right up until the English Civil War in the 1640s, when a parliamentary army took on the king and won.

As the name suggests, the divine right of kings means that the monarch draws authority to rule not from parliaments or elections but directly from God. The monarch is supposed to be, in effect, God's representative on earth and therefore everything he or she does is right and he or she must be obeyed at all times – yes, that is some sort of ego trip.

Nowadays no one believes in the divine right of kings, yet we still have a monarch. However, in a very British-style compromise, the monarch has few actual powers and his or her role is largely ceremonial. See Chapter 11 for more on the monarch and the British constitution.

Understanding Why the UK Doesn't Do Extremism

The British don't tend to do extreme ideologies like fascism or communism and plenty of good reasons exist for that. The UK:

- ✔ **Is a long-established democracy.** The UK is one of the oldest and sturdiest democracies in the world, which makes the job of those who'd like to subvert it very hard indeed.

- ✔ **Has seen other countries go awry.** Britain fought a long bloody war against Nazi Germany between 1939 and 1945. The memory of that war and the crimes of the Nazi regime mean far right ideology is discredited in the UK.

- ✔ **Is a rich, successful country.** History suggests radical ideologies tend to gather wide appeal following military defeats or economic turmoil. Although Britain is no longer as powerful as it was in the 1800s, it is very economically stable, which means it doesn't present fertile ground for revolution.

- ✔ **Has political parties that appeal to a wide range of citizens.** The UK's political parties are well organised with large memberships and have deep roots in local communities. This makes it difficult for smaller, more extreme parties to beat them at election time.

- ✔ **Has a unique electoral system.** The UK has a first-past-the-post electoral system, which means seats are won by those candidates polling the highest number of votes. Again, this makes it harder for smaller parties to get seats in parliament.

✔ **Follows the rule of law.** In the UK, everyone is equal before the law and subject to it, which means that British society has an in-built system of redress which also reduces the chances of totalitarianism and tyranny.

Britain is often referred to as a liberal democracy, which simply means the country is a democracy – where people get to vote to decide who governs the country – and it has strong traits associated with liberalism, such as primacy of the rule of law and acknowledgement of the importance of individual freedoms and liberties. Much of the world doesn't live in a liberal democracy but many peoples would like to.

Chapter 5

Forming the British Political State

In This Chapter

▶ Building up the power of monarchy

▶ Transferring power from the monarch to parliament

▶ Looking at the forming of political parties and the role of the prime minister

▶ Breaking with traditions: Ending the power of the Lords, and votes for all

*I*n this chapter, I look at the big political events that have got us to where we are today – a democracy of some 60 million people with votes for the majority, a free press, an independent judiciary and civil liberties.

From monarchs to Machiavellian prime ministers, this is the chapter to look at for the lowdown on the key steps on the road to the British politics of today.

Getting to Grips with the Normans: From Conquest to Magna Carta

The date 1066 is etched into the history books of Britain – and throughout the world – because it's the year William, Duke of Normandy, in one of the great big gambles of history, successfully invaded England and defeated the Saxon King Harold at the Battle of Hastings. William became known simply as the Conqueror (he'd previously been known as 'the bastard', so this must have been a welcome change). He gave tidy portions of England to the hundreds of French knights who'd helped him, for them to rule on his behalf.

Make no bones about it, the Norman invasion was brutal. The Saxon upper classes suffered the indignity of losing much of their own lands and having to submit to their new Norman rulers, who even spoke a different language. As Saxons slid further down the social scale, they not only saw much of their native culture and customs eradicated but also had to pay substantial taxes and live under a multitude of oppressive laws. All in all, post-Norman Conquest England wasn't a happy place. William and his descendants ruled over what was for much of the time a violent and totalitarian regime – no liberal democracy back then.

A succession of good, mediocre and downright rubbish kings led some of the descendants of the Norman knights, and those Saxons who still had some land and money, to question whether the king really should have total control over the country. In fact, in the reign of the particularly inept King John, in 1215, the great barons of the land rose up in mutiny and forced the king to sign an agreement called Magna Carta – meaning Great Charter – which limited a little the power of the king to go around killing or imprisoning those he didn't like without first having them tried in a court of law.

In effect, *Magna Carta* was a statement of basic rights, which in theory bound the king to act within the law of the land. In particular it set up the right of *habeas corpus*, which means the right to appeal against imprisonment.

Magna Carta is widely seen as the first major constitutional document in the western world – coming a whole five and a half centuries before the American Declaration of Independence.

Although Magna Carta was very important, it didn't mean that everyone in England lived in peace without fear of being wrongly imprisoned or killed without due process. The monarch was still at the top of the tree and had enormous power for the next four and a half centuries and could pretty much anything.

Doing the Splits: Church and State Clash

For the five centuries after the Norman Conquest the monarch wasn't the only powerbroker in the country. The Roman Catholic Church was also a big deal, with huge tracts of land, the right to raise taxes from the public and even its own system of courts to try people who had broken its laws – called canon law. In effect, the Roman Catholic Church was a state within a state. For example, priests couldn't be tried by the king's courts but only by the Church courts.

Now for most of the time the monarch and the Church got on hunky dory. But when the pope refused to let Henry VIII divorce his wife, Catherine of Aragon, the monarch turned on the Church with a vengeance. He had Church lands seized, closed ancient monasteries and melted the gold and silver they held for coins. What's more, Henry had himself installed as head of the Church, which meant the pope was no longer obeyed.

The legacy of Henry II

Henry II, the great-grandson of William the Conqueror, ruled England, parts of Wales and Scotland and even large chunks of western France in the second half of the twelfth century. His reign was a long and successful one and he was one of the great state builders of British history. For starters, he set up the magistrates' courts, which still operate today trying people accused of minor criminal offences. He moved to increase the power of the monarch over the Church and started a system of transparent tax collection. Henry's reforms helped form the basis of how the monarchy governed for the next five centuries.

The battle between Church and monarch was a major turning point in Britain's history. It increased the power and wealth of the monarchy enormously, and because the Church land was sold to wealthy merchants, it also created a new group of landowners, who in time went into parliament and took part in government.

The break with the Roman Catholic Church and the construction of what's called the Church of England, with the monarch as head of the Church, is called the *Reformation*.

The legal framework for the Church of England was set up in the 1530s and 40s, and most of the Church land seizures took place then. It wasn't a straightforward transition; in fact, once Henry VIII died, his daughter Mary reversed the process and again England became a Catholic country. However she died soon after and younger sister (Elizabeth I) chose to break with the Roman Catholic Church once more.

The monarch is still head of the Church of England but nowadays the Church tends to play less of a role in public life, mainly due to a fall in religious observance by the UK population as a whole. At the start of the twentieth century it was estimated that the majority of people attended a religious service at least once a week, whereas today fewer than one in ten do.

Gearing Up for Revolution: Parliament Takes on the King and Wins

The English parliament was set up by Henry II in the twelfth century as a means by which to more effectively govern the country and raise taxes. Over the next few centuries the power of parliament gradually increased as the monarch needed the help of its members to raise more taxes to run the government.

Working hand in hand

Most of the time the monarch and parliament worked well together, pursuing policies that were widely agreed, particularly over the break with the Roman Catholic religion and its replacement with a Protestant one, with the monarch as head not just of the state but the Church too. Elections to the House of Commons – although not the Lords – were held regularly but only landowners got to vote (a very far cry from the liberal democracy of today). But apart from sporadic rebellions and the nasty Wars of the Roses in the late fifteenth century, between rival claimants for the English throne, the country was at peace and government worked well.

Chafing under Charles I and enduring Cromwell

Then along came the diminutive, lisping and rather useless Charles I. He hated ruling with the agreement of parliament and tried to go it alone; at the same time, he raised what were seen as punitive and potentially illegal taxes and even flirted with the Catholic faith, which didn't go down well with Protestants in parliament. The Members of Parliament, many of whom were also rich and powerful merchants and landowners, became increasingly fed up of Charles' style of kingship. Eventually, in 1642, civil war broke out. In 1649, Charles, having been defeated in the Civil War, was executed and the country became a *republic* (without a monarchy) for 11 years under the austere Oliver Cromwell.

Oliver Cromwell was a great general who'd risen through the ranks of the parliamentary army and ultimately swept to power as a military dictator. He fought wars on the Continent and in Scotland and Ireland. He was devoutly religious, even banning some Christmas festivities – bah humbug!

When old Scrooge Cromwell died he was replaced by Charles II, who was more politically astute than his father Charles I. Charles II for a time restored the powers of the monarchy but, after he popped his clogs, another short useless rule, this time by James II, meant another civil war in the offing. However, James was replaced in a relatively bloodless coup in 1688 by the Dutch King William of Orange.

Reaping the benefits of the Glorious Revolution

But the real result of the Glorious Revolution, as it became known, was that parliament was able to wrest control of the levers of state from the monarch.

The Glorious Revolution came about after the unpopular Catholic king, James II, was overthrown in a coup led by leading land owners and parliamentarians. William of Orange – a Dutch Protestant ruler – was offered the English throne and became King William III. The fact that a monarch had been deposed and a new one installed, in effect by parliament, was crucial, as it showed where the political power now lay. In future, although the monarch would at times have real power, he or she would only govern the country with the agreement of parliament. In effect, power shifted from a single monarch to the members of an elected parliament and the unelected House of Lords.

By the reign of Charles I (1625–49), England had swallowed up Wales and, although Scotland still had its own parliament, Charles was king of both England and Scotland, which was a big step towards the eventual union of the old enemies in 1707.

Scotland joined with England and Wales to form the United Kingdom in 1707. In the run up to the signing of the Act of Union many people in Scotland were bankrupted by a failed attempt to establish a colony in North America. In return for having the nation's debts paid off, the Scottish parliament agreed to vote for the Act of Union, and itself out of existence. Scotland didn't have its own parliament again until 1999 (see Chapter 16 for more).

Throwing Political Parties into the Mix

From the Glorious Revolution to the forming of political parties wasn't a great leap. As power became concentrated in parliament, factions arose behind certain policies and certain individuals.

These early political parties weren't parties as you'd recognise them today. They were more a matter of powerful Members of Parliament and wealthy lords coming together either to push through a piece of legislation, or because they shared some common interests. Over time, these fluid factions started to form into what we'd call parties.

The first two great political parties were the Whigs and the Tories – the forerunners of today's Liberal Democrats and Conservatives. In the eighteenth and nineteenth centuries they became bitter rivals, but once one of the parties came to power they had to share out government jobs and privileged positions. Why were the Whigs and Tories at such loggerheads? Well mainly it was because of big religious differences, as the Tories were generally Catholic or Anglican while the Whigs were from a more Calvinist or radical Protestant tradition. Religion in the eighteenth and nineteenth centuries was a big deal and it was the root of the enmity between the two parties. (Turn to Chapter 8 for more on the formation and evolution of Britain's political parties.)

Ending the Power of the Lords

Back in 1908 Lloyd George – later a prime minister – was Chancellor of the Exchequer. He announced a radical budget which for the first time paid people an old age pension and guaranteed some limited welfare payments for those less fortunate.

The bigwigs in the House of Lords hated this budget and blocked it. At the time, the House of Lords could in effect veto any laws drawn up by the House of Commons. But the Liberal government was having none of this and introduced the *Parliament Act* in 1911, which did away with the veto power the House of Lords enjoyed. As a result of the Parliament Act, the House of Lords has the right to scrutinise proposed laws drawn up in the Commons and to ask members of that House to think again three times. If the Lords rejects a law a third time, the House of Commons can say enough is enough and the proposed Act passes into law despite opposition from the Lords. The Parliament Act was a big deal as it finally established the primacy of the House of Commons over the House of Lords as they key legislative body. Any party holding a majority of seats in that House has huge power.

The retreat of the Lords has continued, with it now becoming little more than a debating chamber. Even its membership has changed, with the Labour government of Tony Blair removing many of the hereditary lords – people whose right to sit in the Lords is passed down from parents and not through being appointed by the monarch. See Chapter 12 for how the House of Lords works and what role it plays in the day-to-day government of the UK.

A member of the House of Lords is often referred to as a *peer*, and no, it has nothing to do with your mates.

Expanding the Franchise: Democracy Arrives in Britain

In many people's eyes Britain didn't become a fully fledged democracy until after the second decade of the twentieth century when finally half the population, women, were granted the vote. Prior to this date only men were able to vote and, turning the clock back even further into the nineteenth century, only men who owned property in the form of a house or land. The overwhelming majority of the population didn't have a say in who governed them.

Before the expansion of the *franchise*, the right to vote, the number of people who actually had a vote in some parliamentary constituencies was relatively small. Whereas these days some seats have 60,000 to 70,000 electors, back in the seventeenth, eighteenth and early nineteenth centuries elections involving a few hundred people were commonplace as the population was much smaller and only property owners could vote. Having such a small electorate meant that the ballots were open to being rigged, with wealthy landowners literally bribing electors to vote for their candidates. This phenomenon became known as the *rotten boroughs*, and there were a lot of them.

Earning a stake

The reasoning behind limiting voting just to property owners went that only they had an interest, or stake in the country – merely being born British and living in Britain didn't give you a stake.

Overcoming this idea of only those with an interest being entitled to vote involved a long struggle. A host of political thinkers put forth the idea that all men – rarely back then did anyone say women as well – had the right to cast a vote.

As the population grew and the economy moved from being agricultural and rural to industrial and urban, what would be recognised as the working class formed. But, despite their importance to the wider economy and their numerical superiority to the landowning class, they had no voting power and therefore no representation in parliament until 1884.

Fighting the good fight: Emmeline Pankhurst

Emmeline Pankhurst was the leader of the British women's *suffrage* – right to vote – movement in the late nineteenth and early twentieth century. Starting out by hosting public debates to discuss votes for women and trying to persuade leading politicians of the time of the justness of their cause, Pankhurst became convinced that a more direct approach was needed to shake up society so that votes for women would shoot to the top of the political agenda. To this end, activists inspired by Pankhurst – and her own daughters – took part in vocal protests, threw stones through windows, chained themselves to railings and even indulged in arson and assaults on police. Pankhurst and her activists were sentenced to repeated prison sentences but votes for women became a hot topic and after the First World War – for the duration of which Pankhurst called off militant action – women eventually won the right to vote. In 1999 US magazine *Time* named Pankhurst as one of the most important people of the twentieth century.

Mass movements of people, drawn largely from the working and to a lesser extent middle classes, in the middle of the nineteenth century called for more people to be given the vote as well as a written bill of rights for each individual. Soon after, trade unionism started to take hold in the working classes and they too wanted votes for all. The politicians, worried about the potential for revolution, as had happened half a century earlier in France, started to make concessions to the working class and slowly but surely the right to vote was extended to all men, regardless of whether they were property owners or not. Simply being a British citizen brought with it the right to vote.

Recognising the rights of women

Votes for women took longer, with many mid-Victorian politicians dismissing the idea as madness. But as the male franchise expanded and women's suffrage movements formed, a groundswell of support for votes for women took place too. However, it wasn't until after the First World War, during which women did difficult and dirty work on the home front while men were fighting in the trenches, that the majority of politicians came around to the idea of votes for women. And even then equality in the voting booth wasn't yet in place, as only women over 30 were given the vote in 1918. Only in 1928 were women granted the vote on the same terms as men, from age 21.

Switching Parties: The Ebb and Flow of Party Influence

The government reflects the ideals of whichever party is in power at the time.

Both of the main UK political parties – Labour and Conservative – have what is called a *core vote* that turn out and vote for their chosen party election after election. The key to winning an election for either the Conservative or Labour parties is appealing outside this core vote to what is called *Middle Britain* as their votes swing the poll, particularly bearing in mind the UK's first-past-the-post system (where candidates have only to win the largest number of votes, rather than a majority, to win the seat they're standing for).

Making a play for power: The Labour Party is born and thrives

Looking back from the early twenty-first century and gauging exactly how momentous and fast changing the world of the Victorians was is difficult. In the nineteenth century the UK population nearly trebled and new industries rose and fell as millions migrated from the countryside to the towns and cities. Probably the closest parallel for Britain's industrialisation and modernisation is what's going on in China right now! But such massive changes inevitably bring about political change too.

In the same way that monarchs eventually found that they couldn't hold absolute power over thousands of landowners and rich merchants, those self-same landowners and rich merchants found that they couldn't hold the millions of new working class created in Victorian England in thrall.

The working classes started to become politically active, with shared ambitions and objectives such as more pay, better working conditions, the vote and health care and education. To help achieve some of these ambitions, workers formed unions and from these unions came the Labour Party.

The Labour Party started to field candidates to fight seats in parliamentary and local government elections in the early 1900s. They didn't do well at first but gradually more Labour MPs and councillors started to be elected and once in office they could change things. By the 1920s the old Liberal Party was in decline and many voters had switched allegiance to Labour, so much so that in the 1928 election they won a majority of seats in the House of Commons and formed the government under their leader Ramsay McDonald.

The first Labour government wasn't successful as it was soon hit with the economic cataclysm of the Great Depression of 1929–32 when millions lost their jobs.

In fact, the Labour Party split for a while (the leadership disagreed over government spending cuts) with its leader Ramsay McDonald leaving to form a National Government made up of his supporters in the Labour Party and leading members of the Conservative Party. The big idea of the National Government was that in a time of crisis – such as the Depression and later the Second World War under Winston Churchill – politicians from all parties should come together for the greater good. However, the result was to split the Labour party in two for over a decade and make McDonald's name a byword amongst some in the Labour Party for treachery. But after the Second World War with the sweet scent of military victory in the air, Labour won a landslide on the promise to provide more houses, jobs, schools and hospitals.

Playing musical chairs: Labour and Tories swap power

As far as government power since the Second World War goes, the Labour and Conservative (Tory) parties have been playing their own version of the hokey cokey – one minute one party is in (power), the next they're out. In fact, during the 60 plus years since the end of the Second World War, the Labour and Conservative parties have spent relatively equal time in power.

In the mid-twentieth century the country switched from Conservative to Labour and back again every few years. More recently, from the 1980s on, Britain had first a long spell of Conservative government followed by a long spell of Labour. Some of the reasons for this slight slowing in the game of musical chairs include:

- ✔ During the 1950s to the 1970s, the UK economy did badly, which always reflects on the government in power, so electors voted the current government out fairly regularly, which meant the parties traded being in power.

- ✔ After the Second World War, the Conservative and Labour parties seemed to represent very different ideologies, both of which had wide appeal and offered voters a real choice. Labour won the election in a massive landslide because it offered the voters a new vision for Britain based around the creation of a welfare state, and during the next six years the Labour PM Clement Attlee went about constructing the National Health Service and nationalising key industries.

- ✔ From the 1980s until the global recession of the late 2000s, the UK economy faired much better, which reflects positively on the government, and encourages electors to stick with the party in power.

Over time, the Conservative and Labour parties have come together on many policies. Such consensus makes many voters wonder whether the parties differ at all and offer any real choice. When voters feel they don't really have a choice, they can become apathetic towards voting, an issue I explore in more depth in Chapter 7.

Leaving out the Lib Dems

You may have noticed that (up until now) I've left out the Liberal Democrats (Lib Dems). That's because they haven't gained enough seats to form the government since just after the First World War. In fact, for a large part of the post-war years they've had only a handful of MPs.

In recent elections the Lib Dems have faired better but they're still very much the country's third biggest party and quite a long way behind the Conservative and Labour parties in terms of membership, influence and prospects of forming a government. The UK electoral system doesn't favour whatever party is in third place in the polls. The Lib Dems regularly attain over 20 per cent of total votes in a general election but win under 10 per cent of the seats. (See Chapter 6 for more on voting systems and why the Lib Dems lose out.)

Holding the balance of power: Coalition government

Because of Britain's first-past-the-post electoral system (which I explain in Chapter 6), coalition governments are pretty rare. Normally the Conservatives or Labour find a way of winning enough seats to hold a majority and form a government.

When a party gathers just enough seats to hold power it sometimes enters an informal arrangement with one of the smaller parties along the lines of 'we will follow some of your policies as long as you support ours'.

Occasionally, an election result is very close indeed and one of the big two parties have to form a coalition government with a smaller rival in order to have enough seats to get their laws enacted. What tends to happen is that the prime minister is chosen from the bigger partner in the coalition but leaders of the smaller party get some key cabinet posts. Back in the mid-1970s Labour and the Liberal Party governed in a coalition in what became known as the Lib–Lab pact.

Sometimes coalitions are formed because the country is in crisis due to war or economic woes. For example, in the Second World War Winston Churchill headed up a coalition government and in the 1930s Ramsay McDonald was in charge of a National Government as the country struggled to cope with the Great Depression.

The main advantage of a coalition government is that people from different backgrounds and representing a wide group of electors work together for the greater good. However, often coalition government can be short-lived and acrimonious. For example, the Lib–Lab pact of the mid-1970s only lasted a couple of years and senior figures from the two parties were often at loggerheads.

Concentrating Power in the Hands of the Prime Minister

The British, it seems, love having a head honcho, someone they can focus on when they think of government. In the six centuries after the Norman Conquest the role was performed by the monarch. However, as parliament took over many of the powers of the monarch, prominent figures within the House of Commons or Lords became very important. Groupings that formed in parliament under these figures were the early incarnation of the Whig and Tory parties, and the leading figures in these groupings acquired jobs within government.

Although the phrase *prime minister* (PM) wasn't officially used until the nineteenth century, from the early eighteenth century onwards the person who led the biggest grouping of MPs or the leader of the party holding the most seats in the House of Commons was effectively the prime minister. Like most things in Britain's unwritten constitution, the role of prime minister evolved over a long period of time rather than being created on a specific day.

The prime minister forms a cabinet drawn from members of the party he or she represents to head up the government and divvy out jobs and titles. The post of PM has been at the top of the political tree for around three hundred years. Over that time more and more power has centred on 10 Downing Street – the official home of the prime minister.

Within the cabinet the prime minister is supposed to be the 'first amongst equals', meaning that the PM is a member of the cabinet where each minister's views are given equal weight. However, the PM is the leader of the group and in big matters the final decision rests with him or her.

It's hard to understate the power of the prime minister within the current political system. The incumbent gets to make appointments throughout government and largely forms government policy. That is not to say that the PM can be dictatorial or govern without consent. The PM relies on the support of cabinet members and MPs sitting in the House of Commons.

One of the biggest powers the prime minister has is to appoint members of the cabinet; in effect, the big decision-making jobs in government. Every so often the PM has a cabinet reshuffle, which involves the hiring and firing of ministers. See Chapter 13 for more on the cabinet and reshuffles.

Robert Walpole (1676–1745) is seen as Britain's first prime minister, although he wouldn't have recognised the phrase at the time. Walpole was the most prominent figure in the Whig party in the House of Commons and he was enormously powerful, acquiring jobs, titles and cash during his long career. At the height of his power he controlled the government, making appointments and handing out favours to friends and allies. He was the leader of the Whigs from 1721 to 1742, when he fell from power after a British military defeat.

Breaking Up the Union: Scotland and Wales to Go It Alone?

For much of its history the British Isles has been split into distinctive, separate and independent nations, namely, England, Scotland, Wales and Ireland. As one of these nations – England – became more powerful in terms of trade and military, the other countries through a combination of imperialism and persuasion joined in a political union. Four nations in effect became one. This is why Britain is also referred to as the United Kingdom.

As far as the English were concerned this union worked pretty well – although some people in the other nations may have disagreed. Great Britain, remarkably, became the most powerful nation on the globe in the nineteenth century, with an enormous empire. However, the Irish wanted out, and after years of political and sometimes violent wrangling, in 1922 Ireland became independent – with the six counties in the North of Ireland remaining within the union.

Winding the clock forward about 90 years to now shows growing signs that the Scots and, to a lesser extent, the Welsh also want out of the union so as to become independent nations again.

Since 1999 the Scots and Welsh have had *devolution*, which means that they created a local parliament (Scotland) or assembly (Wales) in order to make laws which apply just to their countries.

Some say that devolution will help the union stay together, as the Scots and Welsh now have more control over their own lives and governance so they don't need complete independence. Others, though, believe that devolution is merely a prelude to independence and that, as people in Scotland and Wales get used to exercising their own power, they and their elected politicians will want to go a stage further and try for full independence.

As an indicator that the latter may be true, at the 2007 Scottish general election the Scottish National Party, which wants independence, became the biggest party in the Scottish parliament and actually formed the Scottish government. Many observers believe that Scotland will be independent within a generation.

Alex Salmond became first minister of Scotland in April 2007 when the party he leads – the Scottish National Party (SNP) – won the highest number of seats in the Scottish general election. Salmond is considered a very capable communicator and has a large personal following, even amongst electors who wouldn't usually vote SNP. Salmond has been a long-time proponent of Scottish independence and may one day be seen as the prime mover towards that goal. Some even say he'll be the leader of an independent Scotland one day soon.

In Wales the main nationalist party Plaid Cymru has also made great strides, but support amongst the Welsh for independence as yet is weaker than the Scots' desire to go their own way. See Chapter 8 for more on the Welsh and Scottish nationalist parties.

As for the English, growing signs exist that many people there are becoming disillusioned by the union and a system which they see as unfair, where more government spending per head goes to the Scots and Welsh than to the English.

Like the rest of the British constitution, the relationship between England and its smaller neighbours Scotland and Wales inevitably changes over time. Since the Norman Conquest there have been periods when they've been closer together and others when they've been further apart; such ebb and flow is bound to mark all these countries' histories.

Encroaching on Britain's Turf: The European Union

Britain has been a member of the European Union since 1973. At that time the EU was called the European Economic Community and, yes, you guessed it, it was all about promoting economic growth in Europe. But since Britain joined the EEC it's increased its remit to include setting out a series of laws and rules that all members must abide by. Some senior European politicians have talked about EU member states actually joining together in some sort of federal European super state. The EU itself has massively expanded its civil service and institutions and raises money from donations from its member states. Meanwhile, the EU has also become a big club, now covering 27 countries and over 400 million people from Ireland to the borders of Turkey. The EU is made up of a parliament, a commission and a council of ministers; it's a really complex setup, with hundreds of politicians and thousands of civil servants. (Chapter 20 gives you a full run down on how the EU goes about its business.)

Gradually, the growing importance of the EU has caused major waves in British politics and is likely to do so for a long time to come. The EU is now virtually a super state which has legal powers within the UK. In addition, some Britons looking for justice take their cases not only to UK courts but also to the European Court in Strasbourg. In short, for the first time since the Reformation and the break with the Roman Catholic Church, foreigners now have real sway over legal matters in the UK. Some welcome this move and think that many good laws come from the EU, which has helped bring about economic growth and enshrine more rights for citizens.

In 1985, the British parliament ratified the *Single European Act*. At the time this didn't cause much of a stir but it was hugely significant because the Act gave laws drawn up by EU legislators equal power with those drawn up by the UK parliament.

Many within UK politics are opposed to the idea of a European super state and want to see the UK either leave the EU or say clearly that it doesn't want to join any sort of political union. These people are *Euro Sceptics*.

Britons get to vote for Members of the European Parliament in what are called European elections. Experts estimate that nearly two-thirds of new laws affecting the lives of Britons result from legislation drawn up by the EU rather than the UK parliament in Westminster.

Part II
Elections and Britain's Parties

'Darren says he's come up with another
idea to get people to vote.'

In this part . . .

1 build on the basic knowledge of politics and get down into the details of Britain's electoral process.

I examine parliamentary, local and European elections and the voting behaviour of the great British public. I take a good long look at Britain's political parties from the big two – Labour and Conservative – all the way through to the minor and emerging parties. I then look at the pressure groups that exert their influence on politicians and the wider public. Finally, I take a look at that most turbulent of relationships between politicians and the media.

Chapter 6

Counting the Votes: Differing Electoral Systems

In This Chapter

▶ Examining the types of elections

▶ Explaining first past the post

▶ Winning a majority of votes

▶ Looking at proportional representation

▶ Peering at the additional member system

▶ Keeping the system as is

*E*lections are a big deal in the UK (and all the other democratic countries around the globe for that matter), from deciding which party should form the government to who should be in charge of the local council; it's the democratic process in all its Technicolor glory.

Although election campaigns can go on for weeks and even months, the vote itself is squeezed into one day when electors are invited to attend a ballot station and cast their vote. It's the time when you and I get the chance to make a difference by saying who we want to represent us, and it's our opportunity to kick politicians out of office who we feel aren't doing a good job. For election day read judgement day.

Get your calculator out now because in this chapter I peer into the polling booths and explain exactly how we elect our politicians.

Listing the Big UK Elections

When you think about British elections your mind probably turns to a general election, with the high-profile national politicians going head to head and the airwaves crackling with everything political. However, the UK has lots of different elections which you have a right to vote in. Here's a quick guide to the UK's election scene:

✔ **General elections.** These elections are considered the biggies, with seats up for grabs in the UK parliament. Traditionally, these elections have the biggest turnouts and receive the most media coverage. Usually a general election occurs once every four or five years.

✔ **Devolved elections.** The Scottish parliament and Welsh and Northern Irish assemblies are big deals to the millions of people living in these parts of the UK. These bodies have lots of powers and in some ways are more important to people living within their compass than the UK parliament. Elections to these bodies take place once every four years and the system used is part first past the post, and part proportional representation (explained in a moment).

✔ **Local government elections.** From county, parish and community councils to mayors, across the UK almost every year a new set of elections is held. These elections may not have the glamour of a general or devolved election but they're important, as local government is responsible for many of the nation's public services, as well as raising council taxes and business rates and approving or turning down planning applications. Chapter 16 has more on the inner workings of local government.

✔ **European parliamentary elections.** In some ways European elections shouldn't be last in this list of elections of note because many of the laws governing the life of Britons actually come from the European Union (EU) (I explain the relationship in Chapter 20). Turnout tends to be low – usually between 30 and 40 per cent of people registered to vote actually bother to do so in European elections – and they take place once every five years, under a very complex system called the D'Hondt method (see 'Dividing in the D'Hondt method', later in this chapter). The last European election was in 2009, so the next is scheduled for 2014.

In total, 736 Members of the European Parliament (MEPs) sit in the parliament building in Strasbourg, France. Of this number, 78 come from the UK, which slightly under-represents the UK's share of the total population of the EU. For example, the UK has a population of 60 million, which works out to roughly an MEP for every 800,000 citizens; meanwhile Malta, with a total population of just over 300,000, has five MEPs.

UK general elections are pure theatre. The prime minister (PM) decides that an election should be called and asks the monarch to dissolve parliament. Once this request is granted, a date is set for a general election – normally around three to six weeks after the dissolution of parliament. During the run up to the election, politics receives almost blanket coverage on television and radio and in the newspapers, with politicians being quizzed by journalists and debating policy. Meanwhile, across the country thousands of party workers go *canvassing* – trying to drum up support for their party's candidate by knocking on constituents' doors, setting up stands in shopping centres, holding public meetings, and so on. On election day itself, the polling stations are open from 7 a.m. to 10 p.m., allowing tens of millions of people to vote. the votes are then counted and usually by the following morning it's clear which party has won the largest number of seats and will get to form the next government.

POLITICAL SPIN

Pick of the bunch: General elections

General elections are the stars of the electoral show. They can be a real watershed for British politics, with genuine policy changes of direction following soon after. The following list highlights some of the big turning point general elections of relatively recent history:

✔ **1945: Goodbye Churchill, hello Attlee.** Prime Minister Winston Churchill may have been instrumental in the UK winning the Second World War but he was still turfed out by electors at the 1945 general election. The Labour Party, under leader Clement Atlee, promised new schools and hospitals, as well as the construction of a more generous welfare state. These policies proved hugely popular with Britain's war-weary voters. Labour duly won and over the next six years the National Health Service (NHS) was set up, key industries nationalised and higher and more wide-ranging welfare benefit payments brought into being. British politics has never been the same since.

✔ **1979: The Iron Lady takes residence.** In the spring of 1979 Britain was ready for a change. Decades of economic underperformance, union militancy and a breakdown of what was called the post-war consensus between the Conservative and Labour parties (meaning they followed similar economic and social policies, on the premise that the government should manage the economy) led to the election of the radical reforming Conservative PM Margaret Thatcher. The Iron Lady, as she was nicknamed, went about reforming the unions, privatising former state industries and cutting taxes. As a result, the country boomed in the late 1980s but relapsed into economic difficulty in the early 1990s.

✔ **1997: Labour promises 'Things can only get better'.** After 18 years of Conservative rule, first under Thatcher and then John Major, the country was again ready for a change. The UK was wealthier than in 1979 and Labour said it wanted to use this newly created wealth to improve the lot of those less fortunate in society. Under the leadership of the charismatic Tony Blair, Labour, which had done badly at the previous four general elections, won in a landslide. Blair acknowledged victory at a televised party to the accompaniment of the pop song 'Things can only get better'.

Coming Up On the Rails: The First-Past-the-Post System

The UK parliament is an ancient institution and the system whereby its members are elected also goes back a long, long way. This long-used system is commonly known as *first past the post* because it has all the characteristics of a race. This is how the first-past-the-post system works: voters cast their ballots on election day, putting an X by the name of the candidate they want to elect. All the votes are counted and the individual with the largest number is declared the winner.

Elections to the UK parliament and local councils are run under the first-past-the-post system.

How many votes the winning candidate wins by is irrelevant – just one will suffice, and actually has done so on the odd occasion. More often than not, though, the winning candidate will have a *majority* (number of votes more than the next finisher) in the hundreds or thousands.

Table 6-1 shows the City of Chester candidates for MP and their vote totals from the 2005 general election:

Table 6-1	The City of Chester Vote Totals in 2005		
Candidate	*Party*	*Votes*	*Percentage of Vote*
Christine Russell	Labour	17,459	38.9
Paul Offer	Conservative	16,542	36.8
Mia Jones	Liberal Democrats	9,818	21.9
Allan Weddell	UKIP	776	1.7
Ed Abrams	English Democrats	308	0.7

Result: Christine Russell (Labour) wins the seat with a majority of 917 votes.

Crucially, under first past the post, you don't need a mathematical majority of votes to win the election, just the largest number. For example, in the election for the City of Chester outlined in Table 6-1, the Labour candidate won despite getting less than 40 per cent of the vote. Look at that figure from another angle and more than 60 per cent of voters in Chester voted for a different candidate than the person who won!

The racing theme is also applicable to the forming of a government in parliament. If a party acquires more than 50 per cent of the seats in parliament, it holds a majority – which means if all the party's MPs vote in the same way it can't lose the vote – and is then asked by the monarch to form the government.

A constituency where the winning candidate enjoys a very large majority – over 10,000 votes – is referred to as a *safe seat*. On the flipside, a constituency where the winning candidate has a small majority is referred to as a *marginal*.

Looking at the advantages

First past the post has been around for a very long time, which means that it must offer something people like. Here's what's good – from some people's perspective – about first past the post:

- **Strong government.** It's possible for a political party to win a majority of seats in the House of Commons without actually getting a majority of votes cast. For example, in the 2005 general election Labour enjoyed a 66-seat majority but only gained around 40 per cent of all votes cast. Holding a majority in parliament means the governing party has a virtual free hand to carry out its legislative programme and often leads to a strong government.

   Under other systems, such as proportional representation – explained in 'Examining Proportional Representation' later in this chapter – parties often have to work together and form coalitions to get legislation through their parliaments.

- **Community-centric.** Voting for an individual candidate to represent them in parliament allows voters to feel more ownership of their MP. In fact, although MPs nearly always belong to a political party, they sometimes put the interests of their constituents over that of their party. For example, an MP may vote against his or her party over plans to close a hospital in the constituency. What's more, MPs meet regularly to hear constituents' concerns, regardless of whether the constituents voted for them or not. Under other election methods, such as the candidate list system – explained in the later section 'Varying PR: The candidate list system' – this connection between a sitting MP and his or her constituents is less strong.

A *coalition government* is made up of more than one political party. Coalitions are rare in the UK because of first past the post, but are much more common in countries that employ proportional representation.

Taking in the disadvantages

Every argument has two sides, and that's certainly true when considering whether first past the post is right for the country. A lot of commentators simply don't like it because first past the post:

- **Often ignores the majority of voters.** MPs are regularly elected with a minority of the votes cast. This means that a majority of voters end up with an MP that they've actually voted against. Many suggest that this outcome is undemocratic.

✔ **Aids the two major political parties and marginalises minor parties.**
Apart from a brief period in 1974 when a Liberal–Labour coalition government existed, for the last 65 years only one of two parties has been in government – Conservative or Labour. The two-party nature of parliamentary election results is no doubt aided by the first-past-the-post system, because it makes it easier for one party to gain a majority in parliament and thereby form the government.

The Liberal Democrats have long disliked the first-past-the-post system, ostensibly because it's undemocratic. However, some self-interest is also at play – what, self-interest from politicians, surely not? Under first past the post, usually the bigger, more popular parties – Labour and the Conservatives – form the government. The Lib Dems – despite enjoying support of up to 25 per cent of the electorate – are in perennial opposition. If first past the post was abandoned, Lib Dem, as the third-biggest party, could expect to be part of a coalition government.

The prominent Labour turned Lib Dem politician Roy Jenkins (1920–2003) was a long-standing proponent of reforming the UK electoral system. After a long career in politics, Jenkins was asked by new PM Tony Blair in 1997 to produce a report on reforming parliamentary elections. Unsurprisingly, Jenkins recommended getting rid of first past the post and replacing it with proportional representation. Blair, equally predictably, ignored the recommendations of the report as he owed his majority in parliament to the first-past-the-post system. Even at its most popular, Blair's Labour Party never polled more than 43 per cent of all the votes cast in a general election.

Securing Over 50 Per Cent of the Vote: Majority Electoral Systems

Nineteenth-century US president Abraham Lincoln summed up democracy in his famous 1863 Gettysburg Address by stating that it was 'Government of the people by the people for the people'. But can any government which attracts less than half the votes cast really live up to Old Abe's ideal? Many think not, and therefore electoral systems do exist that are geared towards ensuring that the winning candidate actually has the support of over half the voters. The next sections cover these three majority systems.

A big advantage of majority voting systems is that the wishes of those voters whose preferred candidate didn't win are still taken account of. These voters may not get their preferred candidate but at least they may be able to avoid getting their least-preferred candidate.

Laying bare the two-ballot system

Basically, in a *two-ballot system*, instead of one vote to decide a winner, two votes are cast on separate occasions.

In the first ballot, voters cast their ballot for their preferred candidate. If one candidate gets over 50 per cent of the votes cast he or she wins and no more voting is necessary. But if no candidate gets 50 per cent of the votes, a second round of voting takes place.

In the second round, only the two candidates with the highest number of votes can stand; candidates who finished third, fourth or lower are automatically eliminated.

The idea is that those who voted for the now eliminated candidates will vote for one of the remaining two candidates in the second ballot. Even if they choose not to vote, it doesn't matter; with only two candidates standing in the second ballot, one of them is certain to achieve over 50 per cent of the votes and thereby win. French presidential elections use this system.

Playing the alternative vote system card

Strap yourself in for an explanation of the *alternative vote system* – it's a bit complicated! Under this system, voters get to rank all the candidates on the ballot paper from the most preferred to the least preferred. If a candidate receives more than 50 per cent of first-preference votes, he or she wins the election and everyone can go home – job done!

However, a candidate getting 50 per cent of first-preference votes is a fairly rare occurrence, which is where the complexity kicks in.

The candidate with the fewest number of first-preference votes is eliminated from the next round of voting. Ballot papers having that candidate marked as first preference are examined and the second-preference selections of those voters are then redistributed to the candidates remaining in the election. If these redistributed votes push one candidate over 50 per cent, he or she wins and, again, job done. If still no candidate has over 50 per cent of the votes, again the candidate with the fewest number of votes is eliminated and the second preferences of that candidate redistributed.

This process of elimination and counting second preferences – and, in some variants of the system, the third, fourth and even fifth preferences – goes on and on and, yes, on, until finally one of the candidates breaches the magic 50 per cent of votes cast.

The election for the mayor of London is carried out under the alternative vote system.

Throwing in the supplementary vote system

The *supplementary vote system* is a pared down version of the alternative vote system explained in the preceding section. Fortunately, it's a little less complex. Here goes: voters fill out first and second preferences. The votes are counted and if one of the candidates gets more than 50 per cent of the first-preference votes he or she's the winner – time to open the champagne! However, if no candidate gets 50 per cent, all but the two highest-polling candidates are eliminated. The second-preference votes are added to the first preferences of the two remaining candidates. This process leads to one of the candidates achieving the magic 50 per cent and is a good deal less long-winded than the alternative vote system.

Examining Proportional Representation

The concept behind *proportional representation* (PR) is fairly clear cut – which is a relief after the alternative and supplementary vote systems, which I cover in the previous sections. Under PR, parties are assigned seats according to the percentage of the votes they gather rather than winning seats through a series of local election races where the candidate with the most votes wins outright.

For example, at the 2005 general election Labour, under first past the post, had a majority of 66 seats yet only won 40.7 per cent of the votes cast. If the election had been run under the PR system, Labour would still have been the biggest party but wouldn't have come near to obtaining a majority of seats. As a result, in parliament Labour would have been forced to rely on the support of other political parties to see its bills made into law. It's not always the case that under proportional representation there will be a coalition government but it happens more often than not. In order to have a majority of seats in parliament under a PR system, one party has to poll more than 50 per cent of all the votes cast in the country and looking at the history of UK general elections that is a very difficult task to achieve.

One of PR's main drawbacks is that, if adopted for elections to the UK parliament, it would break the bonds between MPs and their electors, because voters are voting for the party rather than for individual candidates. Under PR, the politicians elected are drawn from candidate lists which are drawn up by the political parties. The more votes an individual party gets, the more candidates from its party list actually get elected.

Some suggest that coalition governments are a good thing, arguing that a coalition government prevents one party from pursuing extremist policies. If no one political party has a majority, it has to rely on the support of another party or two to govern and the other parties in the coalition tend to rein in extreme policies.

Most European countries operate a system of PR and coalitions are therefore commonplace.

Refining PR: Single transferable vote

Strap yourself in again: this variation on PR is another complex electoral system. Under the *single transferable vote system*, the country is divided into voting regions. The ballot papers contain the names of all the candidates running for election in that region. The voter ranks the candidates in order of preference. Now, if one of the candidates wins enough first-preference votes to breach a pre-set quota – for argument's sake, say 40 per cent – he or she's elected. But when more than one seat has to be filled for the same office – which is common as it's a whole region – the second, third, fourth, fifth and so on preferences of those who voted for the highest-polling candidate are now redistributed to the other candidates. If one of them now breaches the quota level, he or she too is elected. Once the second candidate has been elected, his or her preferences are thrown into the mix, leading to other candidates breaching the quota level and being elected.

A slight variant on this process is that, after the second seat is filled, instead of the other preferences from the voters for that newly elected candidate being counted, the candidate who polled the fewest first preferences is eliminated and lower preferences on the ballots for that eliminated candidate are redistributed to the other candidates, all with the object of pushing another candidate over the quota to be elected.

This process continues until all the seats in the region are filled. This voting system is used in the Republic of Ireland – and it's clearly the one of choice for mathematicians everywhere!

Varying PR: Candidate list system

In the *candidate list system*, the country is divided into voting regions containing lots of seats. The political parties submit a list of candidates for election. The votes cast in the region as a whole are counted and seats given out to the parties in proportion to the percentage of votes each party gains.

For example, say ten seats are up for grabs in the whole of East Anglia. Labour and Conservative get 40 per cent of the vote each, while Lib Dem gets 20 per cent. So, out of the ten seats Labour and Conservative get four each and Lib Dem gets two.

What about those candidate lists? Well, Labour and Conservative will see the first four candidates on their lists elected and Lib Dem the first two. Under this system, electors are voting for political parties rather than individuals.

Dividing in the D'Hondt method

Elections to the European parliament in the UK and the Northern Irish assembly are carried out under a variant of the candidate list system called the *D'Hondt method*. In this system, the party with the highest number of votes wins one of the seats in the voting region. That party's number of votes is then halved and a new calculation made, with the party with the highest number of votes winning a seat and then seeing its vote tally halved. This process continues until all the seats are allocated.

Let me give you a very simple example of a fictional region I'll call Mercia. Out of 935,000 votes cast, the political parties finished up with the following number of votes:

- ✔ Labour 400,000
- ✔ Conservative 300,000
- ✔ Liberal Democrat 110,000
- ✔ Green Party 75,000
- ✔ United Kingdom Independence Party (UKIP) 50,000

Under the D'Hondt method, the region's five seats would be distributed as follows:

- ✔ Seat 1 goes to Labour, as it had the highest number of votes and the candidate at the top of its party list is the new Member of the European Parliament (MEP). Halving Labour's total vote tally results in the following numbers:

  - Conservative 300,000
  - Labour 200,000
  - Liberal Democrat 110,000
  - Green Party 75,000
  - UKIP 50,000

✔ Seat 2 goes to the Conservatives. Its vote tally is halved (again the candidate at the top of its party list is now an MEP), so, for seat 3, the votes stand as:

- Labour 200,000

- Conservative 150,000

- Liberal Democrat 110,000

- Green Party 75,000

- UKIP 50,000

✔ Labour wins seat 3, and the candidate second on Labour's party list is now an MEP. Its voting tally is halved again, so, for seat 4, the votes stand as:

- Conservative 150,000

- Liberal Democrat 110,000

- Labour 100,000

- Green Party 75,000

- UKIP 50,000

✔ The Conservatives win a second seat and the candidate second on their party list is now the MEP. Their tally is again halved, so, for seat 5, the votes stand as:

- Liberal Democrat 110,000

- Labour 100,000

- Green Party 75,000

- Conservative 75,000

- UKIP 50,000

✔ The final seat goes to Lib Dem.

If more than five seats were up for grabs, the process of distributing seats and filling them with candidates from the party lists would go on and on, with even the Greens and UKIP likely to get an MEP. Contrast this scenario with the first-past-the-post system in which neither of these parties would win a seat despite the fact that, between them, they command around 15 per cent of the total votes cast in Mercia.

Looking North and West to the Additional Member System

The additional member system, used for elections to the Scottish parliament and the Welsh assembly, combines the basic fairness of PR with the representative benefits of first past the post. Voters, as a result, still feel a connection with the person they've elected to represent them.

The *additional member system* works in Scotland like this: voters have two votes rather than one – lucky them! The first vote they cast is for an individual candidate to represent them as a constituency Member of the Scottish Parliament (MSP). This election is run according to the first-past-the-post system, with the candidate scooping the highest number of votes winning the seat. For the second vote, the voters simply have a choice of parties. The votes for the parties are tallied up across eight different regions of the country and seats distributed accordingly.

So if, for example, the Scottish National Party (SNP) gets 40 per cent of second votes cast across the country it gets 40 per cent of what are called additional members (additional to the people elected through first past the post as constituency MSPs). As for who gets to sit as these additional members, names are drawn from lists of individual candidates submitted by the political parties.

Of 129 MSPs, 73 are elected via first past the post and 56 through the additional member system.

Those MSPs elected through the additional member system are referred to as *List MSPs*. If one of these List MSPs resigns the seat or dies, he or she is automatically replaced by the next name on the party list. If, however, a constituency MSP resigns the seat or dies, a by-election is held in that constituency, with the new MSP decided by first past the post.

Some commentators suggest that the additional member system was adopted in Scotland to stop the nationalist party, the SNP, ever forming a majority. The combination of the first-past-the-post and additional member systems makes it hard for any party to gain a majority of seats in the Scottish parliament, which in turn makes it harder for the SNP to ever get its wish of forcing a referendum on Scottish independence. However, the SNP has announced plans to go ahead with such a referendum after the next UK general election, in 2010. Whether or not it will secure a big enough vote in the Scottish parliament to be able to go ahead remains to be seen.

Expanding or shrinking according to the boundary commissions

Society doesn't stand still, and population patterns in towns and cities across the UK fluctuate over time. As a result, the parliamentary seat map has to change to reflect population moves. Locations with falling populations lose MPs while those with rising ones gain seats.

This ongoing reallocation of seats isn't done to suit a particular purpose or on the whim of a politician. Instead, every eight to ten years a review of parliamentary seats is carried out by four boundary commissions – one each for England, Scotland, Wales and Northern Ireland. These commissions are politically independent and staffed by civil servants.

The commissions look at each constituency in turn to see whether its boundaries mean it still meets certain criteria. Voting patterns are never part of the boundary commissions' delib-

erations. The boundary commission looks at how many people now live in the constituency and its geographic span and decide whether or not it should remain as it is, be split up into two constituencies, or merged with another constituency.

If the population of the constituency has declined since the last boundary commission review, a chance exists that it may be merged with a neighbouring one; if the population has increased, then part of the constituency may be hived off to a neighbouring constituency or be split into two and a new seat created.

Since Scottish, Welsh and Northern Irish devolution, the job of the boundary commissions has expanded to include constituencies in the Scottish parliament and Welsh and Northern Irish assemblies.

Preserving the Status Quo Rather than Rallying for Reform

Attempts to reform elections to the UK parliament and the first-past-the-post system have come to nothing so far. The reason for that is that changing the system isn't really in the interests of the two main political parties, which have formed the UK governments for the past 70 years or so. If the Labour or Conservative parties were to ditch first past the post and adopt some version of PR or an additional member system, they'd be unlikely to be able to form a majority in the House of Commons. As a result, the UK would probably see a succession of coalition governments.

Such governments work well in countries like Germany and the Netherlands, but the big two parties in the UK – Labour and Conservative – would have to compromise over policy if they had to join forces with a smaller party in a coalition government. No doubt the smaller party in the coalition – most likely Lib Dem – would extract a price in the form of support for some of its policies and jettisoning some of the main party's policies. In addition, the smaller party in the coalition would expect some of its leading members to be picked as cabinet ministers by the PM.

In the UK parliament three parties dominate – Conservative, Labour and Lib Dem. If a coalition government were to form, it would probably be the Lib Dems joining with Labour, as they're closer to each other in outlook and policy than is either with the Conservatives. (Chapter 8 talks about the make-up of the UK's political parties.)

Coalition governments have existed in the past. After the 1992 general election the Conservatives only had a small minority and sometimes relied on the support of the Northern Irish Ulster Unionist Party (UUP) to get their bills through parliament and into law.

Interestingly, because the Scottish parliament and Welsh and Northern Irish assemblies don't operate an exclusively first-past-the-post system, they have a greater chance of a coalition government. In Wales, for example, currently Labour and the nationalist party Plaid Cymru work together in government. In Northern Ireland a grand coalition of all the main parties holds power, while in Scotland, the SNP is in government with a minority of seats but looks to gather support from other parties on a needs-be basis to see some of its Bills make it through into law.

Hanging chads to rotten boroughs: Dubious election results

Whatever electoral system is deployed, no process is ever foolproof. Mistakes happen, controversy arises and sometimes even electoral fraud takes place. A quick delve into the electoral chamber of horrors brings the following problems to light:

✔ **Rotten boroughs.** Going back a couple of hundred years in the UK, lots of what were called rotten boroughs existed. *Rotten boroughs* were parliamentary constituencies containing very few voters – sometimes as few as a couple of hundred – who were often controlled by a local nobleman or landowner. The said nobleman or landowner could literally nominate who he wanted as a candidate and be assured that he (it was always a he in those days!) would win hands down. Some rich and prominent noblemen and landowners had several of these rotten boroughs in their pockets, which provided – indirectly – quite an influence in parliament. After all, the MP who sits in the rotten borough seat is always going to act on the say-so of his benefactor. This abuse continued for years until the Reform Act of 1832 swept away many of the nation's rotten boroughs.

✔ **Gerrymandering.** An American term, gerrymandering involves drawing of electoral boundaries to favour a particular political party at election time. Because the drawing of boundaries is often in the hands of the state governor or legislature, gerrymandering wasn't an uncommon practice in the past. In the UK, gerrymandering is a far less frequent occurrence because the boundary commissions are independent bodies. However, in the 1960s and 1970s in Northern Ireland, there were loud accusations that gerrymandering had taken place with the aim of reducing the impact of the Catholic vote in favour of the Protestant one. These accusations helped fuel Northern Ireland's civil rights movement and are believed to have inflamed the conflict between the Catholics and Protestants.

✔ **Hanging chads.** The US presidential election of 2000 was a very close-run race. At first count, the Republican candidate George W. Bush had defeated his rival, the Democrat candidate Al Gore. However, in the aftermath of the count, reports of voting irregularities in the state of Florida – whose governor just happened to be Bush's brother – emerged, with accusations that many votes for the Democrats had been discarded unfairly. So began the 'hanging chad controversy', so named because up to 70,000 ballot papers were rejected by machine counters because a hanging fragment of paper or *chad* was where a clear punched hole should have been. It may not seem like a big deal but a hanging chad on a ballot paper meant that it was discarded and the individual's vote went to waste. Eventually, after lots of legal to-ing and fro-ing and a Supreme Court decision, Al Gore conceded the election and George W. Bush was declared the president of the United States.

✔ **Postal fraud.** The UK doesn't have hanging chads or counting machines but moves have been made towards allowing more *postal votes* – allowing people to cast their vote through the post. Some welcomed this development as making it more convenient to vote, others have pointed out that more postal voting has led to electoral fraud by some supporters of the candidates standing for election. For example, postal votes have been tampered with and, in some cases, individuals have found that their votes have been stolen – they turn up at a polling station and are informed that they've already voted by post. Of course, they haven't – a fraudster has! In 2005 at an enquiry into voter fraud in Birmingham, Justice Richard Mawrey said that the UK's voting system was 'an open invitation to fraud'.

Chapter 7

Voting Behaviour and Trends

· ·

In This Chapter

▶ Looking at who gets to vote

▶ Sorting out who does vote

▶ Paying attention to what motivates voters

▶ Persuading voters to vote

▶ Accounting for campaigning

▶ Balancing media bias

· ·

'Win or lose, we go shopping after the election.'

Imelda Marcos, former presidential First Lady of the Philippines

S hopaholic Imelda Marcos's husband was famously overthrown in the late 1980s; perhaps she should have paid more attention at election time!

In the UK and the other great democracies of the world, election time is a very big deal. Tens of millions of Britons each year take the time and trouble to vote. They may elect the UK parliament, the distant parliament in Strasbourg or even the local council just down the road. Elections in the UK are varied and colourful, with lots of different candidates and parties.

People often see an election as a major staging post in their life – as with Margaret Thatcher's election in 1979 or Tony Blair's in 1997. They're part of a shared experience, yet very personal as each individual plays their part by voting.

In this chapter, I explore everything you need to know about what influences how people come to a decision over who they vote for or whether in fact they choose not to vote at all. I also take in the tactics used by the political parties to try to get you to put your x by their name at election time.

Looking at Who Can and Can't Vote

Just about everyone over the age of 18 has the right to vote at election time, whether it be UK, European parliamentary or local council elections In order to vote, you must register for the privilege on the electoral roll.

Registering to vote is easy. You can simply ring your local council and ask to register, do it online or wait until the local electoral registration office writes to your address and asks who at that address is eligible to vote. All in all, this means that the overwhelming majority – above 90 per cent – of adults in the UK are registered to vote.

At election time you're sent a polling card which you take down to your local polling station to prove who you are, and then get to cast your vote.

The UK is a democracy but plenty of people are still barred from having their say at the ballot box:

- Young people under age 18
- Foreign nationals
- Prisoners
- People convicted in the past five years of voting fraud
- Members of the House of Lords (on the premise that if you're there already you don't need to have someone else represent you in parliament)

Foreign nationals are barred from voting in UK elections even when they've been granted residency. However, as a bit of a hangover from the days of empire, Irish nationals and people from Commonwealth countries living in the UK can vote in a UK general election.

The monarch is allowed to vote but never does. They're supposed to be neutral and above the cut and thrust of party politics.

Understanding Voter Turnout

Not every eligible voter actually casts a vote; the proportion of voters that do is called the *voter turnout*. Voter turnout varies according to the type of election being held. Generally, elections to the UK parliament – called *general elections* – see the highest turnout as they're seen as the most important. Meanwhile, elections to the European Parliament and local councils are seen as less crucial, so voter turnout is lower – sometimes only half the level seen at a UK parliament general election.

All people of voting age must be registered as a legal requirement. But many people slip off the radar – they may not have a permanent address or simply decide that they don't want to appear on the electoral roll. A study suggests that anything up to six million people living in the UK who should be on the electoral roll aren't and are therefore technically breaking the law. But this six million figure is disputed by many.

Declining voter turnout

Voter turnout has been declining over the past fifty years, gradually at first but more recently at a considerable pace. Turning back the clock to the 1950s, around 85 per cent of all the Britons registered to vote would vote in a general election. In the 1970s this turnout had slipped to around 75 per cent. By the 2001 and 2005 general elections only around 60 per cent of voters actually turned up at the polls, as Figure 7-1 shows.

Figure 7-1:
Percentage
of voter
turnout from
1945 to 2005
(in 1974,
F = February
election,
O = October
election).

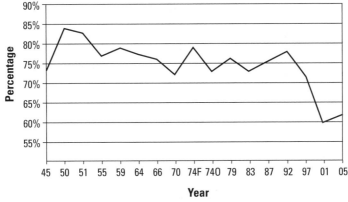

Politicians don't like it when voter turnout is low for a couple of reasons:

  ✔ **Low voter turnout damages their legitimacy.** If the government has only had a fraction of people voting for it, then some may argue it doesn't have a proper mandate to implement its policies.

  ✔ **Low voter turnout highlights political failure.** Generally, if turnout is low it's an indication that politicians are failing to connect with the public. In short, the public is turned off by the policies, message and even personalities of the political parties.

Sometimes voter turnout is low because the result of the election is seen as a forgone conclusion. In effect, voters stay at home because they don't think they are going to make a difference to the final result.

In some parliamentary constituencies voter turnout at a general election is much lower than the national average. At the 2005 general election, for example, some turnouts were as low as 40 per cent.

Political commentators have blamed falling turnout at UK general elections on:

- Declining trust in politicians
- Recent elections being almost a foregone conclusion
- The policies of the UK's big political parties being widely seen as very similar

Falling turnouts aren't confined to the UK. In the United States, for instance, the US presidential elections regularly only see voter turnouts of between 50 and 60 per cent.

Declining local democracy

All people on the electoral register have the right to vote in UK local elections. In areas where there are several tiers of local government – say county, district and parish – voters actually cast several ballots. Council seats are usually contested once very four years and at first glance it seems that local democracy is in rude health.

Turnout at local elections is on average only around half that at general elections and sometimes even lower. The fact that usually only a minority of those eligible to vote at local elections actually do is seen as an indication of the general decline of local democracy across the UK. Here are some of the reasons given for widespread voter apathy when it comes to local elections:

- **Council work is unimportant.** A lot of the work of local councils is viewed as mundane and as a result people rarely get exercised about which group of councillors is doing what.

- **The parties are no different from each other.** Across British politics a view persists that all politicians are the same and that the political parties don't have distinctive enough characters or policies.

- **Councillors aren't representative of ordinary people.** Being a councillor is an unpaid job and this means that a lot of them are retired and have time on their hands. The average age of a councillor in England for example is nearly 60 and this can make some younger people feel that they don't have much in common with their elected representative.

✔ **Councils are powerless to effect real change.** Although councils provide many key services and set Council Tax rates they get most of their money from central government, so many electors associate their daily engagement with government with the party in government in Westminster or Holyrood (in the case of the Scottish parliament) rather than their local council offices.

✔ **Councillors are unknowns.** Councillors tend to have a much lower profile than national politicians – think about it: you may not know the name of your local councillor but you certainly know who the leaders of the three main UK political parties are!

Turnouts at local elections are around the 30–40 per cent mark, whereas national general elections to the UK parliament see around two thirds of people eligible to vote casting their ballot.

Reversing declining voter turnout

It seems that after each general election, politicians and pundits ask what happened to all the voters. Politicians agree that they need to do more to 'engage' with voters. In other words, they need to do a better job of communicating why people need to get out and vote. But more radical solutions to declining voter turnout have been suggested:

✔ **Offering more ways to vote, including via the post and the Internet.** People lead busy lives, sometimes too busy to spare the time to go to the polls. To encourage those who'd like to vote but can't find the time, the idea is to make it easier to vote. Instead of taking their polling card down to the polling station they should be able to send their vote through the post or even go to a website and literally tick a box online in a few seconds. See the nearby sidebar 'When postal ballots go wrong' for a real-life look at some problems associated with alternative voting methods.

✔ **Compulsory voting.** Registering to vote is already a legal requirement, so why not take it a stage further and pass a law so that everyone actually casts their vote or faces a fine? Compulsory voting has been introduced in Australia and is one way to ensure far bigger voter turnout. But in the same way that voting is a democratic right, choosing not to vote, according to some, is also just that.

Traditionally, polling stations are open from early in the morning until 10 p.m. to allow voters the maximum amount of time to cast their vote.

When postal ballots go wrong

After the 2001 general election grave concerns were expressed regarding low voter turnout. In response, the government decided to make using a postal ballot easier for voters. Previously, applicants for a postal ballot had to give a good reason for why they weren't able to turn up in person to cast their vote at a polling station. But making the right to a postal ballot easier to get hold of had unforeseen consequences.

In the 2005 general election and several local government elections instances of voting fraud occurred, with postal votes going missing or people turning up at polling stations only to find that they'd apparently already voted by post. An investigation into voting fraud in the Birmingham area led to the examining magistrate describing the situation as more akin to the practices of a 'banana republic' (a politically unstable and corrupt country).

As a result of these controversies, the further loosening of rules governing the availability of postal votes has been put on hold.

Sometimes people turn up to vote but instead of putting a cross next to the name of a candidate they choose to write a message or put multiple crosses on their ballot paper. Doing so is called *spoiling a ballot paper* and the vote is counted but not assigned to any candidate. As a rule of thumb, you can expect a few dozen or perhaps as many as a hundred spoilt ballot papers at each individual parliamentary seat election. High numbers of spoilt ballots can indicate voter disharmony with the candidates and political parties on offer.

Considering What Sways Voters

Voters put their cross by a particular candidate or party usually for a combination of reasons, including:

- ✔ The attitude of the party or its candidate to a particular issue.
- ✔ The personality of the candidate or of the leader of the party.
- ✔ The social background of the voter.

I explore each of these issues in turn in the next sections.

Often people describe themselves as *traditional* Labour, Conservative or Lib Dem voters. The traditional status normally means that their parents or grandparents usually voted for the same political party all their lives. Pressure from family members and peers on voting patterns is difficult to measure but is no doubt a factor.

Taking in the big issues

Every so often pollsters ask the public what they see as the big problems or challenges facing the country. Some issues come and go but generally the public think the following few specific policy areas are the most important and look favourably on the party that seems to offer the best plan for each:

- ✔ **The state of the economy.** If the economy is doing well and people feel prosperous, this is good news for the government in power. If not, the public will probably want a change – bad news for the current government.

  Former US president Bill Clinton won the 1992 election on the issue of the economy. At the time, the US economy wasn't doing well and unemployment was rising fast. The incumbent president George Bush Senior made foreign policy the centre of his campaign, while the Clinton campaign kept the now-famous phrase 'It's the economy, stupid!' as his motto. Clinton communicated to the electorate that he knew what the real problems facing the US were and painted his opponent as being out of touch. Clinton won a landslide election victory.

- ✔ **Public services.** Normally, *public services* means health and education services. People like to see that hospitals and schools are well funded yet efficient. Under some circumstances many voters would agree to pay higher taxes for these, but they don't want to feel their hard-earned cash is being wasted.

- ✔ **Military conflict.** Wars can change the political landscape in no time at all, particularly when they go badly or well. If the public feel a war is justified and, crucially, won, it can reflect well on the government in power. The opposite, though, is also true.

  In 1982 Tory Prime Minister Margaret Thatcher was very unpopular at home. Then the Argentinians invaded the Falkland Islands, which were inhabited by over 2,000 British citizens. Britain fought and won a war to liberate the Falklands. At the general election the following year Thatcher won a massive victory. On the flip side, Tony Blair's decision to support the US invasion of Iraq in 2003 was hugely unpopular and a key reason why he resigned as prime minister in 2007.

Digging into the growing importance of green issues

The damage being done to the environment and the effects of global warming are becoming increasingly important issues. Conservative leader David Cameron has put the environment at the centre of his policy making. People like the idea that the environment should be protected. However, many also want to see economic growth at the same time. Balancing the need to produce economic growth and using fossil fuels with protecting the environment is likely to join health and big foreign policy as a major issue at election time.

Understanding the power of local issues

Not everyone is preoccupied with the economy, public services or foreign policy; instead some voters make their decision based on single issues, such as the need for a better rail network or opposition to nuclear power.

'All politics is local,' Thomas 'Tip' O'Neill, a long-time Speaker of the US Congress, rightly declared, knowing that people can be swayed to vote for a particular party or candidate because of something happening in their locality. For example, the closure of a local hospital can garner support for candidates who are opposed. Voting decisions aren't all based on big national issues – particularly not at local election times.

Throwing personality into the mix: The leadership wild card

The leaders of the main political parties are central figures in British politics as it's they who vie for the job of prime minister.

Many voters don't agree with the individual policies of the parties, and instead make their judgement on who to vote for based on their take on how capable or otherwise the individual party leaders are. They know that the biggest job in British politics is that of prime minister so they want someone in the hot seat who they think is up to the job and that they personally relate to. A leader who has charisma and can communicate well on television can be a huge bonus to his or her party – and the converse is equally true.

In short, if a party wants to be successful at the polls, it needs a leader who appeals not only to party members but also the general public as a whole. In recent years the personality of the leader has become crucial to election results, probably as a result of the main political parties moving their policies to the centre in order to appeal more to Middle Britain electors.

Former Labour leader Neil Kinnock was favourite to lead his party to election triumph in the 1992 general election. The Tory government at the time was unpopular and the economy was in deep recession. But Kinnock was famous for being verbose and often didn't come across well on television and through the media. In a tightly fought election, Labour lost and many blamed Kinnock for not connecting sufficiently well with the voters.

On the other hand, having a great, popular leader hasn't always been a guarantee of success at the polls. Back in 1945 the Conservatives had Sir Winston Churchill, who'd shown himself to be a brilliant wartime leader, but they were beaten by Labour in a landslide led by Clement Attlee, who some observers suggested unkindly had had a charisma bypass. Labour's stunning victory was the result of their policies homing in on Britons' hopes at the end of the war, such as building a free health care system, which became the National Health Service (NHS).

Personality can also play a part in local and individual parliamentary seat elections. Usually an incumbent who has a good profile in the local community can expect to do well against any opponents, as they have a track record and are known by at least some of the voters.

Looking at the voters themselves

Issues and leaders aren't all that drive voters. All the demographic factors – where you live, how much money you make, your ethnic background, your age and gender – play into how you vote. The next sections take on these factors one by one.

No single factor determines how people vote. Factors such as class, gender or where the voter lives can have more of an impact than age or religion – or the other way around. Normally, a combination of factors influences how people vote.

Voting and class

The class system has always been a big part of British society and experts generally reckon that for most of the post-war period from 1945 to the 1970s people voted in line with their class. Therefore, people who worked in manufacturing and other industries that were heavily unionised voted for the Labour Party, while most non-unionised people voted Conservative and to a much lesser extent Liberal – the forerunner of the Lib Dems.

But in the 1970s this old class–party alignment started to fragment, particularly after Margaret Thatcher's victory in 1979. Despite the fact that she was a Conservative, much of her support came from the working class, partly because of widespread disenchantment with union militancy. In addition, the number actually considered 'working class' has fallen in recent years as heavy industry and manufacturing have declined.

But class is far from dead as an influence on how people cast their votes. Labour, for instance, can still count on big support from those who consider themselves working class or those who don't have a job.

Elections are often won and lost depending on which party appeals to the middle class. This tactic is often referred to as appealing to 'Middle England' and for the big political parties is the key to electoral success.

Even at the start of the twenty-first century, the class system still plays a big part in British society and in how people vote. Although something of a stereotype, the higher up the class system you are, the more likely you are to vote Conservative. Generally, you have more to gain by maintaining the current state of affairs. (Chapter 8 has more on the natural supporters of the political parties.)

Voting and women

Up until the 1920s British politicians didn't have to think about appealing to women because that half of the population didn't have the right to vote. However, after a short matter of several centuries of having elections, women were finally allowed to take part. For the almost exclusively male – often moustached – politicians to work out that they needed to appeal to women in order to get elected took a little longer.

Now women are considered by political analysts the key constituency to swing an election one way or the other. A lot of time and money is spent by the big parties trying to gear their policies and their presentation to be attractive to women. Generally, policies relating to public services, such as health and education, and traditional family values play well with female voters.

Pundits often talk about a Worcester woman whose vote is paramount in an election. When they do, they're not referring to an actual woman, but to a type of voter they want to appeal to. The *Worcester woman* represents females with families in small-town England. These women are often seen as *swing voters*, which means they're open to persuasion rather than having a specific and long-standing preference for a single political party. Having policies which attract Worcester woman can be key to winning a general election in the UK.

In the past the Conservatives use to do well amongst women voters, mainly because of their emphasis on the importance of family values. But in recent elections this situation has changed, as Labour has actively courted female voters.

The Labour Party has had women-only candidate shortlists for several elections. These shortlists are intended to get more female candidates standing for winnable seats at election time. In turn, this tactic has resulted in an increase in the number of female Labour MPs. But, interestingly, male MPs are still comfortably in the majority. Many attribute this paucity of female MPs to women being put off entering politics because of negative public perceptions of politicians and the difficulty of balancing pursuing a political career with bringing up a family – a job still assigned in most minds exclusively to women.

Former Labour prime minister Tony Blair did very well with female voters. Most agree this success was because he often talked about issues that resonated with the female electorate, such as improving schools and hospitals. Blair was also noted as an excellent communicator on television, and his clean-cut family man image no doubt helped too.

Voting and age

Ex-British prime minister Sir Winston Churchill wasn't just a great wartime leader and a lookalike for a very big baby later in life, he was also a dab hand at clever quotes and phrases. One attributed to him is: 'If you're not a liberal when you're 20, you have no heart. If you're not a conservative when you're 40, you have no brain.'

Churchill meant that younger people naturally gravitate towards left-wing parties because their message of greater equality and looking after those less fortunate appeals to the emotions of youth. But as people get older and wealthier and see more of how the world works, they tend to become more conservative or right-wing in outlook, wanting to preserve the country's institutions and retain low taxes.

The figures bear Churchill out and generally the Labour Party does better amongst teenagers, students and those in their early twenties, while the Conservatives traditionally do well amongst the over 65s.

At the 2005 general election 47 per cent of people aged 18–24 voted Labour while just 29 per cent voted Conservative. By the time electors had reached age 65 and above, this situation had virtually reversed. Support for the Lib Dems, interestingly, tends to stay at the same level, regardless of voter age.

Voting and where you live

All the main political parties have what are called *heartlands* – areas of the country where they do best. Political scientists say these voting patterns are due to socioeconomic factors. Put simply, the type of industry that dominates the area, the level of unionisation, and local traditions all play a role in making people in a particular part of the country more likely to vote for a particular party.

The following list gives you the lowdown on what parts of the country are more likely to vote Tory, Labour or Lib Dem and why:

- **The North of England, Wales and Scotland.** The Labour Party tends to do better, as traditionally these are parts of the country dominated by manufacturing and industry, with a strong working-class culture and union movement.

✔ **The southeast of England.** The Tories do better here, as people have higher incomes and a lot invested in maintaining things as they are. They also like the party's expressed commitment to low taxes and free-market economics. Crucially, union membership is lower in this part of the UK.

✔ **The southwest of England.** Here, the Lib Dems tend to do well. This area of the UK is rural but also poor so it doesn't have the same interest in preserving the current state of affairs as the do Tories living in the southeast, but it's also not a working-class area and union membership is low. In short, much of what makes the Tories and Labour appeal to the rest of the UK doesn't strike a chord in the southwest, so the Lib Dems step into the breach and have long-standing support and strong local community ties.

Saying that because someone lives in the north they'll vote Labour or in the southeast Conservative is obviously too simplistic. In fact, at times the Conservatives garner major support in the north or Labour does well in the southeast.

Breaking the north–south divide

For many years in British politics a big dividing line existed, and the Conservatives would do well in the populous and prosperous south of the UK while Labour held sway in the less well-off north of the country.

Today, though, the old certainties of party heartlands have become a little less, well, certain. The UK economy has changed dramatically over the past thirty years, moving from manufacturing to services. With substantial immigration, the make-up of the population has also changed. Communities are no longer as homogenous as they once were; instead, people of very different backgrounds and outlooks live cheek by jowl across the country.

A fragmentation of the class system has also occurred as a result of the economic changes. No longer is it possible to compartmentalise millions of Britons as Labour, Conservative or Lib Dem voters; they're more likely to switch allegiances, which in turn is breaking up the old certainties such as the north–south divide.

All that being said, the south of England is very densely populated, which gives whichever party that does well there a very good chance of winning enough seats in parliament to be able to form the government.

Voting and ethnicity

Apart from younger voters, the Labour Party also tends to do very well amongst Britain's expanding ethnic groups. This appeal is explained by a number of factors:

- ✔ Labour is seen as an anti-racist party and, particularly through the promotion of inclusive policy at local government level, it is seen as pro-immigration.

- ✔ Labour is seen as the party most likely to look after the underdog. This can be important to those struggling to establish roots in the UK.

- ✔ Labour is traditionally strong in the north of the country where much mass immigration has occurred.

Within ethnic minorities differences in voting patterns still exist. For example, British Asians are much less likely to vote for a left-wing party than, say, British Afro-Caribbeans. Economically, British Asians have tended to do better and as a result the Conservative's message of lower taxes and keeping the current economic and political situation as it is resonates.

Conservative leader David Cameron has seen that his party is lagging behind Labour in terms of attracting ethnic minority votes. This situation is bad news for the Conservatives because ethnic minorities account for six per cent of the UK population and that percentage is expected to grow to around ten per cent by the middle of the century according to some estimates. In response, Cameron has tried to increase the number of party candidates, at both local and parliamentary elections, that come from a minority. The hope is to improve the party's image amongst minorities and attract more votes. (See Chapter 8 for more on Cameron's new model Conservative Party.)

Voting and religion

In countries like the US an individual's religion is a big deal at election time and can have a substantial impact on whether they vote Republican or Democrat. In the UK, however, religious observance is much lower and as a result faith doesn't tend have as major an impact on voting intentions. Another factor is that the big political parties have very similar policies on issues such as abortion or stem cell research, which are big bones of contention in the US.

Enticing Voters to Vote: Party Strategies

To win elections, political parties and their leaders have to get their loyal supporters excited enough to get out and vote. But simply appealing to this 'core' vote is never enough – they have to attract enough other voters to beat the other parties at the polls. In political jargon this is called going 'over the top'. The next sections talk about these strategies.

Appealing to the core vote

Generally, the big political parties, even when their fortunes are low in the polls, can rely on a proportion of the population – their *core vote* – to vote for them. A party's core vote can be made up of party members or those who've always traditionally voted for that party. My great-grandmother, for instance, would always turn up at her local polling station right into her nineties sporting a rosette in the colour of the party that she'd supported since she was a young woman.

The parties can thus rely on a core vote but they still have to keep in with these people and not take them for granted or they may choose to abstain from voting (although they're unlikely to vote for an opposition party).

The parties appeal to this core vote through the following methods:

- ✔ Party policy tries to keep close to the outlook of these core voters, representing their hopes and ambitions.

- ✔ Local party members identify core voters and then try to encourage them to turn up and vote on polling day. I know one party worker who ferries elderly and infirm people to the polling station so as to ensure that they cast their votes.

Getting the core vote is crucial. Without it, no political party can hope to do well at an election.

Broadening party appeal

The core vote is important but, in order to win elections, political parties must gather broad support amongst people who've voted for other parties in the past or those who may not usually vote at all.

Political scientists talk about *Middle England* or *Middle Britain*, not referring to a geographical location or even the middle class, but to a group of people who don't naturally support political extremes – neither left nor right – and who may have once considered themselves working class but now have access (or want to have access) to some of what were once seen as the trappings of middle-class life, such as home-ownership and private schooling for their kids. People defined as being a part of Middle Britain don't tend to have deep-rooted allegiance to a particular political party; instead they tend to vote for the party which best matches their ambitions for their families and the country as a whole.

Appealing to Middle Britain is often seen as the electoral Holy Grail – it can be the difference between success and failure.

Some of the do's and don'ts of wooing Middle Britain include:

- ✔ **Don't suggest policies seen as too extreme.** In the 1980s Labour did badly partly because it wanted nuclear disarmament; in the 1990s the Conservatives were seen as adopting extreme policies on immigration and the European Union.

- ✔ **Don't tax too highly.** Middle Britain wants to keep its cash and if it does have to pay taxes it wants the money spent wisely.

- ✔ **Do provide good public services.** For its money, Middle Britain wants good schools and hospitals provided – if not for themselves, for their friends and relations.

- ✔ **Do promote a better society.** Middle Britain likes stability and the idea that they and their loved ones are safe. As a result, policies to tackle crime and ensure a fairer society tend to go down well.

People who shift their allegiances between political parties are called *swing voters*. Much of Middle Britain can be described as being made up of swing voters.

Voting to thwart: Tactical voting

Tactical voting is when someone chooses to vote for a party which isn't their preferred choice in order to prevent their least-favourite party from winning a seat. Tactical voting is unique to the British first-past-the-post system, where MPs and local councillors are elected if they poll the highest number of votes in a particular constituency.

Call a fictional constituency something imaginative like constituency A. Now Labour holds the seat in constituency A with a narrow majority over the Lib Dems, and trailing way back in third place are the Conservatives. These Conservative voters are a bit fed up as they have little chance of ever electing their own candidate in constituency A and they really don't like the Labour Party. In fact, they dislike Labour more than they dislike the Lib Dems. Therefore, some of these disgruntled

Conservatives choose to vote tactically at the next election.

When election day comes around, instead of voting for their own candidate, they put their cross by the Lib Dem candidate's name in an effort to get the Labour Party candidate out. When the votes are counted, the Conservative vote shrinks, Labour holds the same, but the Lib Dems do best and win the seat because just enough Conservative voters switched to vote Lib Dem so as to ensure the Labour Party loses.

At the 2001 and 2005 general elections, tactical voting played a major part in the outcome. In these two elections, generally, a strong anti-Conservative vote was evident, with some Lib Dems voting for Labour in constituencies where Labour had a better chance to beat the Conservative candidate and the other way around.

Gazing at Election Campaigning

Most people don't live and breathe politics; they have important stuff to get on with, such as marriages, bringing up families and forging careers. However, every four or five years a general election is called by the party in government. This election is the voters' big chance to change the party of power or, if they like what's going on, keep the government in the box seat. Suddenly, public interest in politics rises, and the parties, their members and leading politicians start to campaign. Many electors make up their minds as to which party they'll vote for during the campaign.

Typically, during an general election the parties use certain tactics including the following to encourage people to vote for their candidates:

- ✔ Party political broadcasts on TV

- ✔ Adverts taken out in the press, online or on street billboards

- ✔ Party members knocking on electors' doors and telephoning them at home

- ✔ Politicians giving lots of interviews to the media and taking part in debates and answering questions for the public

- ✔ Party leaders touring the country, holding rallies with the aim of getting extra media coverage for their campaign

- ✔ Parties using texts, emails and blogs to contact electors

General election campaigns usually last around three weeks. The newspapers and airwaves are dominated during this time with political discussion.

Modern politics is as much about doing down the opposition as telling the public how good you are. At recent general elections, in the US in particular, politicians have been accused of employing *negative campaigning*, which is focusing the communication effort on exposing what they see as the shortcomings of their opponents.

Glancing at the Effects of Media Bias

Politicians – particularly when they've been beaten at the polls – are keen on pointing out that a lot of the media in the UK is biased against them. This assertion isn't sour grapes because certain parts of the media – in particular the national newspapers – are definitely biased. They have allegiances to a particular political party and often attack its opponents. The newspapers would say they're merely reflecting the views and preoccupations of their readers.

The BBC (British Broadcasting Corporation) is a public service broadcaster and, according to the rule of its charter, is supposed to be independent. Journalists at the BBC have to work within strict guidelines to ensure that they're balanced and fair in what they say, and that they devote equal air time to opposing politicians. Nevertheless, the BBC is regularly accused of bias, often by those on the right of the political spectrum.

In the close-run 1992 general election, Labour leader Neil Kinnock said that the negative attitude of many national newspapers, and in particular *The Sun*, damaged Labour's chances at the poll. On polling day itself, *The Sun*'s front page featured a picture of Neil Kinnock's head superimposed on a light bulb next to the headline 'will the last person to leave Britain please turn off the lights'. Labour lost the election and Neil Kinnock resigned as leader straight after. The next day *The Sun* headline read: 'It was *The Sun* wot won it.'

Newspapers' attitudes towards a particular political party are important but aren't the be-all and end-all. Newspaper circulations are falling, for example, and people get their news from so many different sources these days that one newspaper's bias is easily counterbalanced. (Chapter 10 covers the media and British politics.)

Lord Beaverbrook is widely considered to have been the greatest press magnate of twentieth-century Britain. Not only did he own the *London Evening Standard* and the *Daily Express*, he was also given two key jobs – those of Minister of Aircraft Production and Minister of Supply – in Winston Churchill's wartime government. His newspapers were staunchly loyal to the government during the difficult, bloody and protracted conflict that was the Second World War.

Chapter 8

Homing in on Political Parties

- -

In This Chapter

▶ Introducing political parties

▶ Keeping party unity

▶ Looking at the big three – Conservative, Labour and Lib Dems

▶ Taking a peak at the minor and nationalist parties

▶ Dipping into Northern Irish politics

- -

1n this chapter, I examine everything you need to know about Britain's political parties, big and small, mainstream and at the extremes.

Understanding Political Parties and How They Operate

Put simply, a *political party* is a group of people who come together with the aim of winning government power. These people don't just meet randomly in the street, look each other up and down, and decide that they want political power; they need to have something in common, some sort of shared interest or view of how the country should be governed.

Sometimes a shared interest extends to just one issue. In recent years, parties formed in some parliamentary constituencies with the aim of saving a local hospital or because the local Member of Parliament (MP) has been accused of corruption and people want to see a reputable candidate brought in. These single-issue parties don't tend to last long, as members generally become more preoccupied with other policy concerns and find that they don't have much in common with their fellow members.

Recognising the role of the major UK parties

Britain's big political parties – Labour, Conservative (Tory) and Liberal Democrat (Lib Dem) – have been around in one form or another for generations. A reason for their longevity is that each has a philosophy which a substantial number of people throughout the country identify with.

All the political parties have 'natural supporters' – those people whose social and economic background makes them naturally more attuned to a particular political party, philosophy and policies.

The big parties are totems in British life, with hundreds of thousands, if not millions, of people gathering around them in one form or another. Party supporters do everything from joining up to voting for their party or even espousing the party's views in the pub – if you encounter the latter, best drink elsewhere unless you want earache!

The two biggest parties – Labour and Conservative – have their natural supporters that they can usually rely on. However, the key to electoral success lies in appealing beyond this base to the wider electorate. For example, Labour can't win a general election if it doesn't gain some seats in the Tory stronghold of the southeast of England. The Tories, on the other hand, have to win some seats in the north of England to win a majority.

The most long-lasting model for a political party is one in which a shared philosophy guides positions on many issues and lies behind the policies the party proposes to carry out if it makes it into government. The more people who share this philosophy, the more support the party has and the better its chances of being elected and obtaining power.

Some people feel so strongly about the philosophy and policies of a particular party that they join and become an activist or even stand for election under the banner of that party (Chapter 17 covers ways to get more involved in politics).

Even people who are non-party members often identify themselves as being a Tory, Labour or Lib Dem supporter or voter, as it allows whoever they're telling to gauge the sort of things they believe in.

Forming party policy: The approach of Conservative, Labour and Lib Dem

A political party's policy is crucial because it forms the basis for a *manifesto* – a public declaration of principles and intentions – at election time. As one of the major factors influencing how people vote, this manifesto is a big deal.

If the public like the manifesto, so the thinking goes, the party will get more votes and have a better chance of forming the government.

All the big political parties have a different approach to how party policy is formed; here's a run down:

- **Conservative.** Policies are formed by the leadership, but if a policy is against the wishes of a substantial proportion of party members or senior figures, public disagreements will be likely to ensue. In effect, this ability to disagree provides a check and balance on the leadership and its policies. Crucially, the leader doesn't form policy on a whim; he or she has policy advisers who're normally senior figures in the party.

- **Labour.** *Policy forums* – comprised of people appointed by the party's leader – put together potential policies for consideration by the party's National Executive Committee, which is elected by a ballot of all party members. The forum participants draw up policies to be put before the party's annual conference, where they're voted upon. The leadership does have the power, however, to ignore conference voting outcomes if it wishes.

- **Lib Dem.** As with the way they elect their leader (see the next section), the Lib Dems have a convoluted way of deciding policy – a local and federal system. Policies which affect particular localities, such as Scotland and Wales, are decided and voted upon at small party conferences held in that locality. Policies that affect the country as a whole are debated and voted upon at the national party conference.The leader has a say over the forming of party policy because he or she gets to appoint the members of the Federal Policy Committee, which draws up policy proposals for the national conference and also pens the party's election manifesto.

Lib Dem leaders don't have quite the sway over party policy as do the Labour and Tory leaders.

Choosing and following the leader – and other senior party figures

Much of the power in a political party lies with the leader. He or she is usually elected through a poll of members, although the party's MPs or groups affiliated to the party may have a say as well (for example, the trade unions also influence who gets to be Labour leader).

The three major parties in the UK use three different methods to choose their party leader:

- ✔ **Conservative.** Tory leaders are elected through a combination of a ballots amongst the party's MPs and members. If more than two candidates for leadership are standing, the MPs are balloted and the top two in this poll go through to a final ballot, which is voted on by the entire membership of the party.

- ✔ **Labour.** The leader and deputy leader are elected through an *electoral college system*. This college is divided into three parts, each worth a third of the vote. Labour MPs and Members of the European Parliament (MEPs) get to vote in one section, ordinary party members in another, and individual members of trade unions who are affiliated to the Labour Party in the third. Whichever candidate for leader gets the highest number of votes in each of the colleges wins that college and a third of the votes. So to win the leadership the candidate needs only to win two of the three colleges.

- ✔ **Lib Dem.** The leader of the Lib Dems is selected by the highly complex *single transferable vote system*. In short, party members vote for not only their favourite candidate (called a first preference) but also their second-favourite (called second preference). After the votes are counted, the candidate recording the fewest number of first preferences is eliminated and the second preferences of the people who voted for that candidate are then added to the totals of the remaining candidates – I told you this system was complex! This process goes on as the candidates are whittled down to just two. The ultimate winner is the one that polls the highest number of both first- and second-preference votes.

Although the leader is head honcho, it doesn't mean that he or she can't be challenged. If the people who elected him or her are unhappy with the leader's performance they may elect someone else to the role.

The leader gets to appoint the senior posts within the party, such as spokespeople on particular policy areas like health or the economy, and, when the party's in government, to say who'll be ministers.

The leader also appoints people to help with the day-to-day running of the party, making sure, for instance, that enough funds are raised to fight elections and that party membership remains high. Political parties are big institutions with lots of volunteers as well as full-time employees.

Key party bigwigs include:

- ✔ **Party chairperson.** This person ensures the party's operations are up to speed. The chairperson is a crucial bridge between the high echelons of the party and the grassroots members. A good chairperson can galvanise the grassroots while simultaneously letting the leader know what the grassroots are thinking.

✔ **Party treasurer.** This person's in charge of fundraising for the party, wooing big donors and ensuring the party has enough cash to communicate its message and fund the fighting of elections.

✔ **Head of communications.** This person's responsible for the party's advertising and media strategy. His or her job is to ensure the party is seen in as positive a light as possible in the media and hopefully therefore the country. The communications head may not even be a party member – often, a prominent journalist is employed in this role.

✔ **Head of candidates.** This individual makes sure that the best possible candidates represent the party at election time. Each party has a different approach to how this is done.

The big political parties have different hierarchies. For example, the Labour Party doesn't have a party chairperson; instead, they have a deputy leader who's elected in the same way as the leader.

Whipping up discipline: Keeping party members on the same page

The key phrase for successful political parties is 'united we stand, divided we fall', and parties which endure for generations rather than a few years heed this message. In other words, the party philosophy comes first. If a political party isn't disciplined, it will eventually fall apart as the individuals who comprise it go off pursuing their own policy hobby horses and disagreeing in public.

No single politician – no matter if he or she has wider appeal amongst the electorate – is ever as big as the party as a whole. Parties are professionally organised – a little like a business – with chains of command and internal disciplinary procedures. At the top of UK political parties sits the leader and below him or her are senior party members – such as the deputy leader in the Labour party, party chairperson in the Conservatives or president in the Lib Dems. There are also senior politicians appointed by the leader to be ministers (if the party is in government) or shadow ministers (if they're in opposition). This group of politicians are collectively called *the party leadership* and their responsibility is to oversee the making of party policy and be the most visible representatives of the party in the media. But in order to be successful (get elected, in other words) the party leadership has to seem united and they expect the adherence of other party members. Even amongst people who share the same political philosophy, disagreements can occur over what policy the party should be pursuing. Public disagreements, along with personal scandals, can tarnish the image of the party as a whole.

In modern politics, image – if not quite everything – is still crucial, and retaining good party discipline is key to putting across a good image to the voters!

Leading figures in the party who hold an official role, such as chairperson or minister, are expected to adhere to collective responsibility. This sounds very serious and rather solemn and it is. *Collective responsibility* means that, once the party has made a decision, all the ministers and members in official positions are expected to support that position in public – even if they disagree with it behind closed doors. If someone breaks with collective responsibility, he or she can expect to be sacked from their post. More often nowadays, though, the individual chooses to resign from the post but still remains in the party.

Parties whose leading figures disagree in public often do badly at elections. Generally, the electorate don't like divided parties; they feel they'll never get things done in government as they'll be bickering amongst themselves – and they have a point!

Typical 'crimes' which can lead to punishment by the whips and party leadership include speaking out against the party leadership (criticising the leader is a big no-no) or a key party policy, and personal transgressions such as having an affair, or being involved in corruption. Basically, politicians are expected to behave in a good and morally upstanding manner.

Key ways parties keep discipline so that they present a united front to the electorate include:

- ✔ **Whipping MPs.** Yes, you read it right. Fortunately, whipping in this context doesn't refer to some very dodgy nocturnal practice, and MPs aren't physically threatened. Whipping's all about getting MPs to vote in favour of their party's policy or a measure proposed by the party leadership.

  The whip refers to membership of the party in the UK parliament.

  If an MP doesn't do what the party bosses say, he or she can have the whip withdrawn, which means the recalcitrant MP becomes an outcast from the party and won't be helped out by party workers at election time. See Chapter 12 for more on the inner workings of what's called the mother of all parliaments – and, oh yes, more whipping!

- ✔ **Giving and witholding promotion.** Senior figures in the party often get to decide who moves up the party or governmental ranks. For example, the prime minister makes ministerial appointments. If a party member doesn't toe the line, he or she may not get promoted or lose a position held within the party.

  The ultimate arbitrator of this big appointments merry-go-round is the party leader, who's also the prime minister when the party is in government.

Most party members never have to be disciplined or compelled to 'toe the party line' because these members actually believe in what the party stands for. They may not agree with every aspect of policy but they think that the good the party could do in government outweighs any negatives.

Often, when a senior politician resigns following a scandal, he or she says that the resignation is 'for the good of the party'. Such resignations emphasise the key mantra at the heart of successful political parties: no man or woman is bigger than the party.

Looking at the role of the whips

Whipping is crucial to the UK law-making process. All the major parties have a *whip* who usually also has a couple of deputies. The whip's role is to get the party's MPs to vote the way the leadership of the party wants them to. Whips are key to parties in government as they need to ensure a majority so that it can push its bills into law.

Whips are powerful and often very Machiavellian in their behaviour. Their job is to persuade their fellow MPs to support the party leadership. They have been known to threaten recalcitrant MPs with all sorts of sanctions, from denying them government posts in the future (if a whip tells the PM a particular MP is a trouble-maker then the chances of that MP becoming a minister in the future are slim) to actual de-selection as a party candidate at the next election.

MPs receive weekly instructions from their whips, telling them when they are expected to turn up to the House and how they are expected to vote (I know it all sounds very controlling, and believe me it is!).

The leadership is more bothered about some votes and less concerned about others. For example, it's unusual for the whips to instruct all its MPs to vote down a Private Members' Bill as just a few votes against it will normally suffice.

The whips have a code to indicate to their MPs how seriously they should take an instruction to turn up and vote a particular way:

- **Three line whip.** This means that attendance is absolutely essential and MPs are expected to vote with their party leadership. Failure to follow a three line whip can lead to serious consequences for the individual MP.

- **Two line whip.** Attendance is expected but MPs can *pair off,* which isn't some sort of speed dating game, but instead an arrangement in which an MP finds a member from an opposition party and they both agree not to turn up. In effect they negate each other's vote so the voting mathematics remain the same.

- **One line whip.** This is a request from the whips for the attendance of MPs. It's not the end of the world if this is ignored but still the whips won't be happy.

Some areas of legislation are considered *matters of conscience,* which means that the leadership stays neutral and whips don't issue voting instructions.

These matters of conscience include areas such as the re-introduction of the death penalty and changing the legal limit on abortion. On such occasions MPs are given what's called a *free vote*.

On occasions an individual MP annoys the whip so much that the whip *withdraws the whip*. You may think that's happy days for the MP – no more threats and orders from the whip. Not a bit of it though. Withdrawing the whip is in effect suspension from the party. No MP who has had the whip withdrawn can stand as a party candidate at election. Often withdrawal of the whip is a temporary measure, but if the MP doesn't want to be de-selected as a candidate by his or her constituency party, he or she has to get back into the good books of the whip and have the whip restored.

Ineffective whipping leads to government bills not passing. A government which loses lots of votes in the House of Commons will be seen by the media and the electorate at large as weak and ineffective – hardly vote-winning qualities!

There are whips in the House of Lords, but they tend to operate in a more gentle way – after all they're dealing with the nobility. What's more, the members of the House of Lords don't need party support as they don't stand for election.

Breaking the mould: Famous party schisms and rebellions

All of the big UK political parties have been around for many years, but at times rebellions and splits within them have had disastrous consequences at the polls. Some of the big rebellions in British political history include:

- ✔ **The Gang of Four.** Following defeat at the 1979 general election, the Labour Party adopted more radical left-wing policies, such as nuclear disarmament, which led to four of its most prominent MPs – Roy Jenkins, David Owen, Shirley Williams and Bill Rodgers – leaving and forming their own new party, the Social Democrats (SDP). After some initial success at the polls and a further disastrous defeat for Labour in the 1983 general election, the SDP started to fragment and eventually was swallowed up by the Liberal Party, which then changed its name to the Liberal Democrats. Ultimately, the SDP took a large chunk of Labour's

natural support base and inadvertently helped Margaret Thatcher's Tories win a majority at a couple of general elections.

- ✔ **Maggie kicked out.** Margaret Thatcher polarised opinion across the country in the late 1980s, as the UK was in recession and she pursued unpopular policies such as the poll tax. Eventually, in late 1990, Thatcher was forced to resign as prime minister following a rebellion amongst her own MPs and a leadership challenge from rival Michael Heseltine. The party then elected John Major and went on to a surprise win at the 1992 general election. However, supporters of Thatcher never forgave those who'd deposed her and the Major government was disastrously split, which contributed to a big defeat at the 1997 general election.

✔ **Lib Dem leader merry-go-round.** The Lib Dems often benefit in the mind of the public because they're somehow seen as 'nicer' than the other two main parties – probably because they rarely have to exercise any actual governmental power. However, this goodie-two-shoes image has been damaged in recent years by the party MPs turning on leaders Charles Kennedy and Sir Menzies Campbell. Both men had personal or political failings and were subjected to rebellions by their MPs. This internecine warfare damaged the public's view of the Lib Dems in the mid-noughties and consequently the party has only done modestly at election times.

Living it up at party conferences

Everyone loves a knees up, and that's particularly true of the annual conferences held by the UK's main political parties. These big bashes are often held in seaside towns and offer party members the chance to rub shoulders with leading politicians. They normally take place in the early autumn in what's known as the party conference season. Lively debates and fringe meetings are followed by a fair amount of drinking and socialising.

Party conferences aren't just about having fun, though; they serve the following purposes too:

✔ Party policies are debated, although not often changed at conference.

✔ Fringe meetings encourage new ideas, which may ultimately be incorporated into party policy.

✔ The party conference attracts massive media coverage, making it a good platform for the party to let the wider population know its policies.

✔ Huge funds are raised from party members and party donors, which helps the party fight elections.

In the not too distant past, party conferences were quite dramatic occasions, with huge rows erupting between leading politicians. In the 1970s and 1980s the Labour Party's annual conference, for instance, was the scene of rows about policy and leadership. At the time, party policy was decided on by votes taken at conference, so the decisions taken there really mattered.

However, although party policy is still discussed at conference, no longer does the leadership of any of the three main parties have to follow what the conference decides.

Today's party conferences are stage-managed occasions, with leading politicians making carefully prepared speeches, greeted by often delirious applause from the members stood on the conference floor.

This lack of substantive decision making at conferences doesn't mean a lack of drama – far from it! These days, the drama's to be found in the fringe meetings, where policies and sometimes the future of the leader are debated openly by members. These fringe meetings still retain a little of the old fireworks which used to be seen on the conference floor.

Party conferences are carefully choreographed affairs, aiming to project the party's message and the personality of the leader to the country as a whole.

Forgoing party to form a national government

In the normal course of events political parties are at loggerheads, trying to make their opponents look ponderous and frankly a bit daft and themselves bright and full of answers to the nation's problems. This scenario is particularly the case at the big once-weekly set-piece event when the prime minister gets quizzed on what the government is up to by the leaders of the Tories and Lib Dems, and backbench MPs (who are selected to speak by the House of Commons Speaker). Prime minister's question time is all very entertaining and part of the rough and tumble of party politics.

However, occasions do occur when the country's in such a big mess that politicians realise that being at loggerheads is inappropriate. In short, the public won't stand for rowing politicians – they want united action. Such a situation can lead to opposition parties falling into line behind the government and supporting its policies.

Going further than this, in national emergencies the government may invite leading members of the opposition into government, forming what's called a *national government*. A national government is intended to unite the major political parties to meet the emergency and bring together the country's most talented politicians.

National governments are very rare in the UK as the country tends to be very stable. When such arrangements have been made in the past, they've been in response to the following national emergencies:

- The country is at war and has suffered some serious military reverses.
- The country is in the grip of an economic crisis.

National governments have been formed twice in the last 100 years. The first was in response to the Great Depression in the early 1930s and the second was during the Second World War, after allied forces were defeated in first France and then Norway.

Winston Churchill was prime minister during most of the Second World War. He came to power as the head of a government containing members of the Conservative, Labour and Liberal parties when the UK was facing the very real possibility of being invaded by Nazi Germany. (Chapter 22 lists ten of Britain's great prime ministers.)

A national government results in the following benefits:

- ✔ The country's most talented politicians from all parties are brought together.

- ✔ It has an automatic majority in the House of Commons and so can press ahead with new laws.

National governments are meant to be a temporary response to a particular crisis. In the past, as soon as the crisis has been met, the old parties reform and start competing again. For example, at the end of the Second World War an election was held and Winston Churchill stood as the leader of the Conservative Party, while Clement Attlee opposed him as leader of the Labour Party. Only a few weeks before, Churchill and Attlee had been in national government together. But, on election day, Attlee's Labour Party won a historic landslide victory.

Looking at the Benefits of the Party System

Love them or loathe them, Britain's political parties are crucial to the running of the country. The people who run the government are usually drawn from the most popular political party in an election.

Some of the plus points of the 'party system' include:

- ✔ **Parties bring stability in government.** Party members share the same outlook and philosophy, so in theory they should be able to work well together.

- ✔ **Parties help formulate government policy.** Party members decide what policies they'd like their party to pursue when and if they make it into government.

- ✔ **Parties provide opportunities for advancement.** It's possible for anyone to become prime minister but they'll only do it by rising through the ranks of a political party to become leader – look for the nearby sidebar, 'Climbing the ranks to power'.

✔ **Parties mobilise the wider electorate.** Parties help highlight crucial issues for the electorate and individual members can motivate friends and neighbours to get out and vote. Without strong political parties, voter turnout would most likely be much lower than it is.

✔ **Parties provide scrutiny of government.** When not in power, parties can highlight the failings of government and propose alternative solutions to the country's ills. Sometimes the government will agree with what they're saying and adopt policies recommended by their political opponents – although they rarely admit what they're doing.

Parties bring solidity and permanence to the political system. When in power, they ensure the actions and philosophy of the government are closely aligned to at least a substantial minority of the population, even if not always the majority.

Witnessing Party Breakdowns

In times of great crisis – during war or an economic depression, for example – the political party system can appear to break down. The main established parties no longer seem to have the answers to the problems of the day.

When crises happen, what often follows is that the main parties fragment – lose support and membership – and new parties form, or smaller, single-issue parties see a surge in support. Sometimes this scenario can be healthy, but other times less so. In pre-war Germany, for instance, economic collapse caused a dramatic haemorrhaging of support away from the main established political parties as people sought new answers to their economic woes. One party to benefit was the National Socialists (Nazis) under Adolf Hitler. Hitler took power and a few years later plunged the world into the bloodiest war in history. The rise of Hitler was, at the start at least, facilitated by the breaking down of the established political parties.

Climbing the ranks to power

Previous prime ministers (PMs) John Major and Margaret Thatcher prove that it's possible to start off as virtual unknowns to the average person in the street.

Both former PMs came from relatively humble backgrounds – Thatcher's father ran a corner shop and Major's was brought up in Brixton and spent his early life in the circus! But neither Thatcher nor Major fancied the life of the retailer or juggler and so chose a career in politics instead.

They first went canvassing on behalf of their chosen party's (Conservative) candidates, then stood for election themselves. Then, after many years of climbing up the ranks of the party, they were elected leader, and finally, when their party was in government, became prime minister.

Exploring the Tories

The Tories – or Conservative Party, as they're officially called – have been around in one form or another for a couple of hundred years, which shows they must be getting something right in the wider public appeal stakes.

The term 'Tory' goes right back to the seventeenth century and is short for Toraidhe, an Irish word for outlaw. Originally, Tory was used as a term of abuse for English Catholics and those who supported the monarch over the mostly Protestant parliament. The Tories tend to be referred to as being on the 'right' of British politics, which means that they support:

- ✔ Promoting free trade and enterprise over a big welfare state
- ✔ Retaining important constitutional and cultural institutions
- ✔ Keeping Britain independent from a European super state
- ✔ Maintaining a strong military and retaining Britain's senior position in the world

Generally, the party's policies reflect in some shape or form these key philosophies, particularly its adherence to free market economics.

The Conservative Party is often referred to as being a little old-fashioned. Out of the three main political parties in the UK, its members are the oldest. However, not only ageism makes people brand the Tories old-fashioned; the party's wishing to defend the nation's institutions such as the monarchy and a shared British national identity, even when campaigning in Scotland and Wales, creates this image.

Occasionally, Conservative Party candidates for election to the UK parliament refer to themselves as belonging to the Conservative and Unionist Party. They're still Conservatives but tagging on the word Unionist emphasises to the voters that they believe wholeheartedly in the union between England, Scotland, Wales and Northern Ireland. 'Dipping into Northern Irish Politics' later in this chapter has more on what Unionist means in Northern Irish politics.

The Conservative Party has often been referred to as the most successful in British politics. Despite being the oldest of the big parties, it has had more years in government since the Second World War than Labour and Liberal Democrats combined.

Whigs and Tories square off and give birth to Lib Dems

For about 150 years, up until the back-end of the nineteenth century and the reign of Queen Victoria, the UK had only two main political parties – the Whigs and the Tories.

Put simply, the Whigs believed that parliament should run the country and that the Protestant religion should be the only type of Christianity allowed. The Tories, on the other hand, tended to believe that the monarch should have plenty of power in the constitution – even perhaps more than parliament – and that the Catholics weren't to be persecuted.

For most of this time the Whigs headed up (geddit?) the government as their anti-Catholicism and desire for a parliamentary system was more in tune with the rich merchants, the growing band of industrialists and the wider population in general.

The Whig party started to slowly fragment in the nineteenth century over key issues such as free trade and constitutional reform. This fragmentation left the Tories suddenly centre stage, and to counteract this situation the remaining Whigs formed a new party called the Liberals – the forerunner of today's Liberal Democrats.

Re-inventing the Tories: Cameron's conservatism

When David Cameron was elected Conservative leader in 2005, the party had just suffered its third consecutive crushing electoral defeat. It was at a low ebb and the new youthful leader's response was to give the old party a modern makeover.

Cameron has been trying to change the party's image from being old and fuddy duddy to being bright, new and representing the whole country, not just traditional Conservative voters.

Out went the blue torch logo to be replaced by a green-leafed English oak. Working on the Green theme, Cameron changed the party's policies to make them more environmentally friendly. (Prior to this move, the Conservatives had been widely seen as pro economic growth even at the expense of the planet.) Cameron, a former public relations man, then overhauled the process of choosing MPs and MEPs. (An MP is a member of the UK parliament; an MEP sits in the European parliament in Strasbourg.) He set about upping the number of women and ethnic minority candidates to make the party more representative of the UK population. Cameron's aim was to make the party more electable and in subsequent local and European elections the Conservatives performed better than they had done for over a decade.

Tapping natural Tory supporters

If you asked Conservatives what they believed in, they'd probably say a mixture of keeping things just as they are while creating an easy environment for businesses and individuals to create wealth. In short, making money, while keeping what they think is right about Britain.

These principles have a pretty broad appeal and the party has been in government many times, polling between 40 and 45 per cent of the vote at its best and around 30 per cent at its worst.

The Tories tend to do better:

✔ Amongst older people

✔ With people living in the countryside

✔ In the southeast of England – London and the counties surrounding it

The Tories do better than any other party in southern England because people there have higher average incomes and a lot invested in maintaining the current state of affairs. They also like the party's expressed commitment to free market economics and keeping taxes low.

The south of England is very densely populated, which gives whatever party is doing well there a very good chance of winning enough seats in parliament to be able to form the government.

Looking at the Labour Party

The Labour Party had a difficult beginning but grew with speed into one of the two parties, along with the Tories, that usually gets to form the government in the UK.

Labour tends to be referred to as on the left or centre-left of British politics because the party's supporters believe in some or all of the following:

✔ A more extensive and generous welfare system

✔ Limiting some of the excesses of the free market

✔ Quality public services and the need to tax to pay for them

At general elections, when the Labour Party is popular it tends to poll around 40 to 45 per cent of the electorate, enough to form a government. On the other hand, when the party and its policies aren't popular it can poll around 25 to 30 per cent of votes.

Forming the Labour Party

The Labour Party's difficult birth was the result of where it came from – the trade union movement of the nineteenth century. The British trade union movement struggled desperately for recognition, with many activists imprisoned and even deported for trying to get themselves and their fellow workers a fairer deal. But despite their problems, in time the unions gained recognition and grew into a powerful force.

As the nineteenth century became the twentieth, the union or labour movement as it became known wanted a party that represented the aspirations and concerns of its millions of members. In short, the union chiefs felt that the big parties of the time – the Tories and Liberals – had precious little in common with their mainly urban, working-class membership. The Labour Party was formed to give voice to millions of Britain's workers.

Keir Hardie is often seen as the founding father of the Labour Party, although in reality he was only the most prominent of a whole batch of people who brought the party into being. He's considered so important because he was the first avowed Socialist to be elected to the UK parliament, in 1892. He lost his seat again in 1895 but he wouldn't stop there. A renowned public speaker, Hardie always stayed close to his roots as a coal miner and union organiser. In 1900 the Labour Party was formed and Hardie became one of its first two MPs as well as its leader, a position he resigned in 1908 because he wanted to concentrate on campaigning for votes for women and an end to racial segregation policies in South Africa.

Gauging Labour's followers

Like the Tories, the Labour Party tends to do better among voters with certain characteristics and who live in certain areas of the country, including the following:

- People in the north of England, Wales and Scotland
- Trade union members and public sector workers
- Lower income voters and social housing tenants

The Labour Party's bedrock support is rooted in the working class and the union movement. As a result the party does better in parts of the UK which were once dominated by manufacturing and industry.

Borrowing the other side's clothes: Blairism

Labour suffered a series of electoral defeats in the 1980s and 1990s during what is known as their 'lurch to the left' (which describes their strong left-wing politics at this time) because the party was seen as behind the times and didn't have a wide enough appeal amongst the electorate. The party's links with the trade unions – who'd been comprehensively beaten in a series of industrial disputes by the government of Tory PM Margaret Thatcher – didn't help with this image problem.

Then along came the charismatic Tony Blair. A great TV performer and communicator, Blair set about modernising the Labour Party, changing party policy so that it represented more of the concerns of the general population rather than the hobby horses of the party membership and trade unions.

Blair moved the party into the centre of British politics, accepting many of the changes that had been brought about by the then Tory government. In effect, his pitch was simple: we accept the reforms of Thatcher but in the future we'd like to see a fairer society (through policies such as introducing a national minimum wage). Labour's new stance was alluring to the electorate and in 1997 it was elected to government in a landslide victory.

Breaking with the unions: Hard to do

The once so strong relationship between the Labour Party and the trade unions has become strained in recent years, with some even suggesting that they ought to split. But the unions are still crucial to Labour for the following reasons:

✔ Some unions levy a duty on their members, which is paid to the Labour Party

✔ Union members provide many of the activists and canvassers for Labour Party candidates

✔ Many Labour candidates for election to local government, the UK and European parliaments come from the ranks of the unions

Trade unionists have a key role in the election of Labour's leader and deputy leader.

Taking In the Lib Dems

Like the Tories, the Lib Dems – or Liberal Democrats in full – have been around for a long time. The party can trace its roots back to the Whigs in the eighteenth and nineteenth centuries. However, the party has had a chequered history, sometimes claiming the top prize of government but also almost disappearing altogether in the twentieth century. In fact, for several decades in the twentieth century the Lib Dems had only a handful of MPs.

The simple truth is that, of the UK's three main political parties, the Lib Dems almost always poll the fewest votes. It's often seen as the Cinderella party of British politics, never quite garnering enough support at UK parliamentary elections to form the government of the country.

However, don't feel too sorry for the Cinderella party; it still plays a big role in UK party politics because:

- ✔ It often does well in council elections. In fact, much of UK local government is either run by the party on its own or as part of a ruling coalition with the Tories or Labour.
- ✔ When the two main parties run each other close at a general election, the Lib Dems can hold the balance of power – a concept I explore in the next section.
- ✔ It tends to be seen as the progressive party of British politics. Its policy ideas are often derided by Labour and the Tories but then quietly adopted.
- ✔ It's often said to be at the centre or centre-left of British politics.

Understanding the balance of power

The Lib Dems often talk about holding the balance of power. Sometimes neither the Tories nor Labour get enough MPs to form the government on their own. This means that one or the other needs the support of another party or two with sufficient MPs of their own to join together to form a *coalition government.*

In such situations, the Lib Dems may come into their own. They can lend their support to a larger party, but usually extract a price – some of their senior politicians made into ministers and some of their policies adopted by the government.

Coalition governments are few and far between in the UK and, what's more, the Lib Dems aren't the only game in town. Labour or the Tories can form governments with the help of minor parties – such as the Scottish and Welsh nationalists or the Ulster Unionist party. (I describe these minor but nevertheless important parties later on in this chapter.)

Generally, coalitions are more likely at local government (council) than UK parliament level.

Supporting proportional representation

Elections to local government and the UK parliament in Westminster are run on a first-past-the-post system. Put simply, this system means that the party candidate who polls the highest number of votes wins the seat.

This winner-takes-all scenario doesn't help the Lib Dems or any of the other smaller parties. The Lib Dems often struggle to get enough votes to win the constituency outright but do regularly manage to run a close second to the Tories or Labour.

The Lib Dems would prefer a system of *proportional representation* (PR), whereby seats are awarded according to the proportion of total votes cast. At the 2005 general election, the Lib Dems attracted around 22 per cent of the votes cast in the UK; under PR, this result would have given them roughly 130–140 seats in parliament. However, they only managed to get 47 seats under the current system.

Why isn't the system changed? Well, neither the Tories nor Labour want to change a system which gives them a good chance of forming the government outright. See Chapter 6 for the merits or otherwise of different voting systems.

Looking at Lib Dem supporters

Defining the natural supporters of the Lib Dems is harder than doing it for Labour and the Tories. Some cynics would say Lib Dems are all those who don't naturally gravitate towards the Tory or Labour parties. But this view is a little simplistic. The Lib Dems do have natural supporters and parts of the country where they do better than others:

- ✔ People in the southwest of England
- ✔ People who're very concerned about the state of the environment
- ✔ People who'd like to see the UK play a fuller part in the European Union

When the Lib Dems are popular in the country they can attract around 25 per cent of the electorate; when they're doing less well they can gather only 10 to 12 per cent of UK voters.

Focusing on the Minor Parties

Under the UK's first-past-the-post electoral system, minor parties rarely gather enough votes in one constituency to have an MP elected. But this doesn't stop the minor parties combined taking a substantial proportion of the popular vote – sometimes as much as 20 per cent.

The UK's major minor parties – if you get what I mean – include:

- ✔ **British National Party.** The BNP has been around for many years and has its roots in the British Union of Fascists, which supported the rise of Hitler in the 1930s. The BNP would like to see all non-white Britons repatriated to the country that either they or their ancestors hailed from. Opponents accuse the BNP of being simply a racist party and widespread disquiet is felt about the party's gathering momentum at the polls. At the 2009 European election, for instance, the BNP managed to attract enough votes to get two MEPs elected.

- ✔ **Green Party.** The Greens are preoccupied with promoting more environmentally friendly government with the aim of reducing carbon emissions and saving the planet. It's a big ask, but the Green Party has had some major successes in European and, to a lesser extent, local elections. Its best showing has seen the Greens attract between five and ten per cent of the votes cast.

   The Green Party in the UK is somewhat the poor relation of its counterparts on the European mainland. In Germany, for instance, the Green Party played a part in a past coalition government.

- ✔ **UK Independence Party.** UKIP is a relatively new political party and has made quite an impact in European elections. In 2009, it polled more than ten per cent of the votes cast and has several MEPs. The party is opposed to the idea of the UK joining a federal European Union. In fact, UKIP has said that it would like the UK to withdraw from the EU. (Turn to Chapter 20 for more on the UK's often troubled relationship with the EU.)

In many other EU countries minor parties can play a substantial role in government as a result of their use of a proportional representation electoral system. Under PR, if a minor party gets five per cent of the vote they get five per cent of the seats in parliament. This outcome can mean that the big parties often have to work with the minor parties so that they can have a working majority in parliament and govern the country. The Green Party in Germany and the Communist Party in Italy, for example, have been a part of coalition governments.

The UK's first-past-the-post voting system makes it unlikely that a party polling five per cent of the vote – apart from the Scottish and Welsh nationalist parties – will get any seats at all. Minor parties are thus not as important.

Often a vote for the minor parties is referred to as a *protest vote*, which means that the individual is protesting the policies of the big political parties – Labour, Tory and Lib Dem – by giving his or her support to a minor party.

Embracing strange small parties

The British love eccentrics, and election time brings them out in spades. In fact, one of the most colourful aspects of British political life is all the strange minor parties and weird individuals who stand for election to the UK parliament. Some of the minor parties which have fielded candidates for election in the past and may do so again include the following:

✔ **Monster Raving Loony Party.** Offering policies such as a bottle of gin for everyone, the Loonies are a comic addition to any election campaign.

✔ **Natural Law Party.** This party believes that crime and economic problems can be solved through a type of meditation called Yogic Flying – and, yes, you read that right!

✔ **Mums' Army.** Started by *Take a Break* magazine as a campaign against yobbish behaviour, this small party has fielded candidates in many parts of the UK.

✔ **Fancy Dress Party.** This party's an offshoot of the Monster Raving Loony Party and the candidates insist on wearing – guess what?

Beyond the minor parties, nearly all individuals are allowed to stand for parliament provided they pay a deposit. This easy path to standing for election can lead to some real eccentrics making it onto the ballot paper. My favourite is a man who stood in the Dover constituency in 1979 and canvassed door to door dressed as a circus impresario, leading a friend (presumably) on a chain who was dressed as a mouse!

Minor parties tend to do best at European and local elections as turnout is lower and people perceive that the election is less important than a general election. Registering a protest vote at a European or local election is thus seen as safer than doing so at a general election.

Taking a Look at the Nationalists: SNP and Plaid Cymru

Although the Scots and Welsh nationalists – called the Scottish National Party (SNP) and Plaid Cymru, respectively – can be classed as minor parties as they only attract a small percentage of the total UK electorate, in their own parts of the country they're a very big deal indeed.

In fact, the SNP has been the biggest party in Scotland for the past few years and is currently in government in the Scottish parliament. (I cover the Scottish parliament and Welsh assembly in Chapter 16.) It's looking a distinct possibility that the SNP will eventually achieve its ambition of a Scotland independent from the rest of the UK. At the most recent elections the SNP attracted more than 35 per cent of the votes cast in Scotland.

Plaid Cymru in Wales has also made significant strides in recent years, taking many votes from the Labour Party, traditionally the biggest and most popular party in Wales. However, Wales isn't likely to become independent from England anytime soon, although many within Plaid Cymru would like that to happen. Wales is generally poorer than Scotland and has a smaller population, and many people there worry that it couldn't stand on its own without help from its much bigger neighbour, England. At present, they're probably right!

Both the SNP and Plaid Cymru tend to be on the left of British politics, believing in tight regulation of the free market and strong, well-funded public services paid for, if necessary, through higher taxation.

Neither the SNP nor Plaid Cymru candidates ever stand for election in England, only in Scotland and Wales, respectively.

Not only the Scots and Welsh have nationalist parties; the English do too. For example, in the southwest of England, the Cornish National Party often fields candidates and elsewhere in England, so does the English National Party. However, neither the Cornish nor the English nationalists are anywhere near as popular in their parts of the UK as the Scots and Welsh nationalists are in theirs.

Dipping into Northern Irish Politics

To someone from mainland Britain, the way in which Northern Ireland's society and politics are divided may be difficult to fathom. Parties aren't split along the same lines as in the rest of the UK, but according to sectarian affiliation. Electors vote for parties that represent their own religious ideal.

Put simply, *sectarianism* is a division based on religion – in Northern Ireland's case, the adherence to either the Protestant strand of Christianity or the Catholic.

Yet religion isn't the only factor at play; intertwined with it is nationalism – both British and Irish. Here are some of the realities of Northern Irish politics:

- ✔ People from the Protestant community are often Unionists (also called Loyalists) who believe in being joined with Britain, which is ostensibly a Protestant country.

- ✔ People from the Catholic community are often Nationalists (or Republicans), which means they want Northern Ireland to leave the UK and join with the Irish Republic, remembering that the Republic is ostensibly a Catholic country.

Now this division probably wouldn't matter quite so much if it wasn't for the fact that the population is roughly evenly split between Catholics and Protestants and that, for much of the last 40 years, certain people within both communities have resorted to violence to advance what they see as their cause.

To complicate matters further, not all Catholics are Republicans and not all Protestants are Unionists.

The party politics of Northern Ireland are very different to the rest of the UK, with Labour, Tory and Lib Dem not having much impact. Instead, parties rooted in the Catholic and Protestant communities hold sway and actually even these communities have different strands, each sparking their own party.

The main Protestant parties in Northern Ireland and what they stand for are:

- ✓ **Democratic Unionist Party.** The DUP is currently the biggest party in Northern Irish politics. In the past, it's been staunchly opposed to any closer ties to the government of the Irish Republic in Dublin. However, a deal brokered by the British and Irish prime ministers saw the DUP enter into a power-sharing agreement with the ultra-Irish nationalist Sinn Fein party in 2007.

  For many years, the DUP was led by the firebrand Reverend Ian Paisley, who stood up for what he perceived as the rights of his community. Like his party, though, he too came round to the idea of power sharing.

- ✓ **Ulster Unionist Party.** Throughout the 1970s, 1980s and 1990s, the UUP was the biggest party representing the interests of the Protestant community in Northern Ireland. It held several seats in the UK House of Commons and was often called upon to support Labour and Tory governments when they were struggling to reach a majority. Generally, the UUP was considered to be more moderate in its outlook than the DUP, and its former leader, David Trimble, was key in the early stages of the peace movement in Northern Ireland.

On the Catholic side of the community, the major parties are:

- ✓ **Social Democratic and Labour Party.** Traditionally, the SDLP was the biggest party representing the Catholic community in Northern Ireland, but, like the UUP, it's been supplanted at the top of the polls by a rival party hailing from the same community. The SDLP was for years seen as a moderate voice in Northern Irish politics, looking for union with the Irish Republic through peaceful, democratic means.

✔ **Sinn Féin.** This party is the most controversial in Northern Irish politics as a result of its close links with the Provisional Irish Republican Army (IRA). Sinn Féin was for many years ignored by the British government and its leaders' voices were even banned from being broadcast. Some of the leading members of Sinn Féin are widely presumed at one time or another to have been involved with the Provisional IRA and therefore violence. However, the party was key in arranging an IRA ceasefire and then getting it to renounce violence. As part of a wide-ranging peace agreement, Sinn Féin was invited into government in Northern Ireland and, as a party, is now the biggest in the Catholic community. Currently, Sinn Féin shares government with the DUP.

A few parties have pitched themselves as being 'cross community' – including the Alliance Party of Northern Ireland – but generally they've attracted only minor support.

Northern Ireland has an assembly and a government, which at present is a coalition between Republicans and Unionists, with leading figures from very different parties such as Sinn Féin and the Democratic Unionists sharing the top jobs.

The Northern Ireland Assembly sits in Stormont Castle and has 108 elected members. Its powers are limited, though. For example, the assembly can decide health, education and environmental policy, but over criminal justice and matters of international trade and diplomacy, the UK government in Westminster has control. Interestingly, all Bills passed by the assembly must have royal assent – be agreed to by the UK head of state – to become law.

Until relatively recently, many in the Catholic community felt that their views weren't listened to as many of the top governmental jobs and businesses in Northern Ireland were in the hands of prominent figures from the Protestant community. In the early 1970s, this situation sparked a civil rights movement and the discontent that grew from this perceived inequality led to many young men and women joining terrorist organisations.

Chapter 9

Piling On the Pressure Groups

In This Chapter

▶ Introducing pressure groups

▶ Dividing groups up between 'insiders' and 'outsiders'

▶ Understanding how pressure groups exert pressure

▶ Looking at the role pressure groups play

▶ Lobbying the UK and EU parliaments

▶ Considering the influence of think tanks

*B*ritish politics isn't just about political parties, big-name politicians and close-run elections. Below the theatre of national politics and the every-day workings of local government are organised pressure groups looking to influence government policy and public opinion. These pressure groups aren't to be confused with political parties – they don't seek government office; instead, they have particular objectives in mind which they dedicate all their energies to seeing met.

Whatever the sizes or resources of the pressure groups, they're a key part of our democracy.

In this chapter I explore the world of the pressure group, from the small local organisations – little more perhaps than a single person leafleting and lobbying – to huge well-staffed bodies very savvy at public relations.

Taking In the Universe of Pressure Groups

A *pressure group* is a body or organisation that tries to influence government policy and wider public opinion but, unlike a political party, a pressure group doesn't seek elected office. Pressure groups, particularly in the US, are also referred to in the media as *special interest groups*.

Literally hundreds if not thousands of pressure groups exist in the UK. Some are concerned with a single issue – keeping a local hospital open, for example – but others concentrate on a range of issues with one overarching theme. For example, the NSPCC (National Society for the Prevention of Cruelty to Children) focuses on improving the welfare of children across the country. Some groups represent a particular section of society, such as nurses, lawyers or musicians.

Detailing all the pressure groups in the UK would require a book in itself. They come from all parts of the political and social spectrums. For example, pressure groups exist lobbying for the legalisation of cannabis (the Legalise Cannabis Alliance), representing doctors (the British Medical Association, BMA) and even looking out for the police (the Association of Chief Police Officers). To make things easier, though, pressure groups can be divided into two main types:

- ✔ **Sectional pressure groups** promote the interests of a group of people and are normally related to a profession or occupation.
- ✔ **Cause-related pressure groups** are concerned with a particular social or ethical issue, such as protecting the environment or promoting civil liberties.

Generally, the bigger and more geographically spread the issue or the group represented, the larger the pressure group. Some of these big pressure groups are really sizeable enterprises, employing hundreds of people and needing to raise lots of money to pay wages and to aid the group's lobbying of politicians and the public. Smaller, less well-funded pressure groups have to rely on volunteers to do the administration and fundraising. The bigger bodies, while still using some volunteers, are organised more along the lines of a business, employing lots of staff with skills that should help the group better raise funds and get its message across to the public and politicians alike.

Like political parties, some pressure groups have very long histories dating back fifty and even a hundred years. Why do they have such staying power? Well, the cause they're working for or section of society they represent has widespread support so that the pressure group is adequately resourced and able to exert some influence on politicians and the public.

Sorting out sectional pressure groups

Pressure groups look to promote the interests of a particular section of society. Normally, this section relates to an occupation. By far the best-known sectional pressure groups are the trade unions, each representing the interests of thousands or hundreds of thousands of workers according to their occupation.

Usually, membership of these pressure groups is restricted. For example, a plumber can't join a teaching trade union or become a member of the doctors' body, the BMA. What's more, these sectional groups can often claim a high proportion of people working in a particular occupation or industry as members. Sometimes, in fact, membership of the group is a requirement of being able to practise. For example, dentists have to belong to the British Dental Association, which not only polices good practice in the industry – and can stop wrongdoers from practising – but also represents and promotes the interests of its members.

Not all sectional pressure groups, however, are professional bodies or unions. Groups exist representing business owners, for example, such as the Confederation of British Industry (CBI) and the British Chambers of Commerce.

Sectional pressure groups can have a big say in government policy. For example, no government would dream about reforming the National Health Service (NHS) without at least discussing its plans with the BMA, which represents doctors, who in turn would have to implement any government-inspired reforms.

A sectional pressure group usually sticks to trying to influence policy in a single area of daily life. For example, the Law Society looks to influence how the UK court system operates but won't touch the workings of the NHS.

Seeing to cause-related groups

As the name suggests, these pressure groups look to promote a particular cause. Members of cause-related groups are people from all walks of life coalescing around a particular social or ethical issue. For example, Greenpeace wants to see greater protection of the environment, and in the 1970s and 1980s hundreds of thousands of Britons from all walks of life were members of the Campaign for Nuclear Disarmament (CND).

Crucially, unlike sectional groups, membership of cause-related groups is open to anyone. However, members may be asked to make a regular financial donation to the group so that it can better fund its operations.

Most serious, long-term, cause-related pressure groups achieve some level of success as they continue to lobby and pressure government and persuade the public of the justness of their causes. They tend to make slow progress rather than no progress.

Lobbying failure: The case of CND

In the 1970s and 1980s, the Campaign for Nuclear Disarmament (CND) had a huge membership and attracted widespread media coverage for its campaign for the UK to get rid of its nuclear weapons. They even had a strong influence on the Labour Party, which went into the 1983 general election saying that it would scrap the bomb.

However, Labour lost the 1983 election by a landslide and the Conservative government under Margaret Thatcher retained Britain's nuclear weapons capability. The government argued that CND was too extreme and didn't have enough public support to justify it changing its policy.

Over time, the Labour Party also abandoned its plans to decommission nuclear weapons and CND drifted from being a high-profile pressure group into relative obscurity.

In some cases, cause-related groups are consulted by the government of the day about its policies. For example, the Labour government of Tony Blair in the late 1990s consulted Age Concern, which represents the interests of elderly people, before introducing key reforms to the benefits it paid to this socio-demographic group. It wanted to get Age Concern 'on side' so that when the policy was presented to the media and the wider electorate the government would appear to have the support of a key pressure group. Sometimes this consultation may be a matter of mere courtesy. However, if a pressure group comes out and decries government policy it can persuade some of the electorate who feel strongly about the issue at hand to move their support from the government to the opposition parties.

Generally, cause-related groups find persuading politicians to do what they want them to do harder than sectional groups. Sectional groups tend to be very well organised and can in some cases withdraw their labour if they're angered by a particular government policy – for example, in the past teachers have gone on strike in reaction to the introduction of new working practices. Cause-related groups don't have the option of withdrawing their labour – going on strike – as they come from such diverse backgrounds.

Going Inside, Outside, Up and Down with Pressure Groups

As well as dividing up pressure groups into sectional and cause-related, you can categorise them by which groups have the ear of government on a regular basis – on the inside, so to speak – and those which don't – those on the outside. As you can imagine, a pressure group generally prefers to be an insider rather than an outsider.

Differentiating inside and outside

Table 9-1 shows the main ways to tell if a pressure group is inside or outside.

Table 9-1	Traits of Insider and Outsider Pressure Groups
Insiders	**Outsiders**
Ministers think that the group's objectives are reasonable and desirable.	Ministers think that the group's objectives aren't reasonable and that their implementation is undesirable.
The government needs the group's support to better carry out its policy – for example, reform of the NHS requires the support of doctors' and nursing groups.	The group is unable to block the course of government policy; instead it can only look on from the sidelines.
The group has wide public support or extensive appeal amongst a particular section of society.	The group only appeals to a very limited group of people.
The group employs peaceful methods to achieve its ends and always acts within the law.	Members of the group employ civil disobedience and may actually break the law.
People working for the group have skills and expertise that ministers find useful when they're looking to consult about the group's issue area.	Leading members of the group aren't considered to have useful expertise or are seen as too biased to give objective assessments to ministers.

The phrase 'united we stand, divided we fall' applies well to pressure groups. If members of a group are united, with a strong leadership talking with one voice and expressing coherent themes, the group has a better chance of influencing government policy and wider public opinion than a group with lots of different factions all claiming to represent the members' interests. A group without a coherent stance, whose members are divided over key issues is likely to have outsider status rather than insider access.

The bigger, better organised and more popular the pressure group, the more likely it is to be on the inside rather than the outside. Politicians, after all, rely on electors and if a pressure group has wide support, how much attention the government – or opposition parties – pay to it can influence voter behaviour.

A tale of two pressure groups: One inside, one outside

The Royal Society for the Prevention of Cruelty to Animals (RSPCA) is one of the UK's biggest, richest charities and also a strong pressure group for better animal welfare. The RSPCA enjoys widespread public support, garners lots of media coverage and often advises the government – regardless of which party forms it – on aspects of its policy relating to animal welfare. The RSPCA is very much an insider pressure group.

The Animal Liberation Front (ALF), in contrast, employs direct action as its method of combating what it sees as the systematic mistreatment of animals. In fact, sometimes the actions of the ALF are illegal and, although it does enjoy some support – often among students, the young and those involved in what may be termed Britain's counterculture – it has no real influence on government policies on animal welfare. The ALF is very much an outsider pressure group.

Watching the political ups and downs of pressure groups

Which pressure groups are inside or outside changes over time. For example, trade unions often have significant influence when the Labour Party is in power because the latter draws much of its funding and parliamentary candidates from the trade union movement. This situation gives unions unique access to Labour government ministers and, although their influence has dwindled over time, they're very much on the 'inside' when Labour is in power.

In the 1970s, for example, the leaders of Britain's big trade unions were regularly at 10 Downing Street talking over the minutiae of government policy with the prime minister. These get-togethers were famously dubbed the 'beer and sandwiches' meetings. The unions had huge power and influence.

However, when the Conservatives came to power in 1979 they believed that the unions were too powerful and brought the 'beer and sandwiches' meetings to an abrupt halt. Under Conservative prime ministers Margaret Thatcher and John Major, members of business pressure groups such as the CBI and the British Chambers of Commerce had the ear of ministers. So, groups that were insiders became outsiders to some extent and the other way around.

Looking at How Pressure Groups Exert Influence

Getting the government of the day and the general public to support their goals and to act accordingly is the goal of all pressure groups. To achieve this, pressure groups employ a range of methods and pull many political and public relations levers.

Two tactics that nearly every pressure group uses are:

- ✔ **Having members contact politicians.** Individual members of pressure groups often write to their MPs expressing their views on an aspect of government policy. This approach can have quite an influence, as MPs have to stand for re-election every four or five years, and if they anger their constituents they may not get voted back into parliament.

- ✔ **Employing a professional lobbyist.** This more sophisticated method of influencing MPs instructs the lobbyist to make contact with MPs and put the pressure group's case before them. Professional lobbying has grown apace in the UK in recent years and is now a multi-million pound industry.

  The better the contacts the lobbyist has, the more they can charge the pressure group for their services. However, some pressure groups employ people from within their own organisation – as head of public relations, say – to do the lobbying.

Sometimes pressure groups strongly disagree with government policy and challenge its legality in the courts. Lawyers for the pressure group may argue that a minister has exceeded his or her legal powers or that a policy is discriminatory against a particular group or breaks European human rights legislation. However, legal action can be ruinously expensive, so in many cases it is usually a last resort for the pressure group or not deployed at all.

I sort out some of the main paths to influence in the following sections.

Getting the ear of ministers and civil servants

Government policy is implemented by ministries. At the top of these ministries are a handful of politicians (called *ministers*) aided by senior civil servants. (I talk more about ministers and ministries in Chapters 13 and 14.) Any pressure group which can put its views to these politicians and civil servants has a real chance of influencing what the government actually does.

Understanding that size is important

Usually the more members a particular pressure group has, the more it can influence the formation of government policy and public opinion. This influence results from:

✔ **Electoral impact:** Each member of a pressure group has a vote, and the government is more likely to attract the votes of those members if it listens to or supports the group's objectives. The more members, the more votes and in theory the more likely the government is to want to tailor its policies to reflect the concerns of the pressure group.

✔ **Funding muscle:** The more members, the greater the level of donations and subscriptions, which can help pay for professional staff and advertising campaigns to better get their message across.

✔ **Campaign resources:** More members means a wider pool of volunteers to call upon when the pressure group undertakes marches and demonstrations.

Saying that big equals powerful in the world of pressure groups is a bit too simplistic. Some groups don't have large numbers but do have considerable wealth and therefore influence. For example, the Confederation of British Industry (CBI) is made up of business owners. Now the CBI doesn't ask its members to take part in demonstrations or vote for a particular party but what it says has a great deal of influence in government because its members control much of the wealth of the country and employ millions of people. In short, governments are happy to listen to the CBI because they can see that doing what it says is usually good for the UK economy and ultimately its own chances of getting re-elected. After all, at election time the health of the economy is usually a big deciding factor in terms of whether the government wins or loses.

Once a pressure group is able to grab the ear of a minister or senior civil servant it can be said to be an insider in the workings of government (see 'Differentiating inside and outside' earlier in the chapter).

Why do ministers and civil servants listen to these pressure groups? Well, the relationship is a two-way street: the pressure group gets access and its views listened to; and the minister and civil servant can call on the group's specialist knowledge, gain co-operation for the implementation of government policy and hopefully garner the group's support in public, which can help at election time.

Focusing on backbench MPs

Only a limited number of pressure groups have direct access to ministers and senior civil servants. For one thing, only so many hours are available in the day for ministers and civil servants to listen to the views of pressure groups.

Those pressure groups finding themselves left out in the cold don't just give up; instead, they look to influence the views of backbench MPs. After all, the MPs may one day be ministers themselves. In addition, MPs have the power to introduce legislation to be debated in parliament (although it can be hard for backbench MPs to see this into law without the support of ministers – see Chapter 12 for more on this process). MPs also get to sit on parliamentary select committees, whose job it is to scrutinise proposed government legislation to see if it will work.

So, although individual backbench MPs have limited power, a pressure group that can get enough of them on side and believing in what they have to say can have an influence on the formation of government policy.

Courting public opinion

Pressure groups – even those with access to ministers – look to appeal to the public directly. The big idea is that the government will also listen, as it fears that, if it doesn't, the public will vote for its political opponents at election time. Unlike meeting ministers or lobbying MPs, appealing to the public is an indirect method of trying to change government policy.

Pressure groups look to court public opinion through getting stories in the media that present their ideas in a positive light. To this end, some groups organise media stunts – such as Fathers for Justice staging a protest on the roof of prominent Labour politician Harriet Harman's house – so as to get their name and their cause (basically, greater account taken of father's rights on family breakdown) some coverage in the press. Most attempts to get media coverage are a lot more subtle, though, and involve pressure groups employing professional public relations agencies which have access to prominent journalists.

Sometimes, pressure groups don't try to appeal to the whole public, instead focusing on just the middle class. Many politicians, journalists and so-called *opinion formers* are drawn from the middle class. These opinion formers have high public profiles and are seen as possessing expertise. What they say often attracts media coverage. The idea is to influence ministers and other senior politicians – they're just using a roundabout way.

In 2009 TV actress Joanna Lumley used her high public profile and popularity to campaign for the right of Gurkhas (Nepalese soldiers) who'd served in the British army to live and settle in Britain. Ms Lumley made powerful speeches, organised rallies and confronted ministers in front of the camera to convey her message. Eventually, ministers relented and agreed to the campaign's demands. Ms Lumley's ability to grab the attention of the media and gather widespread public support was what brought pressure to bear on the government so that it changed policy.

Joining the throng at party conference

Many of the UK's biggest and most influential pressure groups try to appeal not only to government ministers, leading opposition MPs (who may one day be in government) and the general public, but also to the rank and file of the big political parties. They do so by setting up stalls at and sending members of their group to the annual party conferences of the big political parties.

As I discuss in Chapter 8, party conferences are big shindigs where party members meet up with leading politicians and ideas are exchanged, policies formed, speeches made and plenty of drinks downed.

Pressure groups show up at conference time to exert indirect influence on the leading members of the party, who may be government ministers or have the potential to be government ministers in the future. This tactic is subtle but it can help move opinions amongst leading politicians and over time influence political debate.

Taking it to the streets: Direct action

Direct action means demonstrations, marches and rallies. The idea is to bring members of the pressure group together in one place so as to show the politicians, the public at large and the media that the group is organised and has strong feelings about a particular issue. People have a legal right to gather together and express their views and direct action makes the most of this right.

Thousands of peaceful demonstrations take place across the UK each year. These gatherings represent pressure group politics at its most raw, and they can have a real effect on government policy if the views of the pressure group strike a chord with the public, the media and the politicians.

Direct action can go further than simply demonstrations. Trade unions, for example, have organised sit-ins and strikes. In the 1980s the Campaign for Nuclear Disarmament (CND) held large-scale protests outside the American nuclear weapons base at Greenham Common.

Appealing over the heads of politicians

Many pressure groups don't target politicians directly, and instead try to mould public opinion to their way of thinking. Usually, this approach simply involves trying to get the press to cover the issues they're concerned about or paying for advertising campaigns to generate support and perhaps attract extra members.

Making poverty history

The Make Poverty History campaign has proved to be one of the most successful pressure groups of recent years. With important figureheads and prominent musicians such as Bob Geldof and U2's Bono, the campaign galvanised hundreds of thousands of people to peaceful protest coinciding with the 2005 Gleneagles G8 summit (a meeting of the world's eight biggest economies plus Russia). The campaign aimed to pressure world leaders to address the problems of poverty in the developing world. Geldof and Bono had simultaneous direct access to UK prime minister Tony Blair and US president George W. Bush.

Eventually, the leaders agreed at the summit to boost aid to developing countries and write off some debts. However, the campaign was only a partial success as some governments made promises at the summit and then reneged on them later. Nevertheless, Make Poverty History was an example of a pressure group getting things done through a combination of peaceful protest and insider access to prominent politicians.

Members of pressure groups have also on occasion decided to influence things by standing for election themselves, perhaps feeling that to beat the politicians they have to join them. In 2001, for instance, retired doctor Richard Taylor stood for parliament. As the Kidderminster Hospital and Health Concern candidate, he was part of a local group worried about the closure of a local hospital. Mr Taylor overturned a substantial Labour majority in the Wyre Forest seat to win by a landslide.

Placing Pressure Groups in the System

Big money is involved in political lobbying and much of the conversation between pressure group lobbyists and politicians goes on behind closed doors. Now that seems like a recipe for potential corruption. However, MPs have to declare in the Register of Members' Interests – a public document – any gifts given to them. Whether the reporting requirement is a factor or not, Britain's politicians generally are considered to be honest and corruption in public life is a rarity – unlike in the case of politicians in many other countries.

However, when multi-million pound contracts are at stake, a little bit of what you and I call corruption to oil the wheels may be very tempting. And politicians nonetheless do enjoy a fair few freebies from friendly lobbyists. For the lobbyist, the idea is to get access to the politician, which in turn helps the client.

Taking in the dark side of direct action

Direct action is usually legal and peaceful but at times it crosses into violent protest. For instance, on May Day 2000 a host of pressure groups gathered in London to protest what they saw as the inequality brought about through economic globalisation.

Many of those involved acted peacefully and merely marched and rallied; a minority though – most involved in anarchist groups (see Chapter 4 for more on these) – rioted, causing millions of pounds worth of damage in the process.

Likewise some extreme animal rights groups are notorious for violent protest. Staff working at the Huntingdon Life Sciences animal research centre have been subject to harassment and intimidation from animal rights campaigners. Nevertheless, the work of the laboratory has continued. What's more, the Animal Liberation Front have in the past broken into labs and released animals used in research. Although many members of the public share the concerns of the anti-globalisation and animal rights activists, the use of violent or illegal protests has lost these groups considerable support amongst the general public and also ensures that they don't have access to ministers and senior civil servants. In short, in the UK violent or illegal direct action rarely results in a change in government policy.

Unfortunately, instances exist in the EU of politicians accepting gifts or freebies from lobbyists in return, it's alleged (yes, I'm being careful for the lawyers!), for the politicians looking favourably on the arguments of the pressure group.

Lobbying is big business in the UK and now, particularly, the EU. According to the most recent estimate, some 15,000 lobbyists work in Brussels and about 2,600 interest groups have permanent offices in the city. Lobbying activities are estimated to produce as much as £200 million a year: that's a lot of wining and dining.

Looking at the downsides of pressure groups

Not everyone thinks that pressure groups are all good. In fact, some people believe that pressure groups can have quite a detrimental impact on our democracy, aside from the potential for corruption amongst politicians through the well-funded lobbying system.

Some of the main criticisms of pressure groups include:

- ✔ **Too powerful.** Pressure groups try to exert influence on politicians through a variety of means. When they're very successful they themselves become powerful and their voices may drown out those of other groups or the wider general public.

✔ **Too limiting.** Some pressure groups have lots of power through the scale of their membership and the specialist skills of those members. For example, doctors are represented by the British Medical Association; if the government want to reform health care, to see its plans carried through it will have to consult with the BMA. This situation makes the BMA very powerful indeed.

✔ **Too disruptive.** Some pressure groups will stop at little to see their objectives met – even committing violent and illegal acts. Their behaviour can have an unsettling effect on wider society.

In the US, pressure groups and the lobbyists they employ are believed to exert huge influence on politicians. According to some, lobbyists representing oil companies and motor manufacturers had a strong influence on the Bush administration's take on environmental policy. For much of his presidency, George W. Bush denied the existence of climate change.

Taking in the plus points of pressure groups

Every argument has its flip side and this is particularly true of whether pressure groups are good for society or bad. The main arguments for the existence of pressure groups include:

✔ **They keep politicians grounded.** Pressure groups can keep politicians informed about the opinions of the wider public or a section of society.

✔ **They help debate.** Pressure groups can inform political debate either within groups of politicians or in the country as a whole, often through the media.

✔ **They protect minorities.** By their nature, many groups represent a section of society. They allow the voice of this part of society to be heard more effectively and stop it from being drowned out completely.

✔ **They provide expertise.** Pressure groups have access to committed and knowledgeable individuals as well as useful information about their area of expertise. This bank of knowledge can be very important when the government wants to consult over the formation of policy.

Identifying the UK's Big Pressure Groups

Thousands of pressure groups operate in the UK. However, not all pressure groups are equal in terms of public appeal or political influence. A golden league of pressure groups don't exactly dictate government policy but definitely have influence both in the corridors of power in Whitehall (the civil service) and amongst the electorate as a whole.

The following sections provide an overview of some of the pressure groups the politicians ignore at their peril.

Business groups

The most prominent business pressure group is the Confederation of British Industry (CBI), but other bodies represent the interests of those who own businesses in the UK as well, including the British Chambers of Commerce and, in the agricultural sector, the influential National Farmers' Union.

Because members of these bodies employ millions of people and the wealth they create pays the taxes for schools and hospitals, they have access to leading politicians and what the group leaders say garners substantial media coverage.

Powerful multinational companies employ professional lobbyists to make contact with leading politicians in order to try to influence government policy as it relates to their particular firm. For example, an oil company may want ministers to ignore objections from local residents over the proposed building of a refinery.

Charities

A staggering 16,900 charities are registered in the UK. Most of these are tiny – some quite literally are one person stuffing envelopes and producing newsletters at home. But whether the charity is big (and some multi-million pound charities exist) or small, they all dream of persuading the public and politicians to adopt their cause.

Some of these charities are well resourced and actually help the government carry out its policies or themselves perform a wider social service – for example, the National Childbirth Trust runs antenatal clinics and the Royal Society for the Prevention of Cruelty to Animals runs animal shelters. These bodies often have direct access to ministers and civil servants.

Another way of exerting influence is through possessing expertise in a particular field and receiving lots of media coverage.

Other notable charity pressure groups include the National Society for the Prevention of Cruelty to Children (NSPCC), the Consumers' Association, the Wellcome Trust (which carries out biomedical research), Cancer Research UK and Mencap (which represents people with learning disabilities and their families).

Human rights groups

Since the terror attacks on America in 2001 and the anti-terrorism legislation that followed in the US, UK and other European countries, civil liberties have gradually risen up the political agenda. Human rights groups have been lobbying for the repeal of anti-terror laws and the continuation of what once seemed guaranteed liberties such as the right not to be held without charge.

Liberty campaigns for greater civil liberties and has come to the fore in recent years as the government has sought to impose anti-terrorism laws in the face of Islamic extremism. Although it has a relatively small membership, Liberty has attracted widespread publicity as it has fought the government over anti-terrorism laws in the court.

Amnesty International is another prominent human rights pressure group. However, it focuses most of its energies on helping draw attention to the human rights abuses of foreign governments. Amnesty has a particularly strong pull for students and other young people.

Environmental groups

Global warming is now a widely recognised reality, and the influence of the environmental lobby has grown apace with increasing knowledge. Groups such as Greenpeace and Friends of the Earth have many thousands of members in the UK and abroad. The reports they issue and policy statements they make can attract considerable media coverage, and more politicians than ever are now adopting green policies. As well as lobbying and using the media, environmental groups often deploy direct action – see 'Taking it to the streets: Direct action' a little earlier in the chapter.

Professional groups

One of the key types of pressure group is that which represents a section of society. The UK has a long history of the professions forming their own pressure groups so to protect their own interests and those of their clients. These groups are normally associated with the public services, such as education or health care. Groups exist for every type of profession but some of the most influential include the Law Society, the British Medical Association (BMA), the Royal College of Nursing and the National Union of Teachers.

If the government wants to enact policy in, say, the National Health Service or the courts, it usually consults the relevant professional body, as it represents the people who'll actually have to enforce new government initiatives.

Trade unions

Nearly seven million people belong to a trade union in the UK. These members pay subscriptions, making unions wealthy. Protecting the pay and working conditions of its members is a trade union's main job but it also gets involved in general aspects of promoting greater social justice.

Most trade unions actively support the Labour Party. Because of this overt party political alignment, the trade unions tend to exert more influence when Labour is in power than when the Conservatives are. In recent years, though, Labour and the trade unions have drifted apart – particularly during the prime ministership of Tony Blair from 1997 to 2007. Nevertheless, the Labour Party still draws a lot of its financing from the unions (see Chapter 8 for more on the key role the unions have played in the development of the Labour Party).

Working on a Bigger Stage: Pressure Groups and the EU

Much of the law affecting the lives of Britons is actually passed by the parliament of the European Union (EU) rather than the UK parliament based in Westminster. From labour relations through to weights and measures, the EU passes hundreds of laws each year. It therefore follows that, if big British pressure groups want to get their message across and see their ambitions reflected in new laws, they need to have influence not just at Westminster but also at the European parliament in Strasbourg and amongst the European Council of Ministers in Brussels. (I explain how the EU works in Chapter 20.)

Ever since the passing of the Single European Act in 1986, laws made by the EU have had exactly the same weight in UK law as those made by the UK parliament.

UK-based pressure groups are unlikely to have large numbers of members across the whole EU, and organising demonstrations, marches or other direct action overseas is thus difficult. What's more, no significant European-wide media exists (instead each country has its own unique media culture, although some overarching international newsgathering organisations such as the BBC or CNN have an international presence), which means putting pressure on EU politicians through a media-savvy campaign isn't easy.

What tends to happen as a result of these difficulties is that pressure groups employ professional lobbyists to get their views across to members of the EU parliament and politicians sitting on the EU Council of Ministers.

For pressure groups looking to gain influence in the EU, it's often crucial to gain good contacts with groups of politicians from across the EU, particularly those who sit in the European parliament, as they can amend proposed legislation. The key is that member states of the EU agree to abide by the laws that its legislative bodies draw up. Any group wanting to see a change in the law has two avenues: their own country of origin's parliament and the EU legislative bodies. In effect, pressure groups get two bites at the cherry of influencing lawmakers: their own national politicians and those such as Members of the European Parliament (MEPs), who make laws for all 27 member states of the EU.

Many UK pressure groups have an office in Brussels or Strasbourg or are part of a bigger European-wide pressure group that shares resources and costs. For example, the UK Law Society is a member of the EU's International Bar Association and the UK's Federation of Small Businesses is part of the European Small Business Alliance.

Some of the bigger, more well-resourced pressure groups operate a *mixed approach* to lobbying, which means that they try to lobby both UK-based politicians and media as well as politicians from the EU. These pressure groups hope to maximise their chances of success by putting their message across to as many politicians as possible. Sometimes a pressure group can see itself ignored in relation to a particular issue in the UK but its feelings reflected in EU law, and the converse is also true. Pressure groups always look to focus their efforts on where the power to make decisions lies, whether that be in London, Brussels or Strasbourg.

Pushing the Intellectual Envelope: Think Tanks

A *think tank* is an organisation that does research and formulates policy ideas which may be adopted by the government. In effect, as the name suggests, think tanks are all about idea generation.

Think tanks have been around for a long time. The left-leaning Fabian Society, for instance, was formed way back in 1884. Generally, most think tanks are seen as being either left leaning – supporting the idea of greater social justice and equality – or right leaning – wanting to see more free market solutions adopted to meet the challenges of government.

Putting a finger on how powerful a particular think tank is isn't easy because it often depends on which political party is in power. For example, think tanks that are perceived as left leaning may not have that much influence when a Conservative government is in power. Conversely, think tanks that are seen as more right leaning may not have the ear of government ministers when the Labour Party is in office.

Think tanks generally take a long-term view. What they propose right now may not carry much weight in government but a few years down the line, perhaps after a change of government or in different economic and social circumstances, suddenly the policy change proposals or insights made by the think tank can be in vogue.

Hundreds of think tanks exist. Some are big operations with dozens of staff, who produce lots of policies and studies for politicians, the media and the wider general public to mull over. Others only have a handful of people working for them, aren't so well resourced and produce papers of variable quality. Actually, some of these smaller think tanks are barely disguised pressure groups and what they say can be seen as a bit biased.

Generally, the media only reports on those think tanks it believes have at least the ear of the politicians and, although they may come from the left or right of the political spectrum, what they say does carry some weight in the world of politics and pressure groups.

My run-down of some of the major UK think tanks includes:

- ✔ **Adam Smith Institute (www.adamsmith.org).** This think tank is named after the great Scottish economist Adam Smith, who believed in the free market over state intervention. Unsurprisingly the Adam Smith Institute tries to suggest free-market solutions to society's and the economy's problems. According to its president, Madsen Pirie, 'We propose things which people regard as being on the edge of lunacy. The next thing you know, they're on the edge of policy.'

- ✔ **Centre for Policy Studies (www.cps.org.uk).** This right-leaning group tries to propose how public services can be reformed while reducing the size and expenses of the UK government. The CPS comes at some of the big issues of the day from the perspective that we need less not more government interference in people's lives.

- ✔ **Institute for Fiscal Studies (www.ifs.org.uk).** This think tank looks at how well government finances are being run, personal debts and the prospects for the UK and international economy.

- ✔ **Institute of Public Policy Research (www.ippr.org.uk).** The IPPR is often referred to as Labour's favourite think tank. It has a big staff and its papers on all matters of British life, from financial inclusion to welfare reform – even to the spread of the Internet – often hit the headlines and draw the attention of politicians.

- ✔ **National Institute of Economic and Social Research (www.niesr.ac.uk).** This think tank receives government financing and is charged with looking at the prospects for the UK economy, as well as tracking important social trends.

✔ **The King's Fund (`www.kingsfund.org.uk`).** This group looks at the provision of health care in the UK, monitors efficiency within the National Health Service and proposes changes to it to bring about improvements.

The list here is just a small sample of some of the think tanks in the UK. Nearly every aspect of public policy, from transport to crime, is informed and reviewed by at least one dedicated think tank, and sometimes more. Some think tanks, including the IPPR and the Adam Smith Institute, conduct research and make proposals in a huge variety of different areas of UK life.

Think tanks don't just form policy or carry out research on British matters. Some, such as the International Institute of Strategic Studies, also look at foreign relations and Britain's place in the world.

The lighter side of chocolate

One of the most influential think tanks in the area of poverty and how to best alleviate it is the Joseph Rowntree Foundation (JFR). Named after the great social researcher Joseph Rowntree, a member of the York-based confectionary-producing family, the JRF has been operating for over a century. At the beginning of the 20th century, Joseph Rowntree used some of his considerable resources to examine the conditions of Britain's poor in cities such as York. These early studies of poverty are considered pioneering works and highlighted for the middle class, perhaps for the first time, the plight of the poor.

Chapter 10

Scrutinising Politics and the Media

· ·

In This Chapter

▶ Exploring the relationship between politics and the media

▶ Looking at national newspapers

▶ Throwing the BBC into the mix

▶ Breaking the news mould with modern media

▶ Taking in election campaigns

▶ Testing the waters: opinion polls laid bare

· ·

*A*lthough Britain is a country of 60 million people, with the fifth-largest economy in the world, it is a small place compared to China, the US, Russia and even France. You can fly from one end of the country to another in an hour. Although the UK is a diverse society with large numbers of immigrants as well as strong independent Celtic culture in Scotland, Ireland and Wales, in terms of media, the UK is remarkably concentrated, with the BBC and the national newspapers able to command large numbers of viewers and readers across the length and breadth of the country.

The UK has probably the strongest cross-section of national newspapers in the world, read by millions each day. At the same time the hugely popular national broadcaster – the BBC – is one of the great newsgathering operations in the world, employing more than a thousand journalists.

This strong national coverage offered by both the BBC and the newspapers means that when they report political events and interview politicians, literally millions of electors get to hear or read about what's going on in the corridors of power. Add in access to new media – blogs, political websites and Twitter – and you have a media market that makes UK voters exceptionally politically educated and knowledgeable.

In this chapter I look behind the headlines and unravel the complex, contrasting relationship between politicians and the media.

Exposing the Uneasy Relationship between Politics and the Media

Politicians and journalists have the archetypal love–hate relationship. Politicians know they need the media to get their message across yet they don't like the awkward questions they get asked or that their personal foibles get splashed over the newspapers and the airwaves from time to time.

Members of the media know that they need politicians as they're the lawmakers, the people in power and a great source of stories and, of course, juicy gossip – the very lifeblood of journalism. Simultaneously, however, many journalists distrust politicians regarding what they say and what they do.

It's a 'can't live with them, can't live without them' attitude on both sides.

Most of the time politicians and journalists get along fine, with politicians being given an opportunity to put their views across and journalists allowed to ask searching questions.

The can't-live-without-politics aspect of media coverage is exemplified by the so-called *silly season* when parliament isn't sitting and MPs are on their summer holidays. Newspapers and TV stations sometimes have difficulty finding material, and often relatively minor stories hit the headlines as newspapers try to fill their pages and TV stations their airtime.

Wheeling out the sound bite

As the media has become bigger and more sophisticated, so has the way politicians deal with it. For a long time after the Second World War – the fifties, sixties and seventies – politicians were treated with deference by the newspapers, television and radio. But society has changed and so has the approach of the media to politicians. These days questioning by journalists tends to be fairly aggressive and pointed.

Journalists are always on the lookout for the story, which can often entail searching for differences of opinion between politicians from the same political party and exposing the failings of individual politicians and their policies. Any slip-ups in speeches or interviews by politicians are broadcast over the airwaves in a matter of minutes and journalists love to talk up the idea of politics and politicians being in crisis.

Partly in response to how members of the media talk to them, politicians in recent years have changed the way they talk to the media.

In the hot seat

Jeremy Paxman has been one of the UK's top journalists for many years, presenting the late-night news programme *Newsnight*. Paxman is famous for his often sarcastic and pointed questioning. A famous moment came in an interview of the then Tory Home Secretary Michael Howard. Paxman asked a question of Howard and asked for a yes or no answer; when Howard dissembled, the combative Paxman asked the question again and again . . . and again – a total of 12 times. Still Howard refused to give him a yes or no answer. Later Paxman revealed that he adopted the tactic because he had to fill time before the start of the next news item but his dogged questioning was seen as a prime example of journalistic interviewing craft at its best.

Modern politicians try to master the art of the *sound bite* – a carefully prepared statement summing up their view, which is brief and succinct enough to have a good chance of making it into newspaper articles and onto television news bulletins and the radio.

A good sound bite serves politicians, who can get their message out unchanged by individual journalists. And, it serves journalists, who get a pithy take on an issue that can serve as a launching point for other facts and opinions.

All the careful thought before speaking can mean that you never get a simple yes or no answer from politicians; instead they turn questions around so they can make a positive point about their own policies or attack those of their opponents.

Opinion is divided on how good for democracy modern media manipulation by politicians actually is. Some suggest that the overuse of sound bites and the media training that many politicians undergo actually turns off quite a few voters who feel they're being spun a line rather than given the simple, straight and honest views of politicians.

Media savvy: The role of 'special adviser'

Nowadays politicians must have a media presence in order to communicate effectively with the electors. Virtually all politicians pay experts to train them in how to deal with questions from journalists and how to best craft their public utterances so they get their message across effectively.

Getting revenge: The media witch-hunt

Occasionally, the relationship between politicians and journalists breaks down quite spectacularly. A particular political scandal or action by a politician can lead to some elements of the media openly attacking individual politicians. Referred to as a *media witch-hunt*, it doesn't involve a ducking stool, lots of pitchforks and an angry mob – although to the politician under fire it can feel a bit like that.

Often a witch-hunt involves the private life of the politician being scrutinised by the media and political opponents and even colleagues, who may take the opportunity to call on the politician at the centre of the controversy to resign.

Probably the biggest witch-hunt of recent years occurred in 2009, when the scandal over MPs' expenses came to light. Many MPs were discovered to be claiming huge expenses, sometimes for quite unnecessary things such as a moat-cleaning service or the construction of a duck house on a private pond. The media – reflecting the public mood – became incensed by some of the items claimed for, and newspapers, TV and radio outlets joined together to pour scorn on MPs in general. This massive story dominated the summer of 2009 and caused several MPs to announce that they wouldn't stand for parliament at the next general election.

Many of the MPs at the centre of the witch-hunt felt that they'd been unfairly treated by the media. For its part, most in the media felt they were only doing their job by exposing a scandal. Generally, the middle of a witch-hunt isn't a good place to be.

Many top politicians now employ special advisers who both advise them on how to deal with the media and act as gatekeepers, making sure they speak to journalists and media outlets that may be sympathetic to what they have to say.

Someone who advises a politician on how they deal with the media is often called a *spin doctor*. The phrase was first coined in the US in the 1990s but was soon widely used in the UK.

Often special advisers come from the world of journalism or public relations, which gives them a unique insight into how the media works.

Probably the most prominent special media adviser in recent decades was Alastair Campbell, confidante and close political adviser to Prime Minister Tony Blair. Campbell was extremely loyal to Blair and highly combative. He would reportedly tear strips off journalists who he believed didn't treat Blair or his government's views fairly. As Blair's right-hand man he was also known to give senior ministers a dressing down if they veered in their public uttering from the agreed party or prime ministerial line on a particular issue.

Campbell would often say that he wanted Blair's Labour MPs and ministers to be *on message* – meaning that they needed to stick to the same line on an argument or issue as that held by the prime minister.

Many say that special advisers have become too numerous and too big for their boots – after all, they're not elected by the public. Special advisers can exercise huge power as they're confidantes of senior politicians and the media will go through them to gain access to their political employers. (Chapter 13 has more about special advisers.)

Reading the UK's Newspapers

The UK boasts lots of national newspapers which appear seven days a week, 364 days a year (no papers on Christmas Day). They can be divided up into three types:

- ✔ **The qualities.** These tend to take a serious approach to the news, covering political stories in detail and often avoiding celebrity gossip.

- ✔ **The mid-markets.** These have more of a mix of politics, social affairs and the inevitable celebrity stories.

- ✔ **The red top tabloids.** These widely read titles feed off a diet of sex scandals and celebrity gossip. They cover politics but not in great detail.

The qualities tend to draw most of their readers from amongst management and professional groupings, while the mid-markets take some from these as well as the public sector and middle management. The red tops, on the other hand, draw most of their readers from the working class.

Most of the UK's newspapers can be divided into those which naturally support Conservative or Labour; no paper overtly supports the UK's third-biggest party, the Liberal Democrats.

The political views of the person who actually owns the newspaper can have a major impact on editorial content. These so-called *press barons* are often courted by politicians as they're believed to have direct or indirect influence on the political leanings of the newspapers they own.

Waning influence – or not?

The great American writer and humorist Mark Twain wrote, after seeing his own obituary printed in a newspaper, 'The report of my death was an exaggeration'. The same may now be said about the great British newspaper trade. According to some commentators – particularly in the blogosphere – newspapers, whether national or local, are over and done with. They've been supplanted by free access to online content.

Shrinking size of the qualities

The qualities are sometimes called the *broad-sheets*, a term referring to the size of the paper used. Broadsheets are big and often have to be folded in two to be read comfortably. In the recent past, the *Independent, Guardian, Times* and *Daily Telegraph* were all broadsheet newspapers. However, a few years ago the *Times* and *Independent* switched to become tabloid-size newspapers. Around the same time, the *Guardian* also shrank in size but only to what's called the Berliner format, which is still bigger than a tabloid. Only the *Daily Telegraph, Sunday*

Telegraph and *Financial Times* are still printed as broadsheets. Nevertheless, the term broadsheet is still sometimes applied by people referring to the *Times, Independent, Telegraph* and *Guardian.*

For many years newspapers had journalists who worked exclusively on the Sunday edition and those who worked on the daily. However, in recent times most nationals have merged these teams and inevitably lost staff.

Although publishers are struggling, readership shrinking and advertising revenue falling, national newspapers still play a huge part in the life of the country. Politicians still want to sweet-talk newspaper editors and tip off prominent political reporters with stories and gossip. A big political story still gets people in the streets, and fuels conversation in homes and offices across the country.

Even newspapers' detractors use them as sources, following up exclusive stories first reported in print. Evidence that what newspapers write can still make huge waves was supplied in 2009. The *Daily Telegraph* – one of the UK's influential national newspapers – got hold of the expenses claims of MPs. Many of the claims were shown to be fatuous and even potentially corrupt in some cases. As a result of the *Daily Telegraph* story, a host of MPs resigned or were *deselected*, which means that they were sacked by their party. The MPs' expenses scandal was one of the biggest UK political stories in decades – see Chapter 23 for the lowdown on what happened – but it also re-confirmed the power of the press in the UK.

Taking in the qualities

The *Times, Telegraph, Guardian, Financial Times* and *Independent* are often referred to as the *quality newspapers*, so called because they take quite a serious approach to the news, reporting stories which wouldn't find space in the mid-markets and the red top tabloids. The qualities tend to produce more pages than other papers and to be less reliant on gossip.

To describe the quality newspapers simply, just replace the word *quality* with *serious*, although some would say plain old *boring* is more apt.

The varied coverage of the qualities mixes politics and business with the arts and, of course, sport. They often do in-depth investigations of political and social matters. The qualities break many of the biggest political stories in the country and carry out lengthy interviews with politicians. Despite the qualities saying that they have strong traditions of journalistic excellence, they all to a greater or lesser extent have their own political axes to grind. In other words, they have particular issues or political parties they like to support and generally present themselves and are perceived as being either left- or right-wing. In very simple terms, *left-wing* means to support the idea of a bigger state, acting to tax more highly and distribute this cash to help the most needy and to work toward equality across society. Being *right-wing* means supporting the institutions of the country, wanting low taxes and promoting free trade. (Chapter 8 has more on what distinguishes right- from left-wing politics.)

Newspapers don't have to appear to be independent in terms of their political stance like the BBC must. In fact, each UK newspaper has its own political slant and position, which I explain in this list:

- ✔ *The Daily Telegraph.* The biggest-selling quality newspaper supports the Conservative Party and often stands up in its editorials for what are seen as traditional British values and preserving things as they are. It is a firm supporter of institutions such as the monarchy.

- ✔ *The Times.* Owned by billionaire and media mogul Rupert Murdoch, the *Times* usually supports the Conservatives but has on occasions switched to Labour. Generally, though, *The Times* is seen as right of centre in its politics.

- ✔ *The Guardian.* Seen as the newspaper most read by people working in the public sector and amongst urban-based intellectuals, the *Guardian* supports the Labour Party, generally, and is concerned often with stories about exposing society's inequalities. The *Guardian* is unashamedly on the left of British politics.

  The *Guardian*'s Sunday edition is called the *Observer*.

- ✔ *The Independent.* This paper is supposed to be, well, independent in terms of party politics. However, the newspaper is an avowed supporter of preserving the environment and promoting a more liberal society and is thus often grouped with the *Guardian* on the left of British politics.

- ✔ *The Financial Times.* The 'Pink 'un', so called because it's printed on pink paper, is the voice of top UK management and City staff. Its predominant focus is on business matters, but it also covers politics extensively. The *FT* tends to be on the right of British politics, supporting free trade and lower government taxes. In the past, though, the *FT* has supported both Labour and Conservatives at general elections but more generally the latter.

On general election day each national newspaper editor writes an editorial setting out which party the newspaper supports and putting the case for its readers choosing to vote the same way. Opinions differ as to whether these editorials really matter. In a close election – like the one in 1992 – some suggest that newspaper editorials made a difference to the result. Back then, the *Sun* – the UK's biggest-selling newspaper – urged its readers to vote Conservative rather than Labour. The Conservative leader John Major went on to win a narrow, surprise victory and afterwards the *Sun* ran with the front-page headline: 'It was the *Sun* wot won it' (misspelling deliberate).

Meeting the mid-markets

The mid-market UK national newspapers are called 'mid-market' for a good reason. In terms of content and outlook, they occupy the space between the qualities' fairly serious approach and the red top tabloids' focus on sex and celebrity. Where the qualities tend to have quite serious, lengthy articles, the mid-markets are a bit – well – lighter in their outlook. The mid-markets cover politics but they throw in a little more gossip – both celebrity and otherwise. The mid-markets don't go anywhere near as far as the red top tabloids, which live off a diet of celebrity and scandal.

The combined sales of the two main mid-market newspapers are actually as great as all the quality newspapers combined:

- ✔ **Daily Mail.** This mass-circulation newspaper sells around two million copies a day. Interestingly, it enjoys a high female following, mainly because of its running of more lifestyle features. Generally, major politicians try to court the *Daily Mail* and are keen to appear within its pages as they know it holds significant influence. When the *Daily Mail* campaigns on a topic, politicians often support that cause. This paper is seen as right-wing and a natural supporter of the Conservative Party.

- ✔ **Daily Express.** Back in the 1950s the *Daily Express* was the UK's best-selling newspaper but those glory days are long gone. The paper still has a large following, though, and tends to tread a similar path to the *Daily Mail*, supporting the establishment and the Conservative Party.

Prime ministers such as Tony Blair and John Major were often known to brief the editors of major national newspapers, particularly the *Daily Mail*, *Sun* and *The Times*, before announcing major policies publicly. They do this to see the press reaction to new laws and fresh party policy. Politicians are always sensitive to shifts in public opinion – as ultimately they rely on votes to stay in office – and the support of the press is seen as crucial to convincing the public to support a particular new law or policy.

Checking out the red tops

The red top tabloids are often seen as embodying all that's good and bad about British journalism. (They're called red tops because the *Sun*, *Mirror* and *Star* all have a bright red backdrop to their names on the masthead.) The tabloids tend to be irreverent, full of humour, simple and straight to the point in ways many politicians – and their constituents – can only dream of, and they have large-scale followings. On the downside, tabloids thrive on scandal, can indulge in tactics many consider unethical to find stories and over-simplify political debate by presenting complex arguments and important matters in glaring black and white.

The tabloids love gossip and celebrity stories and, of course, sex scandals. When politics gets covered it tends to be in only the barest terms, but the millions of readers can be influenced by what line their red top tabloid newspaper of choice takes.

In terms of size, the red top market is bigger than the mid-markets and qualities combined – literally millions of copies of these papers are sold day in, day out.

The main tabloid players and their political leanings are outlined in the following list:

- ✔ **The Sun.** Not just the biggest-selling newspaper in the UK, the *Sun* is one of the biggest in the English-speaking world. It is seen as a benchmark for red top journalism, packed full of celebrity and scandal as well as investigative journalism. It was a strong supporter of Margaret Thatcher and her Conservative government, but in 1997, courted by Tony Blair, it switched to Labour. With Blair's departure, the *Sun* moved back to the Tories and can be seen as once again a staunchly Conservative paper. The Sunday edition of the *Sun* is called the *News of the World* and has a very similar outlook in terms of its politics.

- ✔ **The Mirror.** This paper sells nearly two million copies a day. Whereas its deadly rival the *Sun* is seen as a Tory paper, the *Mirror* has always supported the Labour Party. It has its fair share of celebrity and scandal but gives space to leading politicians to write editorials, particularly from the Labour Party. The *Mirror* has often been viewed as the newspaper of the UK trade union movement, which itself is very strongly linked to the Labour Party (I talk about this link in Chapter 8). The *Mirror* is the biggest-selling paper in what may be seen as the naturally Labour-supporting region of northwest England.

- ✔ **The Star.** The smallest-selling red top carries the least political coverage. Instead it tends to obsess about reality TV stars. Its political allegiances aren't as easy to gauge as those of the *Sun* and *Mirror* but at the last election it supported the Conservatives.

Taking it to the grass roots: Regional newspapers

Although the national newspapers have the readers, and to a certain extent the glamour, literally hundreds of local newspapers give over column inches to politics and local political debates.

At the last general election, one parliamentary candidate told me that the first thing anyone standing for parliament should do is get to know the editor of the local newspaper. At election time, the coverage given to politics by the local newspaper can be crucial in swinging votes in the constituency. In fact at several recent by-elections (those held between general elections to fill a vacancy), local newspaper coverage has been seen as key to the final result.

Generally, local newspapers don't tend to be overtly biased towards one party or another. They tend to look at the individual candidates and explore the major local campaign issues, exposing what they see as any flaws in the arguments of the party candidates.

Scotland has its own 'national' newspapers: the *Scotsman*, *Herald*, *Daily Record* and *Scottish Sun*. Although their circulations are small compared to the UK national newspapers – which sell across the country, including Scotland – they still have considerable influence in the Scottish political scene. The support of a particular newspaper is still sought after by politicians from all the parties, particularly now Scotland has its own parliament and could be moving towards independence (see Chapter 16 for more on the Scottish situation).

Balancing Act at the BBC

The British Broadcasting Corporation (BBC) is probably the most influential public service broadcaster in the world – it's certainly the largest. Generally, the BBC covers politics in great depth with politicians regularly appearing on its TV and radio stations to be closely questioned by journalists. Politicians like to appear on the BBC because they know that it has huge reach and its interviews are reported by other media outlets.

For example the *Today* programme on Radio 4 attracts an audience of millions and its interviews are widely reported in newspapers and even on rival radio and TV networks.

The job of a BBC political correspondent (journalist) is considered to be the pinnacle of British journalism and politicians often give the stories or explain their opinions to these correspondents because the stories they put out get wide coverage within the BBC and outside. However, some politicians accuse the BBC of being biased against them.

Whereas most of the UK's national newspapers are biased towards one or other of the political parties, the BBC as a public service broadcaster is supposed to be completely impartial. In fact, when covering politics the organisation has to obey strict rules on not favouring one party over another. When one politician makes an accusation about a political opponent, the BBC has to give the accused individual or party a right of response. At general election time all the main political parties are given equal airtime and political debate fills the airwaves.

A very large part of the BBC's funding comes from the TV licence fee paid by everyone who owns a television – something like 99 per cent of UK households. The TV Licence currently costs £142.50 and funds the BBC's offerings on television, radio and online.

Not only does the BBC offer TV and radio programmes and online material for the whole of the UK, it also provides TV programmes, radio stations and websites specifically targeted at the regions. The main political programmes offered by the BBC include the following:

- ✔ **Radio.** Radio 5 Live provides 24-hour news and sport coverage; Radio 4 has the *Today* programme, which attracts nearly six million listeners a day, as well as *The World at One*, *PM* and *Today in Parliament*.

- ✔ **Television.** The television arm has a dedicated digital channel screening debates in parliament, catchily called 'BBC Parliament'. The BBC broadcasts news programmes throughout the day and shows *Daily Politics* every weekday lunchtime, *Newsnight* every weekday evening, *This Week* on Thursday evenings and the *Politics Show* on Sunday, not to mention regional political debates. Its flagship political debating programme, *Question Time*, airs on Thursday evening.

- ✔ **Online.** The widely read BBC News website (`http://news.bbc.co.uk`) carries a 'Politics' section and each of the main political programmes on TV and radio have their own dedicated Internet pages.

This list provides just a sample of the political coverage broadcast on the BBC; the organisation also has a 24-hour news channel, covered in the next section.

From time to time the BBC is accused of bias either in the way it reports political stories or in the way TV and radio interviewers ask their questions. Many politicians on the right of British politics – members of the Conservative Party or UK Independence Party – have accused the BBC of favouring the Labour Party. Some argue for abolishing the licence fee that funds the BBC in response to this perceived bias. However, just to confuse matters, on the other side of the coin, Tony Blair's advisers accused the BBC of bias in the run-up to the Iraq war in 2003. According to these people, the BBC was anti-war and therefore against the Labour government. Sometimes, the BBC just can't win!

Offering News around the Clock

Broadcast and online media sources have exploded in recent years. Whereas in the 1970s and 1980s the UK had only a handful of TV stations, now it has literally hundreds. In addition, two 24-hour news stations exist – Sky News and BBC News 24. Add to that the proliferation of political websites, blogs and other modern media, and you have access to news and politics limited only by the speed and availability of your Internet connection.

Political parties are now using new mobile and internet technology to get their message across. In the 2001 UK general election, the Labour Party sent text messages to individual voters' mobile phones trying to get them to support them at the polls. This approach has expanded, with parties regularly emailing potential voters with newsletters from their leaders or criticism of their opponents' plans.

Starting up 24-hour TV

When Sky launched the UK's first national 24-hour TV news channel in 1989, it was unclear how great an impact it would have on the reporting of politics. At the time, 24-hour TV news was seen as a bit of a novelty, with many asking how the time could be filled. By the time the BBC launched its rival channel, News 24, nearly a decade later, it was clear that the cut and thrust of party political debate would fill a lot of the time on 24-hour news.

Politicians are forever making appearances on 24-hour news, talking about policy, the latest political scandal or simply blasting their rivals. Often, debates in parliament are shown live on 24-hour news. The idea is to keep the public informed as to what their legislators are doing, and it's working. The advent of 24-hour news channels has helped increase public awareness of politics and politicians enormously. Viewing figures for 24-hour news stations are often small; however, they shoot up when big political stories break or crises occur. Put simply, 24-hour news has become a key way for many people to get to know their politicians and what they stand for.

Breaking the mould: The world of political blogging

For many people, 24-hour news, terrestrial TV and radio stations and newspapers are all so last century. Growing numbers of people are becoming informed of political goings on online through political blogs and commentaries.

A *blog* is a diary or ongoing commentary posted online about any subject the author wishes to write about.

By their nature blogs tend to be very opinionated and some go further and spread untruths and gossip online. Generally, journalistic standards aren't as high in what's called the *blogosphere* as in traditional media outlets such as TV and newspapers.

The anonymity the web offers allows political bloggers to be a little daring in what they say. Because something is online rather than printed in a newspaper, however, doesn't mean that it's exempt from the UK laws of libel.

In the UK, the world of political blogging and online commentary isn't as developed as it is in the US. However, it's becoming more so. Some of the big beasts of the online political blogging and commentary jungle include:

- **Nick Robinson's blog.** The BBC's political editor writes a regular and lively blog published on the widely read BBC News website (www.bbc.co.uk/blogs/nickrobinson).

- **Order-order.** This blog is authored by 'Guido Fawkes' and spreads political gossip and rumour (http://order-order.com).

- **Party blogs.** Members of the Conservative Party run ConservativeHome (conservativehome.blogs.com) and Labour members run their own website (www.labourhome.org).

- **Commentary blogs.** Sites such as those of Councillor Bob Piper (www.bobpiper.co.uk), A Big Stick and a Small Carrot (bsscworld.blogspot.com), Dodgeblogium (www.andrewiandodge.com) and the very oddly named Chicken Yoghurt (www.chickyog.net) all comment on current UK political matters. In a way, these bloggers are like newspaper columnists.

Some politicians are embracing the new age of blogging. David Cameron was the first UK party leader to set up his own blog, which carries film of him at home and talking directly through his website to the reader rather than through the prism of a newspaper, radio or TV interview. Labour leader Gordon Brown has also tried his hand at new technology. In 2009 he announced a new policy on the highly controversial MPs' expenses, not in parliament, but in a YouTube broadcast. At the time, the move drew much criticism. However, this broadcast is undoubtedly a sign of politicians looking to directly appeal to the electorate – particularly the young – without having to use traditional media outlets.

Political blogging is a big deal in the US. The 2008 presidential election cycle saw an explosion in the number of new blogs. Thousands of Americans were energised by the election of the first black president, Barack Obama. And not only supporters of Obama blogged and commented; those who wanted to see his opponent, the Republican candidate John McCain, win also filled the

Internet. Most blogs only got a few hits but some caught the public imagination and attracted lots of readers.

Viewing politics at street level: Twittering

Twitter is very much the online social networking tool of the moment – which probably means by the time you read this it'll be old hat! Twitter allows people to post thoughts and comments and link with other users so long as the comments aren't more than 140 characters long. Why the limit? Well, Twitter's key feature is that it can be accessed through mobile phones with Internet connectivity. Thousands of people are joining Twitter – I'm on it and so's my mum!

Most Twitter comments are fairly mundane but some are dedicated to politics. Leading politicians like US president Barack Obama and Britain's David Cameron and Nick Clegg (leader of the Lib Dems) use Twitter. However, always bear in mind that many tweets and blogs said to be the work of politicians are actually authored by professional publicists.

Twitter became a huge story during the Iranian elections in 2009. Many suspected that the polls had been rigged by the incumbent president Mahmoud Ahmadinejad. As a result, people took to the streets and organised demonstrations and kept in touch with each other through Twitter. Foreign news agencies, which were banned from moving freely in Iran, kept up with events by checking out Twitter.

Looking at the Media in an Election Campaign

From highlighting a division within a party to policy failings, from government incompetence to a politician being involved in a sex scandal, the media always loves a good meaty political story. But media interest in politics and politicians becomes even more frenzied during an election campaign. Suddenly the newspapers are full of political comment and the airwaves awash with politicians being interviewed and debating with one another.

The leaders of the big political parties run daily press conferences during an election campaign – which usually lasts three weeks or so – during which they make statements and face questioning from journalists. At a local level, party workers go door to door in their constituency and try to persuade people to vote for their party's candidate.

Party election broadcasts

In each national election campaign, whether it be a general election for seats in the UK parliament, European elections, or when lots of local council elections are held at once, each of the main political parties – the Lib Dems, Labour and the Conservatives and, depending on the proportion of votes at the previous election, the Greens and even the British National Party – are entitled to party political broadcasts. These are broadcast by the BBC and ITV during the campaigning period, which normally lasts around three weeks.

These broadcasts are free and last between five and ten minutes. In them, the parties get a chance to explain their policies and tell the public what they'd like to do if they were in power. Increasingly, parties use much of the allotted time to attack their opponents without giving a huge amount of detail as to what they'll do themselves. Party election broadcasts are often supplemented by newspaper, billboard and, increasingly, Internet advertising as part of the campaign.

Crucially, party political broadcasts are scrutiny-free zones; no journalists are there to ask awkward questions and the party is free to say what it wants. However, journalists watch the broadcasts and if the party makes false claims then it will most likely be reported in the media.

Broadcasts are also a good way for a party to convey the merits of its leader. In fact, leaders feature a good deal in broadcasts as they're the individuals bidding to be the next prime minister. The personal appeal of the party leader is a big determinant in how electors vote.

In addition, each party publishes a *manifesto* – a document which sets out the policies they'd pursue if elected to government. The media is always keenly interested in the launch of the big parties' manifestos and closely scrutinises what's in them.

The BBC must abide by strict rules stipulating that it remains politically impartial and doesn't favour one party over another. During the period of an election campaign these rules are adhered to even more strictly, with all of the major parties canvassed for their comments.

Opinion is divided over how much impact election campaigns actually have on the result of a general election. At the last three general elections, for instance, the party that was leading at the start of the election campaign was still leading at the end. In fact, most people vote for the same party election after election and are therefore barely influenced by what goes on in campaigns.

When the two main political parties are neck and neck in the opinion polls at the time the election is called, campaigning can make a difference. For example, in the 1992 general election, Labour had a narrow lead when the election was called by the Conservative prime minister. John Major had a good campaign and the Conservative's party political broadcasts and their press advertising are believed to have been more effective. Result? On polling day, the Conservatives won a narrow victory.

Political parties spend a lot of money at election time. The Conservative and Labour parties have budgets for advertising and other costs of £5 to £10 million. The Lib Dems tend to spend far less. This money is raised through party membership subscriptions, from rich donors and, in Labour's case, the trade unions.

Testing the Temperature: Opinion Polling

Politicians and the media alike want to know what voters are thinking on the big political issues and which party they would vote for if a general election were called. Conducting an opinion poll is the best way to see how people would vote.

Opinion polling methods range from a quick phone call to a cross-section of voters all around the country to in-depth interviews carried out by researchers at people's homes. Increasingly, email is being used to canvass people's opinions. Polls tend to be of a minimum of 1,000 voters – sometimes several thousand. The six main organisations conducting opinion polls in the UK are Mori, Gallup, YouGov, NOP, ICM and Populus.

Much thought, expense and work goes into conducting opinion polls, as they can provide a crucial insight into what the British people are thinking on particular issues or towards the policies of the main political parties.

Generally, during a general election campaign, polls are carried out frequently. Sometimes several newspapers and TV stations will carry out a poll each day so that they can run a story highlighting which party is likely to do well.

Polls aren't confined to an election campaign period. In fact, nearly every week the public is being asked who they'd vote for and what events or policies are likely to influence their decision.

Here's why polls are considered useful and important:

- **Story generation.** The media simply loves polls as they give the perfect excuse to run a story about which party or politician is up and which one is down.

- **Political barometer.** Polls allow politicians the chance to see how popular their policies are and what they may need to change to attract more votes at election time.

- **Signal of next government.** An opinion poll showing one party streaking ahead of the others can be a strong indicator of which party will win the next election and form the government. This information can be useful for businesses making plans in relation to which party they'll have to deal with down the track.

Politicians whose parties are doing badly in opinion polls often say that they take no notice of their results and the only poll that matters is the one at election time. The idea is to appear calm and collected and undeterred from pursuing their policies. Actually, this stance is utter rubbish. Politicians are avid readers of the polls and often make crucial decisions on the back of them.

Opinion polls tend to be very accurate at estimating support for individual parties. They're generally correct to within two or three percentage points – called the _margin of error_. However, polls haven't always been so spot on. In 1992 the opinion polls predicted a win for the Labour Party at the general election but in fact the Conservatives triumphed.

As well as polls carried out for media outlets, the big political parties carry out their own private polling, often with small groups of voters called _focus groups_, to see in detail what voters feel about the policies they're pursuing or their views on particular political subjects.

Part III
The Ins and Outs of Parliament

'Nothing to do with policy – one's a
Campbell and one's a McDonald.'

In this part . . .

*I*n this part I get to the meat of Britain's ancient democracy. I examine Britain's unwritten constitution and the strengths and weaknesses of the British way of doing politics. I examine how Westminster makes laws that affect all of our lives. I take a peek behind the door of 10 Downing Street and see exactly what the prime minister and the cabinet do. I examine the civil service and judiciary, without whom government and the rule of law would break down! Then I get all local, looking at how government at the grassroots works as well as the relatively new Scottish parliament and Welsh and Northern Ireland assemblies. Finally, I show you how to become an MP or local councillor.

Chapter 11

Examining Britain's Constitution

In This Chapter

▶ Introducing the concept of the constitution

▶ Looking at the variety of constitutions

▶ Homing in on Britain's constitution

▶ Cheering on Britain's successful constitution

▶ Moving towards a written constitution

▶ Looking at monarchy versus republicanism

The Constitution is the sole source and guaranty of national freedom.

Former US president Calvin Coolidge

This is the chapter to read if you want to know who calls the shots in the British political system because it's here that I take an in-depth look at what characterises a constitution and give you the lowdown on how Britain's constitution actually works.

Focusing on Why Countries Need a Constitution

In the simplest terms a *constitution* is a set of rules outlining how a nation should be governed. Crucially, a constitution looks to contain the powers of politicians by giving them a set of rules to work within.

Most countries around the globe have a constitution and some of the characteristics many of them share include:

- ✔ **It curtails the power of those at the top.** In every society certain people or groups of people (usually the leaders of political parties) exercise *executive power* – the power of the person or people at the top of the executive branch of the government. Setting limits on what they can do is where a constitution comes in.

- ✔ **It provides a key role for the courts.** Constitutions need to be interpreted to suit everyday situations, which is a responsibility given to the courts. Law courts decide what is and isn't constitutional and politicians exercising executive power are required to obey the decisions of the court.

- ✔ **It sets out who does what in government.** Most governments have several different branches – in the UK we have a cabinet, a parliament and a monarch. A constitution sets out clearly the powers of each governmental branch. The courts can be called on to interpret the constitution and make a ruling when it's believed that one branch of government is exceeding its constitutional powers.

- ✔ **It lists the rights of individual citizens.** Constitutions guarantee certain freedoms for the individual – the rights to free speech, to vote at elections and, even more fundamentally, not to be arrested without due legal process, a right called *Habeas Corpus* in the UK. Again, the courts decide whether these rights are being breached.

Much of a nation's constitution concerns outlining the rights of the individual and the power of the executive to impinge or not on those individual rights. The courts exist to apply constitutional protections to everyday situations. Their decisions result in *legal precedents* – outcomes establishing a principle or rule that a court or other judicial body utilises when deciding subsequent cases involving similar issues or facts. (See Chapter 15 for more on the role of the judiciary in modern Britain.)

Academics can trace human society back some 10,000 years, and against that timescale constitutions are a relatively modern invention. The world's first fully fledged constitution was written in the newly formed United States of America in 1787. The US was a brand new country starting from scratch and the founders felt that a written constitution was needed to contain the powers of government and guarantee the rights of the individual.

Constitutions often come about as a way of preventing tyranny. For example, in the midst of the French Revolution (1789–99) a constitution was drawn up – called the Rights of Man and the Citizen – which was intended to guarantee the fundamental rights of the individual while simultaneously curtailing the power of the monarch. This constitution aimed to prevent tyrannical rule by any future French monarchs. The French revolutionaries did have a plan B, though – namely executing King Louis XVI, which they did in 1793.

Exploring Differing Types of Constitution

Political scientists tend to categorise the different constitutions of individual countries as follows:

- **Written or unwritten.** This one's pretty clear – a constitution is either recorded on a piece of paper, parchment or bark, or it isn't. The UK constitution is unwritten.

- **Unitary or federal.** In the case of a unitary constitution, ultimate power resides in a central government. A federal constitution provides for shared power and bars the central government from overruling the actions of regional governments.

- **Rigid or flexible.** A rigid constitution allows for no changes; a flexible one can be amended.

These categorisations can be a little confusing But basically a constitution can belong to three of the six categories at the same time; a constitution can have one attribute from each pair. So, for example, the US constitution is written, federal and flexible, whereas the UK constitution is unwritten, unitary (although becoming more federal, as I discuss in 'Taking in unitary and federal constitutions' later in this chapter) and flexible.

Just to confuse matters even more, a country can be said to be unitary yet have a degree of federalism (if you really want to know, this set-up's called *quasi-federalism*, which would be worth a big score if you could use it at Scrabble) and differing degrees of flexibility. Although the US constitution is often defined as flexible, amending it is actually very difficult, which means that any statement that the US constitution is flexible has to be qualified in some way.

Classifying constitutions as unitary/federal or rigid/inflexible can be useful, but each nation's constitution is unique and is categorised according to which definition it fits most closely. I think I need a lie down now!

Each nation develops in its own unique way and at its own pace. For example, the US had a constitution in 1787 after it rebelled against British rule. Some countries in Eastern Europe adopted a constitution just in the past decade or so after throwing off rule by the Soviet Union.

Recording the difference between written and unwritten constitutions

Okay, setting out the differences between written and unwritten constitutions is relatively easy and Table 11-1 provides a quick guide to tell one from the other.

Table 11-1	Comparing Written and Unwritten Constitutions
Written	**Unwritten**
A written constitution is one that is enshrined in the law of the land.	An unwritten constitution comes about through many years of tradition, legal argument and custom.
Written constitutions are created – the US's, for example, was written by top politicians and political thinkers of the late 1700s.	Unwritten constitutions come about organically over many years, reflecting the history of the country.

Sadly, I'm going to confuse matters again. No constitution is completely written or unwritten. The UK is often said to have an unwritten constitution which has risen organically over many years, yet much of what we recognise as the key components of a constitution puts limits on the executive branch of government. Guaranteed rights for the individual have come about through laws passed by the UK parliament, and these laws, of course, are written down. So the UK, while not having a single document called the constitution that everyone can refer to and argue over, does have a patchwork of laws that do much the same thing – limiting the power of the government and protecting the rights of the individual.

Most democratic countries have a written constitution – a single document that lawyers, judges, citizens and politicians can refer to. In fact, out of western democratic nations, only the UK, New Zealand and Israel can be said to have unwritten constitutions. Strangely enough, however, a constitution doesn't need to be written down to secure the rights of the individual. Britain has an unwritten constitution and yet we are seen as one of the most stable and most free countries in the world.

Taking in unitary and federal constitutions

The key points relating to federal and unitary constitutions are as follows:

- ✔ **Unitary** – The constitution provides that central government wields supreme power over any locally based government or parliament.

✔ **Federal –** The constitution stipulates that power is in effect shared between a central government and regional-based governments or parliaments. In short, the central government can't encroach on the powers held by regionally based governments.

Up until 1999 the UK could be said to have a unitary constitution without any contradiction. Power was vested in the central government through the UK parliament. However, the establishment of the Scottish parliament and the Welsh assembly means that those parts of the UK get to make their own laws to govern themselves, with some limitations. (Chapter 16 explains the situation in detail.) The UK is still defined as having a unitary constitution but with the qualification that some elements of federalism apply.

Germany offers a good example of a federal constitution at work. After the Second World War a written constitution was established that shared out power between the central government and the parliaments and governments in the regions of the country. Regional governments in Germany have substantial powers and central government is not allowed to ride roughshod over them.

Changing the rules: Rigid and flexible constitutions

Some constitutions are easier to change than others. In a country with a written constitution, it is usually the case that the constitution, as well as dividing powers and enshrining rights of the individual, establishes a process to change the constitution in the future. The constitution is flexible, anticipates that it will be reformed by future generations, and provides the means of doing so. The idea is to allow the constitution to adapt over time so that outdated laws and institutions can be jettisoned and more up-to-date and relevant ones adopted. The ease with which this process can take place is the measure political scientists use to decide how flexible a country's constitution is. A *rigid constitution* is one that's hard to change. This may be a deliberate decision because the people who drew it up don't want the contents to be altered at a later date, perhaps because the individual rights outlined in the constitution needed to be protected through a constitution for ever.

It's crucial to get the process of how a constitution can be changed in the future right from the beginning. Specifying an impossibly high threshold for change – say, everyone in parliament has to agree to any change – risks that the constitution becomes less relevant over time and that it is ultimately ignored as a method to improve the country. On the flip side, make changing the constitution too easy and chaos is likely, as politicians will try to do so when it suits their short-term political objectives. In a worst case scenario, an easily changeable constitution will be a weak one and a dictatorship may result.

Unwritten constitutions are generally seen as more flexible than written ones. However, this flexibility doesn't make them weak. The patchwork of different laws, traditions and customs which together create an unwritten constitution are incredibly difficult to unravel by someone wishing, for example, to form a dictatorship. Take the UK: it's said to have an unwritten constitution yet has been a healthy democracy, with renowned civil liberties, for many years.

Celebrating Britain's Constitution

If you're British, time to puff your chest out with pride. The UK constitution is just a bit, well, special and highly successful. It developed over many hundreds of years from Magna Carta (I talk about this ancient grant of rights in Chapter 5) in the 13th century, to the forming of the civil courts and parliament between the 12th and 16th centuries, to the curtailment of the power of the monarchy in the 17th and 18th centuries, to the extension of voting rights and rights for women in the 19th and early 20th centuries – and that's just to mention a few developments. A few wars and disagreements have occurred along the way but for much of this time Britons have been amongst the freest people in the world, able to express themselves without fear that some unhinged dictator or over-powerful government is going to come along and do them harm.

Think of the UK constitution like a spider's web, with lots of different strands leading in all sorts of different directions and yet remarkably strong at any point you choose to touch.

No such thing as a British constitution document exists; instead, the whole edifice of laws, traditions and customs is supported by the following:

- ✔ **Parliament.** The UK Houses of Parliament are responsible for making *statute law* – the body of laws written by a legislature rather than the executive or judicial branch of a government. Enacting statute law is the single most important support for the UK constitution because statute law made by parliament outranks all the other laws, traditions and customs. Sometimes statute laws merely enshrine other less important laws, traditions and customs. (See the upcoming 'Granting parliamentary sovereignty' section for more on the central role of parliament in the constitution.)

    Changes to UK statute law are made through an Act of Parliament. Basically, a bill is put before the House of Commons; it's then voted upon several times and members are free to table amendments which means that they want to make a change to the wording of a bill. Once the bill passes, it is signed by the monarch and becomes law.

✔ **Common law.** A patchwork of laws based on customs and traditions, common laws often arise through *legal precedent* – a judge's decision in one case becomes binding on all subsequent cases based on the same principle.

For example, in recent years cases individuals have argued that euthanasia (being allowed to die) should be legalised. The ruling in these cases sets a precedent for similar cases in the future.

However, if the government of the day doesn't like the court's ruling, it can seek to alter future interpretations by introducing new statute law through parliament.

✔ **Constitutional conventions.** Defining a convention can be tricky but suffice it to say that constitutional conventions are unwritten rules followed through force of habit and tradition if for no other reason. For example, it is a constitutional convention that the government of the day will call an immediate general election if it loses a vote of confidence in the House of Commons. No law decrees this, politicians and the public just accept that certain actions must follow from a particular event. Constitutional conventions are the most baffling part of the UK constitution for most observers, but they act as a real check on the authority of those in a position of power.

In the UK the monarch is theoretically allowed to make laws – termed the *royal prerogative* – literally on a whim. However, the monarch never exercises this right because he or she's bound by the 17th-century convention that parliament is the place for drawing up laws. The monarchy not taking advantage of its royal prerogative is an example of how conventions influence the UK constitution.

The UK constitution is quite flexible, as incremental changes happen through changes to common law or conventions while bigger changes can be brought about through new statute laws. Changing the UK constitution doesn't take long – in fact, statute laws can be rushed through parliament in a matter of weeks if needed.

No one person has the power to radically change the UK constitution – not even the prime minister. Instead, for changes to statute law a majority must be secured in parliament, while alterations to common law only occur following a court case in which judges decide the outcome. (Chapter 15 has more on the judiciary and its role in the UK constitution.)

Granting parliamentary sovereignty

Parliament makes the law for the UK. The laws passed by parliament have precedent over all the other parts of the constitution. In addition, parliament has the right to repeal or change laws passed by previous parliaments and British courts have to enforce the laws passed by parliament. Parliament is thus pre-eminent in the UK constitution.

This situation means that the UK government is centralised and that much of the power in the country is concentrated in the hands of the people at the top of the biggest political parties sitting in the House of Commons. The prime minister and his or her cabinet therefore have a huge say in the actions of the government and any constitutional changes that take place.

However, what the bigwigs have to say doesn't necessarily go – I talk about the several checks and balances in place in the next section.

Parliament became of central importance over a few hundred years. Originally, it was set up to allow the monarch to better collect taxes but over time, and after the Civil War in the 1640s, parliament supplanted the monarch as the main source of power in the country.

Limiting parliamentary sovereignty

Parliament may have huge power within the UK constitution but there are limits. The main ones are:

- ✔ **Elections.** Parliamentary elections are held every few years. If the laws the governing political party has passed are unpopular, it may be voted out of office.

- ✔ **Party system.** Even the prime minister is accountable as he or she relies on the support of Members of Parliament (MPs), who in turn rely on the support of members of their party. Politicians who use parliamentary sovereignty to push through laws unpopular with the people and with their own party will find it very hard to get re-elected.

- ✔ **Media scrutiny.** The press and TV examine parliamentary laws very closely. Efforts to change the constitution get reported, as do the views of opponents. The electorate pays attention to such issues. (See Chapter 10 for the relationship between politics and the media.)

- ✔ **EU membership.** As a part of its membership of the European Union (EU), Britain has to agree to its laws. In fact, EU law has precedence even over statute law passed by parliament – see the nearby sidebar, 'Witnessing the growing role of European law'. Some say this situation undermines parliamentary sovereignty, but the UK parliament could withdraw from the EU, thereby repealing the right of EU law to precedence over statute law.

Some argue that the courts are a check on parliamentary sovereignty, but even the High Court doesn't have the right to alter statute law passed by parliament. However, the courts do have the right to review allegations that people in government – whether ministers or officials – have acted illegally. So, no government is above the law despite the fact that they create much of it!

Witnessing the growing role of European law

As a member of the European Union, the UK agrees to adopt laws and treaties the EU enters into. In recent years, this situation has had a profound effect on the UK constitution. European laws apply to Britain, as do the judgements of European courts such as the European Court of Human Rights. Whereas in the past individuals wanting to right what they saw as a wrong would go solely to a UK court to argue their case, these days they have the right to take their case to European courts too.

Many see this move as undermining the British constitution and national sovereignty. However, others see the increasing encroachment of EU laws as actually adding to the freedoms and rights of the individual and further limiting the power of the UK government. Chapter 20 has more on how Britain is being altered by its membership of the European Union.

Quantifying the Success of the UK's Constitution

Although the UK constitution has lost some of its gleam in recent decades, it's been admired – but rarely copied – around the globe. Some of the reasons for the constitution's status include:

✔ **The UK is a stable democracy.** Whereas many European countries, such as Spain, Germany and Italy, have succumbed to dictatorships within the past century, Britain never has. Many say that this stability results from its constitution and that its mix of laws, traditions and customs provides an in-built mechanism for preventing dictatorship and retaining a democracy.

✔ **The UK's government is efficient.** The UK constitution concentrates a lot of power in the central government based in Westminster. This means that the government can more easily execute the policies it was elected to carry out without the fear that, for example, the judiciary will stand in its way. All in all, UK governments can take decisive action when required.

✔ **The UK constitution is rooted in history.** The UK constitution has grown organically over a long period of time. According to some, Britons feel protective of, value and respect their constitution much more because it's part of their collective history.

Moving towards a Written Constitution

Some argue that the UK's constitution, resting as it does on a combination of parliamentary statute law, the courts and convention, is past its sell-by date. Political analysts state that what we need is a written constitution so that everyone knows where they stand. This argument isn't new; calls have been made for Britain to have a written constitution ever since the American and French revolutions of the late 18th century.

Critics of the UK's constitution make the following points:

- ✔ **The centralised government holds too much power.** The prime minister and the majority party in parliament can change statute law as they like, which leaves the constitution at the mercy of the majority party.

- ✔ **The centralised government can ignore civil liberties.** Because UK central government is so strong it can ride roughshod over civil liberties at times.

   For example, in 2007 the government proposed detaining terrorist suspects for 120 days without charge – a move which alarmed civil liberties campaigners. However, it's worth noting that the government was defeated in parliament and the detention limit is currently 28 days.

- ✔ **The current constitution lacks definition.** Knowing what parts of the constitution actually stand for can be tricky. Many constitutional conventions change over time.

   For example, in the past a constitutional convention held that government ministers would resign if their senior advisers told a public untruth or acted in an incompetent manner. These days many ministers simply sack the adviser and carry on in their job.

The new UK Supreme Court

The UK's Supreme Court came into being in October 2009. Put simply, this court has swept up the judicial powers of the House of Lords and the Privy Council (which formerly acted as the highest court of appeal for the UK and even some former colonies). The Supreme Court hears appeals against rulings in all the other courts in England, Wales and Northern Ireland (it doesn't have power over Scottish criminal courts though).

The Supreme Court makes legal decisions that set precedents. In turn, these precedents will form part of the nation's unwritten constitution. The Supreme Court can't, however, overturn statute law passed by the UK parliament in Westminster. (Check out Chapter 15 for more on the courts and judiciary.)

The UK is gradually having more elements of its constitution enshrined in law. Unwritten parts of the constitution, such as conventions, have been put in writing. For example, freedom of speech – long seen as a part of the UK constitution but not preserved in law – now forms a key part of the Human Rights Act. Chapter 15 covers the provisions of this key law.

The establishment of the Scottish parliament and the Welsh assembly has moved quite a bit of power away from the UK parliament and, therefore, the UK prime minister – issues I explore in more depth in Chapter 16.

Crowning the Constitution: The Monarchy

For much of Britain's history the monarch – not parliament – ruled the roost. For more than six centuries successive kings and the odd queen were at the pinnacle of the political system and at the centre of what we'd recognise as the constitution. The monarch controlled the army, made political appointments, called and dissolved the House of Commons whenever he or she liked and had all the high offices of state in his or her gift. From the 1540s onwards, the monarch even controlled the Church, appointing bishops and acquiring huge tracts of land which had formerly belonged to the Roman Catholic Church. In short, the monarch was number one.

However, during the 17th century, the Civil War resulted in parliament seizing some significant powers from the monarch – Chapter 5 gives you the full lowdown on how this transfer of power took place. As a result, many of the powers to appoint government officials started to fall into the hands of politicians instead of the sovereign.

But unlike many other Western countries, Britain didn't get rid of its monarchy. Instead, the institution transformed into a *constitutional monarchy*. What this means is that, instead of exercising absolute political power, modern-day monarchs exercise their authority within the confines of the UK's constitution. In short, the monarch acts within certain limits set by accepted conventions of behaviour.

In practice the monarch performs several roles, but his or her power is largely ceremonial, such as:

- Opening and dissolving parliament
- Appointing the prime minister
- Consenting to all bills passed by parliament (without this consent they can't become law)
- Appointing bishops and members of the House of Lords

These powers may seem pretty similar to those being exercised by monarchs way back in the 17th century before parliament took over. However, a crucial caveat applies to the power of the monarch: he or she must always act with the *advice of ministers*. What this means, in effect, is that the monarch does as they're told by the leaders of the government.

For example, the monarch dissolves parliament only when he or she's been told to do it by the prime minister, who wants to call an election.

The power to appoint a prime minister is also illusory because, by constitutional convention, the monarch has to ask the leader of the party which holds a majority in parliament. The personal feelings or wishes of the monarch don't come into it. The monarch's job is to rubber-stamp what goes on in parliament.

Take the relationship between Queen Elizabeth II and ex-Conservative prime minister Margaret Thatcher, for instance. It was widely rumoured that the Queen didn't like Margaret Thatcher nor the policies that her radical, reforming government pursued. However, Her Majesty had to appoint Thatcher as prime minister three times because Thatcher kept winning elections. In reality, the monarch has no choice in who he or she appoints to the role of prime minister.

So what would happen if the monarch decided to disobey his or her ministers – the government – and appoint someone he or she liked to be prime minister or refused to give consent to bills passed by parliament? Well, the majority of MPs in parliament would possibly vote to either ask the monarch to abdicate or even abolish the institution of monarchy altogether.

The monarch has a team of advisers called *privy councillors* who sit – yes, you guessed it – on the Privy Council. The Privy Council has been around for hundreds of years and used to be a very powerful body. These days being a privy councillor is little more than a ceremonial role and its members are drawn from both the House of Commons and the House of Lords – yes, politicians! The monarch appoints privy councillors and they get to sit for life. There are hundreds of privy councillors but the Council only meets in full on two occasions: when the monarch dies and the council proclaims the accession of the heir; and when a monarch intends to marry. The privy council has a judicial wing which acts as a court of last appeal for some Commonwealth countries, sometimes when defendants face the death penalty.

Stirring Things Up: Republicanism

Britain has had a monarch for nearly a thousand years, but for the last four centuries many thinkers and politicians have called for abolishing the monarchy and making the country a republic. England was a republic (it didn't have a monarch) between 1649 and 1660, following the Civil War and the execution of Charles I by parliament.

Most Britons, when asked, support the idea of having a monarchy but a substantial minority (usually around a quarter) would prefer it to be abolished. Table 11-2 sets out the main arguments for and against keeping the monarchy.

Table 11-2   Arguments For and Against Retaining the Monarchy

Arguments For	*Arguments Against*
It still enjoys widespread support as the monarch symbolises national unity.	It's an elitist institution with no real practical purpose – in other words, the institution's powerless, so why keep it?
It's above petty party politics and is a welcome check on the power of the prime minister (although if the monarchy exercised its power independently it would risk being abolished).	Monarchs ascend the throne through the hereditary principle, which many believe is unfair and anachronistic in what's supposed to be a meritocratic society.
As an institution, it provides welcome continuity in a fast-changing, globalising world.	The monarchy is no longer as popular as it once was and incidents such as the treatment of Princess Diana have lessened respect for the institution.
It attracts lots of tourism. Just think of the thousands of foreigners who flock to Buckingham Palace each year and they all spend, spend, spend.	It costs too much to keep it; members of the royal family receive annual payments from the *civil list* – a sum set aside for funding all activities to do with the monarchy – which is funded through taxation.

Although the monarchy has suffered periods of declining popularity, don't expect it to be abolished anytime soon. All the major UK political parties have pledged to keep the monarchy.

Queen Elizabeth II has been widely acknowledged – even by some republicans – as a successful constitutional monarch. She has reigned for over 50 years during a time of political upheaval and fundamental change to society. Nevertheless, she's always carried out her ceremonial duties to the letter and assiduously avoided getting involved in party politics. She may not exercise political power but opinion polls show that she's always been respected by the overwhelming majority of Britons.

Many of the difficulties affecting the institution of monarchy in recent years can be blamed on the behaviour of some of the members of the royal family. Divorce, infidelity and conspicuous expenditure of public money have undoubtedly led some to question the institution as a whole.

Some suggest that the monarchy should be reformed. For example, only the monarch and the heir to the throne should receive money from the civil list and they should have to pay income and inheritance tax on their vast wealth.

Chapter 12

Britain's Parliamentary Democracy

In This Chapter

▶ Exploring parliament – the Houses of Commons and Lords

▶ Looking at the jobs of MPs and peers

▶ Following the passage of government and private members' bills

▶ Putting Commons committees under scrutiny

▶ Appreciating the role of the Speaker and other parliamentary bigwigs

*I*n this chapter I explore the inner workings of Britain's parliamentary democracy, peeking behind the oak-panelled doors of the Palace of Westminster to see where the real power lies in the UK.

Honouring the Mother of Parliaments

The UK parliament is often referred to as the 'mother of parliaments' as a result of its long history and because its traditions and approach to the execution of democracy have been copied and admired around the globe.

Even the building that the UK parliament sits in shouts out history, power and tradition. The Palace of Westminster is recognised as a gothic masterpiece, with its stained glass, medieval timbers and, of course, iconic Big Ben – read more about this building in the nearby sidebar, 'Visiting the Palace of Westminster'.

But the Palace of Westminster isn't just a great building but is also a workplace, with 1,100 offices, 100 staircases and the small matter of 5 kilometres of corridors – all of which help the hundreds of Members of Parliament (MPs) and peers in the House of Lords do their job. And what a job it is – making the laws that govern the lives of around 60 million Britons. These laws are drawn up, scrutinised, debated and voted upon in two legislative chambers:

> ✔ **The House of Commons** made up of MPs elected by the public in individual constituencies
>
> ✔ **The House of Lords** made up of appointees suggested by the monarch (who in turn takes the advice of the PM) as well as some lords who've inherited their title and right to sit in the Lords

The House of Commons is often referred to as the *lower house* and the House of Lords the *upper house*. These terms date back to before the 20th century when society was very different and the House of Lords was more important than it is today. Back then members of the House of Lords were considered to be of high birth, whereas members of the Commons were thought of as, well, common and of low birth. In short, these terms are anachronistic and rooted in Britain's ever-so-complex and long-standing class system.

Within parliament, many committees made up of MPs and members of the House of Lords pore over the small details of new laws and monitor old laws to see how they're working. All of this activity stems from one grand building in Westminster, which is at the very centre of Britain's democracy.

The UK parliament is still of crucial importance, but some of its powers have been *devolved* – in effect, given away – to the Scottish parliament and the Welsh and Northern Irish assemblies. Flick to Chapter 16 for more about devolution.

Visiting the Palace of Westminster

So much of Britain's history has been made in the Palace of Westminster. Here, important laws have been passed, major debates taken place and even a king tried as a criminal (following the Civil War, Charles I was tried and executed for treason in 1649).

The oldest part of the Palace of Westminster – Westminster Hall – was built in the reign of William II, son of William the Conqueror, in the late 11th century. Originally Westminster Hall was the home of successive English kings and queens, right up until the reign of Henry VIII in the 16th century.

It also housed the first English parliaments, whose main jobs were voting on tax-raising measures for the monarch and making the laws of the land, usually on the instruction of the monarch. Despite the fact that monarchs

moved out of the building in 1512, it was still called a palace and its main role became that of home for the House of Commons and House of Lords. After the Civil War (1641–51), the power of the monarchy was broken, and the Palace of Westminster became the centre of power in England and eventually the whole of the UK.

But not all was plain sailing. In 1605 Guy Fawkes and other plotters tried to blow up the Palace of Westminster and kill the country's leading politicians and the monarch. They failed. However, in October 1834 fire gutted much of the building. It was rebuilt in the gothic style of the day according to the plans of architect Charles Barry. One of the most notable innovations from this time was the building of a clock tower at the north-eastern end of the palace, the bell of which became known as Big Ben.

The building was controversial at the time and criticised by some but is now viewed as a masterpiece, attracting hundreds of thousands of visitors a year.

Westminster Palace isn't a museum, though – it's a hive of activity, with each MP having office space and hundreds of staff providing administration, security and even catering. Even restaurants – very good ones, too – and bars are found in the Palace. Yet, despite its huge size, the Palace of Westminster can't house all of government. Many MPs work from nearby Portcullis House and the Norman Shaw Building. Also nearby are individual ministerial buildings housing thousands of civil servants putting into practice the laws drawn up in the Palace of Westminster. Nevertheless, the palace provides one of the iconic images of Britain.

Taking It to the Top: The House of Commons

More so than probably any other institution in the country, what happens in the House of Commons impacts on you in some way or another. The House of Commons is the major law-making body and the laws it makes affect your life for good or ill. For example, consider your car: laws made in the House of Commons dictate that you need to pay road tax and have car insurance and a budget voted upon by its members decides how much tax you pay on the petrol in the tank. The job of the Commons is also to scrutinise the activities of the government of the day (run by politicians from the biggest political party in the Commons) as well as protect the liberties of Britons. Even in this modern media age, what happens on the ancient floor of the House of Commons chamber and in its committees does count as it's at the very heart of our democracy.

Laws made by parliament are called *statute law* or *Acts of Parliament*. They're the most important laws in Britain because no court is allowed to overturn statute law – only another Act of Parliament can do the job.

Looking at the job of MPs

At the 2005 general election, a grand total of 646 people were elected to the House of Commons – each MP representing a constituency. On election, these people become known as Members of Parliament, or MPs for short. Being an MP is a very important job.

Some of the key responsibilities and powers that come with being an MP include:

✔ Voting on proposed changes to the law.

✔ Helping amend existing laws.

✔ Proposing changes to the law through private members' bills, which I explain in the upcoming section, 'Introducing private members' bills'.

✔ Sitting on committees which scrutinise proposed law changes and the effectiveness of existing laws, as well as the actions taken by government ministers and their departments.

✔ Tabling written questions of government ministers and even the prime minister over their actions. Ministers and even the PM are expected to answer these questions fully and truthfully.

✔ Taking part in debates over new laws and matters of public policy concern.

✔ Meeting with constituents to hear their concerns over local matters or wider public policy.

Above and beyond their official duties, MPs do lots of different things:

✔ Host receptions in the Palace of Westminster for pressure groups or noteworthy constituents.

✔ Meet press journalists and give them stories or do TV interviews.

✔ Visit other countries so that they can see how policy initiatives and law changes work in practice.

If you ask a group of MPs how long their hours are they'll probably give you a host of different answers. Some are real workaholics, others less so. Some MPs focus on one or two aspects of the job, such as meeting with their constituents and listening to their concerns, while others love the limelight of the TV studio or like to propose myriad changes to the law. I've even met one MP who took pride in the fact that he routinely killed off law changes proposed by colleagues by talking and talking so that the bill ran out of legislative time. He saw keeping as many laws as possible off the statute books and thereby freeing Britons' lives from red tape as his duty. I suppose someone's got to do it!

And, from being an MP, you can potentially become a minister and even prime minister (PM)! The PM is usually the leader of the biggest party in parliament. Technically, party leaders can come from either the House of Commons or the House of Lords. However, according to convention party leaders come only from the House of Commons. In fact, no leader of a major party and therefore prime minister has been drawn from the ranks of the House of Lords for over a hundred years.

Recognising that the House of Commons holds the power

The House of Lords used to be equally and at times actually more powerful than the House of Commons, but this is no longer the case. Although the House of Lords can vote against legislation sent to it from the House of Commons, it can't kill it. All the Lords can do is propose amendments and ask the House of Commons to think again about legislation. In the final analysis, the House of Lords has an advisory role to the Commons and little real power.

In 1909 Chancellor of the Exchequer Lloyd George proposed a radical budget introducing the first old age pensions. Many in the House of Lords voted against this budget, threatening to kill it off and send government finances into chaos. The Liberal government wasn't having unelected peers telling it what to do over such a crucial issue so it passed the 1911 Parliament Act. In effect, this Act removed the right of the House of Lords to vote down legislation sent to it by the House of Commons.

Britain has an unwritten constitution based on tradition, custom and convention. This situation is best highlighted by the fact that the Parliament Act is used very rarely indeed. In effect, if members of the House of Lords don't like legislation sent to them by the House of Commons they vote against it and ask the Commons to reconsider; on the third and final reading, however, even if their concerns haven't been reflected in amendments to the legislation, they'll vote it through anyway. Why? Well, many peers in the House of Lords recognise that the House of Commons, as the elected body, has the greater rights and opposing its bills isn't their job.

Lording it Up: The Job of Peers

Members of the House of Lords aren't elected by you and me. Instead, they get to sit in that chamber because they're peers of the realm – which sounds very grand and is. Their official title is 'lords'.

Before taking up their seat in the House of Lords, the peer has first to attend a ceremony to swear an oath of allegiance to the monarch. For this occasion, they dress up in ermine-trimmed ceremonial robes.

In the past, being a lord brought all sorts of extra legal rights and powers – in effect, they were considered extra special; some lived in castles and kept their own armed forces. Nowadays, being a lord is less about castles – although some still live in them – and more about ceremony. Modern lords either inherit their title or are appointed by the PM to sit in the House of

Lords. As well as attending the State Opening of Parliament when the monarch reads out the government's legislative programme for the parliamentary session ahead, the lords also have other key jobs to play in Britain's parliamentary democracy, including:

- ✔ Voting on whether to accept or reject legislation drawn up by the House of Commons.
- ✔ Proposing amendments to legislation drawn up by the House of Commons.
- ✔ Debating legislation drawn up by the House of Commons.
- ✔ Introducing new laws to be debated.

The House of Lords does draw up legislation but all the really important laws tend to start their journey through the legislative process from the House of Commons.

Members of the House of Lords don't have a constituency – although their title may refer to a particular part of the country, the association is merely ceremonial. Not having a constituency means not having constituents to listen to and solve the problems of. However, peers often have a specialist area of knowledge, such as education or the military, which means that individuals and pressure groups who also have concerns in these areas will contact them so as to express their views on aspects of legislation.

Until 1999 up to 700 peers who'd inherited their titles – called, catchily enough, *hereditary peers* – were allowed to sit in the House of Lords and take part in votes. However, this state of affairs was deemed undemocratic and most of the hereditary peers were turfed out by the Labour government of the day under PM Tony Blair. As a compromise, a small group of hereditary peers – just 92 – were allowed to keep their seats in the Lords. Nowadays membership of the Lords is by appointment and not through birth (apart from the remaining hereditary peers).

Gauging the independence of the peers

Party loyalty tends to play a less important role in the House of Lords than in the Commons. Peers are often older than MPs as they've had notable careers in industry, the sciences, the military or the House of Commons itself before being appointed to the House of Lords. Lords have been there, done it and got the T-shirt – although lined with ermine, of course! Members of the House of Lords aren't usually in politics in order to carve a career. As a result, they're generally less likely to follow the dictates of a political party leadership and often, in fact, express their own views strongly.

Whereas MPs who go against their party leaders can expect to be ignored when government jobs are handed out, or even deselected by their local party as a future parliamentary candidate, peers have less to lose by being free thinkers. Some say this situation is healthy for Britain's parliamentary democracy because it means that the political party machines aren't all-powerful and leave room for individual expression – which often happens in the House of Lords.

However, the House of Lords has much less real power than the House of Commons, so in effect the free thinking of some peers and independence in voting and opinions has only a marginal impact on the make-up of the laws passing through parliament.

Some members of the Lords don't belong to a particular party grouping. These peers are referred to as *crossbenchers* and they literally sit on benches opposite the throne in the House of Lords rather than on the side of the government or their opponents.

Nominating peers for life

The prime minister has the job of nominating peers to sit in the House of Lords – for life, if he or she wishes. Thus, they're called *life peers*. Once they die, their title lapses.

On the face of it, nominating peers seems a huge constitutional power in the hands of the PM and the PM alone. However, it has become convention for the PM to ask the leaders of the two main opposition parties to submit names for inclusion. So, in practice, in 2009 Gordon Brown as PM asked Conservative leader David Cameron and Liberal Democrat leader Nick Clegg for a list of men and women to include in the list of new life peers.

Usually, the PM – of whatever party – tries to draw up a final list of peers which ensures that their party has a majority of supporters in the House of Lords but also gives the other parties a substantial number of sympathetic peers.

The PM sends the list of life peers to the monarch for approval but this is just a technicality. The monarch always approves the peers that the PM wants because of a constitutional convention that the monarch must always take the advice of the PM. (Chapter 11 explains the inner workings of the British constitution.)

Lots of life peers have a right to sit in the House of Lords but only a fraction of these people regularly do so. Instead, they choose to simply accept the title but not take part in the legislative process.

When an individual is made into a lord, they're *enobled*, which means that they're now a member of the nobility. In Britain's ancient class system the nobility are right near the top of the social hierarchy – just below the monarch in the pecking order, to be precise.

Introducing Bills

In the UK, laws only come about when the House of Commons, House of Lords and the monarch all agree. These days the agreement of the monarch is a given because, according to Britain's unwritten constitution, he or she has to agree to new laws made by parliament (see Chapter 11 for more on this). What's more, the House of Lords can only suggest changes to legislation drawn up by the Commons. So, in a power battle between the House of Commons, House of Lords and the monarch, there'll only be one winner – the Commons.

Laws can emanate from both the House of Commons and the Lords. A proposed new law debated by parliament is called a *bill*. The two types of bill are:

- ✔ **Public or government bills:** These are sponsored by the government, with wording carefully drawn up by civil servants and introduced by the minister responsible for that area of government. So, for example, a bill proposing extending compulsory education to age 18 would be introduced by the Minister for Children, Schools and Families.

   Government bills nearly always become law because the ministers who introduce them can rely on a majority of MPs to support them.

- ✔ **Private members' bills:** These are sponsored by individual backbench MPs in the House of Commons. Private members' bills have only a marginal chance of success – about 1 in 10 bills become law – as the amount of debating time given to them isn't large, and if the government opposes them, they don't have a chance of getting a majority.

Government bills are introduced by the minister responsible for the area the bill affects. For example, a new bill on the future of pensions would be introduced by the Minister for Work and Pensions.

Explaining government bills

Government introduces bills for a number of reasons, including the following:

- ✔ **To fulfil manifesto pledges:** During elections, each party states in their manifesto what they'll do if they get elected. These promises will form the basis of their policies. The party that gets into power is then expected to carry these pledges through by introducing new laws.

✔ **To maintain the regular workings of government:** Each parliamentary session the government is expected to introduce a Budget, or Finance Bill, which sets up the legal framework for the collection of taxes. Without this bill government can't raise the cash to fund day-to-day operations.

✔ **To deal with an emergency:** Sometimes a major event, such as a war or outbreak of disease, means that new laws are needed fast. In this scenario, other Bills are put on the backburner and parliamentary time is freed up to allow the government to introduce its new law.

Often, the government consults pressure groups and interested parties prior to introducing new legislation. (Chapter 9 has more on the role of pressure groups in forming government policy.)

Circulating new ideas: Government Green Papers

Often, before introducing a new bill to parliament, the government checks out what interested parties think by publishing a *Green Paper*. In this document the government sets out its ideas and presents what it thinks are the policy options. Interested parties can then comment on the contents of the Paper and the government can take their views into account when it finally publishes its White Paper, which I explain in the next section.

Green Papers are only appropriate when the government has time to spend on introducing the new law. In the case of an emergency, the government won't bother with a Green Paper, moving straight to introducing the bill to parliament.

Moving the law along: The White Paper stage

A *White Paper* is the final stage before an actual bill is introduced to parliament. The minister whose area of responsibility the bill falls into uses the reaction to the Green Paper and the policy proposals contained within it to inform the contents of the White Paper. Some proposals in the Green Paper fall by the wayside while others make it into the White Paper.

The minister who'll be introducing the bill to parliament shows the White Paper to his or her colleagues in cabinet and to the PM, and they debate its contents. Again, changes may be made, particularly when the Bill could affect many different departments. Usually, following White Paper stage, a bill is drawn up by civil servants and this bill is then introduced to the House of Commons or in some cases the Lords first.

Introducing private members' bills

Although private members' bills have only a slim chance of actually passing into law, it doesn't stop individuals trying. Bills brought to parliament by backbench MPs can be devoted to big issues of the day or to addressing very small local concerns.

Long, hot, stinking summer

Parliament enjoys a long summer holiday – a bit like schoolchildren – as a result of tradition. Until the 20th century, the River Thames gave off an awful stink in the summer months and being close to its banks when the weather was warm was considered very unhealthy. Therefore, it was decided that parliament shouldn't sit during the hot, summer months. This tradition has continued, which some cynics say is very convenient indeed for the MPs and peers.

Time is short, with only 13 Fridays each parliamentary session set aside for private members' bills to be debated and voted upon. What's more, debates often only contain a handful of MPs because many members return to their constituency homes on Thursday evenings.

The four methods MPs use to introduce their private members' bills are:

- ✔ **A bills ballot:** Because only very limited time is allocated to hearing private members' bills, a pre-selection process is in place. MPs put their private members' bills on a list and the 20 most popular according to a ballot of MPs are allowed to be presented to the Commons on an allotted Friday.

- ✔ **Ten-minute bill:** I said debate time was short, but ten minutes? Individual MPs are allowed ten minutes of parliamentary time to present the case for a new piece of legislation. However, these bills very, very rarely make it into law. Generally, a ten-minute bill is used as a chance for the MP introducing it to bring greater publicity to a particular area of concern or to a policy hobby-horse.

- ✔ **Bills from the House of Lords:** Peers are allowed to introduce their own bills in the House of Lords and they can team up with an MP who'll introduce it in the House of Commons as well.

- ✔ **Standing Order No. 57:** I know it sounds like a perfume but this order is actually a parliamentary procedure allowing individual MPs to introduce this type of bill on a Friday (the time set aside for this procedure) without making a supporting speech – which saves on precious time. The MPs literally get to read the bill (if they want) and can vote to debate it if it tickles their fancy. Usually, though, Standing Order No. 57 Bills don't make it to debating stage.

A private members' Bill has the best chance of making it into law if it's introduced in a ballot. Success in the ballot brings debating time and means that a bedrock of support amongst MPs is already in place. However, the overwhelming majority of ballot bills don't make it into law either.

As far as MPs introducing their own private members' bills goes, time is the enemy. Very limited time is allowed for debating and voting on the bill and sometimes MPs will debate a Bill for so long that no time remains for a vote.

Getting Bills Passed: The Process

Parliament operates to a strict calendar. Each year around November or just after a general election – a new parliamentary session begins, with the monarch visiting parliament and making a speech outlining what bills the government hopes to introduce into parliament in the coming session. During this session debates take place and laws are voted on. During Christmas, Easter and over the summer, parliament doesn't sit and is referred to as being in *recess*. The amount of time parliament has in recess varies. If a general election is held, that can alter things. But parliament is often in recess. In the 2008–09 parliamentary session for example, Christmas recess ran from 19th December to 12th January, then Easter recess from 3rd to 20th April and the summer recess ran from 22nd August through to 12th October. Better than school holidays!

Detailing the passage of bills

Bills have to jump over lots of hurdles and undergo oodles of scrutiny before they can become law. But government bills usually have a majority of supporters, hence these bills usually get through even when opposition parties and pressure groups outside the UK parliament don't support them.

A bill must pass through these stages:

- ✔ **First reading in the Commons.** MPs vote on whether the bill will pass to the next stage of the process.

- ✔ **Second reading in the Commons.** MPs vote on whether the bill will now be sent to a parliamentary committee for closer scrutiny.

- ✔ **Committee stage.** Here, the bill is examined by the relevant Commons standing committee. For example, a pensions bill is examined by a committee of MPs put together specifically to examine it (I explain the types of committees in 'Poring Over the Detail: Parliamentary Committees' later in the chapter). Individual MPs can *table* – put forward – amendments to the bill, and these are debated by the committee. The committee then sends the bill back to the Commons with some amendments attached.

- **Report stage.** The House of Commons considers the amendments proposed by the committee and may attach new amendments.

- **Third reading in the Commons.** The bill and its amendments are voted on again. Usually, the amendments are only accepted if the minister who has introduced the bill agrees to them.

  The government will tell its MPs to vote for or against amendments.

  Once the bill passes third reading, it's sent to the House of Lords, where it again goes through a process of first, second and third readings.

The House of Lords has the power to table its own amendments to the bill. The bill is then sent back to the House of Commons and the amendments debated and voted on. The House of Commons does, however, have the ultimate say over whether or not amendments from the Lords see the light of day.

Though rarely used, the House of Lords has the right to vote down a bill. Doing so doesn't kill the bill off, however, it merely delays it for a year. The bill is presented to the Monarch to be given royal assent; however, the legislation doesn't come into force for one year. The exception is the government Budget: if the Lords vote against this it can be sent to the monarch for royal assent and it becomes law straight away.

By taking a vote the House of Commons can choose to bypass the committee stage of a bill. It will thus pass straight from second to third reading. Cutting this stage speeds up the process of law making and is useful in emergency situations.

If the bill falls at any one of the above hurdles, it won't become law.

When little debating time is available in the House of Commons, the government may choose to introduce its bill to the House of Lords for debate first. The bill still has to jump the same number of hurdles – first, second and third reading – but it may do so in a slightly different order. MPs and members of the House of Lords may team up to introduce a bill and they can choose to go through the Commons or Lords route.

Talking it over: Debating

When an MP refers to a fellow member in the House of Commons he or she always prefaces the comment with either 'my honourable friend' or 'the honourable member'. The word *friend* is used to indicate that the MP is on the same side as the MP speaking, while *member* refers to an MP from an opposition political party. So a Labour MP will refer to a fellow Labour MP as honourable friend and a Conservative MP as honourable member.

Sitting by tradition

On the floors of both the House of Commons and the House of Lords even the seating is dictated by tradition and parliamentary custom. In both houses the governing party occupies the seats to the right of the Speaker's chair – from the viewpoint of the Speaker – and government ministers sit on the very front bench. Opposite them sit the MPs from the opposition parties. The biggest opposition party occupies the benches closest to the Speaker's chair, while the third-biggest party and any representatives from minor parties sit in the bottom left of the chamber as the Speaker sees it.

The chambers of both Houses are quite small (though they look much bigger on television), and when all the MPs and lords are in attendance not everyone can sit down and many members have to stand in the gangways. The actual distance between the benches occupied by the government and the opposition parties is also very small. In fact, two red lines roughly two sword lengths apart are marked on the floor of the House of Commons chamber and members from either party aren't allowed to cross them.

The seating arrangement in the Commons and Lords pits opposition parties physically against each other across a small distance and aids what's seen as a very adversarial approach to politics. Debates can often become very heated as members look into each other's eyes. Most other parliaments around the globe have bigger debating chambers, with members sat in rows or in a circle rather than eyeballing one another as happens at Westminster.

The Leader of the House (a position I describe in 'Tying Up the Loose Ends: The Other Parliamentary Players' later in the chapter) dictates how much parliamentary time is spent on a particular bill – with the assistance of his or her party whips – but the Leader doesn't have a completely free hand. The main opposition party, usually either Conservative or Labour, has the right to a set number of opposition days each session, when other business has to be set aside and the opposition gets to debate an aspect of government policy. Generally, opposition days are chosen so as to cause maximum embarrassment to the government. So, for example, a scandal relating to mismanagement in the National Health Service (NHS) would lead to the shadow Leader of the House (the main opposition party's equivalent to the Leader of the House) putting in a request for an opposition day debate on, you've guessed it, mismanagement in the NHS.

Once a debate begins, the Speaker presides and he or she calls individual MPs to speak in the debate. After the time set for the debate has elapsed (and this is set out on a case-by-case basis, from an hour or two to several days), it's up to the Speaker to bring the debate to an end. If the debate is over a piece of legislation, the Speaker calls on MPs to cast their vote to see whether it should move onto the next stage of the legislative process. The result of the vote is announced on the floor of the House of Commons.

Minding your language in parliament

The UK parliament is an ancient institution with all sorts of solemn, confusing and downright silly traditions. Minding your language is one of them. Certain words and phrases are considered inappropriate to use on the floor of either House.

If an MP or lord breaks the rules and conventions of the House, the Speaker (see 'Keeping Order: The Role of the Speaker' later in this chapter) will take action. Such action can involve public censure, asking the MP or lord to withdraw the comment or even, in some cases, suspending that person from sitting in the House – the equivalent of being told to stand outside the classroom at school.

Some of the things you're not allowed to say include:

- **Rude words or swearing:** Parliament is supposed to be a serious place and language that is deemed offensive and insulting is way out of line.

- **Accusations of lying:** MPs and lords may think an opposition member is telling porkies but they're not allowed to accuse them of lying. In fact, any suggestion that a member is being dishonest is ruled out of order. The Speaker will ask any member who accuses another of lying to withdraw the comment.

- **Direct insults:** Personal insults directed at a fellow member aren't allowed. Over time, the Speaker of the Commons has ruled the following words as being out of order: coward, hooligan, git (yes, git!), traitor, stoolpigeon (delightfully 1930s gangster movie language), sod, slime, warty and, wait for it… guttersnipe. Referring to a member as being drunk or under the influence of illegal narcotics is also out of order. The only person allowed to drink alcohol in the chamber is the Chancellor, when delivering the Budget speech.

Even the government is affected by the lack of debating time available in each parliamentary session and has to prioritise which bills it really wants to make into law. As a result, a newly elected government may take a couple of years to introduce the new laws it promised in its manifesto. Government bills get the most parliamentary time while private members' bills have to survive on the scraps.

In an emergency, laws can be passed in a matter of hours or days. The Finance Bill usually takes a few weeks to make it into law. Most government bills do take a few months, though, as they're debated vociferously and scrutinised by committees of MPs.

Members of the House of Commons and House of Lords enjoy *parliamentary privilege*. This privilege means they can say what they want in the debating chambers of these two Houses without fear of action being brought for libel or slander. However, members must be polite. The nearby sidebar, 'Minding your language in parliament', explains what can and can't be said. What's more, members are free from arrest on civil matters within the Palace of Westminster. However, this is not the case if they're sought for a criminal offence.

Icing the legislative cake: Receiving royal assent

Even after a bill has been through the exhaustive process of numerous votes and debates in the House of Commons and House of Lords, it still isn't actually law. No bill from parliament can become law without being signed by the monarch – grandly termed *being given royal assent*. The monarch is presented with the Act of Parliament to sign.

Getting the monarch's signature is partly a constitutional convention but is also meant to be a final check on the law making of parliament. However, the monarch must always follow the advice of ministers, which in this instance means he or she must sign or risk sparking a constitutional crisis.

A few weeks usually take place between the bill passing through parliament and it receiving royal assent and becoming law. In emergencies, though, the monarch's signature can usually be obtained in double-quick time.

Without the signature of the monarch the bill doesn't actually become law. Once it becomes law, the bill changes into an Act of Parliament, which sounds very grand and official, and is!

Poring Over the Detail: Parliamentary Committees

Much of the work of parliament is carried out by committees of MPs and, to a lesser extent, committees of lords. Two main types of committee exist:

- ✔ **Standing committee.** A temporary committee formed to examine a particular bill.
- ✔ **Select committee.** A permanent committee whose job it is to scrutinise the effects of legislation already on the statute book or examine the decisions taken by ministers.

These committees can shadow a particular department or they may look across the activities of a host of different departments. In short, though, parliamentary committees are a big deal, whose meetings are sometimes televised and in which experts from different walks of life are called to give evidence.

Looking at standing committees

Standing committees are set up temporarily to examine a particular bill put before parliament. The job of a standing committee is to debate and consider amendments to the bill they've been asked to examine.

The phrase *standing committee* is very confusing – as with many terms used in parliament. Because the committee is only in existence temporarily, sometimes its work is done and it's disbanded within a few weeks – so it doesn't stand for very long at all.

Membership of the committee is decided according to the number of MPs each party has in parliament as a whole. In a committee with 30 places to fill, the majority of members would come from the government party (reflecting the fact that it has a majority of MPs), a large minority from the biggest opposition party and a smaller minority from the third-biggest party, and so on until all 30 places are filled. The key is that the committee is meant to be a microcosm of parliament and reflect the relative size of the parties (in terms of seats won) as closely as possible. So if one party has two thirds of the seats in parliament its members make up two thirds of the members of each standing committee.

A government with a significant majority of seats in the House of Commons can usually expect to see its legislation go through committee stage without too many unwelcome amendments. MPs may tack on amendments which don't undermine the basic thrust of the legislation and instead look to improve it, and the government may look at these amendments and agree that they're a good idea.

Standing committees tend to have quite large memberships – anything from 14 to 50 members. Interestingly, members of standing committees sit with members of their own party, opposite the opposition parties. Therefore, Conservative members of a standing committee sit opposite Labour members. This seating arrangement can make committee meetings quite adversarial in character.

The individual party whips decide which of their party members get to sit on the standing committees. This is in contrast to select committees (discussed in the next section) where MPs get to choose which of their colleagues will be the chairperson, for example.

Examining select committees

Much of the work of standing committees doesn't gain public attention, whereas select committees – permanent committees that meet regularly – are sometimes televised and have produced real set pieces of political theatre.

Typing select committees

Two types of select committee exist:

- ✔ **Departmental.** These examine the actions of a particular government department or the effects of laws in that area.

- ✔ **Non-departmental.** As the name suggests, these committees aren't related to a particular government department. Instead, they focus on the general operation of government as a whole, the internal running of parliament and even UK relations with the European Union (EU).

Of around 20 departmental select committees, the major ones include:

- ✔ **Treasury.** This influential committee looks at how well the Treasury is performing – is it, for example, collecting taxes and paying benefits as efficiently as it ought? It also examines areas of wider public life relating to finance.

  In recent years, the committee held public meetings with Britain's top bankers to examine how the credit crunch came about and even questioned prominent financial journalists over their reporting of the 2008 worldwide banking crisis.

- ✔ **Foreign Affairs.** This committee launched an extensive inquiry into the reasons for Britain going to war in Iraq in 2003.

- ✔ **Defence.** This committee looks at how the ministry of defence spends its money and equips the UK's armed forces.

- ✔ **Health.** This committee examines how the government manages the National Health Service as well as aspects of public health.

- ✔ **Home Affairs.** This committee examines the workings of the criminal justice system and the police.

- ✔ **Education.** This committee examines the state education and university system.

The relative importance of the select committee reflects the importance of the department whose work it's shadowing. For example, the treasury select committee is considered very important and membership of it is prized by MPs because it shadows the work of the treasury, the most important government department. (See Chapter 13 for more on which ministries are the real powerhouses in British government.)

A whole host of committees don't follow a particular department but still examine an aspect of UK government or the running of parliament itself. Lots of these committees exist but here are some of the most important:

✔ **Public Accounts.** The most prominent non-departmental committee, Public Accounts is well known for examining how government spends its money and bringing waste to light.

✔ **Public Administration Committee.** This examines the work of the parliamentary ombudsman, a position I explain in 'Tying Up the Loose Ends: The Other Parliamentary Players' later in this chapter.

✔ **Standards and Privileges.** This is dedicated to monitoring the behaviour of MPs.

✔ **European Scrutiny Committee.** This looks at laws being passed by the EU.

Like standing committees, places on select committees are allotted according to party size in the House of Commons. Therefore the government has a majority on all the select committees. However, one of the MPs has to chair the committee and he or she's elected to this post through a ballot of MPs (in the case of Commons committees) or peers (in the case of Lords committees).

Working out what select committees do

Committees meet about once a week while parliament is in session. They question ministers and civil servants, and call witnesses from the general public with special skills or knowledge.

Although committees can question ministers and ask for information from ministries, the minister or their civil servants aren't automatically obliged to tell the committee what they know or give them access to private departmental documents. Ministers and civil servants who want to keep their dealings secret can always cite national security for not fessing up and telling the committee everything they know. For example, during the exhaustive Foreign Affairs Select Committee's examination of the reasons for war in Iraq, the committee were often met with the argument that to disclose certain information would put national security or the work of the intelligence services at risk.

The House of Lords has its own committees but these don't tend to play a major role in legislative procedure and often their public meetings and investigations get little or no media coverage. This situation reflects the subservient role of the Lords to the Commons in Britain's parliamentary democracy.

Keeping Order: The Role of the Speaker

One of the most notable figures in parliament is the Speaker of the House of Commons. He or she sits on a chair between the government and opposition benches. The Speaker is an ancient role, dating back to 1376.

GREAT FIGURES

Introducing two notable Speakers

The Speaker is a major figure, not only in parliament but also in British politics. The Speaker may not have the power of the PM or a leading cabinet member but he or she embodies the grand old institution of parliament, and is the protector of its traditions and privileges. Elected by a ballot of MPs, the Speaker is often a larger-than-life and colourful character. Two of the recent sitters in this particular hot seat are:

✓ **Betty Boothroyd** was the first female Speaker of the House of Commons. She acted in the role from 1992 to 2000 and was widely regarded as a highly competent Speaker. Ms Boothroyd often displayed a sense of humour while at the same time maintaining strict discipline. Remarkably,

Ms Boothroyd was used to life in the limelight; as a young woman in the 1940s she'd been a member of the Tiller Girls, a famous dance troupe of the day.

✓ **Michael Martin** became the first Speaker in four centuries to have to resign the post. Martin was deemed by many to be partly responsible for lax monitoring of MPs' expenses. The MPs' expenses scandal of 2009 – see Chapter 23 for more on this – caused widespread discontent amongst the public and the media. What many viewed as Martin's mishandling of the expenses regime and the ensuing crisis led to many MPs calling for him to resign. He duly did so in May 2009.

The Speaker's main jobs are:

✓ Ensuring that the procedures of the House of Commons are followed to the letter.

✓ Deciding which MPs are allowed to speak in debates.

✓ Ensuring that MPs behave themselves and don't use un-parliamentary language (see the 'Minding your language in parliament' sidebar earlier in the chapter for more on this).

✓ Disciplining MPs who don't behave themselves. Sanctions include naming them publicly to suspending their privileges as an MP.

The Speaker of the House of Commons is elected by a ballot of all MPs. This is a free vote, which means the party whips don't try to influence how MPs vote (see Chapter 8 for more on the role of the whips). MPs are presented with a list of candidates – any MP can put his or her name on this list – from which they pick who they'd like to be Speaker. Once elected, the Speaker will sit for the duration of the parliament.

REMEMBER

The Speaker is supposed to be independent and, although a sitting MP and belonging to a particular party, he or she only votes when a tie occurs, which is very rare indeed.

The House of Lords has its own Speaker but he or she is nowhere near as powerful as the Speaker in the Commons. The Speaker of the Lords isn't allowed to call an end to debates or tell members to sit down and shut up. In addition, if two peers want to talk at the same time, the Speaker doesn't get to decide who'll have the floor. Other members – normally through pointing – determine who gets to speak.

Tying Up the Loose Ends: The Other Parliamentary Players

As well as the Speaker (see preceding section), several other significant figures play an important role in the UK parliament:

- ✔ **Leader of the House:** This is a government minister whose job it is to set out what debates and bills will be presented before parliament in the forthcoming session. The Leader's role is crucial because the amount of time given to a debate often dictates whether or not a bill will make it through first-, second- and third-reading stages. The Leader generally gives preference to government bills.

- ✔ **Parliamentary ombudsman** – The basic job of the parliamentary ombudsman is to investigate maladministration by the government which may have harmed the public. The ombudsman generally sticks to big subjects and spends a long time hearing evidence, writing reports and making recommendations about how the government can right its wrongs. As government gets bigger and stretches into different walks of life, the workload of the parliamentary ombudsman steadily increases.

- ✔ **Black Rod:** The role of Gentleman Usher of the Black Rod, to give this person's full title, dates back to 1350. Black Rod is in charge of security in the House of Lords and accompanies the monarch when he or she attends the State Opening of a new session of parliament.

- ✔ **Serjeant at Arms:** This individual is in charge of security in the House of Commons. The Serjeant's job is to escort MPs out of the chamber who've been asked to leave by the Speaker. Usually, the people who become Serjeant at Arms – and Black Rod – are former members of the UK police force or military.

Chapter 13

Gazing at the Summit: The PM and Cabinet

. . . .

In This Chapter

▶ Taking in the prime minister

▶ Looking at cabinet responsibilities

▶ Meeting the bigwig cabinet members

▶ Moving things around in the cabinet

. . . .

*T*his is the chapter to read if you want to know about the real bigwigs in British politics – the ministers and the prime minister – whose decisions affect your daily life, propel the economy into boom or bust, and even send soldiers to war.

The prime minister and cabinet are at the very pinnacle of British politics and in this chapter I explain why they're so powerful and how they run the government day in, day out.

Going Straight to the Top: The Prime Minister

Whoever is prime minister (PM) is the most important person in British politics, the big cheese, the head honcho, the main man or woman – you get the idea!

The PM wields so much power for a whole host of reasons, including that the PM:

- ✔ Leads the biggest political party in the House of Commons, the main law-making body in the country.

- ✔ Gets to appoint ministers who perch at the top of all the main branches of government, called ministries, which I talk more about in 'Concentrating on the Cabinet' later in this chapter.

- ✔ Gets to decide the ministers to sit in the *cabinet*, the key decision-making body of government.

- ✔ Appoints junior ministers and has a say in senior civil service appointments.

- ✔ Usually takes the lead in forming government policy, and when disagreements occur amongst ministers or MPs, the PM makes the final call.

- ✔ Oversees how government is organised, and can actually set up or abolish whole government departments.

- ✔ Chairs meetings of the cabinet, where the government takes key policy decisions and sets the legislative programme for parliament.

- ✔ May not be the head of state – that's the monarch's role – but he or she represents the country when visiting other states and is very much the nation's leader.

Much of the PM's power derives from the fact that he or she also leads the biggest political party in the House of Commons. The role of party leader is also very powerful (see Chapter 8 for more on the inner workings of political parties).

As you can probably imagine, just one of the many jobs a PM has to do would be more than enough for most individuals to cope with. The PM often has to work long hours and is always in the public eye, with his or her slightest move causing comment. In some ways, being the PM resembles being a major celebrity but without the option of selling your wedding photos. Seriously, though, the job of PM is exhausting and deeply taxing and a few of the people who reach this pinnacle aren't always up to the task.

The PM lives and works in 10 Downing Street. From the outside, Number 10 seems little more than a grand Georgian terrace house – which it is – but behind its famous black door exists an inordinate amount of office space. In fact, the PM's residence resembles Doctor Who's TARDIS small on the outside, cavernous on the inside. The PM doesn't live and work at 10 Downing Street full time. As a perk of the job, he or she gets the use of a country estate called Chequers, in which to entertain visiting world leaders.

Facing Prime Minister's Questions

Prime Minister's Questions (PMQs) is one of the great set-piece events in British political life. Each Wednesday when parliament is in session the PM goes to the House of Commons and answers questions from MPs about the governance of the country for around 30 minutes. Most of the time, though, is taken up with questions from the leaders of the main opposition party and the third-biggest party in the Commons (usually the Liberal Democrats). PMQs gives backbench MPs a chance – albeit a very limited one – to put their own questions to the most important politician in the country.

The idea of PMQs is for the head honcho to explain what government is doing and for its actions to come under scrutiny. In recent years questioning during PMQs has often had more than one eye on creating a sound bite for the television news bulletins. However, PMQs is still dramatic and gaffes made by the PM or opposition leaders can become big news stories.

Getting to be the PM

Only one person can be PM at any one time and the job doesn't change hands that often. In fact, since 1979 we've had only four prime ministers. With the thousands of politicians around the UK, the odds on becoming PM are very long indeed. For well over a century all of the PMs have followed this path:

- ✔ **Get elected as an MP.** All PMs for the past century have been members of parliament.

- ✔ **Get elected party leader.** It's a constitutional convention that only a party leader can be the prime minister.

- ✔ **Get a House of Commons majority.** The monarch asks the leader of the party with the majority of seats in the House of Commons to form the government and be prime minister. No majority, no keys to number 10!

The prime minister is appointed by the monarch but in reality the monarch has little choice. By a convention of Britain's unwritten constitution, the monarch must appoint a PM capable of rallying a majority of MPs in the House of Commons. As such, the leader of the largest political party in the House of Commons usually gets the job.

By constitutional convention, PMs must also be Members of Parliament (MPs) as they're supposed to have a majority in the House of Commons. The last time a member of the House of Lords was also PM was way back in 1895, when Lord Salisbury was appointed to the role.

Gauging if the PM is really 'first amongst equals'

The PM is supposed to be *primus inter pares*, which means 'first amongst equals'. The PM is first because he or she heads up the government and is the face that the electorate knows best, but equal because he or she chairs the cabinet rather than telling it what to do.

In theory, each member of the cabinet has an equal say in what policy the government pursues. But theories don't always work out in reality, and despite the pretty Latin phrases and the idea of equality, the power that the PM wields – particularly to hire and fire government ministers – means that he or she is far more than an equal. In fact, usually what the PM says goes and any minister wishing to oppose him or her had better have their arguments well stacked up.

Limiting the power of the PM

Some PMs take a dictatorial approach to the job but even they know that they're not untouchable. The power of the PM is built on powerful pillars but through political misjudgements or bad luck these pillars, over time, can crumble away and the power base of a PM erode. In fact, even the most successful PMs last little more than a decade in modern times and many have to high-tail it out of 10 Downing Street much sooner. Someone once said that all great political careers end in failure and that is especially true for the PM.

Some of the ways the PM can have their power constrained or simply find themselves out of a job include:

✔ **Losing an election.** The PM is always the head of a political party, and if that party does badly at an election then it loses its majority in the House of Commons, which means that the monarch asks whoever leads the new majority party to form the government. In other words, the PM is turfed out along with the government.

✔ **Losing party support.** Much of the PM's power comes from being the head of a political party. However, when it comes to leaders and political parties, power is a two-way street. If the PM doesn't follow policies popular with the rank and file of the party or is seen as ineffective or a bad leader then he or she loses support. Ultimately, the leader can even be replaced as party leader in an internal ballot. If this happens, the job of PM is automatically lost too.

✔ **Losing cabinet confidence.** The PM may be the head honcho in cabinet and have the job of hiring and firing ministers but these ministers have their own following in the party, media and wider general public. In short, certain ministers are harder for the PM to sack or ignore than others. If enough of these minsters gang up on the PM, then the person being turfed out of office may well be the PM. Although they're superpowerful, PMs have to govern with the consent of their cabinet colleagues and, more generally, the MPs and members of the party they head up.

All the main political parties have a mechanism for getting rid of their leader. Doing so often involves a substantial minority of MPs proposing that someone else should be leader. If this candidate has enough support, a leadership election takes place. Very few party leaders survive a serious leadership challenge.

Sometimes MPs want to give their leader a warning to let him or her know that they're unhappy with his or her behaviour. In the past, this warning has led to a leadership election and a stalking horse candidate running for the top job. A *stalking horse* isn't a very serious contender because he or she doesn't have enough support and experience. Instead, the role is to galvanise opponents of the party leader into taking action.

Observing the changing nature of the PM's relationship with the cabinet

It used to be that PMs used meetings of the cabinet as a way to thrash out ideas and genuinely debate policy initiatives. The diaries of former Labour minister Tony Benn revealed that in the 1960s and 1970s, under PM Harold Wilson, cabinet meetings were a real hotbed of discussion. Some meetings would go on for hours, often involving heated disagreements.

But in the 1980s, under Margaret Thatcher, cabinet meetings changed in character, with the thoughts of the PM taking centre stage. Members of the cabinet could argue with the fearsome Mrs T but they needed to come well prepared and accept that sometimes – particularly in her final few years as PM – she wouldn't listen.

In the 1990s and 2000s, under Tony Blair, cabinet culture changed again. Government policy was being formed elsewhere – in cabinet committees or by the PM with his close advisers. Cabinet meetings became less about debate and more about ministers simply reporting their progress in pushing policy through. Instead of lasting many hours, cabinet meetings would be over in an hour or under.

Many argue that, as a result of these changes, the cabinet is no longer as powerful a body in the constitution as it once was. Any idea, therefore, that the PM is first amongst equals must probably be consigned to the dustbin of history.

Concentrating on the Cabinet

The cabinet is a group of the top politicians from the ruling political party and its members are called *government ministers*. PMs can bring anyone they want into the cabinet but generally ministers are selected from the ranks of MPs of the governing party in the House of Commons. The odd lord finds their way into the cabinet but these days convention dictates that it's best if elected politicians rather than peers take the top jobs in government.

The job of the cabinet is to decide what policies the government will pursue, and once a policy is decided it's up to whichever minister is overseeing the pursuit of the policy to report back to the cabinet on progress. The PM chairs the cabinet and he or she, with the help of the cabinet secretary and senior civil servants, decides what will be discussed at weekly cabinet meetings. The number of politicians sitting in the cabinet tends to vary. Not all ministers get to sit in the cabinet but with certain jobs, such as Chancellor of the Exchequer or Health Secretary, it automatically follows that by constitutional convention they get to sit in the cabinet. Ultimately, though, the PM decides which minister gets to sit in on cabinet meetings.

Occasionally, a PM wants to give an individual a seat in cabinet – presumably because the PM values that person's advice or acumen – but all the ministries already have a minister in place. Well, that's not a problem! The PM is free to appoint who he or she likes to the cabinet and can simply bestow the title of *minister without portfolio*, which basically means a minister without a government department.

The cabinet has its own secretary. Now this person's job isn't taking notes, booking meeting rooms and ensuring all the ministers have sufficient tea or coffee. Cabinet secretary is one of the most senior civil service jobs in the country. The cabinet secretary runs the Cabinet Secretariat, which provides vital administrative support services for cabinet committees, ensures decisions are consistent across government, monitors how well ministries are following through government policy and circulates minutes from meetings of cabinet and cabinet committees.

Governing the UK is a massive undertaking, with literally thousands of civil servants based in Whitehall alone. In order to ensure that ministries don't go stepping on each other's toes and contradicting one another, the Cabinet Office exists. The role of the Cabinet Office is to ensure that government action is co-ordinated across ministries. In the day-to-day running of the UK government, the Cabinet Office is very important (see Chapter 14 for more).

Taking in the great offices of state

The PM isn't the only big mover and shaker in cabinet; several other posts within government carry with them enormous power. Some ministerial jobs carry more clout and power than others.

At the top of the tree is the PM, of course, but just below this office are other ministers whose jobs are equally historical and whose positions are important. Here's a run-down – PM aside – of the great offices of state:

✔ **Chancellor of the Exchequer.** The Chancellor is second in importance in the UK government only to the PM. This job involves setting government economic policy and ensuring that public finances work. The Chancellor presents a Budget (spring) and Pre-Budget report (autumn) to MPs in parliament that change tax rates and set government spending. The Chancellor also runs the Treasury, which sets the spending budgets for all the other departments of state. And, in politics as in daily life, power often rests with whoever controls the purse strings.

✔ **The Foreign Secretary.** This person oversees foreign policy. The Foreign Secretary's job involves lots of international travel and diplomacy and is often seen as the glamour gig in the UK government. The Foreign Secretary often acquires a high public profile and he or she has control over a big budget and gets to meet world leaders face to face.

✔ **The Home Secretary.** This minister is responsible for policing, national security, internal affairs, immigration and citizenship. In recent years the job of Home Secretary has been something of a poisoned chalice, with successive ministers being sacked or resigning. In fact, the performance of the Home Office as a whole has come under such close scrutiny that, in 2008, the PM decided to remove some of its powers – such as control of the prison service – and give it a newly formed justice ministry. Nevertheless, Home Secretary is still seen as a top government job.

Observing the big beasts of the cabinet jungle

Even the PM has to tread carefully around certain cabinet members. These figures carry *political weight* – what they say and do normally attracts considerable attention in the media and amongst commentators who refer to them, not entirely flatteringly, as the *big beasts*. A minister's big beast status depends on the following:

✔ Whether they occupy one of the great offices of state such as Chancellor of the Exchequer or Foreign Secretary (I cover the great offices of state in the next section).

✔ Whether the individual is popular in the party, with a personal following amongst MPs and party members.

✔ Whether they have wide appeal amongst the public and are well liked or seen as good at their job.

It is possible for a minister to hold high office but not be a big beast because he or she doesn't have a high public profile or wide popularity in the party – and the converse is also true. Have high office, strong public profile and a following in the party, however, and you're definitely a big beast.

Sensible PMs try to keep big beasts on board by involving them in decision making and consulting them. Collective cabinet responsibility, which I describe in the upcoming 'Explaining collective cabinet responsibility' helps keep big beasts reined in as well.

The biggest beast in Tony Blair's cabinet was undoubtedly his Chancellor, Gordon Brown. Blair, knowing that Brown had a lot of support amongst party members and was seen widely as being a capable Chancellor, let him have an enormous say in party policy, particularly over domestic matters. Blair kept tight control of foreign affairs and diplomacy. Brown's power was so great that it was even likened to having two PMs. However, the two men didn't see eye to eye, and their advisers often bickered and briefed against the other side. In fact, in the Labour Party of the late 1990s and 2000s MPs and advisers were often referred to as either being 'Blairites' or 'Brownites'. Brown eventually replaced Blair as PM in 2007.

Looking down the political food chain to other ministerial posts

Outside of the great offices of state around another 30 ministers attend cabinet meetings, which are held once a week, on Thursday. Some of these ministers are called cabinet ministers as they're expected to attend every meeting. These include:

✔ Health Secretary

✔ Education Secretary

✔ Defence Secretary

✔ Leader of the House of Commons

- ✔ Leader of the House of Lords
- ✔ Work and Pensions Secretary
- ✔ Justice Secretary
- ✔ International Development Secretary
- ✔ Transport Secretary
- ✔ Secretary for Business, Enterprise and Regulatory Reform
- ✔ Environment Secretary
- ✔ Secretary for Communities and Local Government
- ✔ Secretary for Culture, Media and Sport
- ✔ Chief Secretary to the Treasury
- ✔ Secretary of State for Wales
- ✔ Secretary of State for Northern Ireland
- ✔ Secretary for the Cabinet Office
- ✔ Secretary for Children, Schools and Families
- ✔ Secretary for Innovation, Universities and Skills

In addition, several cabinet posts exist which may not mean that much – Chancellor of the Duchy of Lancaster and Parliamentary Secretary to the Treasury come to mind. These positions are often given to the people who act as chief whips for the party in the Commons or House of Lords.

Other ministers attend cabinet meetings when their particular area of concern is likely to be discussed either directly or indirectly. The cabinet secretary lets the individual minister know when he or she's expected to attend cabinet meetings. For example, the housing minister isn't actually a cabinet minister but whenever a matter likely to touch on housing is on the cabinet's agenda along will come the housing minister.

Apart from the housing minister, the following ministers get to attend cabinet meetings occasionally:

- ✔ Europe Minister
- ✔ Minister for Olympics and London
- ✔ Minister for Children
- ✔ Minister for Africa, Asia and the UN
- ✔ Attorney General

Assuming Cabinet Responsibilities

A seat in cabinet comes with certain responsibilities – work that the minister is expected to perform for the government. The PM decides who will and won't be a member of the cabinet and if the minister fails to live up to the responsibilities, he or she is likely to be sacked or demoted by the PM at cabinet reshuffle time.

Explaining collective cabinet responsibility

Ministers are supposed to act according to the catchily named *ministerial code*, which states that 'decisions reached by the cabinet are binding on all members of the government'. In short, this means that ministers can disagree with each other as much as they want behind closed doors – and they often do – but once the collective voice of the cabinet has spoken (if a vote's been taken or a majority agree), it's time to get into line.

This concept of public unity is called *collective cabinet responsibility* and is meant to ensure the government seems united in the eyes of the electorate and speaks with one voice. It supposedly makes government action more effective as well.

Publicly stating disagreement with a decision reached by cabinet colleagues is a ministerial cardinal sin. A minister who states that he or she doesn't like a policy or new bill usually resigns from the cabinet or, in some cases, is sacked by the PM.

One of the most contentious issues of the early 2000s was Britain's decision to support the United States-led invasion of Iraq. The PM Tony Blair very much wanted Britain to go to war and he got the support of most of the cabinet; however one minister, Robin Cook, couldn't agree with the decision so he resigned his post. Cook couldn't accept collective cabinet responsibility so he felt he had to go.

Collective cabinet responsibility is close to the heart of PMs because it means that the government can be seen as acting in unison and the electorate likes to think it's governed by people who have a clear purpose. However, often collective responsibility, while not fully breaking down, does become a little frayed. Ministers, while not publicly disagreeing with policies decided upon by cabinet, will get friends and advisers to talk to journalists to let them know what their real feelings are. This dissent is then reported in the media but attributed to an anonymous source. (This is called *briefing* and is an everyday occurrence at Westminster.)

Taking in individual responsibility

As well as a responsibility to their colleagues, cabinet ministers are also responsible for their own ministry. A minister is thus expected to do the following:

- ✔ Explain before parliament the actions of the ministry. A minister may do so in debates in the chamber of the House of Commons or in front of a select committee – see Chapter 12 for more on debates and committee meetings.

- ✔ Take responsibility when senior civil servants within his or her own ministry make mistakes. Ultimately a minister may resign their job because of a mistake carried out by advisers or civil servants.

In recent times the convention that ministers are responsible for the actions of their civil servants and that, ultimately, they should resign if these mistakes come to light has gone a little by the wayside. Under PMs Tony Blair and Gordon Brown ministers have no longer resigned under such circumstances, although Conservative leader David Cameron has argued that they should.

Ministers can't know everything that's going on in their department. In fact, even some major decisions are left to senior civil servants.

Civil servants are supposed to be both independent and permanent employees – therefore surviving changes of government. However, under PM Tony Blair many commentators argued that some senior civil servants had become politicised, meaning that they were biased towards the government of the day in their actions. (Chapter 14 provides an in-depth look at the civil service.)

Working Behind the Scenes: Cabinet Committees

Many of the big government policy decisions are no longer taken by full meetings of the cabinet. Instead, the PM selects a few ministers – often no more than four or five – to sit on small committees whose job it is to form government policy and then present their work to the PM and the cabinet. Obviously, these cabinet committees are hugely important.

Committees are formed because they work more quickly than the full cabinet, mainly as a result of far fewer members being involved They can also be set up and abolished in double-quick time at the PM's say-so, making them very flexible. At any one time generally between 8 and 15 cabinet committees are operating to review important policy areas.

Some ministers sit on several committees at once. For example, Tony Blair's deputy prime minister John Prescott sat on lots of cabinet committees as chairperson. Later, under Gordon Brown, Lord Mandelson fulfilled a similar role.

Over some topics, the PM will have face-to-face meetings with a minister to thrash out policy in his or her area. This approach is a popular method of government for Labour PM Gordon Brown.

Conservative PM Margaret Thatcher was known for her – how shall I put it? – combative leadership style (put simply, she liked a tear-up). She regularly met with ministers face to face to discuss policy and was noted for holding and espousing strong views at cabinet meetings. Thatcher had a very black and white view of politics, and she famously used to ask even her own cabinet colleagues 'are you one of us?', meaning did they hold similar convictions to her. Eventually, fed up with her dictatorial style, Thatcher faced a rebellion of her own MPs and ministers and was forced out of office in 1990.

Shaking Up the Cabinet

Politics can be brutal, particularly near the top of government. Becoming a cabinet minister can take years of hard work and political manoeuvring but careers can be cut short on the decision of the PM or through having to resign. In addition, new politicians move into cabinet and ministers move into different jobs, all at the behest of the PM. As a result, the membership of the cabinet rarely stays the same for very long.

Some suggest these movements are disruptive to the operation of government and that we need politicians in post for a long time so that they can see government policy through properly (and some cabinet members do stay in the same job for years on end). Others suggest that disruptions reduce complacency – with no job-for-life mentality – and keep ministers on their toes.

The day-to-day work of government is done by civil servants (explained in Chapter 14) rather than ministers, so in some respects, which politician is actually the minister may not matter a great deal.

Falling on their sword: Ministerial resignations

Politics is a brutal business and often careers that look destined for the top crash and burn in double-quick time. Even at the top of government, powerful ministers can be happily ensconced in their ministries one minute and out of office and on the backbenches in the Commons the next.

This fall from grace can be sparked by a sacking from cabinet by the PM – see 'Shifting the seats: Cabinet reshuffles' next – but it can also result from the minister resigning.

Now, unlike you and I, who probably resign to go on to a better job elsewhere, ministers who resign do so because of a political or personal issue that dictates that they simply have to go. Some ministers fall on their own sword – resign of their own accord – and others are persuaded to do so by the PM or his or her advisers.

The three main reasons ministers take the long walk off a very short political pier are

- ✔ **Policy differences.** Ministers are bound by collective cabinet responsibility and are supposed to go along with the decisions made by the cabinet. However, sometimes they just can't do it and as a result resign their post. Doing so is called resigning on a matter of principle and is actually viewed as quite an honourable thing to do.

- ✔ **Mistakes.** Ministers make errors – sometimes huge ones – and in such instances opponents often call for their resignation. These days ministers are more likely to try to sit tight but occasionally the media furore and public anger at the boob is so great that the minister in question feels that resigning for what they often say is 'the good of the party' is best. He or she believes that remaining as the minister will damage the party's chances of getting re-elected.

- ✔ **Scandals.** Here's the juiciest reason of the lot (I explore a host of these tabloid fodder stories in Chapter 23). The minister becomes embroiled in a scandal involving, say, some abuse of office, deception or sexual peccadillo and, as a result, he or she feels that it's best to resign for 'the good of the party'.

Politicians need to take great care when lecturing the public on morality. The government of John Major was severely damaged by the Back to Basics scandal, when Conservative PM Major said that he wanted the country to return to Victorian-style morality. Over the next few months the press exposed a host of Conservative MPs for adultery and dodgy financial dealings. Back to Basics was an absolute disaster for the government but great for the tabloid press.

Shifting the seats: Cabinet reshuffles

Once a year, generally, the PM looks to bring new people into the cabinet and get rid of those seen as not up to the job. The PM may also promote those seen as especially loyal, while offloading those seen as potential future leadership challengers.

Cabinet reshuffles are big occasions in UK politics and journalists love them as an opportunity to gossip about which ministers are going up or down. The PM's advisers often brief prominent journalists which minister is likely to go where or sometimes suggest that a particular minister is close to getting the boot so as to keep that individual on their toes.

On the day of a cabinet reshuffle, the PM calls or sees in person all the ministers he or she wants to promote or remove. Waiting to see what the PM will do is extremely nerve-wracking for ministers and their advisers. Some political careers virtually come to an end on reshuffle day.

Not just cabinet ministers get moved on reshuffle day; junior ministers are also shunted about. These people don't hold cabinet rank but do a job within a ministry. For example, within the Department of Work and Pensions is a Secretary of State for Work and Pensions, who's of cabinet rank; below them is one minister for work, one for pensions and even one for pension reform. These junior ministers, almost to a man or woman, want one day to be a cabinet minister but must first prove that they make a good fist of a more lowly post and then catch the eye of the PM.

A cabinet reshuffle day can be very dramatic. Sometimes, for example, ministers don't want to change jobs, while others are disappointed by the post on offer and decide to leave the government. What's more, the whole build-up tends to be highly secretive – although the PM and ministers brief some journalists regarding which ministers are likely to go down and which up – and makes great theatre.

Sometimes the reshuffle is dramatic and changes the fortunes of the government for good or ill. In 1962, Conservative PM Harold Macmillan sacked seven senior cabinet ministers following the Profumo scandal (see Chapter 23 for more on this). The move became known as the Night of the Long Knives and, although a bold step, it didn't have the desired effect. A short time afterwards Macmillan stepped down as PM on medical grounds but by then his savage cabinet reshuffle had led to him losing the confidence of many of his own MPs and cabinet.

Whispering in the PM's Ear: Special Advisers

One of the biggest changes in modern British politics is the rise of the special adviser. A *special adviser* is someone – often a journalist or expert – whose job it is to advise the minister or, in some cases, the PM. He or she may have particular expertise or just be a long-standing trusted confidante of the minister in question. Regardless, special advisers have an enormous behind-the-scenes influence on government policy and, in particular, its presentation in the media and to the wider public. The role of the special adviser, particularly in relation to media manipulation, is explored in Chapter 10. However, during the daily cut and thrust of government a special adviser acts as gatekeeper for the minister, as well as a trusted sounding board and expert. The government of Tony Blair saw a huge explosion in special advisers in Whitehall. Blair alone had upwards of 50 special advisers, whereas the previous PM John Major had a mere 8.

Tony Blair's fondness for political advisers and gradual marginalisation of the full cabinet led some to suggest that he had a presidential style of government, in that he took more decision making onto his shoulders than many previous PMs rather than relying on cabinet colleagues. In fact, Blair seemed to make many key political or policy decisions with a few close confidantes. As a result, Blair's style was termed a *sofa government*: a relaxed method of debate with a handful of people close to him, most notably his press secretary, Alastair Campbell. However, set against this theory is the fact that Blair also ceded much of his authority in domestic policy matters to his Chancellor, Gordon Brown.

Turning to the Opposition: The Shadow Cabinet

Most government ministers have a shadow. A *shadow* refers to an MP from an opposition party whose job it is to put across what policies that party would do if it were in office.

So, when the Secretary of State for Health sets out a new policy on hospital treatment, their shadow will reveal what the opposition party would do about reforming hospital treatment if elected or simply point out what they see as the failings in the government policy.

The *shadow cabinet* is supposed to be a government in waiting and meets regularly in the House of Commons to plan strategy. A shadow cabinet:

- ✔ Sets out policies the opposition party would pursue.
- ✔ Criticises the actions of ministers and exposes what it sees as failings in government.
- ✔ Acts as a potential government, ready and waiting.

The shadow cabinet may one day become the cabinet after an election.

If an opposition party looks likely to win a general election anytime soon, the utterances of people in the shadow cabinet become more important. In fact, in the run-up to an election, members of the shadow cabinet are given a courtesy briefing by civil servants about the state of their departments – what bills they're set to introduce, what their finances are looking like – so that if they win the election they can hit the ground running in their new role.

It used to be the case that only the main opposition party operated a shadow cabinet. So if Labour is in power, the Conservatives would form a shadow cabinet and vice versa. But over the past three decades the number of Lib Dem seats in the House of Commons has grown from a handful to several dozen and it too has formed a shadow cabinet. In 2009, Labour Chancellor Alastair Darling was shadowed by Conservative shadow Chancellor George Osborne and Lib Dem shadow Chancellor Vince Cable. I know, it's all very confusing; whoever heard of someone having two shadows?

The leader of the opposition appoints members of the shadow cabinet. However, if the leader of the opposition later becomes PM it's not a given that the member of the shadow cabinet responsible for education is appointed Secretary of State for Education. Who makes it into the new cabinet is entirely up to the new PM. In fact, just after an election victory is often seen as a good time for a new PM to clear out the dead wood from the cabinet.

A member of the shadow cabinet is referred to as a *front bencher*. This term derives from the fact that they have the right to sit on the front bench of their party's row of benches in the House of Commons or House of Lords.

The cabinet consists of between 20 and 30 ministers. The shadow cabinet is often a bit smaller, with some members doubling up their briefs and in effect shadowing two ministers rather than one.

Chapter 14

Assessing Ministers and Civil Servants

In This Chapter

▶ Looking at government departments

▶ Seeing who ranks where

▶ Understanding the civil service

▶ Working up to senior civil servants

▶ Measuring good and bad points

▶ Considering changes and reforms

*A*s far as many politicians are concerned, the TV sitcom *Yes Minister* was more documentary than comedy as it laid bare the relationship between government ministers and their civil servants. The series showed a hapless government minister swimming against the tide of events and the machinations of his own senior civil servant Sir Humphrey Appleby.

But despite the jaundiced eye many politicians cast towards their civil servants, one thing's for sure: how ministers and civil servants work together is key to successful governance. Civil servants are the oil in the government machine that keeps the cogs moving.

In this chapter I peer deep into the corridors of power in Whitehall and go a long way to explaining how government gets done in Britain.

Examining What Government Departments Do

Government departments, or ministries as they're called, are at the hub of UK government. Put simply, a ministry is responsible for ensuring government policy is pursued. For example, if the government policy is that all seven-year-olds are given a test at school, then it's up to the education ministry to ensure this happens. So, for example, the Department of Health deals with government policies relating to the National Health Service and the Department for Transport to Britain's road, rail and other transport infrastructure.

Although many decisions over which policies to pursue in government are taken by the prime minister (PM) and cabinet, the departments are responsible for drawing up that policy, proposing new laws and ultimately implementing them. The PM and cabinet may be the showy grille on the front of the car but the government departments are supplying the administrative power beneath the bonnet.

Some departments or ministries are considered more important than others. For example the Treasury, with the Chancellor of the Exchequer at the helm, is responsible for economic policy as well as tax collection and a good deal of benefit payouts. One key reason the Chancellor and the Treasury are so important is that other ministers have to make their case for their departmental expenditure to them. In short, the Chancellor controls the purse strings of government and that brings huge power and influence (see Chapter 13 for a fuller run-down of this role). As a result, the Treasury is seen as much more important than, say, the Department for Culture, Media and Sport.

Ranking the Departmental Hierarchy

Britain is a democracy, which means the decisions of government are meant to be taken by elected politicians. But many decisions need to be made because governing 60 million people is no small undertaking. So over time a strict hierarchy has formed within government ministries. The most senior politician is at the top – a minister – and he or she is served by other less senior politicians. The idea is that instructions from the minister at the top of the department are followed by the less senior politicians and their civil servants.

From top down, the decision-making chain of command goes like this:

✔ **Cabinet minister.** This politician is head of the department. The minister has ultimate say over which policies are taken to the PM or cabinet and makes the really big decisions within the department. It's their job to defend the department to cabinet colleagues and to the PM and to argue the case for more money for the department's coffers from the Chancellor. Cabinet ministers are often referred to as secretaries of state.

- **Minister of state.** Below the cabinet minister are perhaps two, three or even four other ministers whose job it is to look after a particular part of the ministry's work. For example, below the cabinet minister in the Department for Work and Pensions are three ministers of state – one for work, one for pensions and another for pension reform. Ministers of state usually have a great deal of autonomy but on really big matters or matters which cut across the responsibilities of other ministers they refer up to their cabinet minister boss.

- **Parliamentary under-secretary.** This politician's job is to work under the ministers of state. They enjoy the trappings of a minister in that they're paid a bit more than a Member of Parliament (MP) and may have a driver but they're still at the low end of the very greasy ministerial pole, hoping one day to climb up to minister of state, then cabinet minister and even beyond.

- **Parliamentary private secretary.** Finally, down at the bottom of the ministerial pile, is the parliamentary private secretary (PPS). This job is filled by an MP who acts as the go-between for ministers and parliament. A PPS helps to track the opinion of backbench MPs in parliament so that the minister can get a handle on whether or not new policy initiatives or a particular piece of legislation will be well received. Not only are the PPSs at the bottom of the pile in status – they don't even get paid! But they do it because they have ambitions one day to be a minister and they have to start somewhere!

The cabinet minister and ministers of state are often referred to as the *ministerial team*, which suggests that they're supposed to work together. Ministers falling out within the same department is frowned upon by the PM. On a more sociable note, friendships and alliances often form among members of the team, and when the cabinet minister moves on to another department – as often happens after a cabinet reshuffle, which I cover in Chapter 13 – he or she'll take ministers of state along for the ride.

Although, ostensibly, ministers sit at the top of the government departmental tree, they don't actually take every decision. They leave much of their daily decision making to their civil servants, who have expertise and who, in many cases, have been doing their job for far longer than the minister.

The life of a government minister – no matter how junior – is filled with paperwork. On Thursday evening – when many ministers and MPs leave to go back to their constituencies – the minister is given a red box by their senior civil servants, containing all the paperwork he or she is expected to have read and documents to have signed in time for Monday's return to the office.

Of course, nowadays with the rise of special advisers, it's no longer just ministers and civil servants interacting; instead cabinet ministers, even ministers of state, have their own advisers and even press officers, who may well be listened to more than the senior civil servant.

With cabinet ministers, ministers of state, parliamentary under-secretaries and parliamentary private secretaries, you can see that lots of MPs and the odd smattering of lords are active in government. In fact, around 100 politicians – both MPs and lords – are in the government. This means that a high proportion (sometimes close to a third) of all the MPs from the biggest party in the Commons have jobs in the government, from cabinet ministers down to unpaid PPSs, which makes passing its bills through the House of Commons easier.

The PM appoints the cabinet secretary, who appoints the permanent under-secretaries; they appoint other senior civil servants within the department they head up. Importantly, these top-grade jobs aren't in the gift of the permanent under-secretary: there may be an aptitude test and an interview panel where all the interviewers have their say (but it's safe to say that the permanent under-secretary gets who he or she wants).

Oiling the Wheels of Government: The Civil Service

Civil servants are officials who are appointed and not elected. At last count, a staggering half a million civil servants were working across the UK for the government.

Civil servants do jobs ranging from offering employment and benefit advice at the Jobcentre Plus to serving at 10 Downing Street, the residence of the PM. Despite an often mixed press, without a civil service the government would definitely grind unceremoniously to a halt.

At first glance, working out where the civil service starts and where it ends isn't easy. By the accepted definition, the civil service doesn't include members of the armed forces, police officers, people who work for the National Health Service or local government officials. Anyone who works for the state has their job defined by the branch they work for and is referred to as a public sector worker. But within the public sector, you have police, hospital staff and the civil service.

When it comes to pay and conditions, the civil service is currently split into two. Those of senior civil servants are set by the cabinet office – a crucial means of controlling them. Pay and conditions of lower-level civil servants are set by the individual department or government agency they work for. Thus, a senior civil servant in the Department for Environment, Food and Rural Affairs (Defra) has his or her pay set by the cabinet office and the civil servants below make do with pay grades set out by the senior civil servants in their department.

Some suggest that the two-tier approach to civil service pay is divisive, while others say that it acts as motivation on civil servants lower down the pay grades to strive to become members of the senior civil service and therefore enjoy better pay and benefits.

People often assume that all civil servants work in Whitehall or Westminster, but this simply isn't true. In fact, only one in five civil servants actually works in the capital. The others are spread around the country in different governmental departments.

Apart from the UK civil service, under the ultimate control of the cabinet office, two other branches of civil servants exist:

- ✔ The civil service of Northern Ireland, which runs the government of guess where? Yes, Northern Ireland!
- ✔ The Diplomatic Service deals with the implementation of foreign policy and staffs British embassies overseas.

The heads of these two separate branches of the civil service sit on a body called the *permanent secretaries management group*, along with the cabinet secretary and departmental permanent secretaries. The cabinet office is overseen by the cabinet secretary, a role often referred to as *head of the home civil service*.

Becoming a civil servant and doing the job

People looking to enter the UK civil service have to sit examinations testing their intelligence and problem-solving skills.

The entrance exam is just the first of many hurdles that civil servants have to jump during their career. The UK civil service is supposed to be a meritocracy and to this end staff looking for promotion first have to do well at their current post and then fill out an application form, go through interviews and even an aptitude test specific to the job they're applying for. The same round of applications, interviews and tests applies for every rung of the ladder. It can be a long, hard climb to the top of the UK civil service, and a few make it!

Entrance to the civil service is usually through examination but can also involve interviews and aptitude tests specific to the job you're applying for. For example, you may be tested on your writing and communication skills, numeracy or decision-making abilities.

What jobs are done by civil servants? Well, how long is a piece of string? (And there's probably a civil servant who can give you the answer to that one.) Government departments are chock-full of civil servants who have two key jobs to do:

- ✔ Advise ministers on policy matters
- ✔ See through the implementation of government policy

Go to your local job centre and a civil servant will be advising a job-seeker; see a hospital being built and a civil servant will be ensuring costs don't over-run; read about a new airport and a civil servant will be assessing its economic and environmental impact.

The modern civil service doesn't just recruit straight from university but looks to attract people with specialist skills mid-career.

Behaving as a civil servant

Civil servants are bound by a code of behaviour dating back to the 19th century and the so-called Northcote–Trevelyan reforms.

The Northcote–Trevelyan report was published in 1854. It set out a blueprint for how the UK civil service should operate. Crucially, it stated that promotion within the civil service should be on the basis of merit rather than according to who your father was or whether you were the friend of another civil servant – so nepotism and favouritism were supposed to be out.

The principles of the code of behaviour include:

- ✔ **Staying neutral.** Civil servants may hold particular political views but must carry out the instructions of ministers even if they disagree with them.
- ✔ **Staying beneath the radar.** Politicians love the limelight – just try standing between one and a TV camera crew and you can see what I mean – but civil servants are supposed to be always in the background. Civil servants are do-ers rather than public figures.
- ✔ **Staying for the long haul.** Crucially, civil servants are supposed to stay in their jobs even when ministers and governments come and go. This principle aids continuity of government.

GREAT FIGURES

Leaking about the sinking

Very occasionally, civil servants see something going on in their departments which they simply can't live with and feel compelled to reveal confidences. In 1984 Clive Ponting, a senior civil servant in the Ministry of Defence, leaked documents regarding the sinking of the Argentinian battleship the *Belgrano* during the Falklands War to an MP from the opposition Labour Party. The documents showed that the Conservative government had not revealed the whole truth about the circumstances of the sinking of the ship and the loss of over 300 Argentinian sailors' lives. Mr Ponting not only resigned his job over the leak but was also prosecuted under the Official Secrets Act; ultimately he was acquitted by a jury.

This civil service code is intended to improve the efficiency of government action and better allow politicians to carry out the policies they were elected to pursue.

In addition, civil servants are bound by tradition and code to keep secrets. In order to work together, ministers and civil servants have to trust one another, so discussions between ministers and their civil servants are always supposed to be confidential. A civil servant talking to the press about a particular matter just isn't done. For one thing, this behaviour would break the Northcote–Trevelyan agreement on staying in the background. Civil servants leave it up to the minister to decide how much or how little of their confidential discussions he or she reveals to the public or to fellow MPs.

If civil servants were to break confidentiality it could be embarrassing for the minister concerned. Civil service confidentiality is a reciprocal arrangement: in return, ministers take responsibility for the mistakes of their civil servants rather than hauling them over the coals publicly.

Civil servants have a very powerful trade union called the Public and Commercial Services Union to act on their behalf.

Civil servants are supposed to be politically neutral and in fact are barred from standing for election to parliament. If a civil servant wants to become an MP, they have to stand down from their job first.

Climbing the Ranks to the Senior Civil Service

As the name suggests, senior civil servants work at the heart of government. These are the most influential civil servants in the country, often working closely with government ministers. The senior civil servants are the crème de la crème of UK government and are often quite highly paid and have good pensions.

The most recent head count of the civil service suggests that there are some 3,000 to 4,000 senior civil servants.

Running the day-to-day: The permanent under-secretary of state

It's time to meet Sir Humphrey of *Yes Minister* fame. Sir Humph was a permanent under-secretary of state – which is quite a mouthful – but was also the most senior civil servant in a government department. In real life, as in fiction, the permanent under-secretary oversees the day-to-day running of the department, involving jobs such as:

- ✔ **Bean counting.** The permanent under-secretary is responsible for ensuring the department spends the money it has been given properly.

  As part of the job of accounting for departmental spending, the permanent under-secretary can expect to have to answer questions from parliamentary select committees, which I cover in Chapter 13.

- ✔ **Co-ordinating.** The permanent under-secretary chairs committees of other civil servants, helping to ensure that they're doing their job properly and that government policy is being carried out.

- ✔ **Advising.** The permanent under-secretary can be a key adviser for the cabinet minister on policy matters. The secretary has lots of expertise and years of experience, and also knows the fine detail of the inner working of the department. In short, a permanent under-secretary should be able to let a minister know what it is possible and practical to achieve.

The permanent under-secretary (also called permanent secretary) isn't hired by a minister, or by the PM for that matter. A person who achieves this position rises to the job through the ranks of the civil service. The permanent under-secretary is appointed by the cabinet secretary.

Honouring civil servants

Being given an honour is an almost automatic perk of senior civil servant status. The UK honours system is there to recognise longstanding and substantial service to the state or wider society.

Twice yearly – at New Year and on the monarch's official birthday – an honours list is prepared of approximately 1,350 people who deserve recognition. Many different honours are offered, from peerages and knighthoods to OBEs (Officer of the Order of the British Empire), MBEs (Member of the Order of the British Empire) and CBEs (Commander of the Order of the British Empire).

Honours are suggested to the monarch by the PM, and the cabinet secretary puts forward civil servants who he or she believes have served sufficient time, gained enough seniority and done a good enough job to merit one. In fact, as individuals climb through the ranks of the civil service, honours become an addition to the job. For example, if the cabinet secretary isn't a knight of the realm already, they'll be made one on assuming the top job.

The job of permanent under-secretary is considered close to the very pinnacle of the UK civil service and with it often comes an honour – hence *Sir* Humphrey! (I talk about the honours system in the nearby 'Honouring civil servants' sidebar.) However, even permanent under-secretaries have a boss: the cabinet secretary, who's head of the cabinet office and the UK civil service.

The influence of the civil service over policy formation has declined over the past 30 years, mainly because ministers have been keen to employ their own advisers. These days, although still offering policy advice, many senior civil servants focus on overseeing the delivery of government policy as their prime objective.

Serving as a link: The cabinet secretary

At the top of the civil service sits the *cabinet secretary*, who's the link between the leading politicians in the country – the PM and ministers – and the permanent under-secretaries. The cabinet secretary is always a civil service lifer, often a previous departmental permanent under-secretary. However, the cabinet secretary is appointed by the PM with the advice of the retiring cabinet secretary.

The cabinet secretary is a hugely important post, not just in terms of being the head of the civil service but also often as a key adviser to the PM. If the cabinet secretary is a trusted confidante of the PM, he or she has even more power within government. To a certain extent, the cabinet secretary can be the PM's fixer and enforcer.

Although bound by the civil service code and therefore meant to be apolitical and impartial, the cabinet secretary often gets involved in matters some would see as political. For example, the cabinet secretary may investigate where leaks of sensitive information to the press or MPs have come from within government or help enforce cabinet discipline by meeting with ministers who the PM feels aren't living up to their own code of conduct – such as collective cabinet responsibility. (I talk about the cabinet's code of conduct in Chapter 13.) The cabinet secretary may also have a hand in overseeing the Secret Intelligence Service (MI6).

Evaluating the Good and Bad Points of the UK Civil Service

The UK civil service is one of the longest-standing in the world. Its professionalism has often marked the UK out as a well-governed country. Many other countries – particularly from the Commonwealth – have tried to replicate the ethos and structure of the UK civil service. And you can see why when you consider some of its key plus points:

- ✔ **Honesty.** Very few cases have come to light of British civil servants taking bribes or being corrupt. In fact, the UK civil service is noted around the globe for its honesty and incorruptibility.

- ✔ **Professionalism.** Often the civil service is a job for life, the idea being that the individual civil servant's skills and experience built up over many years are utilised to the maximum.

- ✔ **Meritocracy.** The UK civil service is a meritocracy, with competitive exams held for entry and promotion according to ability.

Nevertheless, some do have it in for the UK civil service and reckon that it's not up to scratch. Some of their criticisms are listed here:

- ✔ **Narrow social background.** Senior civil servants graduate almost exclusively from the UK's two great universities – Oxford and Cambridge – and tend to come from an upper middle-class social background. Many argue therefore that civil servants' life experience is too narrow. (Similar arguments are made about the judiciary, which I cover in Chapter 15.)

- ✔ **Self-serving.** Critics say the civil service always looks out for itself when implementing government policy. They argue that new laws and policy initiatives invariably end with more civil servants being employed.

- ✔ **Not accountable.** Senior civil servants may have to answer to ministers and, of course, to the cabinet secretary but mistakes rarely end with a civil servant losing their job. As a result, critics say that even poorly performing civil servants don't face sanction and that this situation doesn't help the efficiency of government.

Reforming the Civil Service

As long as the UK civil service has existed moves have been afoot to reform it. The Northcote–Trevelyan reforms of the 1850s set out the responsibilities of civil servants to their political masters, as well as a structure for recruitment and promotion. But nearly every new government says on taking office that it wants to reform the civil service and thereby end waste in government.

Ignoring the Ibbs Report

Conservative PM Margaret Thatcher went as far as setting up an efficiency unit with the objective of introducing management practices used in the private sector in an effort to reduce costs and head count. The efficiency unit produced the Ibbs Report in 1988, which concluded the following about the UK civil service:

- ✔ It's too big
- ✔ Civil servants always play safe and don't 'think outside the box' when problem solving
- ✔ It spends too much and offers poor value for money

The Ibbs Report made a host of complex recommendations for reform of the civil service, including giving greater autonomy to civil servants and setting them clear goals. However, after a few years it was widely agreed that the report and its recommendations had had only a marginal effect and civil servants were largely back to their old ways.

Reducing head count: The Gershon Review

The most recent attempt to reform the civil service and public services in general was the Gershon Review in 2005. The then PM Tony Blair and his Chancellor Gordon Brown asked Sir Peter Gershon to review the efficiency of the civil and public services in the UK.

Gershon recommended a host of efficiency savings, which would have seen a reduction in the civil service of around 30,000 employees. However, four years on from the Gershon Review and employment in the civil service and public services hasn't yet fallen.

Some suggest that the civil service has become more politicised, particularly during the government of Tony Blair. During his decade as PM, hundreds of special advisers were ensconced in government ministries, which was bound to have quite an impact on the age-old relationship between civil servants and ministers. For one thing, these appointments have helped create different non-official channels to ministerial access. In the past, a pressure group wanting to meet with a minister would have always gone through a senior civil servant; these days, they're just as likely to approach the minister's special adviser first.

Calling the civil service to account

The civil service exists to carry out government policy but who ensures that they're doing a good enough job? Civil servants don't go unchecked. They're monitored or their actions held in check in the following ways:

- **Internal systems.** These days civil servants are targeted by their superiors and receive feedback in much the same way as workers in the private sector do.

- **Tradition.** The civil service has a long history and today's civil servants feel the pressure to live up to the standards of previous generations.

- **Cabinet Office.** The cabinet office is the ultimate power in the civil service and has internal disciplinary procedures for those civil servants who act in an unethical, irresponsible or even illegal way.

- **Parliament.** Permanent under-secretaries often have to appear before parliament to account for the spending and administration of their departments.

- **Civil service commissioners.** This is a board of people appointed by the monarch – not parliament or the PM – whose job is to ensure that recruitment to the civil service is purely on the basis of merit through competitive examination.

Chapter 15

Taking in the Courts and Judiciary

. . . .

In This Chapter
▶ Delving into the UK's three legal systems
▶ Differentiating civil and criminal law
▶ Examining the legal systems of England, Wales and Scotland
▶ Looking at the role of the judges and the courts in the constitution
▶ Judging in the European Union courts
▶ Protecting civil liberties through the courts

. . . .

*T*he courts and judiciary are a key part of the British state and play a huge role in determining the nation's unwritten constitution and protecting the individual from the potential abuses of the state. And increasingly, with civil liberties being squeezed, the courts are becoming a real bastion of British liberties.

In this chapter, I examine the ins and outs of the UK court system from east to west, north to south, small claims court to fancy new UK Supreme Court. If you want to know what goes on behind the doors of the oak-panelled court rooms, this is the chapter for you.

Explaining the UK's Three Legal Systems

For many outside observers, the UK is a very confusing place. It is one relatively small but densely populated country made up of four nations: England, Scotland, Wales and Northern Ireland. Each of these separate parts of the UK has its own distinctive character, history and traditions, with many of the laws made in the UK parliament. But a separate parliament for Scotland and individual assemblies for Wales and Northern Ireland all interact with the UK parliament in different ways. As I said – confusing or what? Now add that across this one country made up of four parts are three very distinctive legal systems. Perhaps you've now reached confusion overload and need a lie-down in a darkened room.

Nevertheless, the UK has three legal systems: one for England and Wales combined, one for Scotland and another for Northern Ireland. Each has its own distinctive way of doing things and different legal precedents but, in truth, what they share in common is far greater than what divides them.

Criminal laws are drawn up by the UK parliament and it's the job of the courts to see that these laws are followed. Laws made by the UK parliament are called *statute laws*. In addition, though, in civil cases judges use *legal precedent* to decide what should happen in a case; that is, they look at what previous judges have decided in similar cases.

The whole justice system – both criminal and civil law, regardless of which of the three legal systems holds sway – is based on a hierarchy, which means that the courts at the top of the pyramid hear the most serious cases and any appeals resulting from cases brought in courts at the bottom of the pyramid.

Recognising the Difference between Civil and Criminal Law

All of the UK's three legal systems are divided into the same two parts:

- ✔ **Criminal law** governs offences against society and fellow citizens. The state usually brings charges in a criminal case.
- ✔ **Civil law** deals with the relationship between individuals or groups of individuals. Civil cases involve lawsuits between people and organisations on matters that don't involve the state.

Civil law is designed to help settle disputes between individuals, while criminal law is about the state taking to task individuals who've offended wider society's accepted norms of behaviour.

The structures of the criminal and civil courts are very different but at the very top – when cases are appealed – they come together.

Committing crimes against the state

Criminal law deals with stuff like burglary or violence against another person. Interestingly, when someone commits a criminal offence such as stealing a car, the crime isn't said to be against the victim but against the state – whether that be England and Wales, Scotland or Northern Ireland.

People charged with a criminal offence are tried by judges or, in the case of crown court cases, a jury, and if found guilty they can be sent to prison or face some other punishment such as a fine or community service. Any punishment is imposed by the court but executed by the state; thus the car thief is sentenced to six months in prison and is then handed over to the state's prison service for the sentence to be carried out. Criminal cases often involve a jury. Trial by jury in criminal cases is seen as a key right of the British citizen.

Suing your neighbours in civil court

Civil law isn't quite as intriguing as criminal law, which is awash with human interest stories, but nevertheless the need for a transparent and fair settling of disputes between individuals is a key component of a properly functioning society. Without the law to settle disputes, might would most likely triumph over right, with the strong riding roughshod over the weak or vulnerable.

In civil law, the state doesn't bring a case against an offender; instead, one person or group of people sues another person or group of people. For example, in a case in which heirs are arguing over who gets what under the terms of a will, no one has done anything against the criminal law but there is a dispute that needs to be settled.

The parties in dispute go to a court for judgement – which is made by a judge rather than a jury. This judgement is based on what has happened in similar cases in the past and the particular circumstances of the new case.

Examining the Basic Rights of the British Citizen

Being British brings with it certain rights and privileges, and one of the jobs of the court is to uphold these precious rights and privileges. Here's a rundown of those rights:

- ✔ **Personal data protection.** Under the terms of the 1998 Data Protection Act information about all British citizens held by government agencies and businesses has to be accurate, secure and up to date.

- ✔ **Freedom of information.** Under the 2000 Freedom of Information Act British citizens are entitled to ask for previously private information from public bodies such as local councils or the government.

- ✔ **Free health care rights.** Britain guarantees its citizens free health care through the NHS. Doctors' appointments, minor and major surgery as well as emergency treatment are all free.

- ✔ **Free state education.** All British children aged 5 to 16 are entitled to attend a free state school to be educated.

✔ **Freedom to work.** All British citizens can work without restrictions. Laws guarantee that workers can't be discriminated against on the grounds of sex, race or religion. In addition, employers have to pay a minimum hourly wage to their employees.

Focusing on the Criminal Courts of England and Wales

England and Wales combined host most of the UK population by a long chalk so here's the logical place to start. The following sections cover criminal courts, from the lowest rung – trying the least serious criminal cases – right to the top and the appeals courts.

Starting off in a magistrates court

Magistrates courts try the overwhelming number of cases – around 98 per cent of all cases pass through them. Crimes such as non-payment of TV licences, shoplifting and drunk and disorderly offences are dealt with by magistrates courts.

Magistrates courts also act as a gateway to the next tier of the criminal justice system by deciding if the evidence in the case is strong enough and the crime of sufficient gravity to be sent to crown court. In the most serious criminal cases, such as murder, the appearance of the defendant in front of the magistrates court is little more than a formality, with committal to trial in front of the higher court a given.

One of the key distinguishing marks of the magistrates courts is that they're presided over by *Justices of the Peace* (JPs). These are ordinary members of the public from all walks of life. The only major restrictions on becoming a JP are that you don't work in the criminal justice system (such as police officers) and have no criminal record. JPs are trained to hear criminal cases, adjudge guilt, pronounce correct and proportionate sentence and to know when the case should be referred on to the crown court. JPs don't do the job all on their own. They have the help of district judges and deputy district judges, who are professional paid members of the judiciary employed by the state.

Interestingly, most people appearing before the magistrates court plead guilty to the crime – if they don't, a greater chance exists of the case being referred to the crown court where the prison sentences handed out can be heavier. Wanting to avoid a longer sentence (and who wouldn't?), the defendant (soon to be a criminal) pleads guilty. It is then the job of the magistrates to pass the appropriate sentence.

When deciding that a particular case should be heard by a crown court, the magistrate may order that the defendant be held *on remand*. Being on remand means that the defendant is held in prison until the crown court case can be heard. Alternatively, the magistrate may allow the release of the defendant on *bail*, which means they're free to go about their normal life – with certain restrictions such as surrendering their passport – but to report to the crown court for trial when summoned.

Approximately 700 magistrates courts operate across the UK. They don't sit every day, mainly because the JPs have ordinary jobs to be getting on with. Around 30,000 JPs sit in these courts.

Many politicians – particularly those not in government – like to paint a picture of the UK as an increasingly lawless society. To support this view they often point to the fact that the UK has some 80,000 people in prison. Now it's true that the UK imprisons more people per head of population than any other western European country, but compared to the United States, the UK only imprisons around one-fifth of the number of people per head of population. In fact, crime rates in the UK aren't much worse than other European countries and when compared to the Americas, Russia, Africa and large parts of Asia, they're a lot lower.

Advancing to a crown court

Crown courts hear the cases deemed potentially serious enough to merit a long custodial sentence; for example, offences such as murder, rape, manslaughter and robbery with violence.

A defendant who pleads not guilty in these cases is entitled to a trial by jury. The case is heard by a jury, normally consisting of 12 members of the public but sometimes a couple more or fewer. The jury delivers its verdict, and it's then up to the judge, who's overseen the trial and advised the jury as to the key facts of the case, to deliver the sentence or let the defendant off if he or she's found innocent.

A jury is made up of people selected at random from the electoral roll. They're told to turn up at a court on an appointed day and once there are assigned a trial in which they'll sit as a juror. Jury service is very solemn and those called have to give a good reason in advance for not being able to attend, or they could face being in contempt of court.

There's no room for well-meaning amateurs such as JPs in the crown court system. Here, the law gets very serious indeed. This court hears the worst crimes. Crown courts are usually presided over by circuit judges or recorders, who are legally trained state employees. The most grave cases are often heard by a *high court judge*, a very senior judge who has lots of experience.

The most famous crown court in England and Wales is the Central Criminal Court at the Old Bailey in London. Normally, this court hears the gravest of the grave cases and has the very best judges and court workers in place to see that justice is best served.

Making your way to the Court of Appeal

Sentences handed out by the magistrates courts can be appealed at the crown court – pretty simple, yes? Verdicts of cases adjudged in the crown court can be appealed in the – you guessed it – Court of Appeal. However, when it comes to appealing decisions made by the crown courts, things get more complex.

The presumption is that appealing crown court verdicts shouldn't be too easy or lots of rightfully convicted criminals would do it. A filtering system is thus in place to prevent frivolous or just plain hopeful appeals being heard. A compelling reason must exist for the case to go to the court of appeal. Legitimate reasons for sending a case to the Court of Appeal include new evidence being found or the original trial being flawed.

The Criminal Cases Review Commission considers the argument for an appeal and then rules on whether the case should go to the Court of Appeal (criminal division). The Court of Appeal then decides whether a retrial is necessary, the appeal is to be turned down or a straight acquittal is in order.

One other stage of appeal is now available, the UK Supreme Court, which has become the legal arm of the House of Lords. I talk about the Supreme Court in the next section, 'Introducing the New UK Supreme Court'.

It's not just the Court of Appeal that can acquit people found guilty of a crime in a crown court. The monarch – on the advice of the Home Secretary – can grant a pardon. If the convicted criminal has already died, it's called a *posthumous pardon*.

Hearing Civil Cases in England and Wales

A civil court's fare is wide and varied, from relatively small disputes over who gets what in a will, to wrangles between neighbours over who owns a bit of garden, right up to headline-grabbing libel actions and ultra-complex contract disputes between individuals or even big multinational organisations.

Gazing at the civil law process

Just like with criminal law (see the 'Focusing on the Criminal Courts of England and Wales' section earlier in this chapter), a hierarchy of courts hear civil cases in England and Wales:

- ✔ **County courts.** This lowest rung of civil court generally hears matters of a financial value of under £50,000. A fast-track case-hearing process is available – called *small claims* – for disputes of a financial value of under £5,000. The vast majority of civil disputes are dealt with by the county court.

  Common cases heard by county courts include personal injury claims, lenders trying to recover unpaid debts by requesting permission to use bailiffs, and landlord–tenant disputes.

  Some 216 county courts operate in the UK, dealing with thousands of cases a year. Most cases are decided by a solitary district or circuit judge.

- ✔ **High Court.** As the name suggests, this court deals with cases of high value and high importance. Many libel cases end up at the High Court. In addition, through its family division, the High Court deals with high profile divorces and disputes over medical treatment.

Appealing civil cases

Appeals against a decision made in a civil case – as in a criminal case – end up at the Court of Appeal, although in the civil division. Three judges normally hear an appeal in the Court of Appeal, reaching a decision by a majority.

Having an appeal heard is far from a given. Everyone has a right to lodge an appeal but first it goes through a filtering system. In civil cases, a single judge who sits in the Court of Appeal decides whether a case is worthy of being heard at a full appeal.

Generally, the appeals process is very long and at times ruinously expensive, particularly as unsuccessful appeals can sometimes end with the losing side paying the winning side's costs, which can run into hundreds of thousands of pounds – ouch!

Taking in the Scottish Court System

Scotland united with England and Wales to form the UK in 1707 but kept its own very separate legal system. Like England and Wales, though, the Scottish system is divided into criminal and civil law. Here's the lowdown on the court system north of the border:

- **Criminal law.** Minor offences are tried in sheriff courts (with more serious cases going to the High Court of Justiciary. All appeals are also heard by the High Court of Justiciary.

- **Civil law.** Most cases are tried in the same sheriff courts which deal with criminal cases. Importantly, no financial limit is placed on disputes that can be heard in a sheriff court, unlike the county courts in England and Wales.

  Appeals go either to the *sheriff principal* (the head sheriff in the area) or to the Court of Session. At the Court of Session a judge reviews the case alone and then has his or her decision scrutinised by a panel of judges.

No equivalent to the crown court exists in Scotland. Instead, the twin jobs of dealing with the most serious crimes and hearing appeals are performed by the High Court of Justiciary.

In civil cases the losers have the right of appeal to the UK Supreme Court. This isn't the case for criminal cases.

Considering the Courts in Northern Ireland

The Northern Irish legal system is almost indistinguishable from that in England and Wales. There's a division between criminal and civil law and judges' decisions can set precedents.

Criminal cases are heard in magistrates and crown courts (the latter for more serious offences) and civil cases in county courts and a high court. A separate court of appeal hears both criminal and civil appeals and its decisions can be reviewed by the UK Supreme Court.

During the Troubles which started in the late 1960s in Northern Ireland, trial by jury in cases where people were accused of paramilitary activities was halted, but was restored in 2007 as the political situation had eased.

Introducing the New UK Supreme Court

The legal systems of the UK aren't noted for radical reform. For instance, the framework of the English legal system has its roots way back in the 12th century and Scotland's justice system was established not long after. However, 1 October 2009 was a red-letter day for legal reform in the UK with the establishment of the UK Supreme Court.

Previously, an appeal against a verdict in either a civil or criminal law case could ultimately go all the way up to the House of Lords in Westminster. There the case would be heard by any one of a dozen appointed Lords of Appeal in Ordinary – or *Law Lords* for short – who were the nation's top judges. Such cases involved a lot of solemn language, arcane procedure and quite a bit of dressing up in robes and donning of horsehair wigs.

But from October 2009, the legal functions of the House of Lords were hived off into a new body – the UK Supreme Court. The Law Lords still preside over the court for the time being, so a bit of dressing up is still likely but that may change in the future with the possibility of judges who aren't lords being appointed.

The UK Supreme Court hears appeals on criminal and civil cases in England, Wales and Northern Ireland and civil cases from Scotland (criminal case appeals will still be heard by the Scottish High Court of Justiciary). The court also has a new power – previously held by the monarch's Privy Council – to decide what issues can be legislated upon by the devolved governments of Scotland, Wales and Northern Ireland and what has to remain the say-so of the UK parliament in Westminster (see Chapter 16 for more on devolution).

Looking at the Role of the Judge

Whether you're considering the legal systems of England, Wales, Scotland or Northern Ireland, one thing's for sure – the judge is key. The judge serves the following functions in a courtroom:

✔ **Umpire.** Each side in a case is represented by a lawyer, and it's up to the judge to make certain that these lawyers follow the rules of behaviour in court. The judge must also ensure fairness, in that both lawyers have the opportunity to have their say, submit evidence, call witnesses and ask questions of those witnesses.

✔ **Interpreting the law.** Oodles of previous cases could set a precedent in the case or parliamentary statutes (laws) could have a bearing on a case. The judge must be aware of these precedents and statutes and correctly apply them to the case at hand.

- ✔ **Making the law.** Wow! Making the law sounds a biggie, and it is. Put simply, if a new set of circumstances has occurred in the case being heard, the decision of the judge will set a precedent for all future similar cases. This evolution of precedents is the basis of common law.

- ✔ **Handing down sentences.** In criminal cases, if the defendant is found guilty it's up to the judge to decide the sentence (working within guidelines set by the Justice Secretary). In civil cases, the judge decides the redress if one individual is found to have wronged another. For example, in a case of libel, a judge sets the damages.

Judges are often selected to preside over prominent public inquiries, such as those held concerning the death of black teenager Stephen Lawrence or into the circumstances surrounding the death of the UK government's weapons expert David Kelly. Judges are preferred in these positions because of their experience in dealing with disputes and witnesses.

Glancing at Courts and the Constitution

Laws made by the UK parliament – called *statutes* – are the ultimate law of the land, which everyone – even judges – has to abide by. However, statutes aren't the be-all and end-all; they can't cover every individual's circumstances. So a web of hundreds of years of different judgements in cases – called *legal precedent* – sets out what is legal and what isn't. The ability of judges to set legal precedent which is then followed in future similar court cases gives them a key role in the UK's unwritten constitution.

So, campaigners for euthanasia wanting people to be free to travel abroad to end their lives without fear that anyone travelling with them will be guilty of the crime of assisted suicide don't go to their Member of Parliament (MP) to get a new statute law enacted. Instead they've taken a series of cases to the House of Lords (now superseded by the UK Supreme Court) in the hope of setting a legal precedent, which in effect sets new law.

The three legal systems in the UK all operate according to a hierarchical system. This means that the decision reached by the highest court in the land – now the UK Supreme Court in most cases – is binding on all lower courts and also sets a future legal precedent. But if a new statute law is enacted which contradicts legal precedent, the statute law takes priority.

Throwing the European Union into the Mix

The UK is part of the European Union (EU) and as a result laws made by European courts apply here.

The two courts for the European Union are:

- **The European Court of Justice (ECJ).** This court is responsible for interpreting EU laws and ensuring consistent application across all 27 member states.

  If a court in a EU member state is hearing a case in which EU law comes into the equation, the judge asks the ECJ to look at the case and provide a ruling. Crucially, the court – even if it is the UK referring the case – has to follow the ECJ's decision.

- **The European Court of Human Rights.** People who feel that their rights under the European Convention of Human Rights have been violated can take their case to this court. However, the person who feels wronged must first have exhausted the legal processes in their own country, which in the UK's case usually means having gone all the way to the Supreme Court.

The European Convention on Human Rights is now part of UK law through the 1998 Human Rights Act. As a result, if someone feels that their human rights have been violated they can go to a UK court and have it decide on the matter instead of going to the European Court of Human Rights in Strasbourg.

Fighting the Good Fight: Courts and Civil Liberties

Increasingly, in reaction to the growing powers of central government, judges see protecting the civil liberties of the British public as part of their job. Most controversially, since the terrorist attacks on the United States on 11 September 2001, the UK government has expanded its powers to detain potential terrorists. Restrictions on civil liberties in Britain over the past few years include:

- **Detention without charge.** People suspected of terrorist activities can be held for questioning without charge for up to 28 days. This is highly controversial and explored in the nearby sidebar, 'Anti-terror laws and the judiciary'.

✔ **Asylum-seeker detention.** People coming to the UK claiming asylum are often kept under lock and key while their application is considered. These people aren't guilty of a crime but the government worries that if they're allowed to roam freely they'll simply disappear.

✔ **Protest restrictions.** Several instances of violence at demonstrations have led to some restrictions being imposed on the right to protest. What's more, accusations of heavy-handed policing at several rallies, in particular surrounding the meeting of the G20 (the world's 20 most economically advanced nations) in London in 2009, have been made.

✔ **Behaviour orders:** People accused of antisocial behaviour may have a court order imposed on them. ASBOs (Anti-Social Behaviour Orders) place restrictions on people's movements and are often given to younger people accused of vandalism, noise disturbance or petty crime. However, civil liberties groups don't like ASBOs as they feel they're imposed willy-nilly and without due legal process, and stigmatise people who haven't been convicted of an actual crime.

At the same time as extra restrictions on civil liberties have been imposed, the Human Rights Act and the Freedom of Information Act (which gives citizens the right to access information from public bodies) have both been adopted and are seen as massive steps forward in the protection of civil liberties.

Anti-terror laws and the judiciary

Few people realised it would be the case at the outset, but the first decade of the 2000s has been a decade of terrorist threat. As a result of the terrorist attacks on New York and Washington in 2001, Madrid in 2003 and London in 2005, governments around the globe are acutely aware that terrorists would like to bring death on a truly horrendous scale.

The reaction of the British government under prime ministers Tony Blair and Gordon Brown has been to increase the period that terrorist suspects can be held and questioned without charge from 7 to 28 days. In fact, both Blair and Brown said that they'd like to see detention periods of 42 and even 90 days. The reason given is that police enquiries are often highly complex as a result of terrorists communicating with each other via encrypted electronic messages. Police thus need longer to hold and question suspects and examine evidence.

However, the government has only got part of what it asked for – even in the aftermath of the 2005 London bombings, a large number of MPs from all parties were willing to vote against detention for longer than 28 days. What's more, leading members of the judiciary and even the police have said that holding suspects for longer than 28 days is both illiberal and unnecessary. Other anti-terror laws have been effectively overturned by the judiciary. In 2004, for instance, the Law Lords ordered the release of nine terrorist suspects who were non-UK nationals held in Belmarsh prison near London.

Chapter 16

Laying Bare Local Government and Devolution

. . . .

In This Chapter

▶ Looking at local government throughout the UK

▶ Checking the devolved institutions of Scotland, Wales and Northern Ireland

. . . .

*I*f you want to know how government works across the length and breadth of the UK, from the tiniest hamlet to the largest city, this is the chapter to check out. I hold up the inner complexities of local government for scrutiny, peer into the powerful parliament of Scotland and show the Welsh and Northern Ireland assemblies in all their Technicolor – or should that be technocratic? – glory.

Understanding that All Politics is Local

Prominent American politician Thomas 'Tip' O'Neill once famously said that 'all politics is local'. He meant that what happens close to home, in the lives of electors, affects the way they view politicians and ultimately the way they vote. If an individual is made redundant or faces a hefty tax bill from his or her local council it's bound to influence the way he or she views politicians prancing on the national stage.

Often political commentators and journalists focus on the inner workings of the corridors of power in Westminster or which cabinet minister says what, but most people really don't care that much about these goings-on. What the regular people see is how politicians and their policies influence their daily lives. It's local government by a long way that has the biggest impact rather than the MPs, ministers and party leaders.

The structure of local government is set out in statute law, which is laws enacted by the UK parliament. For instance, the UK government through an Act of Parliament set up the devolved Scottish parliament and the different mayoral authorities in England and Wales.

Looking at what local government does

The big national policies, such as the setting of income tax, hospital building programmes and even whether to go to war or not, are decided upon by the Westminster parliament or in some instances the devolved parliaments and national assemblies of Scotland, Wales and Northern Ireland.

But underneath all the national action, local governments do the rest of the tasks that need doing to make society work, and what a lot of work it is! Some of the duties that local governments perform include:

✔ Overseeing the running of state schools

✔ Providing social services

✔ Deciding upon planning issues in the locality

✔ Maintaining public roads and local public transport

✔ Ensuring refuse collections are made and enforcing environmental health policies

✔ Providing local amenities such as leisure centres, libraries, museums and parks, to name just a few

✔ Overseeing the local police force and fire and rescue services

✔ Providing local social housing

No wonder that local government – along with the National Health Service – is amongst the country's biggest employers.

Critics of local government often say that they 'only empty the bins', but as you can see from this list local governments are responsible for an awful lot of facilities and services. In fact, if no local government operated, you'd soon know about it. In the winter of 1978–79 many local government workers went on strike and the chaos that ensued, with rubbish not collected and even the dead not being buried in Liverpool, earned the period the nickname, 'the winter of discontent'. The Labour government of Prime Minister Jim Callaghan was held responsible for the strikes and at the subsequent general election of April 1979, Labour was defeated. All politics is local!

Apart from its role in deciding planning issues, local government has no say in the running of hospitals. That job falls to the National Health Service (NHS). Under the current structure of the NHS the decisions over patient treatment, budgeting and even commissioning new building projects are the call of either the individual hospital or group of hospitals called a *foundation trust*.

Funding local government

So who pays for local government in the UK? Put simply, you do. Local governments are funded in two key ways:

- ✔ A grant of money from the central UK government, raised through central taxation such as income tax or corporation tax
- ✔ Council tax levied on residents living in local homes, and business rates

About three quarters of the money spent by local authorities in the UK actually originates from the central UK government.

Why does central government give so much money to local government rather than let it raise more through local council tax? Well, actually the situation's a bit of a power game. If local government was able to raise as much money as it wanted locally, it could become very powerful. By keeping at least partial control of the purse strings, central government lets those in local government know who's boss.

Both local and central government are elected and it's possible for one party to be in charge of central government while another's running a local government.

In the UK cities that have an elected mayor – the most prominent is London – money is raised through a surcharge on the local council tax. (See 'Reforming local government' later in this chapter for more on the mayoral system.)

Council tax is based on property values. Each property is put into a band from A to G. Properties in band A are the smallest and cheapest, rising to band G covering the largest and most expensive homes. At the start of the financial year – in April – the local council decides how much needs to be collected from the occupiers of properties in each of the bands. People who live on their own, are elderly or disabled can claim a discount on their annual bill of up to 25 per cent.

At times, central government is disturbed to see sharp rises in council tax and has the legal right to cap them. It tells the local council to draw up a new budget and to keep its expenditure down so that council tax bills don't rise by too much.

Taking in the structure of local government in England

Local government structure is very complex. Dividing up all the different types of local government into two is thus probably the best approach:

- ✔ **Principal authorities** deal with important local issues, such as schools, planning and environmental affairs. They have lots of civil servants (see Chapter 14 for more on the civil service) and contractors working for them and they receive money from local council tax and grants from central government.

- ✔ **Community authorities** are the most local of local government. They rely on volunteers and don't have a bureaucracy. They oversee the management of local parks and allotments and advise the local principal authority on planning issues. They're the ones who put in requests to the principal authority for work to be done on local amenities.

  Parish councils and *town councils* are the two main types of community authority in England. Prominent figures in the local community stand for election to these councils. Council members are often aligned to a particular political party but a fair number of candidates for parish or town councils stand as independents.

Most people refer to principal authorities, whether they're county or district councils or unitary authorities, simply as *councils*.

The system of principal authorities in England is a real patchwork:

- ✔ In some areas a **county council** is responsible for education, waste management and big planning issues within the county. Below the county council, **district councils** are in charge of local planning and refuse collection, as well as smaller local planning issues.

- ✔ Some parts of the country have only one tier of principal authority – catchily called **unitary authorities**. These unitary authorities in effect do the work of both a county and district council.

- ✔ In larger cities, a combination of **elected officials** and **council members** takes charge of meeting some needs. London, with a population of nine million, has an elected assembly and an elected mayor, as well as 32 separate boroughs responsible for delivering services to the public. Other major urban areas, such as Manchester, Liverpool and Leeds, have their own councils, with separate boroughs actually delivering the services.

Regardless of whether you live in a part of the country that's run by a county council, unitary authority or even a London borough, you get the chance to elect people as councillors. It is the job of councillors to take the big decisions in your locality and ensure that the bureaucrats running the administration do their jobs properly.

Heading north: Scottish local government

Local government structure in Scotland is much more straightforward than in England. A divide between principal authorities and community authorities (instead of parish councils the Scots have community councils) does still exist; but instead of having lots of different types of principal authority, Scotland's local government is divided into 32 unitary authorities. Some are based on county borders (and are geographically quite large) while others are based on the boundaries of the big cities – Edinburgh, Glasgow and Aberdeen.

Elections for councillors in each of Scotland's 32 unitary authorities are held every four years.

Local authorities have a statutory (legal) duty to consult community councils on planning, development and other issues directly affecting that local community. However, the community council has no direct say in the delivery of services.

The Scottish unitary authorities are funded through a combination of council tax and grants provided by the Scottish parliament, which in turn gets its money from the UK central government in Westminster.

Heading west: Wales and Northern Ireland

Like Scotland, Welsh local government is divided into unitary authorities – 22 in total. Some are based on county borders while others take in the big cities such as Cardiff, Newport and Swansea. Below the unitary authorities are communities, which act in the same way as a parish council in England and a community council in Scotland.

As for Northern Ireland, the 26 district councils don't have the same powers as principal authorities in England or unitary authorities in Scotland. Their functions include responsibility for waste and recycling services, leisure and community services, building control and local economic and cultural development. They aren't planning authorities, but are consulted on some planning applications, and have no say over education matters, housing or road building – these are the preserve of the Northern Ireland Assembly, which I talk about in the upcoming 'Priming the peace process: The Northern Ireland Assembly'.

Reforming local government

It used to be the case that after a local election the newly elected councillors would meet to elect the leadership of the council, with members of the biggest party taking the senior posts such as treasurer or head of planning. In 2000, this cosy little system was shaken up when it was decided that English local authorities with populations of over 85,000 would have to choose between one of three new management structures, two of which included the introduction of an elected mayor. The three structures proposed were:

- ✔ Up to ten elected councillors would form a cabinet, with one cabinet member being designated as council leader.

- ✔ Up to ten elected councillors would form a cabinet but instead of one of their number being leader, an elected mayor would fill that post.

- ✔ An elected mayor gets to appoint a manager, who then appoints a management team to oversee the daily workings of the council.

Most councillors chose option one – a cabinet and council leader – rather than an elected mayor. However, those councils deciding that they wanted an elected mayor had to have this decision ratified by a yes vote in a referendum. (In a *referendum* those people registered to vote are asked to vote on a yes or no question rather than for a particular candidate.) If the referendum passed, mayoral elections then took place.

Of only 12 elected mayors across England, by far the most important is the mayor of London (see the nearby sidebar, 'Introducing London's mayor'). And because so few authorities have an elected mayor, the revision of the system is seen by some as a bit of a waste of time.

Critics of the mayoral system were provided with ammunition by the election of Stuart Drummond as the mayor of Hartlepool in 2002. Drummond was the mascot of the local football club, Hartlepool United, and campaigned dressed as a monkey. His one stated policy was simian in nature: he pledged to provide free bananas to schoolchildren. Drummond won by a landslide and has since won a further two terms – which shows that he must be doing something right in the job – although he did renege on his pledge to supply free bananas due to lack of funds.

Virtually all towns and cities in the UK have a mayor, only not one elected by the public. The mayor turns up at public events to represent the council and the job is largely ceremonial. The only real power a mayor has lies in chairing the meeting of the local council. Invariably, local councillors take turns to do the job of mayor.

Introducing London's mayor

Most people's knowledge of the job of London mayor is the story of Dick Wittington who as a boy famously walked to London with his cat, made his fortune and eventually became mayor.

But the role of mayor of London had been a ceremonial one for generations until the elections of 2000. The idea was that a major world city such as London should have a government structure that reflected its size and standing and to a degree aped those of its fellow premier cities, New York and Paris. It was decided that a mayor of London was the only way to get some oversight of London's 32 borough councils and co-ordination of London-wide policy areas such as police and transport.

Now, London has not just one but two mayors! The main one is the mayor of London, who's directly elected by the public and has pretty substantial powers. The second mayor is called the Lord Mayor of the City of London. The role is largely ceremonial and the office holder isn't elected by the public. What's more, the Lord Mayor of the City of London doesn't represent Greater London but the much smaller – in geographic and population terms – City of London, which is the area of the capital containing many banks and financial institutions.

The mayor is also an important figurehead for the capital and the current mayor was instrumental in securing the Olympic Games for London in 2012.

Ken Livingstone, who served as mayor of London from 2000 to 2008, is one of the most colourful characters in modern British politics. He shot to national prominence as head of the Greater London Council (GLC) in the 1980s. At the time he was called Red Ken as a result of his left-wing policies and criticism of the then Conservative PM Margaret Thatcher. In fact, a power struggle ensued between the Thatcher government and the GLC and it only ended when the GLC was abolished in 1985. But Red Ken wasn't finished and in 2000 he stood for election as mayor of London – much to the chagrin of then Labour PM Tony Blair – and won by a landslide. He was back but had toned down his left-wing policies.

The mayor of London is elected by a complex voting system. In short, electors get to cast two votes – one for their first choice for mayor and one for their second choice. The first choice votes are counted and after this round all but the two candidates with the highest number of first-choice votes are eliminated. These two candidates go into a run-off. At this point, the second-choice votes are added to the first-choice and the winner is the candidate with the highest number of first- and second-choice votes. I told you this system is complex! It's called the supplementary votes system and is explored in greater detail in Chapter 6.

Granting Power from the Centre – Devolution

The UK is made up of four nations or parts – England, Scotland, Wales and Northern Ireland. Each of these parts has its own unique system of local government, partly due to – drum roll, please – devolution!

Arguably the biggest constitutional change in the UK since the Second World War, *devolution* involves power being transferred from the UK parliament based in Westminster to the Scottish parliament based in Holyrood, Edinburgh, the Welsh Assembly in Cardiff and the Northern Ireland Assembly in Stormont, Belfast.

Devolution was granted to Scotland and Wales in the late 1990s and the Northern Ireland Assembly came into being in 1999 as a consequence of the ongoing peace process.

The new, devolved system differs from what's called a federalist system – such as operates in Germany and the United States – in two crucial ways:

- ✔ The central government (the UK parliament in Westminster) can take back the powers it has devolved at any time that it chooses by enacting a new law.
- ✔ The devolved parliaments and assemblies can be abolished by the central government.

When it comes to devolution, the UK parliament in Westminster retains certain powers. These powers can be divided into *excepted powers* and *reserved powers*. In short, excepted powers stay with the UK parliament no matter what and forever, while reserved powers may at some later stage be transferred from the UK parliament to the devolved institution.

Although the UK central government has the right to abolish the Scottish parliament or the Welsh Assembly, it's highly unlikely ever to use this power. Such action would be considered undemocratic as it would be going against the wishes of voters in Scotland and Wales who said 'yes' in a referendum on whether to have a working parliament or assembly.

The legal right of the UK central government to take back powers has been used during the Northern Irish peace process. At times, the parties in the Northern Ireland Assembly have either boycotted the government or been unable to work together. In these circumstances, the central government of the UK has taken back the powers that it in effect loaned the assembly but restored them when the parties settled their differences.

A member of the UK parliament is called an MP, of the Scottish parliament an MSP, of the Welsh Assembly an AM and of the Northern Ireland Assembly an MLA. That's an awful lot of politicians and an awful lot of abbreviations!

Handing over power to unelected quangos

As the Welsh, Scots and Northern Irish have become empowered to have a say in their governance and make their own laws, people throughout England have come under the sway of institutions that wield a lot of power but have a name that sounds like a soft drink – quango.

Quango stands for **qua**si **n**on-**g**overnmental **o**rganisation, which in English means an organisation that does work for the government but isn't directly accountable to the public as elected officials are. The head of a quango is usually appointed by government ministers from the UK parliament or the devolved institutions.

The number of quangos has shot up over the past decade as UK government expenditure has soared in a bid to deliver better public services. No one's sure how many quangos currently exist – some are set up to deliver a particular government objective and then disbanded, some stick around for years – but the most recent estimate in 2005 said that over 500 were in existence. Prominent quangos are those in the health care field, regional development agencies and, in transport, Network Rail, which is responsible for the infrastructure of Britain's railways.

Quangos are widely criticised as being too powerful and for controlling big budgets, while subject to little accountability apart from to the minister or senior civil servants in the department they're attached to.

Focusing on the Scottish parliament

Scotland is a nation within the UK with a long history and strong traditions. Up until 1707 – and the Act of Union with England and Wales – it had its very own parliament. With devolution in 1997, it regained some autonomy.

The Scottish parliament is over ten years old but is already a cornerstone of the UK constitution and political state. Of all the devolved parliaments and assemblies, the Scottish parliament is the most powerful and high profile. Even those politicians who opposed its formation probably can't quite imagine the political landscape without it.

The policy areas devolved from the UK central government to the Scottish parliament include:

- ✔ Health
- ✔ Education
- ✔ Agriculture
- ✔ Judicial services and police

✔ Transport

✔ Environment

✔ Tourism and the arts

In short, the Scottish parliament has the say on most of the policy areas affecting the lives of people in Scotland. But some policy areas – called *reserved powers* – are still in the hands of the UK parliament. They include:

✔ The power to negotiate foreign treaties and declare war

✔ Taxation

✔ Defence and national security

✔ The power of the Bank of England to set interest rates

Although tax policies are set by central government, the Scottish parliament can change tax rates. The Scottish parliament has the right to vary income tax in Scotland by up to 3p in the pound. It is then free to spend the money raised as it sees fit.

The Scottish parliament is based in expensive new offices in the Holyrood area of Edinburgh. In total, there are 129 MSPs – Members of the Scottish Parliament – representing Scotland's six million inhabitants.

Elections to the parliament are under the catchily titled *mixed member proportional representation system*, sometimes called the *additional member voting system*. In short, 73 of the MSPs are elected under the first-past-the-post system, which means that registered electors in an individual constituency vote for the candidate they want to represent them and the candidate with the most votes wins the seat. So far, so simple! But on top of these constituency MSPs are additional MSPs who are drawn from party candidate lists. Basically, the more votes the party gathers, the more candidates from its list get a seat in the Scottish parliament.

The biggest party in the Scottish parliament is currently the Scottish National Party (SNP), which wants full independence for Scotland from the UK. However, the SNP is a minority government and as a result needs the support of other parties within the parliament to see its bills pass into law.

Those who oppose the SNP's desire for Scottish independence refer to such a change as a divorce rather than independence. The idea is that calling it divorce gives the notion of independence a very negative connotation in the minds of the electorate.

Laying down the law in Scotland

The Scottish parliament has lots of powers and big bureaucracy. The biggest party in the parliament forms the Scottish government. At the head of this government is the *first minister* – in effect, Scotland's prime minister – and he or she appoints a cabinet, drawn from MSPs.

Like the Westminster parliament, ministers and individual MSPs propose legislation – in bill form – which is then debated and voted upon by other MSPs. The process is roughly based on the Westminster parliament, with bills being proposed on the floor of the parliament and then moving through a committee stage.

Here's how bills in Scotland become law:

- ✔ **Introductory stage.** The minister or individual MSP proposing the law formally introduces the bill to the parliament outlining the general principles behind it, along with supporting documents outlining how much the new law will cost. The bill is then debated and if a majority of MSPs agree, it moves on to the next stage of the legislative process.

- ✔ **Committee stage.** The details of the bill are examined by a committee of MSPs whose job it is to consider amendments to it. This process can be exhaustive and time-consuming.

- ✔ **Final vote stage.** The amendments to the bill made at committee stage are debated and voted upon by a meeting of the full Scottish parliament. After this, the bill as a whole is voted upon. If a majority agree, the bill only needs royal assent from the UK monarch – a constitutional formality – to become law.

Like the UK parliament in Westminster, a bill has a much better chance of becoming law if it's proposed by a government minister rather than an individual member.

Parliament typically sits on Tuesdays, Wednesdays and Thursdays, from early January to late June and from early September to mid-December, with two-week recesses in April and October.

Like in Westminster, it's a job of the parliament to scrutinise the actions of the executive – the Scottish government. To this end, the first minister and other ministers in the Scottish government regularly attend sessions of the parliament. MSPs are free to ask them questions about what they and their departments are doing. The most prominent question time takes place each Thursday between 12 and 12.30 p.m. when the parliament is sitting. Here, MSPs get to grill the first minister on the performance of the government.

Treading the path to Scottish independence

Many observers of how devolution has worked in Scotland suggest that it's merely a first step towards full independence. Their theory is that, once the Scottish people and their politicians have got used to governing themselves in areas such as education and health and the other devolved policy areas, they'll want to go the whole hog and gain control over taxation and foreign policy and become an independent state with membership of the European Union (EU) and the United Nations (UN). This outcome is the avowed aim of the Scottish National Party and first minister Alex Salmond. At present, the other main political parties in Scotland – Labour, Conservative and Lib Dem – are opposed to independence but there's nothing to say that this will always be the case.

In fact, in 2009 the SNP Scottish government said it planned to hold a referendum in Scotland on full independence, as well as on whether or not some of the powers reserved by the UK parliament in Westminster should actually be devolved to the Scottish parliament in Holyrood.

The main arguments for full Scottish independence are:

- ✔ The UK government acts for the whole of the UK and this can sometimes be detrimental to the interests of the people of Scotland.

- ✔ At present Scotland loses out because it's unable to run its own foreign missions and embassies and has to rely on the UK Foreign Office to represent its interests overseas.

- ✔ Scotland has very distinctive traditions and tends to adopt more socialist policies than those in England. Independence would mean the Scots being free of interference from England.

The decline of the Scottish fishing fleet is often cited as an example of the UK government choosing UK-wide interests over Scottish ones. Over the past two decades the Scottish fishing fleet has been systematically reduced due to negotiations on fishing quotas carried out by the UK government with other members of the EU. The argument goes that the UK government, by trying to get a good deal for the whole of the UK, hung the Scottish fishing fleet out to dry.

The main argument against full independence runs that it's better to be part of a powerful country like the UK, with a seat on the UN Security Council and major voting rights in the EU, than to be a relatively small independent country.

The notion of the Scottish parliament having more powers but stopping short of full independence has been called *devolution max*. Under devolution max, the Scottish parliament would have the right to set its own taxes and spend the cash it raised as it saw fit. In 2009 the Calman review of how devolution had worked concluded that it had been a success and should go further, with the Scottish parliament assuming the power to set smaller taxes such as air passenger duty and stamp duty.

Asking the West Lothian question

Devolution is viewed in Scotland as a big success but many people in England don't agree because of a constitutional anomaly dubbed the 'West Lothian question'. The phrase was first used by former Labour MP Tam Dalyell in 1979 when devolution was being debated in the UK parliament. The question is this: should an MP from a Scottish constituency such as West Lothian have the right to vote in the House of Commons in Westminster over laws affecting English domestic matters? This question is particularly moot because English MPs, following devolution, have no say over many aspects of Scottish domestic matters as they're in the power of the Scottish parliament and its MSPs. In fact, the Labour governments of Tony Blair and Gordon Brown were on occasion only able to gather enough MPs' votes in parliament for reforms to health and education in England – both devolved policy areas in Scotland – with the support of Labour MPs representing Scottish constituencies.

What's more, the Scottish, Welsh and Northern Irish enjoy two levels of parliamentary representation: they have their own parliament or assembly whose members they elect and then they also get to elect an MP to the UK parliament in Westminster. The English – who are the overwhelming majority population of the UK – in comparison only have the UK parliament.

Welcoming in the Welsh Assembly

The Welsh Assembly, or National Assembly for Wales as it's more formally known, was introduced at around the same time as the Scottish parliament. However, the Welsh Assembly doesn't have quite the same powers as the Scottish parliament. The assembly can make laws – called *assembly measures* – but these laws can be vetoed by the Secretary of State for Wales, who's a minister in the UK government based in Westminster.

The Welsh Assembly is allowed to legislate on pretty similar policy areas to those of the Scottish parliament, including:

- ✔ Agriculture
- ✔ Education
- ✔ Environment
- ✔ Health
- ✔ Transport
- ✔ Tourism and the arts

Wales shares its legal system with England so the assembly doesn't need power related to the judiciary or courts; this is left up to the UK parliament in Westminster.

The Welsh Assembly doesn't have powers to raise taxes or even to vary income tax rates.

A total of 60 elected members sit on the Welsh Assembly. As in the Scottish parliament, members are elected by a combination of the first-past-the-post and additional member systems.

Currently a coalition of the Labour Party and the nationalist Plaid Cymru holds a majority in the Welsh Assembly. Somewhat controversially, the assembly has used money from the UK government in Westminster to provide Welsh residents with free NHS prescriptions, charge students less for university tuition and offer discounted local authority care home fees. The controversy arises because these are all things that people in England have to pay more for, which has prompted critics to suggest that devolution favours Scotland and Wales at the expense of the English majority.

Although Plaid Cymru is a nationalist party – like the Scottish National Party – it doesn't, as yet, have a policy of full independence – unlike the SNP. Instead, it wants to see greater devolution from Westminster, with the Welsh Assembly getting the same legal powers as the Scottish parliament.

Priming the peace process: The Northern Ireland Assembly

The Northern Ireland Assembly is no ordinary legislative body; it's the embodiment of a long-cherished desire for peace, an end to conflict and a new age of co-operation. It was born as a result of the Good Friday Agreement in 1998, which finally brought some peace to Northern Ireland and ultimately an end to armed conflict between the warring paramilitary groups of the republicans who wanted Northern Ireland to join with the Republic, and the loyalists who wanted to keep Northern Ireland within the United Kingdom.

The Northern Ireland Assembly has law-making powers but with a twist – the assembly's constitution is designed to breed co-operation between the political parties rather than conflict, as is so often the case in the Westminster system. For example, its executive – in effect, the cabinet – isn't made up of members of the biggest party in the assembly (as it would be in Westminster). Instead, seats on the executive are distributed according to the number of seats a party has in the assembly. So, for example, the Democratic Unionist Party currently has 36 of 108 seats in the assembly, which is equivalent to just over a third of all the seats and, as a result, it also holds just over a third of the ministerial posts in the executive.

Although the Northern Ireland Assembly is as much about breeding co-operation and peace as devolved government, at times the parties in it simply haven't been able to get along and work together in government. As a result, the assembly has been suspended four times since its inception – the longest period being between 14 October 2002 and 7 May 2007. When this happens, the powers of the assembly are assumed by the Northern Ireland Secretary, a government minister in Westminster.

The Northern Ireland Assembly can make laws in the following policy areas:

- ✔ Agriculture
- ✔ Culture, arts, leisure and tourism
- ✔ Education
- ✔ Employment
- ✔ Environment
- ✔ Health
- ✔ Trade and investment

Two of the most important jobs in the executive of the Northern Ireland Assembly are the first minister and deputy first minister. The leaders of the two biggest parties in the assembly (by number of seats) fill these two positions.

As in Scotland and Wales, the Northern Ireland Assembly has no right to legislate in certain areas, such as on foreign and defence policy. In addition, the Northern Ireland Assembly can't legislate on criminal law or the police service, as well as – more bizarrely – consumer protection matters or telecommunications.

Chapter 17

Joining the Lawmakers: Becoming a Politician

· ·

In This Chapter

▶ Getting into the party

▶ Running for local office

▶ Going for a seat in parliament

▶ Leading the life of an MP

▶ Rising in government ranks

· ·

Don't just want to read about UK politics but want to get involved? Then this is the chapter for you. From local councillor or justice of the peace all the way up to the top jobs in British politics, this chapter shows you how to help make the laws of the land and even do your bit to shape the political scene.

Becoming Part of the Party System

British politics is based around the party system. The main political parties – the Conservative, Labour and Liberal Democrat – and some smaller ones compete for political offices around the country, fielding individual party members as candidates.

Helping these candidates get elected are other party members who volunteer to undertake work such as canvassing door to door and posting party literature through residents' letterboxes. The cost of printing materials is funded by the party, which in turn gets its money from members' annual subscriptions and donations.

Political parties only select members of the party to stand for election.

What does all this mean if you have ambitions to hold elected office? Well, it will be much easier to reach your goal if you're a member of a political party.

Most electors, even in a small council ward, never actually get to meet any of the party candidates in the run-up to an election. They may rely on information contained in the local press or party leaflets pushed through their letterbox to decide who they'll vote for. More often than not, though, electors have a particular party they favour – based on family and social background as well as their own life experience – who they'll vote for time and again, regardless of the character or reputation of the party's candidate. Candidates for the big political parties can usually be sure of a certain level of support at election time merely because they're their party's candidate. (Chapter 8 talks about what prompts people to support a particular political party.)

Sometimes it's possible for people who aren't members of one of the big recognised political parties to achieve political office. They do so by standing for election as an independent. However, these independents are normally only successful at parish council or local council elections. I cover running in local elections in the upcoming 'Stepping onto the First Rung of the Political Ladder: Local Elected Office'.

Setting out on the journey: Joining a political party

Joining a political party is the first step to becoming a politician, although in some respects that's the wrong way around. Most people join a party because its policies best reflect their thinking on the big events shaping society, from how to tackle crime and inequality to promoting greater wealth and retaining Britain's place in the world pecking order. Only after becoming a member of the party do people start to think that they'd like to represent that party at an election and thus join the ranks of Britain's politicians.

Not every member of a political party wants to become a candidate at an election. In fact, only a relatively small percentage of party members ever get close or show any desire to be a candidate. Most of the time party members are happy doing volunteer work, or simply giving silent support through an annual membership subscription and ensuring they vote for their party of choice at election time.

Becoming a candidate for election can be very time-consuming, impinging on family life, and to be frank, the glare of publicity that election campaigning brings is very few people's cup of tea.

Lots of political parties exist in the UK, some with only a few members, to ones with hundreds of thousands of members and a long, proud history going back, in the case of the Conservatives and Lib Dems, over 200 years. The history and relative strengths of the UK's political parties are explored in Chapter 8. Generally, the candidates of the bigger political parties –

Conservative, Labour, Lib Dem and the nationalist parties in Scotland, Wales and Northern Ireland – do the best at election time.

Moving from party member to candidate

The politician's life may not be for everyone but being selected as candidate for election still involves stiff competition. The crucial thing to understand is that party members select the candidate they want to represent the party at election. For example, a Labour Party member looking to stand as a Labour candidate in elections to his or her local council ward has to be selected by a vote of fellow Labour Party members in the locality.

In essence, this means that if you want to become a candidate, you have to convince your fellow party members that you're the right person for the job and will do well at election time.

Your best chance for being selected lies in ticking the following boxes:

- ✔ **Be a longstanding party member.** Anyone wishing to be a candidate has to show that they're committed to the party and its causes and one way to do that is to remain a member, paying annual subscriptions for several years.

- ✔ **Be a volunteer.** Being selected as a candidate is easier if you have a high profile in the local party. One way to raise your profile is by volunteering to help people who've already been selected as candidates. Many of the country's leading politicians started out by door-to-door canvassing and leafleting trying to get someone else elected.

- ✔ **Build a political CV.** Don't just get involved in volunteer work for the party, also look to help with fundraising and attend the party's annual party conference (which can be quite raucous affairs in the evening, involving lots of drinking). Becoming a candidate is about the three Ps: profile, profile and, yes, more profile.

- ✔ **Be sure of yourself.** Do you have the time and the home set-up to allow you to spend the time it takes to battle your way to being a party candidate? You may wait many years before getting a chance to stand at an election and most people with ambitions to be a politician never even get that far.

To stand for election to parliament or local council, you must be at least 18 years old and a British citizen, or a citizen of a Commonwealth country with indefinite leave to stay in the UK. You can't be an MP if you're a civil servant, an undischarged bankrupt, a member of the clergy, police or armed forces, a prisoner serving more than a year in jail, or if you've been found guilty of certain electoral offences. In addition, people looking to stand for election to a council have to have lived in the locality for at least 12 months prior to the election date.

Stepping onto the First Rung of the Political Ladder: Local Elected Office

Standing for election to local government office – and winning – is often the starting point for many great political careers, whilst for others it represents the peak of their ambition.

The vast majority of politicians in this country aren't full-time politicians; instead, they're everyday people who give up their spare time to help run local government.

Local government in the UK is based on the council system. Put simply, a *council* administers local government; it does everything from looking after the highways to ensuring the rubbish is collected to approving or rejecting planning applications. At the top of the council are elected officials – *councillors* – who make the big decisions, supported by a professional civil service. In the overwhelming majority of cases these councillors are elected by the public as candidates of a particular political party.

Being a local councillor first isn't a prerequisite of becoming a Member of Parliament (MP), Member of the Scottish Parliament (MSP) or assembly member in Wales or Northern Ireland, but it certainly can be a big plus point in getting selected as a candidate to stand for election.

In England, below county and district councils in England are parish councils. A *parish council* looks after such things as the upkeep of the local parks and alerts the local council of any issues in their area which need attention – such as potholes in the road.

The parish council is the very lowest political rung in the UK but even here the parties have a hold, as candidates are more often than not members of a specific political party.

In Scotland, the community groups do a similar job to that of the parish councils in England. The ins and outs of local government throughout the UK are explored in detail Chapter 16.

Aiming for a Seat in Parliament

All three main national political parties in the UK have their own methods of selecting a candidate to stand for election to parliament or the devolved national assemblies (see Chapter 16 for more on devolution).

The following list offers a basic guide to the hurdles that have to be jumped by candidates for each of the three main national parties:

- ✔ **Conservative.** Party members have to make it onto the *approved candidate list*. Selection for the list is via an application form, interviews and a half-day assessment programme. If you're successful and make it onto the list, you're free to apply to individual constituency Conservative Party associations. The members of these party associations choose who will stand as candidate for the election.

- ✔ **Labour.** The Labour Party has a tradition of devolved selection of candidates, but in recent years the party bigwigs working at Central Office have had more of a say in who should be a candidate for parliament.

  Like the Conservatives and Lib Dems, the Labour Party operates a central list of approved candidates that local parties can select from. The party's National Executive Committee chooses who should be on the approved list. Unlike the other parties, though, members of the local Labour Party can choose candidates not on the approved list but nominated by a trade union or individual council ward. Again, final selection of the candidate is down to a vote of party members in the individual constituency.

  The Labour Party's National Executive Committee (NEC) is made up of its MPs, prominent local councillors and trade unionists. Its job is to help form party policy and impose discipline on party members. Drawing up the list of approved party candidates is another of its key roles.

- ✔ **Lib Dem.** A party member wishing to become a candidate for election to parliament has to make it onto a centrally approved list. Just like going for an ordinary job, application forms need to be filled in and interviews conducted. Once the person has made it onto the list of candidates, he or she can start applying to individual constituency Lib Dem associations, which will conduct interviews with potential candidates and make its selection via a secret ballot of local party members.

From the time when an individual is selected by a party to stand for an election to the UK parliament, until the calling of the general election, he or she's referred to as a *prospective parliamentary candidate*.

Generally, the more winnable a constituency is for a particular party, the greater the number of people looking to become a candidate. For example, the constituencies in the southeast of England are often won by the Conservative Party. When one of these candidacies becomes available, therefore, competition amongst people on the party's approved list of candidates tends to be very fierce indeed. On the flip side, the Conservatives do less well in the north-east of England and Scotland so competition to become a candidate in those seats is less heated. (See Chapter 8 for more on the inner workings of all the main political parties.)

Getting more women into parliament

At present, despite making up the majority of the population, fewer than one in four MPs are women. The Labour Party has a policy of increasing the representation of women. To this end, in 2002 Labour introduced women-only shortlists in what it termed winnable seats. This meant that the local party could only pick a female candidate to stand for election as MP. This move has been highly controversial, with some arguing that women-only lists mean that candidates don't make it on merit alone.

The Conservative Party at first openly disapproved of Labour's women-only shortlist policy, but under leader David Cameron has been actively trying to increase the number of women and ethnic minorities standing as candidates. The party has done so by favouring female and ethnic minority candidates when drawing up its approved list. However, selection is still the choice of constituency members.

The Lib Dems have always rejected the notion of women-only shortlists, stating that favouring one gender over the other is illiberal. Recent reports, though, suggest that the Lib Dems are struggling to attract as many women to stand as parliamentary candidates as the party leadership would like.

Targeting your constituency

The odds are stacked against even ambitious party members becoming parliamentary candidates. Looking at the Conservative Party, for instance, in 2009 it had some 500–600 people on its approved candidate list, all fighting for around 30 or 40 candidacies available at that time.

Against such odds, if you'd like to be adopted as a parliamentary candidate, adhere to these few key rules or risk becoming merely a wannabe politician:

✔ **Limit the number of constituencies you apply to.** The party members who select candidates like to think that there's something special about their constituency and don't take kindly to people who apply to lots of others. Limit your application to say five or six constituencies.

✔ **Be prepared to live in the constituency.** All prospective parliamentary candidates are expected to have an address in the constituency in the run-up to election day. As a candidate, you bear the costs of this constituency home.

✔ **Get to know the constituency.** Anyone applying to be a candidate will be expected to know about the constituency. You need to be aware of any local controversy, know who's the biggest employer in the constituency and which areas of it are likely to vote for or against your party's candidate.

If you want to become a party candidate at an election, make sure that you get to know the important political issues affecting the constituency you wish to represent.

Some people fight and lose an election or two before eventually winning a seat in parliament. They may be chosen as a candidate in a seat which the party they're representing doesn't have much chance of winning. By putting in a good showing, however, even in defeat, the candidate may improve their chances of securing a more promising candidacy at the next election.

When selecting a constituency to apply to, going for one with which you have a natural affinity – where you were born, went to university or lived in the past – is best.

Preparing for an election

A person selected to represent a party as a candidate at an election needs a lot of patience. Often parties select candidates a year or more before the likely date of an election. In the case of a general election, the government gets to choose the date, so in theory it can call an election any time. Constituency parties don't want to be caught out by not having a candidate when the prime minister calls a snap general election. What's more, selecting a candidate well in advance of the election gives the candidate time to increase their profile in the constituency.

But as election day approaches, if you're a candidate, you have to take care of some admin, including the following:

- ✔ **Get your nomination in.** You have to fill out a nomination form, available from the local council or Electoral Commission offices before you're allowed to stand as a candidate at election. It must be countersigned by ten electors and returned by the candidate in person!

- ✔ **Pay your deposit.** Each candidate, whether belonging to a big party or standing as an independent, has to pay a deposit of £500 before they're allowed to stand for election to parliament. This deposit goes up to £5,000 in the case of European elections, whereas people standing for election to the local council don't have to pay a deposit at all.

  The deposit paid by all candidates standing for election is repaid if the candidate gets more than five per cent of the votes cast. If they fail to reach this level of support, they lose the deposit. Candidates from the big parties rarely lose their deposit.

- ✔ **Appoint an election agent.** Having an agent may seem the preserve of film stars and Premier League footballers, but every parliamentary candidate has to have one too. But instead of negotiating big money contracts and transfer moves, the job of a *parliamentary agent* is much more mundane: he or she is charged with co-ordinating the candidate's election campaign.

Counting the votes: Election night

On the day of a general election the polling stations across the country open at 7 a.m. and close at 10 p.m.

As soon as the polling stations close, the big TV broadcasters – the BBC, ITV and Sky – announce the results of their nationwide exit poll. This is involves sending people to a handful of polling stations around the country and asking those coming out who they voted for. The answers are used to predict the likely result of the general election: which party will secure a majority or whether there'll be a *hung parliament* – which means that no single party has enough seats to be in the majority.

Meanwhile, across the country the ballot boxes are collected and taken to the local town hall or community centre to be counted by election workers. The whole procedure is carefully monitored and if any dispute occurs over the result or the counting process, the ballots may be counted again before the result is announced.

Counting takes a few hours and most results are announced in the early hours of the morning.

The whole counting process is overseen by a *returning officer*, who also declares the result of the election for that constituency. The declaration is pure theatre. The returning officer reads out the names of the candidates and the party they belong to in the order they appear on the ballot paper and the number of votes each gathered. The atmosphere is usually very charged, with dozens of people in the hall all rooting for their own candidate and cheering and booing as each result is declared. After all the candidates' votes have been announced, the returning officer declares the winner – the person who'll represent his or her party in parliament as MP. Each of the candidates then makes a speech thanking the returning officer, the people who've helped ensure the election was fair and above board and, of course, their own supporters.

Several MPs I've spoken to say that getting to know the editor of the local newspaper is crucial for a parliamentary candidate. The editor knows what's going on in the constituency and the newspaper's coverage of the election campaign may prove pivotal to its outcome.

Parliamentary candidates are entitled to free delivery of one small leaflet to every house in the constituency (but the Royal Mail will refuse to take offensive material!).

A general election campaign lasts about three to four weeks. Once an election is called, the local party volunteers hit the streets, canvassing door to door and attending the candidate's rallies and photo opportunities. Party volunteers work in their spare time to create a buzz around the candidate they support in a bid to get him or her elected.

Getting to Grips with Life as an MP

At first glance, the life of an MP seems just a bit glam – for starters, you're part of the key law-making body in the country and what you do each day can make a real difference to the lives of your fellow citizens. In addition, as an MP you take part in the key debates about the country's future and are part of the history of a democracy which goes back centuries. You even get to work in the Houses of Parliament, one of the iconic buildings of Britain – if not the world.

But the life of an MP isn't all taking part in crucial debates, making laws and fighting for what you believe in. No, an MP's lot involves loads of administrative work, travel and long, long hours spent in musty committee rooms.

Some of the key duties of an MP include:

- ✔ **Looking after constituents.** Much of an MP's time is spent answering letters and fielding calls from constituents. MPs often take issue with public bodies that may have wronged a constituent in some way, writing a letter on their behalf and making other representations.

- ✔ **Keeping in with the local party.** MPs have to stand for re-election at least once every five years, and to have the best chance of success they need the support of their local party (volunteer workers in particular). As a result, MPs spend a lot of their time helping with party fundraisers and meeting with leading figures of their party in the constituency.

- ✔ **Obeying the party whips.** Each party has *whips*; MPs whose job is to maintain discipline amongst their fellow MPs on behalf of the party leader. They often instruct MPs in the party to turn up and vote at the House of Commons. MPs who ignore the whips are likely to pay a high price in terms of blocked career advancement.

- ✔ **Attending committee meetings.** Most of the work of parliament takes place in committees. MPs are expected to attend and contribute to debates about bills going through parliament. Some committees are quite high-profile, such as the defence select committee or the public accounts committee, but the overwhelming majority are pretty mundane and don't get much public attention.

Each week an MP is expected to hold a *surgery* in their constituency – but it doesn't involve nurses, scalpels and swabs. An MP's surgery is an allotted time when members of the public can drop by and discuss their problems. Often the MP can't do anything about a problem facing a constituent (apart from point them in the direction of someone who can help); occasionally, though, they can actually do something and will take up the case.

The job of MSPs in the Scottish parliament and assembly members in Wales and Northern Ireland is very similar to that of MPs in Westminster. They're expected to vote on bills, see constituents and attend committee meetings.

Occasionally an MP gets involved in a campaign that takes on a life of its own and becomes a crusade. For example, in the 1980s and 1990s Labour MP Chris Mullin became convinced that six men found guilty of bombing two pubs in Birmingham in 1974 as members of the IRA were in fact innocent. He campaigned for years for a retrial, going on TV, giving interviews and writing books and articles. Eventually Mullin got his way and the Birmingham Six, as they were known, were acquitted.

After the expenses scandal of 2009, when dozens of MPs were found to have made dishonest claims, support grew for a *recall law*. If an MP was seen as failing in their duty and enough people in the constituency were unhappy with the job they were doing, this law would mean the MP could be recalled from parliament and replaced with someone from the same political party.

Climbing the Greasy Pole to the Top Jobs in Government

The climb to high position is often referred to as the 'greasy pole' for good reason – it's very easy to slip back down.

Most MPs have ambitions above simply being a good constituency MP; they want to make a real difference by becoming a minister who gets to pilot government legislation through the Houses of Parliament and has a real say on government policy potentially affecting the lives of millions of Britons. However, only a small number of MPs become ministers or rise further up the ranks to the highest jobs in government, such as the Home Secretary, Foreign Secretary, Chancellor of the Exchequer and, of course, the top slot, prime minister. In fact, if you're an MP representing an opposition party rather than the party of government, you have no chance of becoming a minister until and unless your party secures a majority of seats in the House of Commons and therefore forms the government.

But even for those MPs on the government benches in the Commons, making it into ministerial office can still be very hard. Many get close to the summit but don't quite make it.

The path to ministerial power is outlined in the following list. Each step is normally ascended in turn and reaching the top can take many years.

✔ **Parliamentary under-secretary.** This minister's job is to support the departmental minister of state – usually a more senior MP. An under-secretary basically does the work that the more senior minister doesn't have time for.

✔ **Parliamentary private secretary.** This job is the first rung on the ladder to the top ministerial posts. The PPS acts as the go-between for ministers and parliament. He or she helps keep track of backbench MPs' opinions as they relate to the minister and the legislation they're trying to introduce in parliament.

✔ **Minister of state.** Below the cabinet minister are two, three or even four other ministers whose job it is to look after a particular part of the ministry's work. For example, in the Ministry of Defence is a minister for defence procurement, whose job it is to oversee expenditure on weapons and equipment, as well as ministers for the armed forces and international security co-operation.

✔ **Cabinet minister.** This politician heads a government department. Their job is to defend the department to cabinet colleagues and the PM and to argue the case for more money for the department's coffers from the Chancellor of the Exchequer. Cabinet ministers are often referred to as secretaries of state.

Ministers are appointed by the prime minister. Ambitious MPs courting ministerial office need to keep the PM sweet and they do so by remaining loyal and voting the way they're told to by the whips. (Chapter 14 talks more about the role of ministers in government.)

Part IV
Politics Worldwide

'The Chancellor of the Exchequer was on TV again talking about pensions.'

In this part . . .

1 get all global, looking at Britain's relationship with the super-powers the United States and the European Union. I examine the key role of the United Nations, the Commonwealth and the emerging global trade blocs in international affairs. I examine the changing face of NATO and the rising power of China. Closer to home I explain the intricacies of the European Union, its constitution and treaties. Finally, I travel to the Land of the Free, the United States, to look at how the world's most important democracy works in practice.

Chapter 18

Understanding Britain's Place in the World

. . . .

In This Chapter

▶ Moving from empire to somewhere in the middle

▶ Cosying up to the European Union

▶ Maintaining a special relationship with the United States

▶ Reckoning with China

▶ Heading up the Commonwealth of Nations

▶ Policing the world

. . . .

*B*ritain may be an island but it has always engaged with the rest of the world, from the days of exploration and empire through to the export of British music and culture.

In this chapter I take an honest look at Britain's relationship with its close neighbours in Europe and further afield to the former colonies, the rising powerhouse China, and, of course, the United States.

Declining Fortunes: From Empire to the Middle Ranks

If you find yourself an old atlas – and I'm talking early 20th century, here – and turn to a map of the world, you see an awful lot of countries coloured in pink – India, the West Indies, large tracts of Africa and even Canada and Australia. Are they pink because they're hot countries and therefore suffer a bit of sunburn? No, pink was the colour used to indicate which countries belonged to the British Empire.

At its height, the British Empire spanned around a quarter of the globe and held sway over the lives of hundreds of millions of people. As Cecil Rhodes, the Victorian imperialist, once said, 'To be born British is to win first prize in the lottery of life' and indeed for those Brits who got to travel the world and govern other people as imperial civil servants this may have seemed the case. It was also said at around the same time that the sun never set on the British Empire – an expression of both its geographic spread and what seemed its eternal nature.

However, within a century the British Empire had considerably diminished and Britain's role in the world also shrank. What happened? Well, Britain got involved in the two world wars, which virtually bankrupted the country and drained its natural and manpower resources. Meanwhile, many of the countries in the empire developed their own independence movements, perhaps buoyed by Britain's sudden fragility.

When the end of the empire came, it did so relatively quickly. Encouraged by the US government – who wanted to expand their own influence and to whom the British government owed huge debts – the empire was rolled up. First India became independent, followed by colonies in the West Indies and finally those in Africa. In fact, within 25 years of the end of the Second World War, Britain's once massive empire consisted of a handful of islands and far-flung outposts.

Britain's empire lasted for a few hundred years and once even contained territories that became the United States. It was a deeply racist institution and white people from the empire were granted self-government early on while countries in Africa and the West Indies had to wait a long time for self-government or independence. Put simply, many British politicians of the 19th and early 20th centuries didn't believe that non-whites could be trusted to run their own affairs – I told you it was racist!

Probably the most famous figure who protested British rule was the Indian Mahatma Gandhi. He was an inspiration to tens of millions of ordinary Indians and he believed passionately that the country should rule itself rather than be ruled by Britain. He led a boycott of British goods and embarked on hunger strikes and peaceful protests. He gathered much support in Britain for his aims and eventually, shortly after the end of the Second World War, India was granted its independence. However, Gandhi didn't live to see his newly free country blossom, as he was assassinated in January 1948.

Forging a New Role in Europe

With Britain's empire gone and the economy struggling under the debts and other burdens of the Second World War, Britain started to view its role, not as a superpower like America and Russia, but as a leading nation within Europe on a par with France and Germany.

UK and Europe: Growing together or growing apart?

In many respects the UK hasn't been as close to the continent politically and economically as it is today since the Reformation in the mid-16th century. The UK is part of the *single European market*, which means that goods and people can move freely across the whole of the EU – 27 countries and 500 million people. In addition, many of the laws affecting the daily lives of Britons are initiated in the institutions of the European Union.

English is very much the language of business on the continent and millions of Britons travel there for work or pleasure each year. In many respects it could be said that Britain has become part of a European super-state. Whereas 20 years ago it was a given that the EU was moving towards being a super-state and that Britain had a choice of joining in or going it alone, the nature of what was once called the 'European project' has changed.

The expansion of the EU into the former Warsaw Pact countries in 2004 has been key in diluting the idea of an EU super-state. The nations of the east survived under Soviet tyranny for four decades after the end of the Second World War and, having newly gained their independence, many are now loath to sign over more powers to a centralised EU state. So the reluctance to join the European project felt by a majority of Britons – according to opinion polls – which angered many of the EU's partners such as France, Belgium and Germany, is now echoed in eastern Europe. The EU's march to super-state status isn't so self-assured and, although membership of it has changed Britain, ultimately Britain's membership has also changed the EU; it was the UK which was instrumental in bringing the former Warsaw Pact countries of eastern Europe into the EU.

To this end, throughout the 1960s and 1970s the British tried to join the newly formed European Economic Community (EEC), now called the European Union (EU), in the hope of improving trade with the continent. The UK's entry was initially objected to by the French, with President Charles de Gaulle famously vetoing it. But the UK was finally allowed to join in 1973.

Conservative prime minister Edward Heath negotiated Britain's entry into the EEC. It was the culmination of years of diplomacy – particularly when it came to easing the fears of the French – and a triumph for Heath. He often said that he saw Britain's place as a part of Europe rather than as a go-it-alone power. He recognised that Britain had declined as a military, financial and economic power and saw that it could only retain influence on the world stage by working with other nations of similar populations, such as France and Germany.

And not only in terms of trade and the EU did the UK start to look to the continent of Europe rather to than the wider world. The Cold War and threat to western Europe from the Soviet Union led to the formation of the *North Atlantic Treaty Organisation (NATO)*, a military body meant to ensure collective security. The UK, with a strong military, was a leading member of NATO, often working closely with the US.

By the 21st century the majority of Britain's trade was with its EU partners (before the Second World War less than a quarter of the nation's trade was with Europe) and much of its diplomacy was carried out jointly with the other members of the EU, particularly France and Germany.

Not all British politicians are enthusiastic towards the EU. Many argue that the EU is trying to become a super-state and reduce the power of the nation state. Critics suggest that the EU's institutions, such as the commission and parliament, are corrupt and that the famous Common Agricultural Policy (CAP) – see Chapter 20 for more on this – is a massive waste of resources. People critical of the EU who think that Britain would be better off out of it are called *Eurosceptics* and can often be found in the Conservative and UK Independence parties.

Assessing the Special Relationship with the United States

Watch any of the 24-hour news channels for long enough and you're bound to hear the phrase *special relationship* in reference to Britain's close ties with the United States. In this case, a special relationship doesn't mean that Britain and the US are going to move in together, pick furnishings and share a toothbrush holder. Instead, it harks back to the Second World War when the UK and US were allies and fought and beat Nazi Germany and Japan. The two countries worked incredibly closely together and this relationship carried on into the post-war period when western Europe was threatened by the Soviet Union. The countries share the same language and both are democracies. In addition, a long history exists of Americans working and living in Britain and vice versa. The bonds between the two countries are indeed strong and are historical, economic and cultural in nature.

However, it's often said that the UK lays too much store by the special relationship and, according to some critics, that the UK follows US foreign policy too slavishly. For example, during the run-up to the war in Iraq in 2003 the British PM Tony Blair was caricatured as a poodle of the US president George W. Bush because not only did he support the US-led invasion, he also sent thousands of UK military personnel into the conflict.

The phrase *special relationship* was first coined by British PM Winston Churchill in the aftermath of the Second World War. Churchill felt the closeness of Britain's relationship with the US not only because of the co-operation between the two nations during the war but also because his mother was American. (Winston Churchill was one of Britain's great PMs and is covered in more detail in Chapter 22.)

We may not be in the throes of a world war, and the threat from the old Soviet Union (now just plain old Russia) has subsided, yet the US and UK military and intelligence services still cooperate and share an awful lot of information. Often the two nations find themselves together on peace-keeping duty around the globe and with the same diplomatic goals. Why is this? Well, both countries are democracies and have strong cultural and economic ties, so it's understandable that their national interests often coincide.

Looking Further Afield to the Rise of China

If you want to see proof of the dramatic rise of China, look no further than your own sitting room. The TV you watch, the sofa you sit on, the coffee table you place your mug on – chances are they're all manufactured in China.

China is very much the workshop of the world – the title held by Britain at the start of the 19th century. Its growth is awe-inspiring and at this point looks almost limitless. It's estimated that within 20 years the Chinese economy will be bigger than that of the US. Already many of its banks and financial institutions own large numbers of Western businesses. In fact, some suggest that what's happening is a form of reverse imperialism: the Western countries – such as Britain, the US, Germany and France – are now finding the businesses, land and natural resources they once owned around the globe being rapidly supplanted and taken over by Chinese firms, all backed by what's still ostensibly a communist Chinese government.

Britain exports very little to China; in fact, Scotch whisky is probably the biggest export. In contrast, China exports large quantities of manufactured goods to the UK. But with China racing to superpower status, much of Britain's future fortunes will be tied to how well it can forge trading and other links with it. Developing this relationship is one of the major challenges of the rest of the 21st century and with it rests the UK's future prosperity – or lack of it!

The UK currently has the fifth-largest economy in the world behind the US, Japan, China and Germany. Generally, the UK economy – and population – is on a close par with those of France and Italy.

Leading the Commonwealth of Nations

Britain may have lost an empire but it's gained what's called the *Commonwealth of Nations*. The Commonwealth is an international organisation made up almost entirely of former member states of the old British Empire including Australia, India and South Africa as well as lesser known countries such as St Kitts, Lesotho and Malta, whose aim is to promote peace, economic growth and cultural co-operation. There are 53 member states (plus the UK) in the Commonwealth – around a quarter of all the countries in the world.

When the Commonwealth was formed it was called the British Commonwealth, which was a nod to the UK's top dog status as the former imperial power. However, this name was changed to the Commonwealth of Nations, reflecting perhaps the decline of Britain's power around the globe and the desire of the member nations to appear to be a collection of equal nations rather than being under the banner of a former imperial power.

The head of the Commonwealth is the British monarch. This role is largely ceremonial, with the monarch making speeches and turning up for the opening session of the biennial Commonwealth conferences. Interestingly, the British monarch is the actual head of state of 16 of the 53 member states of the Commonwealth. Although the title is largely symbolic, the current British monarch takes her role as head of the Commonwealth very seriously indeed.

Members of the Commonwealth are supposed to adhere to the 1971 Singapore Declaration. This states that members should try to promote peace, human rights, individual liberty, equality and free trade. However, members have often broken with the ideals of the declaration, with some having very dodgy human rights records.

Member states which move too far away from the ideals of the Commonwealth can be suspended from the organisation. Nigeria, Pakistan and, more recently, Zimbabwe have all been suspended over concerns related to human rights or election fraud. Even the idyllic island of Fiji was suspended between 1987 and 1997 after the democratic government was ousted by a military takeover.

Every two years the heads of government of all the Commonwealth nations meet for a big conference. Prime ministers and presidents from all around the globe jet in to discuss all manner of stuff, from improving global trade to issues of security and international development. These heads of government meetings last several days and are usually held in a nice sunny location.

The Commonwealth has its very own civil service – the Commonwealth Secretariat. Based in London, the Secretariat's wide-ranging job includes:

 ✔ Organising the heads of government meeting and drawing up agendas for this important biennial shindig.

✔ Providing economic and social development help to poor member states – in effect, providing them with a professional civil service.

✔ Working to encourage member states to talk to one another so as to increase co-operation and ensure peace.

The Commonwealth Secretariat has a politician sitting at the top making the big calls: the Commonwealth secretary general. He or she's elected by a vote at the heads of government meeting every four years. The Commonwealth secretary general's job is to be a mouthpiece for the Commonwealth, embodying the organisation's shared aims, such as preserving human rights and supporting free trade. The present secretary general is Kamalesh Sharma, an Indian politician.

One of the fun things about the Commonwealth – apart from the sunny locations that host the heads of government meetings – is that membership brings with it the right to field a team at the Commonwealth Games. The *Commonwealth Games* resembles a mini-Olympics and is held every four years. Top athletes represent their nations by competing in all manner of sporting and athletic events. The next Commonwealth Games will be held in Delhi in 2010.

Many of the Commonwealth nations share traditions relating to the old British Empire, for example playing cricket and rugby, driving on the left-hand side of the road and enjoying Westminster-style parliamentary democracy. And above and beyond all this, of course, is the English language, which is spoken as a first or second language in many parts of the world.

Ruling the Waves: British Overseas Territories

You may not realise it but the British Empire actually still exists in the 21st century. It may not cover huge tracts of the globe and hold hundreds of millions of people in its sway but some states called *British Overseas Territories* are, in essence, still run by the UK.

Fourteen British Overseas Territories exist in total, many of which you may not have heard of: Anguilla, Bermuda (very nice and sunny), British Antarctic Territory (very chilly), British Virgin Islands (no comment), Cayman Islands, the Falkland Islands (their flag has a sheep on it!), Gibraltar (rocky, warm and famous for its monkeys), Montserrat, Pitcairn Islands, Saint Helena, Ascension and Tristan de Cunha, South Georgia and the South Sandwich Islands (tasty place I hear), the sovereign base areas of Akrotiri and Dhekelia in Cyprus, and finally the Turks and Caicos Islands.

In population terms, the British Overseas Territories are tiny. The most populous by far is Bermuda, with around 65,000 people; the smallest is the British Antarctic Territory, which has a dozen scientists and a few million penguins. In fact, if you were to add up the population of all 14 British Overseas Territories, it would come to fewer than 300,000 – around the same size population as Northampton or Stoke!

Why does Britain still retain these territories and furthermore why do the local people still want the Brits hanging around? The simple answer is that Britain wants to retain rights to have military bases in these countries, but also stays out of a sense of responsibility. Many of these countries are so small that they'd find it very hard to survive without the government services and investment that being a part of Britain brings. Many of the people have strong historic ties with Britain. The Falkland Islands, for instance, has fewer than 3,000 people but most of them are descendants of British whalers and emigrant farmers in the 19th century. Plus, people from the Overseas Territories are entitled to full British citizenship, which means that they're allowed to work anywhere in the European Union.

Playing the Role of World Police Officer

Britain may no longer be a world superpower but it's no slouch in the military stakes. It's famous for having well-trained, completely volunteer armed services (most European nations rely on conscription), which can be deployed in trouble spots around the globe in double-quick time. Britain's a key member of NATO and a permanent member of the UN Security Council, which I talk about in the next section. In fact, over the past 20 years the UK has acted as peacekeeper in places as diverse as Bosnia in the Balkans and Sierra Leone in sub-Saharan Africa. The UK has also become embroiled in two bloody wars in Iraq and Afghanistan in support of the US's action in what's been dubbed the 'war on terror' following the 11 September 2001 attacks on the United States.

Under PMs Tony Blair and Gordon Brown, Britain became a leading proponent of helping out poorer nations in the developing world. Both Blair and Brown cajoled other leaders into writing off some African countries' debts, as well as committing more cash in the form of aid and grants to help the poorest nations in the world improve their infrastructure.

Deterring the unthinkable: Britain and the bomb

One of the reasons the UK is still ranked as a bit of a military powerhouse is because it retains a nuclear deterrent. Through missiles carried on its fleet of nuclear submarines, the UK still has a nuclear strike capability. The full horrors of this power are probably not worth thinking about but the retention of what was dubbed the *nuclear deterrent* was a powerful symbol of Britain's and the West's ability to face potential Soviet aggression in Europe. Britain's nuclear power status was hugely controversial in the 1980s, with peace activists calling for the country to disarm.

Nowadays the Soviet threat no longer exists, yet Britain retains its nuclear weapons capability along with the US, Russia, China, France, Israel, India and, most recently, Pakistan. Why does Britain keep its weapons now that the Soviet Union is no more? Well, the politicians (and most politicians from most parties support Britain keeping its nuclear bombs) say that it's essential for Britain to keep its nuclear weapons in a world where nations such as Iran and the tyrannical North Korean regimes are all making efforts to acquire nuclear weapons of their own.

Sitting at the Top Table: The UN Security Council

The UK, due to its status as one of the five victorious powers at the end of the Second World War, has a place on the United Nations (UN) Security Council. The Security Council is the muscle behind the UN (an organisation I talk about in detail in Chapter 19). It can deploy peacekeepers and impose sanctions.

Each of the five 'permanent' members – the US, the UK, Russia, China and France – has the power of veto; as a result, the Security Council can only decide that something should be done if the five members are in agreement. Membership of the UN Security Council gives the UK a lot of power in international diplomatic circles.

The power of veto is useful, if rarely used by the UK. Since the UN started in 1947, the UK has vetoed some 32 resolutions out of a total of nearly 2,000. The US, on the other hand, has vetoed 82 and the Soviet Union/Russia 123.

Fifteen members make up the Security Council: the five permanent member countries and ten other nations elected by the full membership of the UN (around 200 countries), each of which remains on the council for two years. These non-permanent members can vote on UN resolutions but have no power of veto.

The UN produces resolutions – about 40 to 50 per year, on average – telling members how they should behave, which can be backed up by military force if the Security Council agrees.

Some suggest reforming the UN Security Council, as its five permanent members reflect the international power politics of the mid-20th century rather than the 21st. To this end, according to some, both the UK and France should lose their permanent status and be replaced by a representative from the European Union. However, unsurprisingly both Britain and France are opposed to this idea and suggest instead that other major powers, such as Brazil and India, should become permanent members – although without the power of veto – of the Security Council.

Chapter 19

Taking In the International Stage

· ·

In This Chapter

▶ Establishing the United Nations

▶ Monitoring financial groups – the G8 and G20

▶ Forming trading blocs

▶ Partnering with the World Trade Organisation

▶ Noting the rise of China

▶ Joining NATO for military support

· ·

*Y*ou live in a rapidly changing, globalising world. What goes on in neigh-bouring nations and faraway countries has an impact both big and small on your life and the prospects for the UK as a whole. In this chapter, I cast the net far and wide to outline the big international organisations whose actions are helping to shape the world in the 21st century. If you want to know more about the wider world, this is the chapter for you!

Starting at the Top: The United Nations

The United Nations, or UN, as it's most commonly known, is the closest thing the planet has ever had to a world government. No fewer than 192 nations are members of the UN, accounting for some 99 per cent of the population of the globe. Each member state sends its own ambassador and team of diplomats to the UN so that they can meet other diplomats, talk about the shared prob-lems of humankind, and resolve and prevent conflicts – or that's the theory. The great British prime minister Winston Churchill once said that 'to jaw-jaw is better than to war-war' and the UN is the ultimate exercise in 'jaw-jaw'.

The UN was formed at the end of the Second World War – a war that claimed the lives of over 50 million people. Leaders of the countries involved in the conflict decided that, after such a cataclysm, having an international body where nations could debate and air their views was necessary and to this end established the United Nations in 1945.

In essence, the UN is supposed to be a force for good in the world, doing its best to prevent war and aid those who are economically disadvantaged, starving or at risk of catching infectious disease.

The UN is an immensely powerful organisation because it expresses the collective will of 192 nations. The moral weight the UN carries gives it a lot of legitimacy. Governments which ignore it or act against its wishes may not survive for long. A government which flies in the face of UN resolutions can find that other nations refuse to trade with it – a process called *sanctions* – or be subject to military action from an international force under the banner of the UN (I talk more about the UN and its military muscle in the upcoming 'The Security Council').

The UN has six official languages – Arabic, Chinese, English, French, Russian and Spanish. All documents are printed in each of these languages. However, ambassadors from member states can use their own language to make speeches as literally hundreds of interpreters work at the UN, translating what each member says.

Amongst diplomats and politicians you often hear the phrase, 'the will of the international community'. More often than not, this phrase refers to the opinions of the UN as expressed through its resolutions. It's not advisable for governments to go against 'the will of the international community'.

The UN's headquarters are in New York City, in the United States. Since the end of the Second World War the US has been widely recognised as the most powerful nation in the world, so it's probably appropriate for this international organisation to be based there.

The small plot of land around the HQ of the UN, although located in New York, is actually *international territory*, which means that the US government and local police force have no rights there. The UN headquarters is, in effect, its own state.

Delving into how the UN works

The UN isn't just a talking shop. It has its own civil service, called the UN Secretariat, and a host of satellite organisations through which it works to achieve its aim of facilitating peace and development around the globe. The UN even has its own court – the International Court of Justice – which oversees the trials of people who've committed war crimes or crimes against humanity. The next sections cover the five principal parts of the UN and the role of each in how the organisation works.

The UN has its own constitution called the *UN Charter*, which sets out the jobs of each of the five parts, as well as the role of the UN Secretary-General. In addition, the charter sets out certain rights that individuals can expect in relation to how their government treats them, such as the fairly fundamental 'right to life'.

The General Assembly

The General Assembly is where all 192 member states meet to discuss world affairs, such as admission or suspension of new member states, whether or not UN members should send food or economic aid to a state, or where one country's border should stop and another one start. Basically, anything that occurs in international politics can be discussed by the UN General Assembly.

The General Assembly may make recommendations for a course of action after taking a vote. Once a recommendation is made, member states are expected to abide by it. In effect, the General Assembly can tell countries what to do.

Each member state has one vote in the General Assembly, so voting rights aren't weighted in terms of population or economic power. China, with over a billion people and a massive economy, has one vote, while the Cook Islands, with a tiny population and an even smaller economy, has the same.

Usually, a two-thirds majority is needed for a recommendation to pass, but on some minor matters, a majority of nations voting in favour is enough.

However, the General Assembly doesn't have the right to make recommendations relating to peace and security – when countries are at war or close to war – as this is the preserve of the UN Security Council, which is covered in the next section.

The Security Council

The Security Council is the body providing the UN's muscle. It's made up of the biggest military and economic powers – as they were in around 1945 – as well as a host of nations voted into their seats by all General Assembly members for a two-year term. The Security Council is important for two reasons:

- ✔ First, it deals with matters of international security and peace. Resolving and preventing conflict was, after all, the main reason for setting up the UN in the first place.

- ✔ Second, whereas the General Assembly can recommend that nations follow a course of action, the Security Council can resolve that they do. The difference lies in the fact that a resolution from the Security Council can be followed up by action. Ignoring a resolution can lead to sanctions and even military action from other member states. In addition, only the Security Council can authorise the deployment of peacekeepers to the world's trouble spots.

Saddam, the UN and WMDs

Back in 2002 the United States and allies such as the UK and Australia got very hot under the collar about Iraqi leader Saddam Hussein. The US said that Hussein was arming his nation with so-called weapons of mass destruction (WMDs).

The UN Security Council had passed a resolution calling on Hussein to allow UN weapons inspectors to check out if he had any WMDs. After years of fleeting co-operation, UN inspectors concluded that Hussein had questions to answer over WMDs. This conclusion was seized upon by the United States, which used Hussein's widely perceived non-co-operation with a UN resolution as the legal justification for launching a war on Iraq.

Eventually Hussein was deposed (and subsequently tried and hung for war crimes) but no WMDs were found in Iraq.

Meanwhile, a bloody civil war started in Iraq and many nations not allied to the US argued that what it had done – under the guise of a UN resolution – was illegal. The controversy continues, and the cost in Iraqi lives is estimated to be in the hundreds of thousands.

The UK is one of the five permanent members of the UN Security Council – along with France, the US, China and Russia. This gives the UK extra-special powers – no, not the ability to scale tall buildings in one bound or see through walls – including the permanent right to sit on the UN Security Council and to veto resolutions. Only the five permanent members of the UN Security Council have the right of veto, which means they can stop any resolution under discussion.

The power of some of the permanent members – such as France, the UK and, to a lesser extent, Russia – has dwindled since 1945. Some argue that they should be replaced by new powerhouse nations such as India, Brazil, Japan or Germany. However, none of the 'big five' wants to make way just yet!

A UN resolution is a very big deal. Since 1945, fewer than 2,000 resolutions have been passed and countries are expected to follow them.

The United Nations Charter gives it the power to keep international peace through military intervention if necessary. Now the UN doesn't deploy peace-keepers to every conflict zone; the Security Council normally requires some sort of ceasefire or peace process to already be in place. The role of the troops on the ground is to try to stop war breaking out again and to create the right atmosphere for a lasting peace.

Member states of the UN don't just support it with money and the provision of ambassadors and diplomats; they also supply troops for UN peacekeeping duty when asked. For peacekeeping duties, troops are usually drawn from a host of nations – sometimes as many as two dozen – who all obey the orders of a single force commander appointed from the senior military of one of the nations supplying troops. Meanwhile, the diplomatic side of the peacekeeping operation is taken care of by a representative of the Secretary General, normally a senior world statesperson.

UN peacekeepers are often referred to as *blue helmets* or *blue berets* after their distinctive headwear.

The UN can't be everywhere and sometimes it asks a regional military organisation such as NATO (see the 'Providing the Military Might: NATO' section, later in this chapter) to do the peacekeeping for it. Although UN peacekeepers generally aren't expected to fight, NATO has traditionally taken a more robust role. In the war in Kosovo in the late 1990s, NATO actually went on the offensive against Serbia and its allies in order to ensure eventual peace.

The UN Secretariat

The Secretariat is effectively the UN's civil service. Its jobs include carrying out studies, providing information and executing administrative tasks for the Security Council and other UN bodies. The Secretariat is expressly charged with meeting the needs of UN bodies and not UN member states. So, for example, a British person working for the UN Secretariat takes his or her instructions from the appropriate UN body rather than the British government.

The Secretariat is headed up by the UN Secretary-General. This post is usually held by an eminent politician from one of the General Assembly's member states. The Secretary-General picks Secretariat staff; generally, they're noted civil servants from member governments around the globe.

The UN Secretary-General is one of the most important roles in world politics. This is so not only because the Secretary-General is in charge of the UN Secretariat and is the figurehead of the UN, speaking for the collective will of the General Assembly and Security Council, but also because he or she's allowed under the UN charter to bring matters to the attention of the Security Council for its consideration. The current holder of the post is the former South Korean prime minister Ban Ki-moon, who took over from Kofi Annan in 2007.

The Economic and Social Council (ESC)

The ESC is a group of member states charged with promoting economic and social co-operation and development around the globe. In particular, the ESC's main objectives are as follows:

- ✔ Promoting higher standards of living, full employment, and conditions of economic and social progress and development.

- ✔ Helping to solve international economic, social and global health care problems.

- ✔ Encouraging international cultural and educational co-operation as well as respect for human rights.

Yes, I know, even just one of the objectives of the ESC is massive. So how does it try to achieve what looks almost impossible? The ESC looks to co-ordinate the work of the main UN agencies (more about these in the upcoming section 'Taking in UN agencies'), governments and even non-governmental organisations (NGOs), such as big international charities, around the globe. The theory is that solutions to really huge problems – such as the spread of HIV/AIDS in the developing world – can only come from nations, charities and UN agencies all working together in a co-ordinated fashion so as to target aid and education. The ESC provides a forum for all these governments, different NGOs and the UN's own agencies to gather and formulate action plans.

The ESC has 54 member states. All the large, powerful nations such as the US, China, India and Japan are represented, as are France and the UK. The ESC holds several meetings throughout the year, preparing for a four-week session in July each year. The really big discussions about and decisions on the problems of the world occur at this session.

The International Court of Justice (ICJ)

As the name suggests, the ICJ is the legal arm of the United Nations. It's where politicians and military leaders who commit war crimes or crimes against humanity can be sent to trial. The ICJ is located in The Hague in the Netherlands rather than New York where the rest of the UN is headquartered.

The ICJ (or *international criminal court* as it's also known) doesn't sit that often but exists for when wrongdoers are arrested. In part, it's supposed to act as a deterrent, to stop government leaders from committing barbarous acts. The most prominent ex-leader recently tried at the ICJ is the Bosnian Serb Radovan Karadží, accused of committing war crimes in the former Yugoslavia at the end of the 20th century.

The ICJ exists to try leaders who've committed terrible acts against their own people or those of other nations. The idea is that any leader thinking of perpetrating such crimes can expect to eventually be brought to justice – if not by their own people then by the UN through its Court of Justice.

Taking in UN agencies

Much of the work of the UN isn't done in New York at the General Assembly or by the Secretariat, but instead by UN agencies. The 17 UN agencies range from low-profile ones dealing with global postal services right up to those bringing aid to the world's starving and promoting better health and education in the developing world to the very big and important World Bank.

Some countries really rely on these UN agencies; in fact, without them it's fair to say that some already troubled nations would slip into absolute chaos. Hunger, illness and acute poverty would present even greater problems than they do already.

The following list contains some of the big UN agencies, many or all of which you may have already heard of in the media:

- ✔ **United Nations Scientific and Cultural Organisation (UNESCO).** UNESCO is meant to contribute to peace and security by promoting international collaboration through education, science and culture in order to further universal respect for justice, the rule of law, human rights and fundamental freedoms. To bring extra publicity to its work, UNESCO employs a series of celebrity ambassadors including actor Angelina Jolie and tennis ace Roger Federer.

- ✔ **World Food Programme (WFP).** As the name suggests, the WFP is about feeding people who are starving. It's the biggest of the UN's humanitarian organisations. The WFP is based in Rome and has offices in more than 80 countries. The main job of the WFP is distributing food to people who are suffering drought or famine. It saves the lives of hundreds of thousands of people each year and, in some years, millions.

- ✔ **World Health Organisation (WHO).** The WHO's objective is to combat disease, especially infectious diseases – new threats such as H1N1 (swine flu) and SARS, as well as established ones such as malaria – and to promote the general health of the people of the world. As part of its work, WHO organises mass vaccination programmes.

- ✔ **World Bank (WB).** This body acts like, well, a bank, making loans to countries for development programmes whose stated goal is to reduce poverty.

- ✔ **International Monetary Fund (IMF).** The IMF oversees the global financial system and the economic policies pursued by individual countries. It tries to ensure that governments follow sensible policies – not borrowing money that they can't afford to pay back, for example – and looks to create a global financial system whereby all countries can enjoy growth.

Many argue that the United States is too powerful within the IMF and World Bank as a result of its government providing much of the finance for the loans and aid distributed by the two organisations.

Saving the planet (hopefully): The UN and climate change

One of the most pressing issues facing the world and therefore the UN is climate change and how to confront it. Every reputable scientist agrees that the earth is warming at an alarming rate and that something has to be done to avoid an ecological catastrophe.

Through the 'Earth Summit' in Rio de Janeiro in 1992, the Kyoto protocol in 1997 to the Copenhagen UN climate change summit in 2009, the leaders of the world's nations are trying to find a way to reduce carbon emissions

and at least halt climate change if not ultimately reverse it.

Organised by the UN, the Copenhagen summit hopes that world leaders will agree a plan to reduce carbon emissions beyond 2012, for the good of the planet. In the run-up to such a major international conference, the diplomats from the member nations discuss their relative positions with the objective of reaching final agreement at the conference table.

Bringing out the Big Guns: The Role of the G8 and the G20

The UN isn't the only big international organisation. Consider also the *G8*, or *Group of Eight*, which started as the Group of Six in 1975 and expanded to its current size in 1997. The G8 organised the seven largest world economies of the time, plus Russia.

But, times have changed, and in 1999 the *G20*, or *Group of Twenty*, formed. Composed of finance ministers from the 19 countries with the largest economies, plus the European Union, the G20 seeks to find ways to stabilise the world economy.

The G8 and G20 are, of course, really big deals, but they aren't the only game in town. The World Economic Forum, held in Davos, Switzerland each winter, brings together the shining lights of world business – tycoons, lobbyists, intellectuals, big-name politicians and the small matter of a few thousand journalists. They talk about trends in the world economy, technological development and the environment.

Starting small with the G8

The G8 is made up of seven of the largest world economies, plus Russia. Its members are Canada, France, Germany, Italy, Japan, the UK, the US and (by invitation rather than size of economy) Russia. The leaders of the G8 nations take it in turn to be the president of the organisation and to host the annual summer summit.

The G8 was originally formed to increase economic co-operation and promote growth amongst member economies, but its role has expanded to include international development (in particular amongst the world's poorest countries), environmental concerns, international law enforcement and even world health issues.

Unlike the UN, the G8 itself isn't a powerful body – for example, it can't deploy peacekeepers. Instead, it gains its clout from the fact that the member states are the most economically powerful in the world, and when the G8 countries agree to do something and carry it through, it can have a huge influence on global events.

The leaders of the G8 nations – the presidents and prime ministers – meet once a year at a big summit to discuss a wide variety of topics and formulate common policies which members should pursue – such as cutting global CO_2 emissions or forgiving the debts of poorer countries. These summits are a very big deal, with literally thousands of diplomats gathering as well as representatives from other nations, the European Union and the United Nations and its agencies, such as the World Bank.

In recent years, the three days of the G8 summit have drawn protests from anarchists and anti-capitalist and environmental groups. Sometimes these protests have become violent; at other times, such as the 2005 summit in Gleneagles in the UK, not so much. Gleneagles saw 225,000 people taking to the streets of the nearby city of Edinburgh to urge the G8 leaders to do more to alleviate poverty in Africa.

The G8 isn't just about presidents and prime ministers getting together and having a chinwag every year. Throughout the year the finance and environment ministers of the G8 meet to maintain co-operation between summits.

The G8 is an exclusive and wealthy club. The eight member states represent some 14 per cent of the world's population but nearly 60 per cent of its wealth. In addition, the G8 nations have military might too; £7 out of every £10 spent globally on defence comes from the G8 countries.

Changing times: G8 morphing into G20

The world's altering fast, particularly with the rise of China and India, and all major international organisations are racing to catch up. The G8 may have seven of the largest economies in the world as members but it doesn't have *the* seven largest economies in the world. China on some measures has a bigger economy than Japan, while India is racing into the top ten largest economies. Meanwhile, some of the established G8 nations are slipping down the pecking order, with Canada recently being overtaken by Spain in terms of economic size.

To deal with these economic shifts, in 1999 the G8 group of nations decided that, instead of the finance ministers of the G8 meeting regularly to decide world economic policy, the finance ministers of the 20 biggest economies in the world should meet. Thus, the G20 was born. Suddenly, countries like Argentina, Indonesia, Saudi Arabia and, of course, India, Brazil and China got a seat at the top table and a say on some of the big issues affecting the world economy. The world financial crisis of late 2008 emphasised the shift of economic power away from the West to the East and the developing world.

The G20 nations account for a staggering two thirds of the world population (thanks in no small part to China's inclusion), as well as 85 per cent of all the world's wealth.

The G20 concerns itself primarily with economic co-operation and ensuring stability and growth in the world economy; its brief is therefore a lot less wide-ranging than that of the G8.

Looking at the Regional Trading Blocs

Nations that are near each other geographically often do most of their trading with each other. For example, the UK's biggest trading partner isn't the United States or China, it's Germany, which is only a short flight away.

As a result of shared trading interests, the world is divided into trading organisations which look to promote co-operation and free trade in their own parts of the globe. These organisations don't stop at just negotiating trade deals between member states and outside countries, they also often delve into other areas of politics such as shared diplomatic objectives or addressing environmental concerns. In many respects these trading blocs have developed into power blocs; although short of being federal states, they still look to carry members in a similar direction.

The idea's a simple one, if you think about it: in a globalising world, relatively small nations, like the UK for instance, have a better chance of exerting influence on world events through membership of a bloc of countries. Some of the major trading or power blocs are:

✔ **European Union (EU).** This is the bloc the UK belongs to. Its 27 member states account for 500 million people, with a combined wealth even greater than that of the United States. (See Chapter 20 for the full lowdown on the EU.)

✔ **North American Free Trade Agreement (NAFTA).** This contains Canada, Mexico and the US, and looks to encourage the free movement of goods and people within the three member states.

✔ **Asia-Pacific Economic Cooperation forum (APEC).** This is the bloc for countries fronting on the Pacific Ocean, as the name suggests. A total of 21 member states comprise APEC, including China, Russia and the United States.

✔ **Cairns Group.** This bloc contains some of the world's leading food producers and exporters rather than nations sharing borders or even an ocean. Argentina, Australia, Brazil and Canada are leading members.

The Chinese government recently stated that it wants to establish a new trade bloc with its relatively near neighbours in Asia, such as Korea and Indonesia.

Factoring in the World Trade Organisation

The World Trade Organisation (WTO) promotes the free movement of goods and services around the globe. It encourages member states (all 151 of them) to abolish or reduce tariffs placed on imports and to stop paying subsidies to their own industries. Negotiations are often mired in controversy, however, and can take a long time; the present round of world trade talks, for example, has been going on since 2001!

The WTO is the only international agency overseeing world trade and ensuring that every nation sticks to the agreements it's signed up to. When nations are involved in trade disputes – for example, the US is always trying to get the EU to let in more of its beef exports – the WTO judges who's in the right and who's in the wrong. However, the WTO prefers to let nations discuss compromise solutions, which can take years to agree upon.

The WTO can impose trade sanctions on countries which it thinks are breaking the rules and imposing unfair tariffs on imports or subsidising their own industries to give them an unfair advantage. However, sanctions are rare as they tend to damage everyone concerned.

Playing the Power Game: China Taking Over from the United States

According to political scientists, the 20th century was the American century but the 21st century will belong to the Chinese – and it's certainly looking that way!

In the last two decades, the Chinese economy has gone from being mostly agriculturally based to being technologically advanced and producing stunning growth. Some of the statistics emerging from China are amazing: a new power station is built each week; a million and a half Chinese people move from rural areas to cities (that's the equivalent of the population of Birmingham) every month; 320 million people are under the age of fourteen (that's five and a bit times the entire population of the UK); and more people now use the Internet there than in the US. China isn't just an arriving world power; it's arrived. It used to be said that 'all roads lead to Rome'; a truer phrase nowadays would be 'all roads lead to China'.

Yet China still has a long way to go to catch up with the old 20th-century superpower the United States in terms of wealth and military might. The US spends roughly ten times as much as the Chinese on its military, while car ownership in the US is seven times greater than in China. What's more, the average American enjoys wealth and a standard of living that the average Chinese person can barely dream of. Life expectancy in China is still five years less than in the US. China, though, is undoubtedly flexing its political as well as its economic muscles and, many believe, at the expense of the West and the US.

Some of the key ways China is trumping the US in the global power politics game include:

- ✔ Looking to form trading and political blocs with near neighbours and other emerging economies.

- ✔ Securing natural resources from African and Arab nations through bilateral trade and aid agreements, sometimes negotiating with regimes which many in the West view as having poor human rights records.

- ✔ Stockpiling large amounts of money made through having a substantial trade surplus and using it to buy US government debt. This situation is worrying for some because if China was to sell this debt in a hurry, it could cause US government finances to collapse.

China is the world's biggest exporter, particularly of manufactured goods, whereas the US is the world's biggest importer. In fact, China enjoys a massive trade surplus with the US – which means that it sells many more goods to, than it imports from, the US.

Comparing the rise of communist China with that of the world's largest democracy

Many in the West are frankly frightened by the onward march of China, partly because it's not a democratic country. In fact, China is a communist regime (see Chapter 4 for the full ins and outs of communism), which many in the West abhor. What's more, the Chinese government routinely suppresses civil liberties and is alleged to have carried out atrocities in Tibet. The Chinese state also executes thousands of its own citizens each year for crimes which, in some cases, would merit only a short prison sentence in the UK.

Against this backdrop, many in the West are looking at the equally stellar growth of the Indian economy for a ray of hope. India – unlike China – is a democracy; in fact, many of its institutions are based on the British model, as it used to be a British colony. Yet, like China, India has a huge population (in excess of one billion) and its economy is growing at a furious rate, particularly in providing services and new technology.

Political scientists may have got things wrong and the 21st century may be the Indian century rather than the Chinese one. If that's the case, many in the West will be mightily relieved.

Providing the Military Might: NATO

The West still has a few cards up its sleeve regardless of the seemingly unstoppable march of China. Led by the United States, the West has by far the strongest and best-equipped military machine in the world, embodied in NATO. The 28 member states in NATO include Canada, France, Germany, Poland, Spain, Turkey, the UK and the US.

Simply put, *NATO (North Atlantic Treaty Organisation)* is a military alliance set up after the Second World War in response to a widely perceived threat from the Soviet Union. This alliance is based on the simple statement that an attack on one NATO state is an attack on all. Three of the member states – France, the UK and the US – can back up this statement with nuclear weapons.

The immediate reason for NATO's existence – the threat from the Soviet Union – disappeared along with the Berlin Wall after 1989 and many questioned whether or not the organisation still had a purpose. However, civil wars in the Balkans in the 1990s highlighted the need for its existence, as it was NATO that eventually imposed peace on the troubled region.

Rather than reducing its membership since the end of the Soviet threat, NATO has in fact increased in size. Many nations which were previously members of the Warsaw Pact – and thus allied to the Soviet Union – are now members of NATO.

More recently, NATO got involved in conflicts outside of Europe and the North Atlantic, most notably in Afghanistan against the Taliban, a group closely allied to the extremists who carried out the 11 September terrorist attacks on the US in 2001.

The UK has been one of the two leading countries in NATO – in terms of military spending – since its inception, but it's the US which supplies most of the troops and money underpinning it.

France has had a difficult relationship with NATO. Former French president Charles de Gaulle actually withdrew the nation's troops from NATO command in 1959, arguing that the US and UK were too powerful. Gradually, though, after de Gaulle's death, the French re-integrated into NATO and their troops now take part in exercises and combat operations when required.

Chapter 20

Expanding Horizons: Europe and the EU

In This Chapter

▶ Recognising the European Union's importance and its goals

▶ Building relationships inside and outside the EU

▶ Agreeing to major EU treaties

▶ Examining EU budgets

*I*n this chapter, I take you on a tour of the UK's nearest neighbours and look into the inner workings of an institution – the European Union – which has a massive influence on everyday life in the UK. Many say that the UK's future is as part of what amounts to a united states of Europe; others disagree. Read this chapter to get a better idea of what they're going on about.

Understanding the EU and How it Works

The European Union – or EU, as it's known – is an extraordinary institution. It can trace its roots back a couple of centuries to when Tsar Nicholas of Russia talked about a union of European states. More recently, in the 1940s, British wartime prime minister Winston Churchill envisaged a United States of Europe. But these two great leaders could have no idea just how powerful an institution would emerge in the late 20th century when the Europeans – who'd been fighting each other from year dot – finally decided to pull together.

To appreciate why the EU came about you have to understand that its formation came a little over a decade after the end of the Second World War, in 1957. For its originators, the EU was seen as a way of reducing national competition and antagonisms which had so disastrously plunged the continent into war. I talk more about the history of the EU in the nearby sidebar 'Expanding the EU: Six become 27'.

The key facts in the following list highlight just how big a deal the EU is to the UK – which is part of it – and in the wider world:

✔ The EU encompasses 27 countries from the Russian Steppe in the East, the Arctic Circle in the North, the shores of Africa in the South to the coast of Portugal in the West.

✔ Up to 500 million people live in the EU member states (roughly one and two thirds the number of people who live in the United States).

✔ The economies of the EU combined comprise the biggest economy in the world, bigger even than that of the US.

✔ The EU may be made up of separate states but citizens across all countries are allowed to work in any state.

✔ The EU is a huge free trade area, called the Single European Market, with all member states able to sell goods and services to each other free of tariffs or quotas.

✔ The EU has its own currency, the euro, which most member states trade in. The euro is one of the world's great currencies, rivalling the dollar for the number of transactions carried out using it.

To be able to join the EU, a state must meet the Copenhagen Criteria, named because they were agreed upon in the Danish capital. The criteria say that member states have to respect human rights and the rule of EU law (which I talk about in the upcoming 'Looking at law-making and the legal system'), as well as open their borders to trade and workers. Generally, a country has to be in Europe to be a member of the EU. However, the bulk of Turkey's land mass is in Asia and yet is still being considered for EU membership.

The UK refused to join the EEC (forerunner of the EU) at its inception in 1958 – we really didn't want much to do with those foreigners, don't you know old chap! – and instead went about forming its own economic club, the European Free Trade Association (EFTA) with nations such as Denmark (five million people) and Switzerland (seven million people). But some UK politicians realised that EFTA wasn't quite as good as belonging to the EU, which had France and Germany in its ranks, and began negotiations for the UK to join it.

Four western European states – Iceland, Liechtenstein, Norway and Switzerland – aren't members of the EU. However, they do have trade and border agreements with the EU allowing goods and people to move freely among these countries and EU member states. In 2009, Iceland applied for membership of the EU following an economic crisis caused by the collapse of the nation's banks.

Expanding the EU: Six become 27

The EU has undergone a tremendous transformation in the more than 50 years of its existence, no less than in the number of countries which belong. Originally, the Treaty of Rome (1957) which set up the EU was signed by six countries – Belgium, France, Germany, Italy, Luxembourg and the Netherlands. But back then the U word – union – was scrupulously avoided; instead, the new organisation was called the very exciting sounding European Economic Community (the forerunner, formed in 1951, was called the European Coal and Steel Community – most riveting!). However, the diplomats at the signing said that the Treaty of Rome was 'the first stage in the federation of Europe'. In other words, economic co-operation today, constructing a new state called Europe sometime tomorrow!

The European Economic Community was a roaring success, with member states' economies booming. Soon other states – including the UK – wanted to join. However, the six original members knew they were onto a good thing and took some persuading to let other countries join their now wealthy club. First up, Denmark, Ireland and the UK were allowed to join in 1973, followed by Greece in 1981, and Spain and Portugal in 1986. In 1995 Austria, Sweden and Finland came in.

But by far the biggest expansion of the EU took place in 2004 when the Czech Republic, Estonia, Hungary, Latvia, Lithuania, Poland, Slovakia and Slovenia were allowed into the EU, as well as the small Mediterranean island states of Cyprus and Malta.

EU expansion hasn't stopped there. Bulgaria and Romania became members in 2007, and even more countries are trying to join, including Albania, Bosnia and Herzegovina (worth lots of points in a game of Scrabble if you could use proper nouns), Croatia, Iceland, Macedonia, Serbia and Turkey. It's even rumoured that Israel will join one day, as may some of the North African states and, who knows, maybe even Russia.

Checking the goals of the EU

European politicians often disagree about the EU's purpose. Some see it as merely a free trade area; others view it as much more a precursor to a United States of Europe. But everyone can agree that the EU looks to achieve some fundamental goals, which include:

✔ Promoting free trade between all member states and the free movement of people to work where they want.

If you're British, or any other EU nationality for that matter, you're free to move to and work in any country in the European Union. That freedom is quite a big deal for many people.

- ✔ Preventing an unfair trading advantage being gained by any member state through its government subsidising domestic industries.

- ✔ Ensuring greater harmonisation of national laws relating to business and the consumer.

- ✔ Protecting EU businesses from unfair competition from countries outside of the EU.

Jacques Delors, the French politician and former president of the European Commission (see 'The European Commission' a bit later on for more) is widely seen as the spiritual father of *European federalism*: the belief that a United States of Europe should exist. Delors campaigned for closer integration of member states and the establishment of the *euro*, the single European currency. For a while in the early 1990s Delors became a hated figure for some in the British press because he was seen as trying to strong-arm Britain into joining a United States of Europe. Famously, one *Sun* newspaper headline of the time read 'Up yours Delors', accompanied by a picture of a hand holding up two fingers – most rude!

Examining EU institutions

The EU can be broken down into four parts, each having its own role and powers. They're covered in the following sections.

The Council of Europe isn't an EU organisation at all, but a group of 47 European states whose collective objective is to encourage peace, understanding and democracy in Europe.

The European Commission

The European Commission is the executive body of the European Union. Major decisions are made by this body and it draws up laws for consideration by the European Parliament and Council of Ministers.

The Commission has 27 members – one for each member state – appointed by their respective governments. Each commissioner fills a specific role and is meant to act in the interests of all member states rather than the nation he or she hails from. Currently heading the Commission is the Portuguese politician José Manuel Barroso. The president's role resembles that of the UK prime minister – orchestrating meetings of the Commission, which in turn works a bit like the UK cabinet.

As far as the UK is concerned, commissioners are often senior politicians in the twilight of their political careers. They may have been prominent government ministers in the past but have now been appointed to the role of commissioner by the prime minister.

Some of the Commission's major powers include:

- ✔ It drafts EU law.
- ✔ It represents the EU at trade negotiations such as those of the World Trade Organisation (see Chapter 19 for more on the WTO).
- ✔ It develops trade and political strategies for the EU as a whole.

Jobs are shared out between the 27 commissioners and their countries. As a rule, the most important jobs go to the commissioners from the biggest countries in the EU – France, Germany, Italy, Spain and the UK. Often countries try to secure the right to appoint a commissioner to a role that suits their national interests. So, for example, the French president may get to decide who's agriculture commissioner, while the British PM gets to appoint the competition commissioner.

The Council of Ministers

Laws and directives drawn up by the European Commission have to go through the Council of Ministers before they actually become law. Again, the Council is made up of representatives from the individual states but this time they're not meant to remain neutral – as commissioners are. Ministers are specifically in place to represent the interests of their member states.

What's more, unlike the egalitarian make-up of the Commission, where each state gets a commission appointee, in the Council of Ministers each country is allocated a block of votes relative to its size. So, for example, the countries with the biggest populations – France, Germany, Italy and the UK – get 29 votes each (which is a little unfair on the Germans as they have by far the highest population) and other countries get fewer votes. For example, Poland gets 27 votes, the Netherlands 13, and tiny Malta (with only 300,000 people) gets 3. Bear in mind, though, that the number of votes isn't completely relative to the population size; it's only a broad approximation, with some of the smaller countries being over-represented and the bigger ones under-represented.

The purpose of assigning these voting blocks is so that the Council can reach a majority and therefore decide to pass or reject laws drawn up by the Commission. But actually it's not a majority that's needed – nothing so simple in the convoluted world of the EU – instead, two thirds of the states must agree *and* 74 per cent of all the votes cast across the Council have to be in favour for a law to pass. This outcome is catchily called a *qualified majority*. Under this system of voting, no single member state can effectively stop laws which the others agree on. Having said that, qualified majority doesn't apply in some policy areas and all member states have to agree to pass laws affecting issues such as taxation, social policy, defence and foreign treaties.

The representatives of the Council of Ministers are often senior politicians from the member states, and each country has a representative for each of the big policy areas. For example, the UK has a representative whose speciality is the environment and another who's an expert on trade, and so on. These specialist representatives often meet to thrash out agreements in their individual policy area. Meanwhile, behind the scenes much of the negotiating is carried out by civil servants from the member states.

The Council of Ministers is often referred to as the Council of the European Union – not to be confused with the European Council (outlined in the next section). Yes, there really are too many councils; perhaps it's time for some renaming!

The member states of the EU are seemingly forever wrangling about the number of votes they get in the Council of Ministers and what constitutes a qualified majority. At the most recent summit, for instance, the Poles argued that they shouldn't have their number of seats reduced (although they have a disproportionately high number compared to their population) and, as a result, a compromise was reached which will see their seats decrease over many years – such is the horse-trading that goes on in the EU.

The European Council

The European Council is made up from the heads of government from all the member states. It meets twice a year, at least, to discuss the major issues affecting the EU, such as its international relations and what future EU treaties will cover.

The European Commission drafts the laws for the EU while the Council sets the broad framework of policy direction. So, for example, if the European Council says it would like to see closer harmonisation of rules governing trade amongst EU member states, then it's up to the Commission to draft specific laws to see that happens.

In terms of actual powers, the Council doesn't have many apart from the right to appoint the president of the Commission, which itself is quite significant as it's often the president who sets the agenda for law-making in the EU and acts as its figurehead. But despite only having limited powers, the Council is incredibly important within the structure of the EU because of the authority of the people who attend. They are, after all, the leaders of governments so what they say – if they agree – usually goes in the EU.

Meetings of the European Council are often dominated by arguments over how the EU is spending its money and whether or not the powers of the EU should be expanded – inevitably at the expense of the powers of the nation states.

The Treaty of Lisbon establishes a new role in the EU: the president of the European Union. This is largely a figurehead role. The president is supposed to co-ordinate the work of the European Council and represent the EU at world summits. In December 2009 the first person to assume the role of president was decided during a meeting of the leaders of member states. Herman Van Rompuy, a former prime minister of Belgium, was chosen for the role.

The European Parliament

Finally, we get to a body that you may be aware of because, lo and behold, you actually get to vote on its membership. Every five years voters from all 27 member states get to choose their Member of the European Parliament (MEP) (see Chapter 6 for the lowdown on how this election works).

But what powers does the European Parliament actually have considering that laws are drawn up by the Commission and approved by the Council of Ministers? Well, the main task of the European Parliament is to debate and suggest amendments to the laws drawn up by the Commission. The parliament is full of elected representatives – unlike the Commission or Council of Ministers – and when they vote to amend or to say that a law shouldn't go ahead, what they say has considerable sway on the debate. After all, to completely ignore the parliament and what it says would be undemocratic.

The powers of the European Parliament have grown in recent years. Under the terms of the 1997 Amsterdam Treaty – yes, the EU loves its treaties – the parliament was given 'co-decision' status with the Council of Ministers. Under the procedure set up in the treaty, the Commission presents a proposal to parliament and the Council which can only become law if both reach agreement. If the two bodies disagree, a conciliation committee – made up of MEPs and councillors – meets to thrash out a compromise. If either body rejects the draft law, it's then up to the Commission to either amend the law and reintroduce it to the Council and the parliament or withdraw it altogether.

Some suggest that the EU is more autocratic than democratic because so much of the law-making power is in the hands of the European commissioners who are appointed by the governments of the member states rather than directly elected by the people.

Looking at law-making and the legal system

The EU is now much more than a club with members striving for free trade and to promote economic growth. It actually has many of the hallmarks of a state. It has its own parliament, president, courts and even, crucially, laws. (The preceding 'Examining the EU institutions' covers the various arms of the EU.)

In member states – including the UK – EU law has the same weight (and sometimes more) as laws made by the domestic parliament. In 1986 the UK parliament passed the Single European Act, which in effect provided the green light for EU law to be binding on the UK. At one stroke, laws made by the EU had precedence over laws made by the UK parliament. This was a big day in the history of Britain's unwritten constitution, which I talk about in Chapter 11.

In areas concerning competition and the operation of what's called the *Single European Market* (in essence, the free movement of goods and people), EU law actually has precedence over domestic laws. So, for example, a law made by the UK parliament stating that the number of cars imported from Germany will be limited would be superseded by the EU law that there be no quotas on any goods coming from a fellow member state.

Two main types of EU law exist:

- ✔ **Direct effect law.** This comes about when member states sign up to an EU-wide agreement. The terms of the EU agreement supersede any national laws.
- ✔ **Directive law.** Under this type of law, basically the EU directs the member states to do something and they then have to alter their own domestic laws in order to conform to the EU directive.

Nearly all EU laws originate with the European Commission, which is made up of representatives from member states.

The EU has an ambassador to the United Nations, and the president of the European Commission attends meetings of the G8 group of nations (discussed in Chapter 19). In addition, the EU has its own flag and, that crucial trapping of nationhood, a national anthem: Beethoven's Ode to Joy.

Getting litigious: The European Court of Justice

Just like a nation state, the EU has its own court system. However, this court system is designed to augment the courts of member states rather than supplant or rival them.

The European Court of Justice (ECJ) is responsible for interpreting EU laws and ensuring consistent application across all 27 member states. If a court in an EU member state is hearing a case which involves EU law, the domestic court asks the ECJ to look at the case and then give a ruling. The domestic court is then bound by the decision of the ECJ.

Protecting human rights in the European Court of Human Rights

As well as the ECJ, there's the European Court of Human Rights. It was set up by the Council of Europe to uphold the European Convention on Human Rights, which sets out basic freedoms that each person in the EU can expect such as the right to life, liberty, and freedom from torture, and to a fair trail, privacy, and to marry who they want.

If an individual feels these freedoms have been contravened, he or she can take the case to the European Court of Human Rights. However, the person who feels wronged must first have exhausted the legal processes in his or her own country. The European Court of Human Rights is only ever a last resort and the process of getting a case heard there can be painfully slow.

Forming Relationships Within and Outside the EU

The EU is more than an economic club but slightly less than a fully fledged state. Over time its influence over member states and on the international stage has grown, and whenever major decisions in world politics are being taken a representative of the EU is normally involved. But as well as playing a role at the top table of international politics, the EU is concerned with issues such as expanding its membership, securing natural resources – most particularly oil and gas for its massive industries – and helping ensure peace and security within Europe itself.

All EU member states have to agree to the entry of a new member state before it can happen. In effect, any member can veto a country trying to enter the EU.

Representatives of the EU – whether they be civil servants or the president of the Commission – are in attendance at the meetings of all the world's main international bodies (such as the UN, G8, World Bank or World Trade Organisation) and major conferences such as those held to discuss climate change.

Looming giant: Russia on the doorstep

The EU's relationship with Russia is a knotty one. Russia was once one of two world superpowers but has now lost this status. However, this giant country, with a population greater than Germany, the UK and the Netherlands combined, is still formidable. Russia has a massive army and a difficult history with western Europe, having been invaded by the Germans, the British, the Turks, the Swedes and the French over the past couple of centuries. In the aftermath of the Second World War Russia controlled eastern Europe through installing a series of brutal puppet regimes, and for 40-odd years squared up to NATO in what's known as the Cold War. In short, there's plenty of history between Russia and the countries of the EU.

Arguing against EU expansion

Some politicians within the EU – particularly in France and Germany – have been less than pleased about its huge expansion in the early years of the 21st century. They have several problems with this expansion, such as:

✔ The new members have voting rights in EU institutions which have diluted the power of the bigger countries, in particular France and Germany, who've been used to getting their own way on some of the big key issues.

✔ Many of the newer member states are poor and thus a drain on the EU's development and common agricultural budgets.

✔ The migration of people from the poorer new member states to the richer western European states in search of jobs and a better standard of living is worrisome.

Former French president Jacques Chirac, although ultimately accepting expansion of the EU, wasn't particularly happy about it. He famously told the leaders of the new members in 2004 that they needed to get 'better manners' and was furious when they sided with Britain – and against France – over a series of key decisions.

But the simple truth is that the EU needs good relations with modern Russia because it happens to be one of the most oil- and gas-rich countries on earth. With massive pipelines carrying gas from east to west, it's pretty certain that if energy supplies were cut off, most of western Europe would be plunged into darkness. But Russia needs the EU, too, as the money it earns from the economies of western Europe is of huge importance to its economy and government.

Many fear, though, that Russia will use the fact that the EU is so dependent on the energy it supplies as a means to exert political pressure – and, frankly, Russia would be a mug if it didn't, at least in some ways. As a result, some members of the EU – most notably Germany – have tried to forge good relations with the Russian government. Meanwhile, the UK, which is seen as close to the US diplomatically and is less reliant on Russian energy, has what is widely seen as poor relations with the government of Russia.

Testing question: Is Turkey really part of Europe?

The question of Turkey is perplexing many leading EU politicians. Put simply, Turkey would love to join the EU and some countries such as the UK are quite happy for it to do so. However, some countries – most notably France – are worried that Turkish entry into the EU would change the EU for the worse. Some of the reasons given for not allowing Turkey entry into the EU include:

✔ Turkey is poor compared to most of the EU nations; it also has a massive population in excess of any member of the EU.

✔ Turkish agriculture isn't very advanced compared to the EU; as a result, the country may be a major drain on the resources of the common agricultural budget.

✔ Turkey is a Muslim country while the EU is made up of ostensibly Christian states; some suggest this would alter the character of the EU.

✔ Turkey is actually geographically in Asia rather than Europe.

✔ For many years Turkey has had a poor human rights record and its government stands accused of mistreating its Kurdish minority.

✔ Turkey is in disagreement with Cyprus over the existence of a separate Turkish-backed state in the north of the island.

While the anti-Turkey lobby raises quite a few issues, some very good reasons also exist for allowing Turkish entry; some of these simply involve seeing the negatives (as perceived by entry opponents) as opportunities:

✔ Turkey is poor but huge and presents a great development opportunity and export market for EU goods and services.

✔ Accepting a predominantly Muslim country as a member of the EU will help build bridges with the Islamic world and promote peace.

✔ Turkey, although part of Asia, has always played an important role in European affairs and many of its institutions are more European than Asiatic.

✔ Turkey's human rights record has improved, as have recognition of individual liberties and freedom of the press, and many suggest the improvement is because the Turkish government seeks EU entry.

Britain is believed to favour Turkish entry into the EU while France generally doesn't. However, neither government has come out and explicitly laid out its position but they'll have to do so when Turkish entry comes up for discussion in 2010.

Bringing peace to the Balkans

Fighting in the Balkans region of Europe ended late in the 1990s, but the images of ethnic cleansing and bombing of civilians scars Europe's collective consciousness well into the 21st century.

The peace process in the Balkans has seen the gradual break-up of the old Yugoslav state and greater autonomy for the Croats and Bosnian Muslims from the majority Serbs. These changes are due in no small part to diplomatic efforts of the EU – backed up with the military stick of NATO.

The EU exerted pressure not just through its economic might and the fact that its members – most notably Britain and France – are strong military powers, but also by offering the long-term carrot of eventual membership in the EU to those countries which follow the path to peace.

In the 1990s, Serbia, for example, was effectively at war with NATO and the militias it supported had perpetrated the worst war crimes seen in the European continent since the end of the Second World War. Nowadays, the Serb government no longer backs these militias, has handed over war criminals responsible for brutality and wants eventually to become a member of the EU.

The EU doesn't have a standing army but many of its states are also members of the North Atlantic Treaty Organisation (NATO), which is the most powerful military machine in the world.

Understanding Britain's thorny relationship with the EU

The UK may have been a member of the EU for nearly 40 years (it joined in 1973) but its relationship with other members has at times been strained. In fact, things got so bad in the early 1990s that some politicians from other EU states actually suggested that the UK should leave – however, doing so was never a serious possibility.

At the heart of the UK's problems with the EU has been a difference in vision of what the EU should be about. Put simply, most British politicians and political parties would like to see the EU remain purely concerned with promoting free trade and movement of people. Yet amongst some EU states – most notably Germany, the Netherlands, Belgium and Luxembourg – there's a drive to change the EU from an economic union of states into an actual political union of states – a United States of Europe. These politicians, called *federalists*, would like to see member state governments become subservient to an overarching pan-European government. For these people, the EU isn't an end in itself but a means to an end – a staging post along the way to a European super-state.

In the UK many people are opposed to the EU gaining more powers and having further influence over British life. These people are generally referred to as *Eurosceptics*.

The UK's relations with the EU have eased in recent years mainly because membership has expanded to 27 states and many of these new members – such as Poland and the Czech Republic – are less keen on the idea of an EU super-state. Nowadays the UK is less likely to find itself in a minority of one.

In recent years the federalist agenda has taken a bit of a back seat in Europe, with many governments preferring to retain their autonomy rather than sign up to the idea of a European super-state.

The two major UK political parties – Labour and Conservative – may both have had their spats with other EU members, but ultimately all the main parties believe that the UK is better off within the EU. From a purely financial viewpoint, the vast majority of UK exports are bought by other EU members.

Putting Pen to Paper: Major European Treaties

The EU should have a 'work in progress' sign above its door because, although it's over 50 years old, it seems to be forever changing. The biggest changes have been brought about by an expansion of membership – from 6 to 27 members in less than 40 years. Meanwhile, the wider world hasn't stood still, with trading blocs rising across the globe (see Chapter 19 for more on these) and, of course, the massive economic and political progress of China and India. Against such a backdrop and adding in new global challenges, such as tackling climate change and poverty amongst the nations of the developing world, it's understandable that the EU seems to be forever examining itself, its institutions, how it does business and its relationships with member states.

This self-examination has led to the creation of a series of key treaties, which have resulted in profound changes to the EU and, indirectly, Britain's relationship with it.

A rundown of the big European treaties and what they've meant in practice follows:

- ✔ **Maastricht (1992).** This treaty paved the way for the creation of a single European currency called the euro (see the nearby sidebar, 'One currency to fit all'). In addition, the treaty increased judicial co-operation between states, set out some key social rights for citizens of member states (such as not being forced to work long hours) and bid member states to work towards forming a single EU foreign policy rather than each state pursuing its own agenda on the world stage. The Maastricht Treaty was seen as a victory for those who supported the idea of a federal European super-state.

The negotiations before the signing of the Maastricht Treaty were highly controversial in the UK. The UK government at the time – led by the Conservative PM John Major – demanded and won opt-outs from the social rights part of the treaty and the move towards a single European currency. When Tony Blair's Labour Party swept to power in 1997, it dropped the opt-out on social rights but chose to remain out of the single currency; the UK thus still has its own currency – the pound – whereas most countries in the EU use the euro.

- ✔ **Amsterdam (1999).** This treaty looked to inject a little more democracy into the EU law-making process. The European Parliament, with its elected members, gained more rights to approve or block laws drawn up by the European Commission. The free movement of people within the EU was also guaranteed under the terms of this key treaty.

- ✔ **Nice (2004).** This treaty was all about reforming the institutions of the EU to cope with the ultimate expansion of membership to 27 states. Seats on the Council of Ministers and in the European Parliament were redistributed.

- ✔ **Lisbon (2007).** More powers for the European Parliament and a tweaking of how voting in the Council of Ministers would work were two of the administration highlights of this treaty. In addition, a charter of fundamental rights – a bit like the Human Rights Act – was made binding on all member states. The treaty also set up the post of a new European Union president. This treaty was ratified by all member states in late 2009.

Just because a government signs an EU treaty doesn't make it law. In most member states the treaty has to be *ratified* – voted upon and debated – in the domestic parliament before it's actually made into law. An EU treaty only comes into law across the EU if every member state has ratified it.

Holding the Purse Strings: EU Budgets

Just as in many a marriage, some of the biggest tear-ups in EU history have boiled down to one subject – money. Under EU rules, each member pays a levy roughly proportionate to the size of its economy and this money is then collected together to pay for the following:

- Bureaucracy – the EU civil service
- MEPs' pay and expenses
- The Common Agricultural Policy
- Grants to member states to help fund infrastructure projects
- Grants to help areas of member states suffering severe economic deprivation

The arguments arise when member states meet to discuss who should be paying what into the EU. The German government, for example, gets back only half of what it contributes in terms of grants and payments under the Common Agricultural Policy. On the other hand, Poland gets around four euros for each one it contributes to the EU budget. Little Luxembourg does best, though, getting around five times as much as it pays in, and that's one of the richest countries – measured in euros per head of population – in Europe. Go figure!

The EU's budget is set each year by the Council of Ministers and the European Parliament. The Council gets to set the budgets for the Common Agricultural Policy (explained in the next section). The parliament decides other expenditures, such as grants to member states to improve infrastructure or for job creation schemes in deprived areas. The Council and parliament draw up their budget estimates and the Commission consolidates them into a draft EU budget. Both the Council and the parliament can amend it and both bodies have then to approve this final budget.

Accounting for the Common Agricultural Policy

Nearly half of all the money the EU spends goes towards carrying out the *Common Agricultural Policy (CAP)*. To understand why agricultural policy is so important, you have to go back to the aftermath of the Second World War when much of Europe was starving. Many leading politicians in France and

Germany decided that making sure that Europe could feed itself in future should be a key objective of the EU. They didn't care whether this goal was achieved through direct aid from the EU or by raising tariffs on imported food. As a result, the CAP was born. This policy guarantees EU farmers a minimum price for their crops, while preserving the rural heritage of the EU.

With the promise of having their products bought by the EU even if the consumer didn't want them, EU farmers just produced more and more. In the 1980s the CAP was brought into disrepute when the EU purchased and stockpiled unused foodstuffs – dubbed 'the butter mountain' and 'the wine lake' by the British press. At the same time, an offshoot of the CAP, called the *Common Fisheries Policy*, was causing controversy because it was leading to the large-scale decommissioning of fleets in Scotland.

In recent years, though, the CAP has started to change, with farmers in the nations that joined the EU in 2004 benefiting from subsidies and investment to modernise their agriculture. Much of the EU's budget has been spent on aiding these countries' agricultural industries and funding infrastructure projects. However, amongst many British politicians, CAP is still a byword for waste and protectionism.

Getting a rebate

Compared to the amount of money that member state governments spend each year, the EU is quite frugal. In 2007, for instance, it spent less than 10 per cent of what the UK government spent that year.

Each year the UK gets a rebate on its contributions to the EU because it has a small agricultural sector which receives limited sums from the EU. Yet, as one of the biggest economies in the EU, the UK has to stump up billions of pounds in contributions. The UK's rebate is a way of trying to redress the balance. Basically the UK makes its contributions to the EU and then receives money back in the form of aid. At the end of the year the EU works out how much the UK has given and how much the EU has spent on the UK. The UK then receives a rebate based on this difference. The rebate is calculated as approximately two thirds of the amount by which UK payments into the EU exceed EU expenditure returning to the UK. The retention of the rebate has caused several arguments at meetings of heads of state in the past, particularly with the French!

One currency to fit all

No world economic power would be complete without its own currency. And, guess what? The EU has its own currency – the euro – which you've probably used if you've holidayed on the Continent in the past few years.

The euro is currency across 16 of the EU's 27 member states and all the big nations in the EU (excluding Britain) use it. In fact, a grand total of 327 million out of the EU's 500 million inhabitants use the euro.

Internationally, the euro has proved a big hit in a relatively short period of time, with only the US dollar being used in more transactions across the globe. So successful has the euro been that some countries which don't currently use it, like Bulgaria and Latvia, are planning on doing so in the future.

As for the UK, Gordon Brown's Labour government set a series of criteria for deciding if the UK should ditch the pound in favour of the euro. As yet those criteria haven't been met and the debate over whether or not the UK should adopt the euro has now slipped beneath the political radar.

Chapter 21

Leading the Free World: US Politics

. . . .

In This Chapter

▶ Charting the US's influence in the UK and around the world

▶ Focusing on how the US government works

▶ Getting laws passed in the US

▶ Judging disputes: The work of the Supreme Court

▶ Looking at political parties and influences

. . . .

*T*he United States is the only superpower in the world at the moment. Although some argue that the US is in decline, it's still at the heart of international politics. Ask any British politician which relationship is most important to the UK and they'll answer that with the United States. No understanding of the wider world, and for that matter Britain's place within it, is possible without knowledge of the inner workings of the US political system from the role of Congress and the Supreme Court to that of the president, unarguably the planet's number-one politico.

If you want to know more about the premier nation in the world and why so often what the president says goes, this is the chapter for you.

Understanding US Influence in the Wider World and in the UK

Whatever the critics of America say – and there are plenty of those, even in a friendly country like the UK – it's still the number-one democratic nation in the world. Despite the rise of China, the US is also the number-one economy, with the most widely used currency – the dollar – in the world. In fact, the scale of America's wealth and influence around the globe is difficult to overestimate.

Some of the keys to America's dominance on the world stage include the following factors:

- **Military might.** The US has the most expensively equipped and best trained military in the world. In brutal terms it's top dog at making war and this fact guarantees huge influence.

  For example, if the US threatens military intervention in one of the world's trouble spots, generally the warring parties sit up and take notice. The US armed forces are probably the only military capable of placing huge numbers of troops on the ground virtually anywhere around the globe in a matter of weeks. In essence, the US carries an awfully big military stick around with it and that spells power.

- **Cultural output.** Been to the cinema lately or turned on a music radio station? Well, if you did you probably had a taste of American culture. US culture dominates the planet, with teenagers and adults around the globe – from China to Chile – wanting a little slice of the American way of life. Their news channels and television programmes inform debate around the world. American actors, artists and even politicians are widely known, demonstrating that the US is still the pre-eminent cultural influence on the planet.

- **Economic powerhouse.** The military and cultural might of the US is probably nothing compared to its economic influence. US businesses employ millions all over the world and are involved in securing natural resources and marketing their wares on a global scale. What's more, the American consumer is responsible for huge wealth generation. Without the seemingly insatiable desire amongst Americans for cheap manufactured goods, no Chinese economic miracle would be under way.

- **Technological leadership.** The US undoubtedly has a disproportionate number of great academic institutions, which have helped produce some of the key advances in technology over the past few decades. From the Internet to successful pharmaceuticals to the iPod, the US is the world's biggest technological power. In fact, its military and private sector research and development are several years ahead of even those of western Europe and China. This situation gives it a lead when designing new products to sell globally. It's often said that what's happening in the US this year will happen in the UK the next, highlighting just how advanced the good old US of A actually is!

The US has a population of around 300 million, making it the third most populous nation in the world behind India and China. It's also the fourth largest by size behind Russia, Canada and (only just) China.

The president of the United States is often referred to as the most important person in the world, and the long drawn-out US election process often attracts huge global media coverage. For example, the election of the US's first black president, Barack Obama, in 2008 sparked intense interest around the world. On a visit to Germany, Obama spoke to a crowd of over 100,000 people in Berlin. This phenomenon was dubbed Obama-mania and he was portrayed by some commentators – particularly in western Europe – as the saviour of America's reputation in the wider world.

Being buddies: The US–UK special relationship

The phrase *special relationship* was coined by the British wartime PM Winston Churchill in 1946. Churchill, who I cover in detail in Chapter 22, was himself half-American and had just spent four years working closely with two US presidents helping beat Nazi Germany, so he had personal reasons to big-up the US–UK relationship.

But the special relationship phrase struck at a truth. The two countries share a common language, a lot of history and a very similar culture. In fact, the British often refer to the Americans as the 'cousins', emphasising this closeness.

But the special relationship isn't all about being misty-eyed and chummy; the two nations' governments have, since the end of the Second World War, often held similar foreign policy objectives and their intelligence and armed services work very closely together.

Some of the key reasons the special relationship between the UK and the US is still alive and kicking more than half a century after it was recognised include:

- **Military alliances.** And we're not just talking Second World War here; in fact, US and UK troops have fought side by side in lots of major conflicts in the past 60 years, including the Korean War in the 1950s, two wars in Iraq and, most recently, in Afghanistan.

  The US and UK are both members of the North Atlantic Treaty Organisation (NATO), which was set up in 1949 to defend Europe from Soviet invasion. In addition, both countries are permanent members of the United Nations Security Council (Chapter 19 has more on this important international body).

- **Cultural links.** I could write a whole book on the cultural links between the two countries. In music, literature, advertising, television and even blogging, the common language and often shared cultural experience mean that American and British citizens often see the world through the same prism.

✔ **Common values.** Both the US and UK are democracies. In fact, they're two of the oldest democratic nations in the world. In addition, both have a long history of respecting individual liberty and free speech. These values may seem the norm to you, but for most people around the world free speech and democracy are either alien or relatively new concepts. These common values between the US and UK deepen and widen the specialness of their relationship.

Growing apart? Recent problems with the special relationship

Not everything's rosy in the US–UK garden. In recent years the political and even cultural links between the two countries seem to be getting less pronounced. Some say that the special relationship isn't so, well, special anymore.

Some reasons the special relationship between the UK and US may be in trouble are:

✔ **War in Iraq.** The US-led invasion of Iraq in 2003 was hugely controversial around the globe. Many saw it as an illegal and aggressive war waged on the admittedly despotic regime of Saddam Hussein. The decision by UK PM Tony Blair to follow the US into Iraq was very unpopular amongst the British people. Overall, the Iraq war and the subsequent retaliation by Islamic militants led many in the UK to question the special relationship and the motives of the US.

✔ **Population change in the US.** Much of the special relationship is based on use of a common language, yet the US population is changing and a large proportion of people in America now speak Spanish as a first language. In fact, some suggest that within 50 years there'll be more Spanish than English speakers. This situation is bound to weaken one of the key bonds between the two countries.

✔ **Growing bonds between the UK and Europe.** The UK is very much a key player in the European Union these days (see Chapter 20 for more). This means that much of the UK's trade and diplomacy is done with near neighbours like France and Germany rather than with the US. As a result, although still hugely important, the strong ties with the US are no longer as crucial to the UK economy as they once were.

✔ **Rise of China.** On the flip side, the UK is no longer as important a trading and economic partner to the US either. In fact, the US takes most of its imports from China, the rising superpower in the East. The government in Washington sees its relationship with Beijing as now far more important than the one with London or, for that matter, western Europe.

✔ **Trade disputes.** The UK and US are now in opposing economic blocs, which I talk more about in Chapter 19. The UK is a part of the

European Union (EU) and the US signed the North American Free Trade Agreement. These blocs are in constant dispute over the imposition of import tariffs and paying of subsidies, which is bound to loosen the bonds between the US and UK.

✔ **Catching criminals.** The US, as part of its 'war on terror', has detained without trial hundreds of people from around the globe in its facility at Guantanamo Bay in Cuba. Some of these people are British citizens, a fact that angers many civil liberties campaigners. At the same time, the UK has signed a treaty agreeing to extradite people accused of crimes in the US, which critics suggest is unfair and one-sided in America's favour.

Such was the level of support shown by Tony Blair for America's policies in Iraq and Afghanistan that he was referred to by political opponents in the UK and even internationally as America's poodle – hardly a flattering image for a British prime minister.

Looking at the US System of Government

The US national anthem, the Star Spangled Banner, refers to America as the 'land of the free' and this is how millions around the globe see the place. Much of the positive press the US receives has its roots in what's widely seen as the nation's strong democracy. But backing up this democracy is one of the most famous documents in the world – the US Constitution.

The American War of Independence eventually gave birth to the world's first written constitution – oddly enough called the US Constitution – which was adopted in 1787. The constitution lays out what all the branches of American government do and lists their individual powers, as well as setting out the relationship between the government and the citizens it serves.

The US Constitution is alterable, and in fact has been amended 27 times. The first ten amendments were added nearly as soon as the ink on the constitution was dry. Those first ten amendments are called the Bill of Rights and they set forth civil liberties such as freedom of speech, association and the press. The amendment process isn't one to be undertaken lightly or quickly. An amendment may be proposed by two thirds of the members of both houses of Congress, then ratified by three quarters of state legislatures. Alternatively, two thirds of state legislatures can call for a constitutional convention to consider amendments, which would each need to be ratified by three quarters of the state legislatures. So far, all amendments have been passed using the first method.

The US Constitution is a very valuable and precious document and is kept under lock and key. The next sections offer a basic rundown of what's in it and the institutions of governance it establishes.

Starting off by breaking with the British

It's a little hard to believe that the most powerful nation in the world was once a colony of farmers, fur traders and merchants ruled by the British Empire. However, a little over two and a quarter centuries ago that's exactly what the United States was.

Several countries had a go at colonising the North American continent – the French, Spanish and even the Russians – but it was the settlers from the UK that made the biggest impact. From a few boats full of settlers in the early 17th century, the American colony grew until it rivalled the UK in terms of population and wealth.

At that point, the relationship changed. Unhappy with the way they were governed – and taxed – from London, the American colonists revolted and after a long, bloody and humiliating war (from Britain's perspective), the American colonists gained their independence from the UK and the United States of America was born.

George Washington isn't just a great figure he's probably *the* greatest figure in American history. He was the general who led the American forces in their victory over the British (after escaping death and defeat several times). He was also America's first president, and a picture of him can be found in nearly all American schools, as well as on the one dollar note. George Washington's a massive figure state side, even having his face carved into the rock of Mount Rushmore.

British–American relations took a long time to improve after the War of Independence. In fact, the two countries were at war again in 1812, during which British troops burned down the White House. Later down the line, during the American Civil War, the British supported the Confederate states in the South who were eventually defeated by the Unionist northern states. And in the last century, 1931 to be precise, US President Hoover drew up plans for a naval war with Britain following trade disputes between the two nations.

Building the Houses of Congress

The US Congress is made up of two elected chambers: the House of Representatives and the Senate.

The 435 members of the House of Representatives each represent a district in an individual state – like a constituency in the UK – and serve a two-year term. The House is meant to be directly responsive to the people.

Each of the 50 states elects two senators. The Senate is supposed to be a more deliberative body than the House, and senators serve six-year terms, with the idea that they'll be less influenced by the whims of popular opinion and more forward-looking.

Elections to the US Senate are staggered so that one third of the membership stands for election every two years. So, for example, in 2010 a third of all senators will stand for election and in 2012 another third and in 2014 another third. In 2016 the senators who were elected in 2010 will have to stand for re-election and in 2018 the ones who were elected in 2012 will face the voters again and so on.

Congress has the following powers:

- ✔ To levy taxes and to authorise the government's budget

- ✔ To make laws

- ✔ To declare war

- ✔ To issue patents and copyright and set weights and measures (it may not sound as big as the other three but this power has a huge impact on everyday life!)

Members of Congress introduce new Bills – which are in effect proposed changes to the law. Often laws are proposed at the behest of America's powerful lobbying groups (I discuss how pressure groups work in the UK in Chapter 9). A staggering 40,000 lobbyists are active in Washington alone, which works out to around 75 lobbyists for every member of Congress.

Because of its power to veto presidential appointments and treaties, the Senate is considered the more powerful of the two houses of Congress.

Establishing the presidency

The head honcho, the main man, the numero uno, the big cheese; however you want to describe the president of the United States, one thing's for sure: no job in the world is bigger.

The powers of the president under the US Constitution are as follows:

- ✔ To appoint a cabinet to head up US government ministries (called agencies or departments in the US)

- ✔ To appoint justices to the Supreme Court (see the upcoming 'Judging disputes: The US Supreme Court' for more on this body)

- ✔ To enter into international treaties, with Senate approval

- ✔ To act as commander in chief of the armed forces. In wartime the president has final say over strategy

- To veto laws passed by Congress
- To grant pardons or reprieves to people who've been convicted of crimes or those facing trial for an offence

Congress, not the president, has the power to declare war, but as commander in chief of the armed services, the president has the power to send troops into military conflict for up to 60 days before having to get Congress's permission. So, in effect, the president has the power to make war.

Only the president gets to nominate cabinet members and top judges, but all appointments have to be 'with the advice and consent' of the US Senate. The president says who he'd like for a particular job and that appointment is then discussed and ratified by the Senate, normally with senior senators sitting as a committee interviewing the president's candidate.

Treaties negotiated by the president must be ratified by a two-thirds majority vote in the Senate to take effect.

Since the US Constitution was amended in 1951 (after Franklin D. Roosevelt was elected president four times), the president can only be elected to two, four-year terms of office.

Exploring the mystique and power of the presidency

The president may have plenty of powers under the US Constitution but it's more than that which gives the person who works from the Oval Office of the White House in Washington a mystique and aura quite unlike that surrounding any other high office in world politics.

Some reasons the US president has such a hold on international attention, include:

- The president is the head of state – in effect, the embodiment of America internationally.
- The president's role of commander in chief puts him in charge of the most powerful military in the world.

It may be helpful to think of the president as a combination of the UK prime minister and the UK monarch – a head of state and the pre-eminent politician rolled into one.

The president may only have the power to veto bills from Congress but in reality he'll often get a friend or party ally in Congress to introduce a Bill he'd like to see become law. In effect, the president has the right to introduce bills to Congress but they have to go through the same consideration process as any other bill.

Electing a president

The election of a president of the United States every four years is always a big deal and an exhaustive process. Long before election day, leading politicians from each of the two main political parties – Republican and Democratic – compete in a series of state elections called *primaries*, in which mostly party members vote. Candidates win a certain number of votes from each primary which convert to votes for that candidate at the party's convention, held in late summer. The votes of each candidate are totted up and whoever has the most is declared winner. That individual then becomes the party's presidential candidate at the subsequent nationwide election in November.

On election day itself, voters in each state have a choice between the two party candidates, and sometimes a third-party candidate if they can qualify to get on the ballot. Unlike in the primaries, the candidate who receives the most votes in a state wins all that state's electoral college votes. So, for example, whoever polls the most votes in Florida wins that state and gets to take all the votes for that state in the electoral college, regardless of the size of the actual victory margin. Electoral college votes are awarded according to a state's population, so the more populous states come with more electoral college votes.

At the end of the night, all the electoral college votes collected by the candidate are totted up and whoever has the greatest number is declared the winner and will be the next president of the United States.

Exploring presidential perks and perils

The president has his own private jet aircraft called Air Force One, which is no small two-seater, but a jumbo jet the size of a commercial airliner. Why so big? Well, this plane is supposed to be a working office for the president which can house dozens of staff members and, of course, provide a safe haven in case of war. The idea is that in times of crisis the president can be safe from harm on Air Force One so that the government still has a leader.

The goodies don't stop with a plane. The president has access to a huge nuclear bunker and a country retreat called Camp David . Camp David doesn't involve tents and queuing at the shower block but is a luxurious property where the president can entertain world leaders and get away from it all. The prime minister in the UK has something similar – although a lot smaller – called Chequers.

The job of president of the United States isn't a particularly safe one, and I don't just mean there's a danger of getting thrown out of office. In total, there've been 44 presidents since the first, George Washington. Of these, four – Abraham Lincoln, James A. Garfield, William McKinley and John F. Kennedy – have been assassinated whilst in office. President Ronald Reagan managed to survive being shot in an assassination attempt in the early 1980s. Perhaps one of the first things a newly elected president should do is call a life assurance broker!

GREAT FIGURES

Looking at great US presidents

There've been good, bad, mediocre and even great presidents of the United States. Here's a look at some of the real stars of the Oval Office:

- **Thomas Jefferson (1801–09).** The third president of the United States and principal author of the Declaration of Independence wasn't just a president but also a great political thinker, horticulturist, architect, archaeologist and even palaeontologist. He was very much in favour of individual states being allowed to get on with their own affairs without too much interference from the federal government in Washington. He also cut taxes, added the state of Louisiana to the US and made importing slaves into the US illegal.

- **Abraham Lincoln (1861–65).** The giant 16th president of the US led the victory of the northern states (called the Union) over the Confederate southern states in the bloody American Civil War. He reformed taxes and the army, made some incredible political speeches and crucially declared the abolition of slavery. He was assassinated by John Wilkes Booth on a night out at the theatre in 1865.

- **Franklin D. Roosevelt (1933–45).** Another wartime president, this time the Second World War, this polio-struck president was elected in the midst of the Great Depression and his economic 'New Deal' programme is often seen as crucial to helping alleviate terrible poverty and unemployment in the 1930s. In wartime he led the US very ably against Nazi Germany and Imperial Japan until his death in 1945.

- **John F. Kennedy (1961–63).** Often simply JFK, Kennedy was one of the most iconic of presidents. Youthful, good-looking and charming, he seemed to have everything. He was elected in a narrow victory in 1960 but proceeded to inspire the nation with great speech-making and by facing down the Russians over the Cuban missile crisis. He set the country on course for its successful moon landings. His assassination in 1963 shocked the world and gave him an added aura of potential cruelly denied. In public opinion polls Kennedy consistently emerges as one of the great presidents.

The president has a vice – no, not drinking too much or being over-friendly with the opposite sex (although quite a few past presidents have done both!) – but a vice president; in effect a deputy. The vice president advises and campaigns at election time with the president and should the latter no longer be able to serve, the vice president steps into the breach and becomes president until the end of the four-year term of office.

Impeaching the president

The president may be the most powerful politician in the world but that doesn't mean that he can do anything he wants. The US Constitution was designed specifically to prevent the rise of a tyrannical figure – like a Stalin in Russia or Hitler in Germany – as president. The system has inbuilt checks on the power of the president, such as only the Houses of Congress being able to make laws and wars having to have their approval. And then of course there are a series of individual citizen rights set out in the constitution.

Congress's ultimate check on the president is the power of impeachment. *Impeachment* is the removal from public office of the president or other official on the grounds that they've acted unlawfully in some way.

In an impeachment proceeding, a committee of the House of Representatives passes, by majority vote, articles of impeachment. In effect, articles are just like being charged with a crime. The full House of Representatives then holds hearings to investigate the claims of the articles of impeachment. If a simple majority of House members votes for impeachment, the trial moves to the Senate, where a two-thirds majority is required for conviction. Once impeached, the president is, well, no longer the president. The job then falls to the vice president, who serves the remainder of the four-year term of office.

Impeachment is a very serious undertaking and has happened very rarely in US history. Two presidents have undergone impeachment proceedings:

- ✔ Andrew Johnson was narrowly acquitted by a vote in the Senate in 1868.

- ✔ More recently, President Bill Clinton was accused of lying to a grand jury over his actions regarding an affair with White House intern Monica Lewinsky in 1998. (Chapter 23 has more on this scandal.) The House of Representatives approved the impeachment articles but the majority of Senators voted against impeachment, which meant Clinton was acquitted and remained in office.

However, even the threat of impeachment can have a big effect on the actions of the president. Richard Nixon in 1974 became the first president to resign from office following widespread calls for his impeachment over the Watergate scandal.

Impeachment isn't reserved for the president. Other senior office holders in US federal and state government can also be impeached if they're believed to have committed crimes. In fact, since the process of impeachment was set up in the US Constitution in 1789, the House of Representatives has initiated such proceedings against 63 individuals.

Judging disputes: The US Supreme Court

Apart from the president and the Houses of Congress, the other major cog of US government is the US Supreme Court, whose job it is to act as the protector of the constitution. The Supreme Court is the highest court in the country and hears cases in which constitutional questions are at stake.

The head of the court is the Supreme Justice of the United States. Working alongside him or her are eight other Supreme Court judges for a grand total of nine justices. The fact it is an odd number is significant, as this ensures that a tie never occurs in votes taken by the justices. The court only requires a majority to deliver a verdict, even five votes to four carries the day.

The president appoints new Supreme Court justices and generally he looks to install people who share his political and social viewpoints. For example, a Republican president may look to appoint a justice who has quite conservative views on political and social issues. However, the appointment of a Supreme Court justice has to be approved by the Senate and senators hold hearings in which they interview the candidate to ensure that he or she's experienced and capable of doing the job.

The Supreme Court decides whether the circumstances of the case in front of them is constitutional or unconstitutional. The court also acts as a final court of appeal for the country's lower courts.

The Supreme Court employs a filtering system for cases it should or shouldn't hear. It will only hear cases which comply with any of the following three reasons:

- ✔ To resolve a conflict in the interpretation of a federal law or a provision of the constitution

- ✔ To correct a major departure from the accepted and usual course of judicial proceedings

- ✔ To resolve an important question of federal law, or to expressly review a decision of a lower court that conflicts directly with a previous decision of the Court

Only if the case ticks one of these complex boxes will the Supreme Court hear it.

Once appointed, Supreme Court justices have *life tenure*, which means that usually only the grim reaper can remove them from office! Of course, they can choose to retire from the job.

Probably the most controversial case heard by the Supreme Court in modern times is Roe versus Wade. This case dates back to 1970 and concerned abortion. A pregnant woman named Roe (an alias) wanted the legal right to have an abortion in the state of Texas, which outlawed it. She took her case to the state court, where the district attorney, Henry Wade (hence Roe versus Wade), argued against the right to have an abortion. Eventually the case found its way to the Supreme Court as it was considered potentially unconstitutional to make a woman have a baby she didn't want. The Supreme Court decided that Roe could have the abortion and this decision set a precedent across the country. Many Christian groups and Republican Party members argue that the Supreme Court decision was wrong and would like to see the decision reversed.

Considering the not-so-great US presidents

A total of 44 presidents is bound to produce a few duffers. Here are some of the men (no woman has yet scooped the top job) who really didn't make a good fist of things in the Oval Office:

✔ **Warren Harding (1921–23).** In polls of political scientists, Harding constantly comes out at the bottom of the pile. Why? Well, he appointed his cronies to the top jobs in government and they were, to put it bluntly, corrupt. Dogged by scandal, he dropped dead from a heart attack (mid-conversation with his wife) after only two years as president.

✔ **Herbert Hoover (1929–33).** He was president at the onset of the Great Depression in the 1930s which saw millions of people worldwide thrown out of work. His economic policies were widely seen as having made the disastrous economic situation even worse, so much so that the shanty towns which sprang up to house the homeless around some of America's big cities were called Hoovervilles. He even wanted to ban beer – not a vote winner!

✔ **Richard Nixon (1969–74).** Old Tricky Dick, as he was nicknamed, was a consummate politician who opened up a political dialogue with China, entered into nuclear disarmament talks with the Soviet Union and even started to scale back the unsuccessful war in Vietnam. All these are good things, so why the bad reputation? Well, Nixon had to resign from office after the Watergate scandal, in which he and his advisers were revealed to have broken the law. See Chapter 23 for the lowdown on Watergate.

✔ **George W. Bush (2001–09).** Initially seen as a hero after the terrorist attacks on the US by Islamic extremists in 2001, George W. proceeded to embroil the country in an expensive, bloody and ultimately highly unpopular war in Iraq. What's more, during his presidency the world came to the brink of economic collapse due to a banking crisis. He was often derided by critics as inarticulate and simply not up to the job.

Passing a Bill into Law

Bills are introduced by individual members of either the House of Representatives or Senate or sometimes by members from both houses. They're then considered by the relevant standing committee. For example, a bill relating to agriculture will be considered by the agriculture standing committee of the body it was introduced in.

Committees usually hold open meetings in which they invite interested parties to testify about the bill or the issue it addresses. At the end of the hearing committee members vote on whether to recommend the bill to the full body. If the vote is no, the bill is effectively dead, but if the committee recommends the bill, it's placed in front of the relevant House for consideration. The House debates and may amend the bill, followed by a vote.

A bill approved by one House is sent to the other, which may pass, reject or amend it. In order for the bill to become law, both Houses must agree to identical versions of it. If the second House amends the bill, the differences between the two versions are considered by a conference committee made up of members from both Houses. The committee produces a final draft of the bill, which again is voted upon by the two Houses of Congress. If the bill gets the green light, all well and good but it's not law yet – it needs the approval of the president first.

Bills which propose levying a new tax have to originate in the House of Representatives rather than the Senate, according to the US Constitution.

The US is a federal state, which means it's made up of lots of largely autonomous individual states. Laws passed by Congress apply to the whole country but in many areas, such as criminal justice, the states are left to decide their own policies without interference from Congress.

Often Congress is referred to as *Capitol Hill* because of the area of Washington where it's located. In the same way, the British refer to their own parliament as Westminster after the area of London that the Houses of Parliament stand in.

Throwing Political Parties into the Mix

The US political system, like the UK's, has political parties right at its heart. The two main parties are the Democratic and Republican parties, both of which are chock-full of history. If a politician wants to get anywhere at election time, he or she has to represent one of these two parties.

Not only leading national and state politicians represent political parties. People stand for election as representing a political party in all manner of local elected offices. For example, the person standing for election to be in charge of refuse collection in a town or city signs on as a Republican or Democrat on the ballot paper, as do people standing in local mayoral elections.

Some people have tried to break the stranglehold of the two main parties on American political life by launching a third party. The most recent – and certainly best-funded – example was the billionaire businessman Ross Perot, who formed the Reform Party and ran for president in 1992 and 1996. His platform promised to fight drugs, control the sale of guns and tax foreign imports. His policies were very popular with the American public but Perot, personally, was less so. However, in the 1992 presidential election he scooped 19 per cent of all votes cast. At the 1996 election he was less successful, attracting just 8 per cent of all votes cast.

Each main party has its own symbol. The Democrats are represented by a donkey, which you may feel isn't particularly flattering (donkeys are hardly noted for their skills in government) but actually refers to a former Democratic leader depicted in a cartoon riding a jackass (again, not flattering). The Republicans are represented by an elephant, which again harks back to the days of political cartoons. Symbols do have a practical purpose, though, because they often appear alongside the name of candidates on the ballot paper. A voter seeing a donkey next to a candidate's name automatically knows that person represents the Democratic Party.

After the 2008 elections, the Democrats were in the ascendancy. President Barack Obama won the White House and Democrats held a majority of seats in both Houses of Congress. But the fortunes of the political parties tend to ebb and flow. In the 1950s, 1980s and early 2000s the Republicans were in the pole position but in the 1960s, 1970s and 1990s the Democrats often had control of Congress and the presidency.

Voting with the Democrats

The older of the two parties, the Democratic Party traces its roots back to the elections of 1800. It tends to gain most of its support along the eastern and western seaboards, amongst ethnic minorities and in the big cities. Some of the great Democratic presidents include Franklin D. Roosevelt and John F. Kennedy.

The Democratic Party tends to pursue more liberal, left-wing policies, believing in a degree of state intervention to help the poor and neediest in society. Democrats favour a minimum wage and government action to protect the environment.

Siding with the Republicans

The more socially and politically conservative of the two parties, Republicans stand for minimal government interference in people's lives and in the affairs of individual states by the federal government. Republicans tend to believe in letting business get on with what it's good at – making money – and support low taxes but strong national defence.

Republicans have had their fair share of admired presidents, such as Abraham Lincoln (the first Republican president), Dwight D. Eisenhower and Ronald Reagan.

Rallying the religious right

One of the most significant developments in modern American politics has been the growth in power and influence of what's been called the *religious right*. The US is a deeply religious country, with the majority of citizens regularly attending a place of worship.

Many Christian groups have taken their observance a stage further, looking to see their religious faith expressed through politics. More often than not, these people – and we're talking tens of millions of people across the country – have gravitated towards the Republican Party. This situation has proved both a blessing and a curse for the Republican Party at election time. A blessing because the religious right supporters are very keen on turning up to vote, which in a society with very low voter turnout – often fewer than 60 per cent of eligible voters actually do so in Congressional and presidential elections – can be quite a boost to the Republican Party. A curse because the views of the religious right can be quite unpopular amongst many Americans (for example, they're staunchly anti-abortion), which turns off many moderate voters who the Republican Party needs to attract to win elections.

Some of the key policies that the religious right would like to see pursued include:

- Criminalising abortion
- Retaining the death penalty
- Doing away with welfare benefits
- Holding of Christian prayers in schools across the country, every day
- Teaching the creationist interpretation of human history alongside the scientifically accepted doctrine of evolution

During the 2008 presidential election, the Democrats undertook a massive Internet campaign to encourage more people to vote. They reckoned that only through increasing voter turnout could they overcome the effects of the religious right turning out and voting Republican. This tactic obviously worked a treat, as their candidate Barack Obama beat the Republican candidate John McCain in the election.

Many of the policies that the religious right would like to see pursued have actually been adopted by Republican Party candidates.

Linking up: UK and US political parties

The special relationship between the UK and US also applies to the two nation's political parties. The Democratic and Republican parties in the US and the Labour and Conservative parties in the UK have close ties, and share ideas, information and even personnel.

Naturally, the Conservative Party has closer ties with the Republican Party than it does with the Democrats, mainly because they're both on the right of politics and share similar ideals such as a smaller role for central government and low taxes. On the flip side, the Labour and Democratic parties are close because they share ideals such as the state providing better welfare for the less fortunate.

During the 1992 US presidential election the Conservative Party of John Major, who was also prime minister, gave quite a lot of assistance to the campaign to re-elect the Republican president George Bush Senior (father of President George W. Bush). Some suggested that this help included giving the Bush campaign information on Democratic candidate Bill Clinton's time as a student at Oxford University in the UK, when he grew his hair long, had a terrible beard and may have partied a little hard. Nevertheless, George Bush Snr lost to Clinton and the new president was known to have been deeply unhappy with the help that Major had given his opponent.

Part V
The Part of Tens

'I sometimes think the Green manifestos are too biodegradable.'

In this part . . .

*E*very *For Dummies* book includes a Part of Tens; chapters that each contain ten or so interesting pieces of information. For this book my choices are guaranteed to get you debating. Who are the greatest British Prime Ministers? What were the ten most significant (and at times sordid!) political scandals of all time? What major events have formed the modern political world? And what are the political and economic trends to look for in the future?

Chapter 22

Ten Great Prime Ministers

. . . .

In This Chapter

▶ Leading with aplomb

▶ Reforming and improving

▶ Taking care of the people

. . . .

*T*he role of prime minister (PM) is the top job in British politics. Although technically just a Member of Parliament (MP) and a servant of the monarch, the reality is that the PM has huge powers, from appointing the heads of government ministries to negotiating treaties with foreign powers. But of the 51 people who've been British PM, plenty of them have been mediocre performers, and some have made a downright bad fist of the job. Yet a select band of men and one woman have been, well, rather special, making an extraordinary contribution to shaping Britain and the wider world.

In this chapter I look at the brightest stars in the prime ministerial sky. If you want to know who's made the biggest splash while occupying 10 Downing Street, this is the chapter for you.

Our Finest Hour: Winston Churchill (1940–45 and 1951–55)

Although this chapter is about the greatest prime ministers, one stands head and shoulders above the rest. In the BBC's poll of the Greatest Ever Britons, conducted at the end of the last millennium, Winston Churchill came top.

As prime minister during the Second World War, Churchill proved the truth of the maxim 'cometh the hour cometh the man'. An avowed hater of the tyrannical Nazi regime (which had overrun neighbouring France in May 1940), Churchill, through his force of character and will, galvanised the British people into believing that they could win the war and that what seemed like the darkest hour of the Blitz bombing of London in 1940–41 was actually the nation's finest hour.

When the war was won in 1945, Churchill was recognised as a truly great world leader, yet the electorate still voted him out of office in favour of a Labour Party which promised to construct a welfare state. Churchill wasn't finished, though: he won the 1951 election and, although past his best as a politician, he still bestrode the international stage as a colossus, forging stronger relations between the UK and the United States.

Even with politics out of the equation, Churchill was still a great person; a journalist, wit, brave soldier and winner of the Nobel Prize for Literature – his was a life less ordinary. It's easy to see why the word 'Churchillian' means strong, committed leadership.

The Welsh Wizard: David Lloyd George (1916–22)

War is a crucible of politics that exposes leaders prone to dithering and incompetence and brings to the fore those who are highly capable and charismatic. In 1916, with the First World War going badly for Britain, the nation needed new leadership. Herbert Asquith, the prime minister at the time, was largely seen as indecisive and not up to the task. In his cabinet, the munitions minister David Lloyd George had dramatically overhauled the production of artillery shells and he seemed like the only man with a plan. Lloyd George deposed Asquith as prime minister and set about reforming government with the sole objective of winning the war. Britain won in 1918 and Lloyd George was instrumental in constructing the peace at the Versailles Conference, which followed in 1919. Lloyd George served as PM until 1922 and granted votes for certain women in 1918 (full female suffrage was granted in 1928).

For much of his political life Lloyd George was an outsider. For starters, he was the only PM whose first language wasn't English – it was Welsh. He also didn't come from an aristocratic background. Lloyd George was seen by many colleagues as deceitful in his dealings and as PM was embroiled in a scandal over the sale of honours. He was also the last leader of the Liberal Party to make it to the post of prime minister.

Iron Lady: Margaret Thatcher (1979–1990)

Britain's one and only female PM makes it into the list not because of her gender but because she's widely recognised as the single most important driving force in British politics since Churchill. Margaret Thatcher, the daughter of a grocer from Grantham in Lincolnshire, went on to study Chemistry at Oxford University. In a sexist environment, in the most old-fashioned of political parties – the Conservatives – Thatcher managed to get herself selected as a parliamentary candidate, elected as an MP, and into the cabinet. She became leader of the party in 1975 following the Conservatives' two election defeats the previous year. In the 1979 general election many of the senior men in her party were expecting Thatcher to fail in the heat of battle but she managed to win a majority in parliament. She stayed in the role for 11 years, fighting a successful war in the Falkland Islands against Argentina, reforming public services, passing anti-union laws, lowering taxes and overseeing a rebirth of British business. By any estimate, she was a great PM.

However, Thatcher was a deeply divisive figure; she didn't like criticism from colleagues, could be domineering of her cabinet, and was intolerant. Many people in the industrialised north of England see her as responsible for the destruction of their jobs and communities. The miners' strike in 1984 (which was about the planned closure of pits) – which led to the defeat of the strikers and a victory for Thatcher – is seen as the embodiment of a bitter, divided Britain overseen by the PM dubbed the 'Iron Lady'.

The Trailblazer: Robert Walpole (1721–1742)

Robert Walpole was the first politician to be recognised by historians as prime minister – although the phrase prime minister wasn't used at the time – and was in power from 1721 to 1742. He inherited a difficult economic situation, with thousands of Britons having lost their life savings in the speculative 'South Sea Bubble' in 1720 (when people invested in the South Sea Company, only for the bubble to burst). His policies successfully dealt with these economic problems and the country enjoyed huge wealth. Walpole was a major figure on the international stage, negotiating favourable treaties for Britain and keeping the country out of a bloody continental war over succession to the throne of Poland.

The Walpole era is seen as a crucial one in the development of Britain as a world power, with the country consolidating its empire – including in North America – and major cultural figures, such as Jonathan Swift and Samuel Johnson, doing their thing. Despite all this, probably Walpole's biggest legacy was the establishment of the job of prime minister itself.

Robert Walpole was the first PM to occupy 10 Downing Street in London, the official residence of British prime ministers ever since. The house was originally three houses, but was knocked into one under King George II.

The Great Reformer: Clement Attlee (1945–51)

To look at, Attlee had a bald dome head, trimmed moustache and seemed every inch the chartered accountant. But still waters run deep. Attlee – a capable deputy prime minister in the wartime coalition government run by Winston Churchill – had risen seamlessly in the ranks of the Labour Party to become leader at the election in 1945. The party's pledge to create a welfare state helped win it a landslide against Winston Churchill's Conservatives, and Attlee, the small man from working-class roots in Putney, was PM. The next six years saw nothing less than the creation of what many people would consider Modern Britain; the National Health Service was founded and large tracts of industry were taken into public ownership. Britain's poor could suddenly expect financial help from the state instead of a cold shoulder. Attlee oversaw the education system overhauled and inequality reduced. Internationally, Attlee took the first steps in dismantling the British Empire, with India finally granted its independence in 1948. In six years, Attlee's government changed Britain forever. The reward was to be defeated by a resurgent Conservative Party under Winston Churchill in 1951.

The First Spin Doctor: Benjamin Disraeli (1868 and 1874–1880)

Britain's one and only PM of Jewish heritage, (pretty extraordinary in what at the time was a deeply Christian country) Disraeli was the master of the art of public relations at a time when PR was unknown. He was the first major British politician to sell the idea of Britain as a major world empire to the public. He made Queen Victoria – with whom he shared a warm friendship – Empress of India and worked to extend the British Empire into the Middle East and Asia upon which 'the sun would never set'. He was noted for getting Britain involved again in Continental European politics. Since the end of the Napoleonic Wars in 1815 Britain had deliberately stayed out of European affairs, adopting a policy dubbed 'splendid isolation'. Disraeli, though, became actively involved in major treaties and negotiations with Continental powers, particularly at the Congress of Berlin in 1878 when, through skilful negotiations, he limited the growing influence of Russia in the Balkans. Some of Disraeli's other foreign adventures were less successful; the British invasions of Afghanistan and the land of the Zulu in South Africa resulted in some military defeats. One of Disraeli's domestic policy achievements was the Reform Act 1867, which increased the number of people (all men back then, of course) who were allowed to vote.

Outside Number 10, Disraeli was no slouch with the pen, writing best-selling romantic novels: from PM to Mills and Boon!

The Grand Old Man: William Gladstone (1868–74, 1880–85, 1886 and 1892–94)

Disraeli's arch-rival was the great Liberal politician and four times prime minister, William Gladstone. The Grand Old Man (GOM), as he was nicknamed, was noted for his very, very long speeches and apparently Queen Victoria once criticised him by saying 'he talks to me as if I were a public meeting'. His bitter rival Disraeli twisted the GOM nickname, saying it actually stood for God's Only Mistake.

Gladstone was a giant of late Victorian politics. He was a major proponent of free trade and the removal of tariffs on imported goods, and supported electoral reform allowing more men to vote. To his credit, Gladstone was opposed to the expansion of the British Empire into the heart of Africa in search of natural resources, although ultimately he could do little about it. Closer to home, he wanted the Irish to have home rule (in effect, self-governance), and if he'd had his way the troubled history between Britain and Ireland of the last century may have been very different. However, Gladstone couldn't get his way because his Liberal Party only enjoyed a slim majority in parliament and there was considerable opposition to home rule.

Gladstone had a high moral code that was adopted by many Victorian men of means. Even as prime minister he used to walk the streets at night trying to persuade prostitutes to give up their way of life and go to church. He eventually gave up being PM aged 84, drawing to a close probably the most eventful and long-lasting political career of 19th-century British politics.

Shaking Things Up: Robert Peel (1834–35 and 1841–46)

Robert Peel was one of British history's great do-ers. Prime minister twice, he was also responsible for setting up the British police force – the police nickname Bobby is short for Robert, and they were originally called Peelers!

Peel was alarmed at the increase in crime and, in face of fierce opposition from those who feared that the police could be used by a tyrannical government to crush opposition, he went about replacing the old method of policing by city watches and sheriffs with a uniformed and professional police force. So next time you get stopped for speeding, you know who you have to thank!

Another crucial contribution by Peel was repealing the Corn Laws. Imported corn was taxed which, although protecting the livelihoods of many British farmers, meant that many poverty-stricken industrial workers had to pay way over the odds for that most basic of foodstuffs, bread. Scrapping the Corn Laws opened Britain up to the mass importation of foodstuffs from the prairies of North America and sent bread prices tumbling. British workers could afford bread but many farmers in the UK went to the wall in the last three decades of the 19th century in what historians dub the Victorian agricultural depression.

Repealing the Corn Laws split the Tory party of the day down the middle and left Peel out of office. His own party, the Tories, had failed to support the repeal and Peel had had to rely on votes from the rival Whig party. Peel's reforming zeal didn't stop at the Corn Law; he also introduced the Factory Act 1844, restricting the number of hours that women and children could work. Less happily, he re-imposed income tax, which had been suspended in 1815.

The Second Master of Spin: Tony Blair (1997–2007)

The fresh-faced and affable Tony Blair promised, in the words of his Labour Party election song of 1997, that 'things can only get better' for Britain under him as prime minister. It seemed for a few years that he was right. The country boomed economically and culturally, with the advent of Brit Pop and Cool Britannia. Britain seemed to be going through a giant make-over and would come out the other side more attractive and vibrant.

Working alongside his Chancellor and successor Gordon Brown, Blair introduced the minimum wage and tax credits for families and made the Bank of England independent from government interference. He also helped bring peace to Northern Ireland after a quarter of a century. Britain's relations with the European Union improved, with Blair instrumental in the expansion of the EU from 15 to 27 member states. In Africa, too, Blair made significant strides in persuading other world leaders to forgive debts of the poorest countries and up their aid commitments. So far, so good. Then came Iraq.

On the premise that the Iraqi dictator Saddam Hussein had weapons of mass destruction, Blair took Britain into an invasion of Iraq alongside the United States. Many British and international politicians suggested that the war was illegal and unnecessary and the case against Blair deepened when, after Hussein's defeat, no actual weapons of mass destruction were found. A bloody civil war in Iraq followed and Blair was portrayed in some media as 'Bliar' and even a war criminal for his actions. What's more, many of the media manipulation techniques which had been deployed by Blair's powerful press secretary Alastair Campbell (see Chapter 10 for more on him) started to backfire, with the Blair government accused of being more about political spin than substance.

Dogged by criticism, Blair retired as PM in 2007 to make way for Gordon Brown. His timing couldn't have been better – he narrowly avoided the world economic crisis which started in summer of 2007. No wonder he was nick-named 'Teflon Tony' for the way scandal never stuck to him.

Wiser than His Years: William Pitt the Younger (1783–1801 and 1804–1806)

Just 24 when he became prime minister, William Pitt the Younger was the son of a previous PM; the aptly named William Pitt the Elder. Although barely out of his school uniform, William Pitt the Younger is one of the greats. In a time when PMs were lucky to last a few months in the role (the three previous PMs had managed just 18 months between them), he was a real survivor and was in place for a whopping 18 years, winning three general elections. Even after his resignation in 1801, he was back again three years later for another two-year term before dying in office at the age of 46.

But it's not just political – if not actual – longevity that marks Pitt out. He was ultra-effective in the top job. He set about reducing the national debt, called for reform of the *rotten boroughs* (parliamentary seats with only a few elec-tors – in effect the property of local landowners and they could get who they wanted elected), he was a staunch opponent of the slave trade and even, from 1793, a wartime leader against France. His second period as PM saw Britain win the crucial battle of Trafalgar as well as form key alliances against France with Russia and Sweden. Pitt even introduced income tax, but the less said about that the better!

All in all, not bad for a man given the top job at just 24 years old.

The not quite so great prime ministers

For every great prime minister there've been at least a couple of total duffers. Here's my list of the worst PMs in British history:

✔ **Lord North (1770–1782).** Through incompetent diplomacy and military tactics, North managed to lose the United States colony to the American revolutionaries.

✔ **The Duke of Portland (1807–1809).** Only in office for two and a half years, the duke spent most of that time infirm, despite the fact that the country was at war with France during his prime ministership and needed strong leadership. He left the cabinet to its own devices to such an extent that two members of it, George Canning and Lord Castlereagh, even fought a duel over a dispute over whether British troops should be sent to Portugal or the Netherlands. The result of the duel? Canning missed by a mile and Castlereagh shot him in the thigh, with non-fatal consequences.

✔ **The Duke of Wellington (1828–30 and 1834).** The duke was an awful politician, and about as far from a conciliator as you could begin to imagine, alienating friends and opponents alike and becoming massively unpopular in the country. In his second stint as PM in 1834 most senior politicians refused to work with Wellington so for a few months he was PM, Chancellor of the Exchequer, Foreign Secretary and Home Secretary and was lousy at all of them!

✔ **Neville Chamberlain (1937–40).** Chamberlain was no doubt a very capable politician but his greatest folly was his belief that he could appease Nazi Germany. He couldn't. After shamefully allowing Germany to grab large parts of its neighbours, Britain was forced into declaring war anyway after the invasion of Poland in September 1939.

✔ **Sir Anthony Eden (1955–57).** Debonair and brave, Eden seemed every bit the politico but he got Britain involved in a disastrous scheme to snatch the Suez Canal in 1956 from the Egyptians (whose country it happened to be in) and was forced to back down by the threat of American economic sanctions. Eden resigned soon after what became known as the 'Suez Crisis'.

Chapter 23

Ten Major Political Scandals

In This Chapter

▶ Call girls, spies and sex

▶ MPs' expenses and government at war

▶ Politicians falling foul of the law

▶ Scandals across the pond

*I*n this chapter, I look at some of the major scandals to rock the political scene in Britain over the past century, and three from over the pond in America. Some scandals have led to the downfall of presidents and party political leaders, others to imprisonment and disgrace . . . all have provided fine fare for the press.

A Very British Sex Scandal: John Profumo

The news of an affair between the dashing (married) Conservative minister John Profumo and call girl Christine Keeler exploded over the British political scene like an atom bomb. The two had met at a party hosted by a member of the aristocracy and had embarked on a short affair in 1961. The story had the added spice that Keeler had also been having an affair with a Soviet spy: you couldn't make it up! The James Bond style espionage overtones gave the press a field day.

Facing difficult questions, Profumo lied about the affair to the House of Commons and from that moment his fate was sealed. Profumo resigned in June 1963 but the story was far from over. Leading judge Lord Denning conducted an investigation to see whether the affair had led to any UK state secrets finding their way to the Soviets. The Denning Report was published in September 1963 and within weeks the Conservative prime minister Harold Macmillan had resigned after being diagnosed (wrongly, it turned out) with cancer. Macmillan was replaced by the affable old Etonian Sir Alec Douglas-Home.

The Profumo affair had a tragic postscript, as the socialite Stephen Ward, who'd introduced Profumo to Keeler, killed himself after being found guilty in a court of law for living off immoral earnings (legal-ese for being a pimp).

The effect of the Profumo affair was to blow away the veil of privacy surrounding the private lives of British politicians once and for all. Whether or not MPs and ministers were having affairs was now fair game for newspaper coverage. Head to Chapter 10 for more on politicians and the media.

From Moats to Maltesers: The MPs' Expenses Scandal

In 2009, the highly secretive expenses system of MPs was exposed to public scrutiny and scorn when the *Daily Telegraph* published details bought from a source working within the Houses of Parliament. MPs had been due to release limited details of their expenses but the *Telegraph* story trumped this. The editor of the newspaper had a team of over 20 journalists trawl through the expenses data and expose what amounted to sheer extravagance and in some cases even potential criminal activity.

MPs were found to have claimed for items such as cleaning their moats, building duck houses for their private lakes and repairing swimming pools. At the other end of the scale were claims for trivial items such as sweets, chocolate biscuits and toilet brushes for their fully furnished second homes. It seemed to many people that MPs were trying to milk the system for all that it was worth. The worst examples of alleged expenses fiddling related to second home allowances, where MPs can claim mortgage payments and other expenses on a second property that they're meant to live in when parliament is sitting.

The story ran throughout the early summer of 2009 and public anger grew, with headlines screaming that MPs simply 'Don't get it' and that they were taking advantage of ill-defined rules to do what looked to many like fiddling expenses.

Eventually, MPs agreed to reform their expenses and Michael Martin became the first Speaker in four centuries to resign his post. Several dozen MPs announced that they'd step down at the 2010 general election and some may be liable to criminal prosecution.

Running Out of Control:
The Westland Affair

Whether or not struggling UK helicopter firm Westland should merge with a European or American rival is the sort of decision that comes across the desk of cabinet ministers every day of the week. But somehow this routine event nearly led to the collapse of the Conservative government of Margaret Thatcher in 1986.

The Secretary of State for Defence Michael Heseltine wanted Westland to merge with European rivals while Trade and Industry Secretary Leon Brittan preferred it to go with an American firm. At a heated cabinet meeting, Brittan carried the argument and Heseltine stormed out saying that he hadn't had a proper hearing and announced his resignation. This was pure political theatre and turned a disagreement between ministers into a full-blown political crisis.

Worse was to follow for the Thatcher government, as Heseltine claimed publicly that the prime minister had been stubborn (not an unknown trait of Margaret Thatcher; see Chapter 22 for more on her). Earlier, a letter criticising Heseltine's conduct, written by a senior civil servant, had been passed to the press in what was widely seen as an attempt to smear the former defence minister. It turned out that the letter had been released at the behest of Heseltine's bitter rival, Brittan. The result of this political bun fight was that Brittan resigned and the competence of the Thatcher government was called into question.

During a parliamentary debate to discuss the scandal, Thatcher reportedly had a resignation note drafted in her handbag. However, she never delivered it as she gave a sterling defence of the government's policies.

Nevertheless, the Westland affair damaged the government and four years later Heseltine ran against Thatcher in an election for the leader of the Conservative Party. Thatcher won the first ballot but was fatally weakened by the lack of support she'd been shown by Conservative MPs and resigned. The complex Westland affair can be seen as the root of the downfall of Thatcher, one of the 20th century's most controversial but also highly capable prime ministers.

Scandal of Mass Destruction: The David Kelly Affair

Britain's involvement in the war in Iraq in 2003 was heavily based on the premise that the Iraqi dictator Saddam Hussein had been stockpiling weapons of mass destruction (WMD). But Iraq didn't have any WMD (more than likely, Hussein had destroyed them a few years prior to the war), and many politicians and commentators questioned whether the government had lied to the British public over the reason for going to war with Iraq.

Journalists and politicians started to investigate the run-up to the war and the official government documents that had been released to support the claims of Prime Minister Tony Blair that Iraq had WMD.

Particular attention was paid to a dossier which had been released by the government outlining what the UK intelligence services knew about Iraqi WMD. The 'dodgy dossier', as it came to be known, claimed that Iraq could make a military strike with chemical weapons within 45 minutes. BBC journalist Andrew Gilligan interviewed the government scientist David Kelly over the claims. Gilligan said that Kelly had told him that the claims made in the dossier had been 'sexed up' by Blair's press secretary Alastair Campbell. This was sensational stuff and parliament started to investigate the claims.

Under huge pressure, David Kelly tragically took his life and a special investigation under the judge Lord Hutton was set up to explore the circumstances surrounding his death. The investigation found that the BBC report had been poorly put together and that the claim that the WMD dossier had been 'sexed up' couldn't be supported by the evidence. Within hours the BBC's top management resigned and Campbell said that he'd been vindicated. Longer term, though, the government's victory seems to have been tarnished. The claim of the existence of WMD in Iraq became discredited and many members of the public sided with the BBC, suggesting that the Hutton Report was a whitewash. Campbell left his post soon afterwards and so did Blair in 2007, with his poll rating plummeting and some suggesting that he'd tricked the country into going to war in Iraq.

Roll Up, Roll Up; How Much for This Knighthood?

The UK honours system (awards given by the state to notable individuals) is meant to recognise outstanding contributions to society, culture and government. The prime minister recommends who should receive an honour and the monarch bestows it. The highest bidder shouldn't be able to simply buy an honour! But from 1920, Prime Minister David Lloyd George allowed the government to basically sell honours bestowed by the monarch for cash donations. A few tens of thousands of pounds could buy a knighthood; more and you could buy a peerage. Lloyd George seems to have wanted the money not for personal gain but to help fund a new political party with, of course, him at the helm. But many members of the aristocracy who'd held their titles for hundreds of years were furious that Lloyd George was devaluing the honours system. However, Lloyd George wasn't acting against the law – although selling honours did later become illegal. Lloyd George failed in his mission to form a new party and after 1922 was never prime minister again.

The practice of selling honours was outlawed by Act of Parliament in 1925.

The scandal has an echo in events of 2007 when senior fundraisers of Blair's Labour Party were accused of giving out honours to party donors. The cash for honours affair involved a police investigation and Tony Blair was interviewed. However, no charges were brought and the case was dropped.

How the Mighty Fall: Jonathan Aitken and Jeffrey Archer

Lying in court is a serious offence – just ask two former Conservative MPs, Jonathan Aitken and Jeffrey Archer. Both men were involved in separate high-profile libel actions.

Aitken was defending himself against embarrassing but not illegal allegations that a stay in a Paris hotel room had been paid for by a Saudi prince. He lied on oath and tried to get his family to cover up for the lie. When it became clear that Aitken had committed perjury he admitted what he'd done. He resigned and spent seven months in jail (he was sentenced to 18). He spent his time inside writing about his experiences and became a campaigner for prison reform. The costs of the libel action he'd taken against the *Guardian*, which had exposed his links to the Saudis, left Aitken bankrupt.

The fall of novelist and politician Jeffrey Archer was even more dramatic than Aitken's. The flamboyant Archer won a libel action in 1987 against a tabloid newspaper that alleged he'd slept with a prostitute. He won record damages and his political career rocketed – so much so that he was nominated as the Conservative candidate for Mayor of London in 2000. But Ted Francis, a friend of his (and with friends like this, who needs enemies?), said Archer owed him money and revealed that the alibi which had helped convince the court that Archer was telling the truth in his libel action 13 years before had been fabricated. The whole sorry saga unfolded; Archer resigned his candidacy and was put on trial for perverting the course of justice – an even more serious offence than perjury – and was sent to jail for four years. While inside Archer penned a three-volume book outlining his experiences, called simply *Prison Diary*.

Murder Plot? The Jeremy Thorpe Affair

Jeremy Thorpe was leader of the Liberal Party in the 1960s and 1970s. He was a brilliant orator with a shrewd mind but he seemed to have skeletons galore in his cupboard. A married man, Thorpe was alleged to have embarked on an affair with male model Norman Scott in the 1960s (when homosexuality was still illegal). Scott made several allegations to senior Liberals and to members of the British establishment about the affair he said he'd had with Thorpe. In 1975 a former airline pilot, Andrew Newton, confronted Scott with a gun and shot the dog Scott was walking – the poor beast's name was Rinka and in the press the story became known as Rinkagate. Newton claimed that he'd been hired by Thorpe as a hitman. Thorpe was arrested and tried at the Old Bailey in London in 1979. By this time Thorpe's once great career was in tatters, although he was found innocent at his trial.

The Fall of a President: Watergate

Political scandals don't come any bigger than Watergate; there's even an Oscar-winning movie called *All the President's Men* about it! In the run-up to the 1972 presidential election there was a break-in at the Democratic campaign headquarters at the Watergate complex in Washington. The burglars were found to have links with members of successful Republican candidate Richard Nixon's administration. This was bad enough but attempts to cover up the links between the burglars and people in the Nixon administration later emerged – including the withholding of sound recordings made in the president's office.

A Senate investigation was launched following a series of newspaper stories by *Washington Post* reporters Bob Woodward and Carl Bernstein. Members of the Nixon administration started to testify against one another. It was said the scandal acted as a cancer on the presidency over a period of months, with member after member of the administration coming forward to testify. No one's sure how much Nixon knew about the break-in or the attempts at a cover-up but ultimately he lost the confidence of the American people and the Senate. Facing the possibility of *impeachment* – a trial which could lead to the removal of office; see Chapter 21 – in 1974 Nixon became the first president in US history to resign his office. Several of his close aides and allies in the White House subsequently served jail sentences for their role in the cover-up.

The effects of the Watergate scandal were so great – after all, it brought down the most powerful politician in the world – that other scandals are often given the moniker 'Gate'.

More Sordid Scandal Stateside: The Monica Lewinsky Affair

President Bill Clinton was always known as a bit of a ladies' man but few realised just how much until he was elected president of the United States. His brief affair with intern Monica Lewinsky nearly cost him the presidency when, while giving testimony in a sexual harassment case, he swore that he didn't have sex with her. Unluckily for him, and hygienically minded people everywhere, Lewinsky still had the stained dress to prove it.

Clinton had to retract his statement and apologise to his wife and country on live television for his lewd activities.

Despite attempts to have him impeached, Clinton the family man remained popular and is considered by many to have been a highly effective president. He served two terms before retiring in 2000; Lewinsky went on to sell a book about the affair. And hopefully visited a dry cleaner.

Dodgy Property Deal: The Whitewater Affair

Scandal was never far away from the Clinton presidency of the 1990s. The Clintons were directors of a company called Whitewater, which was involved in a dodgy land deal. The Clintons argued that they had nothing to do with the company's land deals but a police investigation followed and friends of the Clintons were convicted of their involvement in the scandal. In fact, nearly everyone with any association with Whitewater found themselves in the dock apart from Bill and his wife, now US Secretary of State, Hillary Clinton.

But the Clintons didn't get away scot-free. The special counsel appointed to investigate the scandal, Kenneth Starr, became a thorn in the side of the presidency. Starr spent three years investigating the affairs of the Clintons and was criticised by some as over-zealous and politically motivated. He presented evidence to the House of Representatives that Bill Clinton was guilty of perjury but this didn't lead to an impeachment. Starr didn't give up and set about investigating the sexual misconduct of Bill Clinton in the Lewinsky affair. Many accused Starr of going outside his brief and conducting a 'witch hunt'.

Chapter 24

Ten Political Events that Shaped the Modern World

In This Chapter

▶ Beating down the Berlin Wall

▶ Coming together for peace and prosperity: The European Union

▶ Bringing a new age of terror: 9/11

▶ Emerging into freedom: Nelson Mandela and South Africa

▶ Gazing over the brink: The financial crisis

*W*hen asked by a journalist what was likely to blow his government off course, former British prime minister Harold Macmillan quipped, 'Events, dear boy, events.' And it's true that events, however minor they seem at the time, change the political landscape forever.

In this chapter, I choose ten events that fundamentally altered the political world we live in at the start of the second decade of the 21st century.

Hell on Earth: The Second World War

What to say about a conflict that saw the deaths of over 50 million people, the mass extermination of minorities such as the Jews, and other atrocious war crimes – apart from acknowledging that between 1939 (the outbreak of war) and the final defeat of Nazi Germany in 1945, many parts of the European continent and the Soviet Union were transformed into hell on earth. Eventually though the allied nations – Britain, the US, France, the Soviet Union and China – defeated the axis powers of Nazi Germany, Japan, Italy and several assorted puppet regimes.

The world was changed forever. The old empires of France and Britain were disbanded, Germany was divided for over forty years, Japan moved from a country governed by a god-like monarch to a flourishing democracy and China became a communist state. These are just some of the political implications of the terrible war.

Following the end of the Second World War, Europe was divided into two major military power blocs. The western European nations and America formed NATO (North Atlantic Treaty Organisation) and the eastern European nations and the Soviet Union formed the Warsaw Pact. Both of these military power blocs kept large numbers of troops in Europe in preparedness for war with one another. This sometimes very tense stand-off is referred to by historians as the *Cold War* and it lasted from the late 1940s until the fall of the Berlin Wall in 1989.

Breaking Down the Barriers: Nixon and China

US President Richard Nixon is famous for being the first holder of the office to resign his post, following the Watergate scandal (see Chapter 23 for more on this almighty political tear-up). But one of Nixon's enduring legacies is that he was the first US president to actively seek to improve relations with the Chinese government.

Prior to Nixon's visit to China in 1972, American–Chinese relations had been poor. Put simply, the richest nation in the world, America, didn't get along with the most populous nation. This discord was primarily the result of China being a communist state and America a capitalist one. The two countries had actually fought a war in Korea in the 1950s and the Chinese disliked the fact that the Americans supported Taiwan, which was basically governed by anti-communist Chinese.

But Nixon's decision to visit broke the ice between the two nations and, although not exactly ushering in an immediate period of co-operation and friendship, it did open up genuine channels of communication which could help forge peace. Nowadays, the Chinese and American governments communicate on a very regular basis, with the two nations sometimes co-operating on the world stage. Nixon's visit also heralded China's opening up to Western ideas such as freeing up markets and promoting individual enterprise. Chinese communism is now mixed with a healthy dose of Western capitalism, which has provided a huge impetus to the stellar growth of the Chinese economy since the 1990s. In fact, the Chinese economy has grown so large that many economists predict that within a generation it will exceed America's. Nixon's visit paved the way for China's assent to world superpower status.

Ending Communism in Europe: The Fall of the Berlin Wall

Many Germans who lived through the events of November 1989 still have to pinch themselves to check that it really did all happen. The tyrannical East German regime, which for four decades had been backed by the communist Soviet Union, literally fell apart in a matter of days, mostly through people power.

The Berlin Wall, which was built in 1961 and divided the German capital between east and west, had been a potent symbol of the Cold War that had been going on since soon after the end of the Second World War between the capitalist West, led by the US and the UK, and the communist Soviet Union. The wall had been constructed to stop East Germans fleeing to the more prosperous and democratic West Germany. Undeterred, hundreds of East Germans had tried to get over or under the wall; many were captured, imprisoned and even shot.

It seemed that the wall would last forever but in 1989 the East German regime started to crumble. The Soviet Union was changing its approach to the world under the leadership of Mikhail Gorbachev. The Soviets were trying to improve relations with the West and Gorbachev saw the Berlin Wall and the repressive East German regime as, quite literally, a major barrier to good relations with the West. Gradually, opponents of the East German government started to detect that the Soviets wouldn't intervene in any uprising.

Slowly but surely East Germans started to take to the streets in protest and the East German government leaders realised that the game was up and that they couldn't rely on Soviet military intervention to quell the protests.

The East German government resigned and within a couple of days the guards on the Berlin Wall had opened its gates to allow anyone to enter free West Berlin. For many East Berliners, this was their first chance to see the West and they liked what they saw. Within a few weeks, Germany was on the way to re-unification; no longer split between East and West Germany but unified as a democratic powerhouse of over 80 million people in the middle of Europe.

Other East European states soon followed East Germany's lead and threw off their old communist regimes. Now these former Soviet bloc countries are part of the European Union and all are democracies. The fall of the Berlin Wall is probably the single most important event in European politics in the past fifty or so years.

GREAT FIGURES

Choosing peace over war: The Gorbachev experiment

Much of the credit for the peaceful transference of former eastern European communist regimes to democracies belongs to the Soviet leader of the late 1980s and early 1990s, Mikhail Gorbachev. Although a communist, he saw that the Cold War between the West and East was impoverishing his own and other eastern European people. He wanted to reduce repression and encourage free enterprise – a sort of communism-lite. However, within a few years, the communists were out of power in the Soviet Union and the power and influence of the old world superpower was diminished. However, the policies of openness and free enterprise resounded around eastern Europe and when the crunch came and the people rose up to overthrow their communist regimes, Gorbachev, against the advice of his military, chose to let the eastern European nations go their own way. He chose peace over war and was awarded the Nobel Peace Prize in 1990.

Coming Together: The March of the European Union

When the European Economic Community was formed by the Treaty of Rome in 1957, it wasn't seen as a particularly big deal. In essence, six countries (France, Germany, the Netherlands, Belgium, Luxembourg and Italy) were simply signing an agreement to help boost economic co-operation. But what they were doing was laying the groundwork for what has become, as the modern European Union, one of the world's great trading blocs (with an economy bigger than the United States) and a super-state in its own right, with its very own flag, currency and parliament (refer to Chapter 20 for more on how the EU institutions work).

The European Economic Community (the EU today) expanded to include the UK, Denmark and Ireland in 1973, Greece in 1981, and Spain and Portugal in 1986. The biggest influx of new members was in 2004, when many of the former communist eastern European states such as Poland and the Czech Republic joined. Today the EU encompasses 27 members and now even has a president.

REMEMBER

Over its history the EU has helped to create a massive free trade area and managed to ease many of the ancient rivalries between European states which lay behind the two disastrous world wars of the 20th century. Peace in Europe is in no small part due to the advent of the EU.

Throwback to Another Time: Balkan Wars

Despite the rise of the EU and the reduction of Soviet power in Europe, the Balkans (south-eastern) area of Europe burst into violent conflict in the 1990s. The fall of the communist government of Yugoslavia had led to nationalist movements coming to the fore. First the peoples of Slovenia and Croatia and then Bosnia wanted their own nation states rather than being part of a Yugoslavia dominated by the majority Serbian population. After decades of repression the people wanted to govern their own affairs but this angered the Serbian population and its leaders – based in Belgrade – who'd been used to controlling things in the old Yugoslavia.

A series of small wars broke out, fuelled by the ancient religious and cultural rivalries between the different peoples of the Balkans. Old historical scores were settled and war crimes perpetrated by armed militias on all sides.

Many western European countries could scarcely believe that war was being waged on the continent again after many years of peace and (at least for EU members) prosperity. Some commentators suggest that European governments were paralysed by the spectacle and dithered for too long. Examples of genocide started to be reported; most notably the massacre of Bosnian Muslim men by Serbs at Srebrenica.

Such horrific events sparked NATO into action and, using military strikes against Bosnian Serbs, a peace settlement was imposed which saw Bosnia become an independent state. Now all the nations of the Balkans are applying for membership of the EU and there is peace, although the old rivalries still remain.

Long Wait for Freedom: The Release of Nelson Mandela

The apartheid regime of South Africa is recognised as one of the most despicable of modern history. The state was run on the premise that white South Africans were intrinsically superior to the black majority who were deemed only good for performing menial tasks. That such an evil doctrine could survive into the 1990s is difficult to believe, but it did.

Successive apartheid governments in South Africa kept the black majority poor, ill-educated and in a position of subjugation to the wealthy whites. Blacks were forced to live in poverty-stricken townships and attend poorly financed black-only schools, while the whites owned the farmland, had the best schools and all the professional jobs.

Anti-apartheid groups such as the African National Congress (ANC) clashed violently with the police. ANC leading light Nelson Mandela was imprisoned off the coast of Cape Town in Robben Island jail for 27 years, charged with treason. During his long incarceration, Mandela became a symbol of hope for millions around the world that one day the evil doctrines of apartheid would be defeated and all South Africans treated equally regardless of the colour of their skin.

Slowly but surely international pressure told on the South African regime; sanctions hurt the white ruling classes and they started to see that at some stage in order to be accepted in the wider international community they must dismantle apartheid.

Like the fall of Soviet Union-backed governments in eastern Europe at around the same time, the end of apartheid was quick and surprisingly bloodless. Mandela was released from prison in February 1990 and in a press conference broadcast worldwide he called for an end to apartheid but also for peace and reconciliation between black and white. The once political prisoner Mandela was elected president of the new Republic of South Africa in 1994.

Mandela's message of peace and reconciliation undoubtedly helped heal some of the wounds of South African society and his time as president saw the country take its place again in the international community. Mandela was awarded the Nobel Peace Prize in 1993.

Terror from the Skies: 9/11

Few who lived through 11 September 2001 will forget it. Planes hijacked by Al-Qaeda terrorists struck the twin towers of the World Trade Center in New York and the Pentagon building in Washington. Thousands of innocent people died and a terrorist group only a few people had heard of became worldwide news. Al Qaeda wanted to force the US to stop supporting Israel and to remove troops based in the Middle East.

The implications of 9/11, as it became known, were far wider and deeper than the atrocities of the day. The US government under President George W. Bush started to detain people around the globe who it suspected of being linked to Al-Qaeda. The US, aided by Britain, invaded Afghanistan, the base of operations for Al-Qaeda and removed the governing Taliban regime. In Iraq, a rather tenuous link between the country's dictator Saddam Hussein and Al-Qaeda was used as one of the justifications for a US-led invasion.

On the other side of the coin, 9/11 was used as a rallying call for other Islamic extremist groups, who detonated bombs in Bali, Madrid and London. The US 'war on terror' has dominated international events ever since the moment the first of the twin towers was struck by the hijacked planes.

Bringing Down a Dictator: War in Iraq

The regime of Saddam Hussein had long been in the sights of the Americans. Hussein's invasion of neighbouring Kuwait in 1990 had sparked a massive counter-strike by an international force led by the US. At the time, Hussein had come within an ace of being deposed as dictator, yet he clung on to power.

Twelve years later the US decided that the Iraqi dictator's continued flirtation with weapons of mass destruction and alleged involvement with international terrorism was justification to go to war again. This time around the US was supported by a limited group of countries, including most notably the UK and Australia.

The invasion of Iraq was over in double-quick time and Hussein was captured and later put on trial and executed by his own people. However, the presence of so many US troops attracted insurgents from neighbouring countries Iran and Syria, who started a guerrilla war against the US and its allies.

The violent conflict continued for several years and more than a thousand American and several hundred British soldiers lost their lives. Much of Iraq descended into bloody civil war and the Iraqi government backed by the US struggled to survive.

Gradually, a massive deployment of American forces helped quell the violence but seven years after the US-led invasion of Iraq there are still thousands of US troops on Iraqi soil and relations between the US and several neighbouring Arab states have worsened.

Gazing Over the Brink: The Great Credit Crunch

In 2008 a host of American, British and European banks came to the brink of bankruptcy due to the poor investments they'd made. If the major banks had gone under, the world could have fallen into an economic depression at least as great as that of the 1930s, with tens if not hundreds of millions of people losing their jobs and life savings.

Facing a financial Armageddon, the US, UK and European governments bailed out the banks by effectively transferring the bad debts onto their own books. Suddenly the taxpayer was in hock for hundreds of billions of pounds, having taken on what are called *toxic debts*. Governments will be paying the bill for the crash for a generation to come.

But longer term, one thing's for sure: the financial crash of 2008 struck at one of the major props of American power. The American government owes huge sums to the Chinese and much of the wealth of the West now flows to the East. When the history of the world in the 21st century is written, the financial crash of 2008 may be seen as a key staging post in the transfer of world power from West to East.

Crazy for You: Obama-Mania

The election of the first black president of the US, Barack Obama, is one of those 'pinch me, am I dreaming?' moments. Obama, a lawyer by profession, was a rank outsider for the Democratic nomination to run as president. Not only had no black politician made any real headway in a presidential election before, but Obama was seen as inexperienced and an unknown quantity. But Obama has charisma and star quality in bucket loads. He fought and won a tight contest with political heavyweight Hillary Clinton (wife of former president Bill Clinton) for the Democratic position and then beat the Republican candidate John McCain hands down in the final presidential ballot.

But Obama's success isn't just about one notable politician pulling off a major coup; it's fundamentally about a country with a huge black and Hispanic minority – many of whom have felt disenfranchised by the white population – becoming, well, much more equal. One of his first acts was to abandon the unpopular foreign policies of his predecessor George W. Bush. Many in western Europe breathed a sigh of relief when Obama was elected because they felt that a calming influence had emerged onto the world stage to take on the most difficult but most powerful job in the world.

Chapter 25

Ten Political Trends for the Future

In This Chapter

▶ Voting online

▶ Modernising India and China

▶ Replacing the dollar

▶ Living with global change

*F*ormer British prime minister Harold Wilson once said that 'a week is a long time in politics'. But what about one, five, ten or even twenty years?

In today's fast-paced, interconnected, rapidly globalising world, political careers can end in a jiffy, international alliances form and then fragment in double-quick time, and the fortunes of great nations can rise and fall overnight. Plotting these changes is the work of journalists, historians and that wacky group of funsters, the political scientists, but here's my attempt to gaze into the crystal ball and predict the future of politics.

In this chapter, and in no particular order, I look at some of the political trends that may well play a big role in future politics in Britain and around the world. Some are educated guesses, others seem nailed-on certainties; only time will tell!

Broadening Democracy: Internet Voting

Great democracies like the UK and US are suffering from low voter turnout; anything up to a half of electors are failing to cast their ballots (see Chapter 6 for more on this). Some commentators put this down to a widespread disillusionment with politicians and political parties in general – you know, the man or woman down the pub saying 'politicians are all the same'. But another reason for low voter turnout is that many people are too busy to make their way to a polling station, queue up and cast their ballot.

The logic is that if voting were made easier, more people would vote, which means turnout would be higher, helping to really validate the election process. People could vote online, simply logging into the election website, keying in a personal identification number and ticking the box by their chosen candidate. Internet voting would be cheaper to boot, with fewer staffed polling stations open on election day. Internet voting would also make it possible for voters to express their views on individual topics such as whether or not a particular piece of legislation should be passed. In effect the Internet opens up the possibility of easy-to-organise referendums.

The technology is already available and the Scottish parliament is consulting a group of voters via the Internet on particular policy matters, to get an insight into what the public think.

Some people are worried that Internet voting could lead to fraud, and wonder who'll monitor the machines that tally up all the votes. In addition, some fear that whoever operates the Internet voting system could tell who voted for which candidate, which destroys the secret element of the ballot. Nevertheless, in both the US and UK, a growing groundswell of opinion is in favour of Internet voting.

Rising Power: Indian Modernisation

India is the world's biggest democracy, encompassing more than a billion people. The economy is rapidly expanding, literacy rates are rising and the country also has millions of English speakers able to deal with companies and individuals in the US and UK. India also has a three-hundred–million-strong 'middle class' with generous disposable incomes. India is one of the growing forces in the world economy and may even eventually replace the US as the world's most prosperous democracy.

In the not too distant future, India is likely to take its place at the top table of international politics. It will soon have a large enough economy to enter into the G8 group of nations and there's talk of it having a permanent seat on the United Nations Security Council (see Chapter 19 for more on the UN).

Loosening the Shackles: Chinese Democracy

When the pro-democracy protestors pitched up in Tiananmen Square in Beijing in 1989, the end of the Chinese communist regime seemed at hand. Even when the communists brutally crushed the protest and imposed martial law, it still only seemed a matter of time before democracy would come to

China. Since then, though, the communist leadership has been remarkably adaptable. They've overseen a massive liberalisation of the economy, allowing some people to own their own property and businesses and accumulate wealth. In effect, communism has survived by ditching much of what communism actually stands for (refer to Chapter 4 for more on this ideology). But survived it has. The Chinese Communist Party's position seems unassailable. It even controls people's access to media, and curtails the use of the Internet, not allowing access to websites deemed anti-Chinese.

Many commentators argue that, as the Chinese economy continues to expand, the Chinese will ultimately want more freedom to express themselves and elect a different government. In short, as China becomes more Western in terms of wealth, it will eventually become more Western in terms of its politics. The progress – or otherwise – of democracy in China is a key trend to watch for in the 21st century.

China has the third- or fourth-largest economy in the world and is growing annually at around 8 to10 per cent. Compare this to the US or Europe, where economies are growing by 2 to 3 per cent. You can see why China is rapidly catching up with the Western countries in terms of economic growth.

Securing Natural Resources: Chinese Control of Africa

For hundreds of years, Western nations strived to secure the abundant natural resources of Africa, such as minerals and precious metals. But in the first decade of the 21st century the Chinese have looked to conclude trade agreements and buy up large tracts of land and industries within Africa.

China says that it's simply securing resources for its industries, which in turn supply the West with goods. However, some observers suggest that what's happening is no different from previous 'scrambles' for Africa: paying local corrupt governments in order to get natural resources on the cheap, ultimately providing little or no benefit to the ordinary people of Africa.

China's presence in Africa is an emotive subject but one that's bound to see the country even more powerful globally and even, who knows, replace the US as the world's biggest economy.

Out with the Old: Replacing the Dollar

Ever since the end of the Second World War the major currency around the globe has been the US dollar. In fact, nearly seven out of ten international trading transactions are done in dollars. Barrels of oil and ounces of gold are priced in dollars, not pounds, euros or Japanese yen. The dollar is called the world's *reserve currency*, which means many countries hold a large amount of dollars that will always be acceptable to international markets if another currency becomes untradeable because of an economic crisis.

But the mighty dollar isn't as mighty as it once was, particularly after the financial crisis affecting Western banks in 2008 (refer to Chapter 24 for more on this momentous event). The crisis resulted in a massive expansion of US government debt and weakened the dollar's hold on being the world's reserve currency. Some experts suggest that oil or gold should be traded in euros or Chinese yuan.

No longer using the dollar as a trading currency would make it harder for the US government to persuade other countries – China in particular – to buy its debt (the fact that most world trade is carried out in dollars makes it more attractive for investors to buy bonds issued by the US Treasury). The decline of the dollar would be a key sign that the balance of the world economy was shifting from the US to China and India.

Constructing a Super-State: Expanding the European Union

The European Union (EU) is a major trading bloc; a super-state in the making. The EU currency, the euro, is used widely around the globe and with a population of 500 million people in 27 member states and an economy bigger than that of the US, the EU is increasingly invited to the top table of international events; for example, the president of the European Commission – a part of the EU 'government' – attends meetings of the G8 group of most powerful nations. Talks are under way to bring Iceland and the Balkan countries into the EU, and also Turkey, which has a massive population.

However, not all within the EU are happy with the idea of an EU super-state. Some powerful politicians in the UK, Ireland and east European nations are reluctant to surrender national sovereignty to EU institutions such as the Commission and the parliament. In fact, some suggest that the drift of law-making powers from parliaments of member states to the EU has dwindled and that the EU will stop short of becoming the super-state envisaged by many.

World Going Dry: Shortages of Water

Sat in the seemingly permanently raining UK, believing that the world could be running short of drinking water is a bit difficult. However, a massively expanding population combined with global warming and mass deforestation is turning once fertile wetlands into desert. Some parts of the world, particularly the Middle East, are already relying on technology to make seawater drinkable.

Some political scientists suggest that, in future, wars will be fought over securing vital water supplies rather than over territory or oil.

The United Nations estimates that up to 880 million people around the globe – that's roughly one in eight of the global population – have access to barely adequate or inadequate water supply. This doesn't just mean that people go thirsty; dirty water also leads to disease. The World Bank says 88 per cent of all deaths from disease are related to inadequate water supply.

Black Gold: Scrambling for Oil

Oil companies have drained many of the world's big oil fields and are now trying to drill in areas of outstanding natural beauty such as Alaska and possibly one day even Antarctica.

Experts reckon that the peak of oil production was struck some five years ago and now the world is on a downward path to running out of the most precious of fossil fuels. But just as the world's stock of oil is dwindling, demand is rising, thanks to the massive industrial growth of China and, to a lesser extent, India and Brazil. No wonder the price of oil has shot up five-fold since its lows at the start of the millennium. Many said that the US-led invasion of Iraq in 2003 was motivated by the need to secure oil supplies.

A world without oil is looking like a distinct possibility by the middle of the century. The doomsayers suggest this will lead to a massive fall in industrial production, people will have to give up their cars and power supplies will be under threat. But others say that oil is a dirty, polluting fuel and we'd be better off without it; technologies are available to help the world cope without oil, to enable people to drive their cars, and for industrial production to continue.

How the world learns to live without oil will be one of the great political, economic and social stories of the 21st century.

Risking Our Future: Global Warming

The world has heated up more in the past century than in the previous three thousand years. Most scientists blame human activity, saying global warming has coincided with global industrialisation and that pollution means the planet is retaining more heat from the sun. A smaller group of scientists suggest that the temperature of the planet varies over time and that increasing *greenhouse gases* (gases that purportedly heat up the atmosphere) are due to the natural release of carbon into the atmosphere rather than human activity.

The effects of global warming could be catastrophic for humanity as sea levels rise, countries disappear, deserts expand and millions are made homeless.

If human activity is to blame, then global warming can only be slowed by getting governments, individuals and industry to curtail the release of greenhouse gases into the atmosphere. Many of the world's leading industrial nations have agreed to reduce greenhouse gas emissions by 2020 to help slow global warming but the economic expansion of China and other developing countries means putting these changes in jeopardy. The world's major governments met in December 2009 in Copenhagen to discuss what to do but no one's holding their breath for a radical solution. Some measures that may help are the development of cleaner fuels and helping developing nations adopt greener technology to reduce their dependency on fossil fuels.

Upping Sticks: Global Population Moves

Some of the problems facing governments around the globe, such as global warming and water shortages, are going to have a huge impact on the lives of ordinary people. Some scientists suggest mass population moves in Africa and Asia will occur due to parts of the globe becoming difficult to farm and live in. The majority of the world's population lives in the countryside, working on farms and looking after livestock. If global warming makes these places uninhabitable, the people are going to have to move to neighbouring countries in richer parts of the world such as Europe or parts of Asia.

Immigration is going to be a big issue in the 21st century for most nations around the globe.

Index

• *Numerics* •

1, 2, and 3 line whips, 123
1 nation conservatism, 58
2-ballot system, 89
9/11 terrorist attack, 32, 368–369
10 Downing Street, 216
10-minute bills, 204
24-hour TV, 172

• *A* •

activists, 33–34
Acts of Parliament. *See* statute law
Adam Smith Institute, 158, 159
additional member voting system, 94, 264
Africa, Chinese presence in, 373
age
  of liberals versus conservatives, 109
  minimum for candidates, 273
Age Concern pressure group, 144
agencies (UN), 300–301
aid projects, 31–32
Aitken, Jonathan (politician), 359
alternative vote system, 89
Amnesty International, 155
Amsterdam treaty (1999), 322
anarchism, 61–62, 152
Animal Liberation Front (ALF), 146, 152
Anti-Social Behaviour Orders (ASBOs), 254
appointments
  of ministers by PM, 281
  of PM by monarch, 191, 192
  political power of, 122
Archer, Jeffrey (politician), 359–360
Aristotle (Greek philosopher), 37
Asia-Pacific Economic Cooperation forum
    (APEC), 305
assemblies, 9. *See also* Northern Ireland
    Assembly; Welsh Assembly
asylum-seeker detention, 254
Athenian direct democracy, 37
Attlee, Clement (PM), 85, 106–107, 127, 350
authority models for politics, 22

• *B* •

Back to Basics scandal, 227
backbench MPs, 15, 148–149
bail, release on, 247
balance of power, 134
Balkans war, 319–320, 367
ballot for bills, 204
Bank of England, 29
BBC (British Broadcasting Corporation),
    115, 170–171, 175
Beaverbrook, Lord (press magnate), 115
Benn, Tony (Labour minister), 219
Berlin Wall, fall of, 365
Bernstein, Carl (reporter), 360
big beasts of the cabinet, 221–222
Big Stick and Small Carrot blog, 173
Bill of Rights (US), 331
bills
  amendments to, 205, 206
  debate of, 204, 205, 206–208
  defined, 202
  government or public, 202–203
  Green Papers for, 203
  private members', 202, 203–205
  royal assent for, 209
  Scottish, 265
  stages of, 205–206
  US, 339–340
  White Papers for, 203
Black Rod, 214
Blair, Tony
  Age Concern consulted by, 144
  anti-terror laws under, 254
  cabinet culture under, 219
  debt forgiveness sought by, 31
  devolution under government of, 9
  election of, 85
  electoral reform sought by, 88
  as great PM, 352–353
  hereditary peers removed by, 200
  Iraq war supported by, 224, 330
  Labour Party reformed by, 55
  newspaper editors briefed by, 168

Blair, Tony *(continued)*
  popularity with women voters, 109
  seen as America's poodle, 288, 331
  special media advisor of, 164, 229
  terrorism fought by, 33
  war and resignation of, 105
Blairism
  New Labour approach of, 55, 133
  one nation conservatism compared to, 58
  origins of, 50
blogs, political, 172–174
blue helmets or blue berets, 299
Boothroyd, Betty (Speaker), 213
British Broadcasting Corporation (BBC),
    115, 170–171, 175
British Citizenship Test For Dummies
    (Knight), 44
British Commonwealth, 290–291
British Empire, decline of, 285–286
British History For Dummies (Wiley
    publication), 40
British Medical Association (BMA),
    142, 143, 153, 155
British National Party (BNP), 136
British Overseas Territories, 291–292
Brittan, Leon (Westland affair principal), 357
broad church perspective, 50
broadsheets. *See* qualities (newspapers)
Brown, Gordon
  anti-terror laws under, 254
  as Chancellor during Blair's government,
    222
  debt forgiveness sought by, 31
  euro criteria set by, 325
  YouTube broadcast by, 173
Bush, George, Senior (US president), 105, 343
Bush, George W. (US president),
    32, 153, 288, 339
business pressure groups, 154

• C •

cabinet. *See also* ministers
  big beasts, 221–222
  changing nature of, 219
  committees, 225–226
  ministers (secretaries of state), 232, 281
  offices of the state, 221
  other ministers, 222–223
  overview, 220
  PM's need for confidence of, 219
  reshuffles, 228
  resignation of ministers, 227
  responsibilities of, 224–225
  secretary, 220, 235, 239–240
  shadow, 229–230
Cabinet Secretariat, 221
Cairns Group, 305
Cameron, David (Conservative leader),
    105, 130, 173
Campaign for Nuclear Disarmament (CND),
    143, 144, 150
campaigning for elections, 114, 174–176, 278
Campbell, Alastair (media advisor), 164, 229
Campbell, Menzies (Lib Dem leader), 125
candidates for election. *See also* standing for
    election
  approved candidate lists, 275
  becoming a candidate, 273
  candidate list system, 91–92
  competition for candidacy, 275
  head of candidates, 121
  parliamentary, prospective, 275
  party hurdles for, 275
  Unionists, 129
  women-only shortlists for, 108, 276
CAP (Common Agricultural Policy),
    288, 323–324
capitalism, 53–54, 63
Capitol Hill, 340
carbon emissions, limiting, 30
cause-related pressure groups, 142, 143–144
CBI (Confederation of British Industry),
    143, 148, 154
Central Criminal Court, 248
Centre for Policy Studies, 158
chairperson of parties, 120
Chakrabarti, Shami (Liberty campaigner), 53
Chamberlain, Neville (PM), 354
Chancellor of the Exchequer, 29, 221
charismatic leaders, 22, 106–107
charities, as pressure groups, 154
Charles I, 52, 70, 71
Charles II, 70
Chicken Yoghurt blog, 173
China
  African presence of, 373
  blaming global warming on, 30–31
  democratic ideals in, 11, 372–373
  increasing power of, 33

India compared to, 307
Nixon's visit to, 364
rise of, 289, 306–307, 330
Chirac, Jacques (French president), 318
Church of England, 69
Churchill, Winston
  charismatic authority of, 22
  as great PM, 347–348
  leadership during WWII, 26
  on liberals and conservatives, 109
  loss in 1945 election, 85, 106–107
  as national government head, 127
  'special relationship' coined by, 288, 329
  United States of Europe vision of, 309
citizenship
  being a good citizen, 46–48
  rights of, 43, 245–246
  tests for, 44
city council (England), 258
civil courts
  England and Wales, 249
  Northern Ireland, 250
  Scotland, 250
  Supreme Court, 248, 251
civil law
  criminal law versus, 244
  defined, 244
  in England and Wales, 248–249
  in Northern Ireland, 250
  process of, 245
  in Scotland, 250
civil liberties. See human rights; rights of
    British citizens
civil servants
  branches of, 235
  cabinet secretary, 220, 235, 239–240
  code of behaviour for, 236–237
  defined, 234
  examinations for, 235–236
  head of the home civil service, 235
  honours given to, 239
  as independent and permanent, 225
  monitoring of, 242
  number of, 238
  pay and conditions, 235
  permanent secretaries management group,
    235
  permanent under-secretary of state,
    238–239

  responsibilities of, 234, 236
  senior versus lower-level, 235
civil service, 13, 25, 240–242
civil service commissioners, 242
class, 50, 107–108
climate change, 29–31, 63, 302, 375–376
Clinton, Bill (US president),
    27, 105, 337, 343, 361
Clinton, Hillary (US Secretary of State),
    361, 370
CND (Campaign for Nuclear Disarmament),
    143, 144, 150
coalition governments
  with additional member voting system, 94
  compromises with, 95–96
  defined, 87
  Lib Dems role in, 134
  with proportional representation, 90–91
  rarity of, 77, 87
  in Scotland, Wales, and Northern Ireland, 96
coercion, authority versus, 22
Cold War, 364
collective responsibility, 122
committees
  bill passage through, 205
  cabinet, 225–226
  Scottish parliament, 265
  select, 209, 210–212
  standing, 209, 210
Common Agricultural Policy (CAP),
    288, 323–324
Common Fisheries Policy, 324
common law, 187
Commons. See House of Commons
Commonwealth Games, 291
Commonwealth of Nations, 290–291
Commonwealth Secretariat, 290–291
communism, 56–57, 60, 365–366
The Communist Manifesto (Marx
    and Engels), 57
community authorities, 258, 259
competition
  for candidacy, 275
  socialist versus capitalist view of, 53–54
compulsory voting, 12, 103
Confederation of British Industry (CBI),
    143, 148, 154
conferences, party, 125–126, 150
Congress (US), 332–333

conservatism, 50, 57–59
Conservative Party. *See also* political parties
  advertising budget of, 176
  approved candidate list, 275
  blog, 173
  Cameron's re-invention of, 130
  conservative ideology of, 50
  core vote of, 74
  heartland of, 110, 131
  issues supported by, 129
  leader election by, 120
  natural supporters for, 118, 131
  newspapers supporting, 18, 165,
    167, 168, 169
  older voters favouring, 109
  policy formation by, 119
  power swap with Labour, 75–76
  recent turning point elections, 85
  socialist policies of, 54
  tactical voting against, 113
  ties with US Republican party, 342–343
  as Unionists, 129
ConservativeHome blog, 173
constituency
  competition for candidacy, 275
  politicians' role regarding, 26
  targeting for candidacy, 276–277
constitution (UK)
  common law supporting, 187
  conventions supporting, 187
  criticisms of, 46, 190–191
  defined, 181
  importance of, 181–182
  methods of changing, 24, 25
  movement to put in writing, 190–191
  parliamentary sovereignty in, 187–188
  statute law supporting, 186
  strengths of, 189
  unitary and flexible, 183
  as unwritten, 10, 45, 183, 184
constitutions
  as historically recent, 182
  rigid versus flexible, 183, 185–186
  UN Charter, 297
  unitary versus federal, 183, 184–185
  US, 182, 183, 331, 333–334
  written versus unwritten, 183, 184
Cook, Robin (minister), 224
Coolidge, Calvin (US president), 181
core vote, 74, 112

Cornish National Party, 138
corruption by pressure groups, 151–152
council members (England), 258, 274
Council of Ministers (EU), 313–314
council tax, 257
county courts, 249
Court of Appeal, 248, 249
courts. *See* judiciary and courts
crime rates, 247
Criminal Cases Review Commission, 248
criminal courts
  Court of Appeal, 248
  crown courts, 247–248
  magistrates courts, 69, 246–247
  Supreme Court, 248, 251
criminal law, 244–245, 250
crisis, politicians' role during, 25–26
Cromwell, Oliver, 70
crossbenchers, 201
crown courts, 247–248

Daily Express, 168
Daily Mail, 168
Daily Telegraph, 166, 167
Dalyell, Tam (MP), 267
Das Kapital (Marx and Engels), 57
Data Protection Act of 1998, 245
de Gaulle, Charles (French president),
    287, 308
Delors, Jacques (French politician), 312
democracy
  alternatives to, 11
  Athenian, 37
  characteristics of, 11
  defined, 35
  digital, 41–42, 103, 371–372
  direct, 37–38
  evolution in UK, 9–10, 39–41
  first home of, 39
  health of British, 10–12
  key traits of elections, 36
  liberal, Britain as, 65
  liberalism of, 51
  representative, 38
  strengths in UK, 44–45
  US compared to UK, 38
  weaknesses in UK, 45–46
Democratic party (US), 335, 340–341, 342–343

Democratic Unionist Party (DUP), 139
demonstrations. *See* direct action and demonstrations
departmental committees, 211
deregulation, 28
devolution. *See also specific governments*
  defined, 9, 262
  federalist system versus, 262
  loss of parliamentary powers due to, 196
  need for, 9, 79
  overview, 261–262
  powers excepted and reserved with, 262, 264
  quangos with, 263
  West Lothian question, 267
devolution max, 266
devolved elections, 84
D'Honte method, 92–93
digital democracy, 41–42, 103, 371–372
Diplomatic Service, 235
direct action and demonstrations
  by activists, 34
  by anarchists, 62, 152
  democratic right to protest, 11
  illegal or violent, 146, 152
  by pressure groups, 150
  restrictions on, 254
direct democracy
  Athenian, 37
  digital, 41–42, 103, 371–372
  referendums as, 38
  Scottish, 42
direct effect law (EU), 316
directive law (EU), 316
Disraeli, Benjamin (PM), 350–351
district councils, 258, 259
divine right of kings, 64
Dodgeblogium, 173
dollar (US), decline of, 373–374
Drummond, Stuart (Hartlepool mayor), 260

• *E* •

ECJ (European Court of Justice), 253, 316
Economic and Social Council (ESC), 299–300
economic issues
  base interest rate, 29
  deregulation, 28
  as election issues, 105
  financial crash of 2008, 369–370

government spending, 28
  growth, 28–29
  prevailing during elections, 27–28
  quantitative easing programme, 28–29
  recession, 28–29
  tax policies, 28
e-democracy, 41–42, 103, 371–372
Eden, Anthony (PM), 354
education, British right to, 43, 245
EEC (European Economic Community). *See* European Union (EU)
elected officials (England), 258
election agent, 277
elections. *See also* candidates for election; first-past-the-post system; standing for election; voting behaviour and trends
  additional member voting system, 94, 264
  counting process for, 278
  democratic, 36
  D'Honte method, 92–93
  to the European parliament, 8, 84
  exit polls for, 278
  gerrymandering, 96–97
  hanging chads, 97
  majority electoral systems, 88–90
  media role in campaigns, 174–176
  of MEPs, 8, 84, 315
  of MPs, 15–16, 46
  non-democratic, 36
  parliamentary sovereignty limited by, 188
  party broadcasts during, 175
  for political party leadership, 219
  postal fraud in, 97
  proportional representation, 90–93, 135, 264
  requirements for running in, 47, 137, 273, 276, 277
  right to vote, 40–41, 43, 72–74
  rotten boroughs, 73, 96, 353
  safe versus marginal seat, 86
  single transferable vote system, 91
  spoiling a ballot paper, 104
  standing for election, 274–275
  types of (UK), 8, 83–84
  US president, 335
  women's suffrage, 41, 52, 62, 72, 73, 74
electoral college system, 120
electoral roll, persons missing from, 48
Elizabeth II, Queen, 192, 193
emergencies, government bills for, 203
Engels, Friedrich, 56–57

England
  civil cases in, 248–249
  criminal cases in, 244–245
  judiciary, 16
  legal system, 244
  local government in, 258, 260–261
English National Party, 138
ennobled persons, 202
environmental issues
  as election issues, 105
  global warming, 29–31, 63, 302, 375–376
environmental pressure groups, 155
environmentalism, 63
ESC (Economic and Social Council), 299–300
ethnicity and minorities
  apartheid in South Africa, 367–368
  pressure groups' protection for, 153
  racism, 60, 136, 286
  voting trends and, 110–111
euro (currency), 19, 310, 325
European Commission, 312–313, 314, 315
European Convention on Human Rights, 16
European Council, 314–315
European Court of Human Rights,
    253, 316–317
European Court of Justice (ECJ), 253, 316
European Economic Community (EEC). *See*
    European Union (EU)
European federalism, 311
European parliament
  elections, 8, 84, 315
  overview, 315
  powers of, 315
  role of laws created by, 16, 18, 156, 189
  UK representation in, 84
European Union (EU). *See also* European
    parliament
  Balkans peace process, 319–320
  budgets and spending, 323–324
  Common Agricultural Policy, 288, 323–324
  Common Fisheries Policy, 324
  Copenhagen Criteria for joining, 310
  Council of Ministers, 313–314
  court system of, 253
  criticisms of, 288
  euro (currency), 19, 310, 325
  European Commission, 312–313, 314, 315
  European Council, 314–315
  European Court of Human Rights,
      253, 316–317
  European Court of Justice, 253, 316

  expansion of, 311, 318, 321, 366, 374
  formation of, 80, 309, 311, 366
  goals of, 311–312
  impact on British politics, 80, 156–157
  key facts, 310
  legal system of, 315–317
  overview, 18–19
  parliamentary sovereignty limited by, 188
  pressure group issues, 156–157
  rebate to UK from, 324
  as regional trading bloc, 304
  Russia's relations with, 317–318
  treaties affecting, 315, 321–322
  Turkey's relations with, 318–319
  UK's entry into, 287, 310
  UK's relations with, 320–321
  western European states not members
      of, 310
examinations for civil servants, 235–236
excepted powers, 262
executive power, constitutional limits on, 182
exit polls for elections, 278
expenses scandal of 2009
  Daily Telegraph role in, 166
  elections affected by, 11
  overview, 356
  recall law support after, 280
  Speaker resignation due to, 213
  witch-hunts during, 164

• F •

Fancy Dress Party, 137
fascism, 60
federal constitutions, 183, 184–185
federalism
  devolution versus, 262
  European, 311
  quasi, 183
feminism, 62–63
financial crash of 2008, 369–370
Financial Times, 166, 167
first among equals, 218
first minister of Scotland, 79, 265
first-past-the-post system
  advantages of, 87
  City of Chester example, 86
  coalition government rare due to, 77, 87
  defined, 85
  disadvantages of, 87–88

elections run under, 86
electoral reform desired for, 16, 46
extremism reduced by, 64
minor parties disadvantaged by, 136
reasons for status quo, 95
tactical voting with, 113
flexibility of British democracy, 45
flexible constitutions, 183, 185–186
focus groups, 177
Foreign Secretary, 221
foundation trust, 257
France
  constitution of, 182
  democracy in, 39
  NATO relations, 308
  two-ballot system in, 89
franchise (right to vote), 40–41, 43, 72–74
Freedom of Information Act of 2000, 245
freedom of speech, 11, 43
front benchers, 230

• G •

G8 (Group of Eight), 19, 31–32, 302–303
G20 (Group of Twenty), 19, 31–32,
  302, 303–304
Gandhi, Mahatma (Indian hero), 286
Garfield, James A. (US president), 335
General Assembly (UN), 297
general elections
  defined, 8, 12
  process and coverage of, 84
  recent turning point elections, 85
  turnout for, 8, 84, 99
Gentleman Usher of the Black Rod, 214
George, Lloyd, 71, 199, 348, 359
Germany, federal constitution of, 185
gerrymandering, 96–97
Gershon Review, 241–242
Gladstone, William (PM), 351
global poverty, 31–32
global warming, 29–31, 63, 302, 375–376
Glorious Revolution, 25, 40, 70–71
Good Friday Agreement of 1998, 268
Gorbachev, Mikhail (Soviet leader), 366
government bills, 202–203
government ministers. *See* ministers
government spending, growth regulated
  by, 28
green issues. *See* environmental issues
Green Papers, 203

Green Party, 63, 136
Group of Eight (G8), 19, 31–32, 302–303
Group of Twenty (G20), 19, 31–32,
  302, 303–304
Guardian, 166, 167

• H •

habeas corpus, right of, 68, 182
hanging chads, 97
Hardie, Keir (Labour founder), 132
Harding, Warren (US president), 339
head of candidates, 121
head of communications, 121
head of the home civil service, 235
health care, British right to, 43, 245
heartlands of political parties, 109–110
Henry II, legacy of, 69
Henry VIII, 68–69
hereditary peers, 200
Heseltine, Michael (Westland affair principal),
  357
High Court, 249
high court judge, 247
High Court of Justiciary (Scotland), 250
history of British political state
  devolution, 9, 79, 261–269
  European Union's impact, 80
  Glorious Revolution, 25, 40, 70–71
  increase of parliamentary power, 69–71
  Magna Carta, 68
  Norman invasion, 67–68
  Parliament Act of 1911, 13, 25, 72, 199
  political parties, 71, 74–77
  prime minister's origins, 77–78
  Reformation, 68–69
  right to vote, 40–41, 43, 72–74
  UK formation, 78–80
Hitler, Adolf, 61, 128
Home Secretary, 221
honours
  for civil servants, 239
  selling, 358–359
Hoover, Herbert (US president), 339
hospitals, running of, 257
House of Commons. *See also* Members of
  Parliament (MPs); parliament
  House of Lords compared to, 12–13, 199
  impact on citizens, 197
  legislative powers of, 12, 13
  as lower house, 196

House of Commons *(continued)*
  party leaders from, 198
  primacy established for, 72
  Speaker, 207, 212–213
House of Lords. *See also* parliament; peers
  bills from, 204
  House of Commons compared to, 12–13, 199
  legislative powers of, 12, 13
  as upper house, 196
  veto power removed from, 13, 25, 72
House of Representatives (US), 332, 333, 337
Howard, Michael (Home Secretary), 163
human rights. *See also* rights of British
    citizens
  in China, 307
  Commonwealth suspension over, 290
  pressure groups, 155
  US Bill of Rights, 331
Human Rights Act, 16, 43, 253
Hussein, Saddam (Iraqi leader), 298, 330, 358

• *I* •

Ibbs Report, 241
ICJ (International Court of Justice), 296, 300
ideologies
  anarchism, 61–62
  broad church perspective, 50
  classes supporting, 50
  communism, 56–57
  conservatism, 50, 57–59
  defined, 49
  divine right of kings, 64
  environmentalism, 63
  extremes, reasons the UK avoids, 64–65
  fascism, 60
  feminism, 62–63
  liberalism, 50–53
  Marxism, 56–57
  of political parties, 50
  socialism, 50, 52, 53–57
  theocracy, 61
  of totalitarian regimes, 60–61
immigration issues, 376
impeaching the US president, 336–337
imprisonment
  anti-terror laws, 253, 254
  asylum-seeker detention, 254
  per head of population, 247

right of *habeas corpus*, 68, 182
  with US war on terror, 331
The Independent, 166, 167
India
  blaming global warming on, 30–31
  China compared to, 307
  increasing power of, 33
  independence of, 286
  modernisation of, 372
inside pressure groups, 145–146
Institute for Fiscal Studies, 158
Institute of Public Policy Research (IPPR),
    158, 159
International Court of Justice (ICJ), 296, 300
International Monetary Fund (IMF), 300
international politics. *See also* European
    Union (EU); *specific countries*
  British Overseas Territories, 291–292
  Commonwealth of Nations, 290–291
  decline of the British Empire, 285–286
  decline of Western dominance, 33
  economic issues, 27–29
  environmental issues, 29–31
  G8 and G20, 19, 31–32, 302–304
  global poverty issues, 31–32
  links with China, 289
  North Atlantic Treaty Organisation,
    19, 299, 307–308
  nuclear deterrent capabilities, 293
  overview, 19
  peacekeeping role, 292
  regional trading blocs, 304–305, 321
  special relationship with US, 288–289,
    329–331, 342–343
  UN Security Council, 19, 293–294, 297–299
  United Nations, 19, 31–32, 293–294, 295–302
  World Trade Organisation, 305
Internet, the
  BBC News online, 171
  digital democracy via, 41–42, 103, 371–372
  increasing role in politics, 18
  political blogs, 172–174
involvement in politics, 46–47
Iran, 61, 174
Iraq war, 224, 330, 339, 358, 369
Ireland, Republic of, 91
Irish Republican Army (IRA), 140
'Iron Lady'. *See* Thatcher, Margaret (PM)
'isms', 50. *See also* ideologies
ITV, party election broadcasts on, 175

• J •

James II, overthrow of, 25
Jefferson, Thomas (US president), 336
Jenkins, Roy (electoral reform proponent), 88, 124
Johnson, Andrew (US president), 337
joining a political party, 272–273
Joseph Rowntree Foundation (JRF), 159
judges, role of, 251–252
judiciary and courts
    anti-terror laws, 253, 254
    civil cases in England and Wales, 248–249
    constitution interpretation by, 182
    county courts, 249
    court challenges by pressure groups, 147
    Court of Appeal, 248, 249
    criminal courts, 246–248
    criminal versus civil law, 244–245
    crown courts, 247–248
    EU legal system, 253, 315–317
    hierarchical system of, 16, 244, 252
    High Court, 249
    judges' role, 251–252
    legal precedents, 16, 182, 244, 252
    magistrates courts, 69, 246–247
    Northern Irish court system, 250
    overview, 16
    pardons granted by monarch, 248
    restrictions on civil liberties, 253–254
    right to fair trial, 43
    Scottish court system, 250
    as strength of British democracy, 45
    Supreme Court, 248, 251
    three legal systems, 243–244
jury, trial by, 247
Justices of the Peace (JPs), 246

• K •

Keeler, Christine (call girl), 355
Kelly, David (scientist), 358
Kennedy, Charles (Lib Dem leader), 125
Kennedy, John F. (US president), 335, 336, 341
King, Mervyn (governor of Bank of England), 29
King's Fund, 159
Kinnock, Neil (Labour leader), 106, 115
Knight, Julian (*British Citizenship Test For Dummies*), 44

• L •

labour movement, 132
Labour Party. *See also* political parties
    advertising budget of, 176
    approved candidate list, 275
    Blair's reform of, 55, 133
    blog, 173
    CND influence on, 144
    core vote of, 74
    electoral college system of, 120
    ethnic voting patterns for, 111
    formation of, 132
    heartlands of, 109, 110, 132
    issues supported by, 131
    liberal ideology in, 52
    National Executive Committee, 275
    natural supporters for, 118, 132
    newspapers supporting, 18, 165, 167, 169
    origins of, 74–75
    per cent of votes for, 131
    policy forums of, 119
    power swap with Conservatives, 75–76
    recent turning point elections, 85
    socialist ideology of, 50, 54–55
    ties with US Democratic party, 342–343
    trade union ties to, 146, 156
    unions' relationship with, 133
    women-only shortlists of, 108, 276
    youth favouring, 109
LabourHome blog, 173
language rules for parliament, 208
Leader of the House, 214
left-wing newspapers, 167
legal authority, 22
legal precedents, 16, 182, 244, 252
legal system. *See* judiciary and courts
legislation. *See also* bills
    as key role of politicians, 24
    powers of Houses for, 12, 13
Lewinsky, Monica (affair participant), 337, 361
liberal democracy, 65
Liberal Democrats (Lib Dems). *See also* political parties
    advertising budget of, 176
    approved candidate list, 275
    balance of power held by, 134
    chequered history of, 133–134
    first-past-the-post system disliked by, 88
    formation of, 130

Liberal Democrats (Lib Dems) *(continued)*
  heartland of, 110, 135
  ideology of, 52
  internecine warfare in, 125
  liberal ideology of, 50
  natural supporters for, 135
  per cent of votes for, 135
  policy formation by, 119
  proportional representation supported by, 135
  single transferable vote system, 120
  strengths of, 134
  weak position of, 76
liberal feminists, 62
liberalism, 50–53
Liberty organisation, 53, 155
life peers, 201
Lincoln, Abraham (US president), 35, 88, 335, 336, 341
Lisbon treaty (2007), 315, 322
Livingstone, Ken (London mayor), 261
lobbyists, professional, 147, 156
local government
  all politics as local, 106, 255
  in England, 258, 260–261
  funding of, 257
  in Northern Ireland, 259
  power of local issues, 106
  reforms, 260
  requirements for candidates, 273
  responsibilities of, 256–257
  in Scotland, 259
  standing for election, 274
  statute law providing structure for, 256
  in Wales, 259
local newspapers, 170
local politicians
  elections for, 84, 86
  low turnout for elections, 8, 102–103
  national politicians versus, 8
Lord Mayor of the City of London, 261
Lords. *See* House of Lords; peers
lower house, 196. *See also* House of Commons
Lumley, Joanna (actress), 149

• *M* •

Maastricht treaty (1992), 322
magistrates courts, 69, 246–247
Magna Carta, 68

Major, John (PM)
  Back to Basics scandal, 227
  business peer groups cultivated by, 146
  difficulties of government of, 124
  election win in 1992 by, 168, 175
  humble background of, 128
  newspaper editors briefed by, 168
majority electoral systems, 88, 89, 90
Make Poverty History campaign, 151
Mandela, Nelson (South African leader), 367–368
manifestoes
  defined, 14
  formation of, 118–119
  government bills fulfilling, 202
  media interest in, 175
Marcos, Imelda (former First Lady of the Philippines), 99
margin of error for polls, 177
marginal seat, 86
Martin, Michael (Speaker), 213
Marx, Karl, 56–57
Marxism, 56–57, 60
May Day 2000, 152
mayors, 258, 260, 261
McDonald, Ramsay (National Government leader), 75
McKinley, William (US president), 335
media. *See also specific media*
  activist coverage by, 34
  blogs, 172–174
  concentration of, 161
  in election campaigns, 174–176
  elections affected by bias of, 114–115
  manipulation by politicians, 162–165
  newspaper industry, 18
  opinion polling by, 176–177
  parliamentary sovereignty limited by, 188
  party head of communications for, 121
  PM favoured over MPs by, 15
  political reporting by, 17
  sound bites for, 162–163
  special advisors for dealing with, 163–165, 229
  24-hour TV, 172
  Twitter, 174
  witch-hunts by, 164
Members of European Parliament (MEPs). *See also* European parliament
  election of, 8, 84, 315
  UK representation, 84

Members of Parliament (MPs). *See also*
    House of Commons
  backbench, 15, 148–149
  declining importance of, 15–16
  election process for, 15–16, 46
  expenses scandal of 2009, 11, 164,
    166, 213, 280, 356
  first-past-the-post system for elections,
    86, 87–88
  front benchers, 230
  hours worked by, 198
  requirements for candidates, 273
  responsibilities and powers of, 197–198,
    279–280
  shadow, 229
  surgeries of, 26, 279
  West Lothian question, 267
Members of the Scottish Parliament (MSPs).
    See also Scottish parliament
  election of, 84, 264
  polls emailed to, 42
  responsibilities and powers of, 280
Middle Britain, winning the votes of, 112–113
mid-market newspapers, 165, 168
military conflict, as election issue, 105
ministers. *See also* cabinet
  advice required for monarch, 192
  appointment of, 281
  cabinet, 232, 281
  cabinet reshuffles, 228
  cabinet responsibilities of, 224
  chain of command, 232–234
  defined, 147
  ministerial team, 233
  ministry responsibilities of, 225
  parliament seating for, 207
  parliamentary private secretary, 233, 281
  parliamentary under-secretary, 233, 281
  path to becoming, 280–281
  pressure groups' influence on, 147–148
  resignation of, 227
  Scottish, 265
  of state, 233, 281
  without portfolio, 220
ministry responsibilities, 231–232
minorities. *See* ethnicity and minorities
Mirror (tabloid), 169
mixed member proportional representation
    system, 94, 264

monarchy
  advice of ministers required for, 192
  arguments for and against, 193
  divine right of kings, 64
  history of, 40
  life peers approved by, 201
  pardons granted by, 248
  powers of, 17, 191–192
  privy councillors to, 192
  royal assent for bills, 209
  royal prerogative, 187
  subjects versus citizens, 43
  support for, 17
  totalitarian leadership by, 61
Monster Raving Loony Party, 137
Mullin, Chris (Labour MP), 280
Mums' Army party, 137

• *N* •

National Assembly for Wales. *See* Welsh
    Assembly
National Executive Committee (NEC), 275
National Government party, 75
national governments, 126–127
National Health Service (NHS), 143, 155, 257
National Institute of Economic and Social
    Research, 158
national interests, politicians' role regarding,
    26–27
national versus local politicians, 8
nationalist parties, 137–138
Natural Law Party, 137
New Labour approach, 55, 58
newspapers
  elections affected by bias of, 114–115
  influence of, 17, 165–166
  left- versus right-wing, 167
  mid-markets, 165, 168
  party support by, 18, 165, 167, 168, 169
  press barons, 165
  qualities, 165, 166–168
  red tops (tabloids), 165, 169
  regional, 170
Nice treaty (2004), 322
Nicholas of Russia, Tsar, 309
9/11 terrorist attack, 32, 368–369
Nixon, Richard (US president),
    337, 339, 360, 364
non-departmental committees, 211, 212

Norman invasion, 67–68
North, Lord (PM), 354
North American Free Trade Agreement
    (NAFTA), 305, 331
North Atlantic Treaty Organisation (NATO),
    19, 299, 307–308, 320, 364
Northcote–Trevelyan reforms, 236
Northern Ireland
    Catholic parties, 139–140
    civil rights movement in, 140
    civil service of, 235
    legal system of, 244, 250
    local government in, 259
    political issues of, 138
    Protestant parties, 139
    religious issues in, 138–139
Northern Ireland Assembly
    central government right to abolish, 262
    coalition governments in, 96
    elections, 84
    formation of, 9
    members' duties, 280
    overview, 140
    peaceful nature of, 268
    responsibilities and powers of, 268–269
Northern Ireland Secretary, 269
north–south electoral divide, 110
nuclear deterrent capabilities, 293

• *O* •

Obama, Barack (US president),
    329, 341, 342, 370
Observer, 167
oil, running out of, 375
on message, 164
one line whip, 123
one nation conservatism, 58
O'Neill, Thomas 'Tip' (US politician), 106, 255
opinion formers, 149
opinion polling, 176–177
Order-order blog, 173
outside pressure groups, 145–146
Owen, David (SDP co-founder), 124

• *P* •

Paine, Thomas (politician), 37
Palace of Westminster, 195, 196–197
parish councils (England), 274

parliament. *See also* bills; European
    parliament
    assemblies versus, 9
    boundary commission review for seats, 95
    committees, 205, 209–212
    dissolved by monarch, 191, 192
    evolution of, 40, 69–71
    excepted powers of, 262
    House of Commons, 12–13, 72, 196, 197–199
    House of Lords, 12–13, 25, 72, 196, 199, 204
    language rules for, 208
    legislative chambers of, 195–196
    recess time for, 205
    reserved powers of, 262, 264
    Scottish, 9, 42, 84, 94, 96, 262–267
    seating traditions for, 207
    sovereignty of, 187–188
    standing for election, 274–275
    summer holiday of, 204
    traditions of, 13
    upper and lower houses of, 196
    women in, 276
Parliament Act of 1911, 13, 25, 72, 199
parliamentary agent, 277
parliamentary ombudsman, 214
parliamentary private secretary, 233, 281
parliamentary privilege, 208
parliamentary under-secretary, 233, 281
parties. *See* political parties
party leadership, 121
Paxman, Jeremy (journalist), 163
Peel, Robert (PM), 351–352
peers. *See also* House of Lords
    crossbenchers, 201
    defined, 13
    as ennobled, 202
    hereditary, 200
    independence from parties, 200–201
    life, 201
    responsibilities and powers of, 199–200
permanent secretaries management group,
    235
permanent under-secretary of state, 238–239
Piper, Bob (Councillor), 173
Pitt, William, the Younger (PM), 353
Plaid Cymru party, 79, 138, 268
Plato (Greek philosopher), 7
PM. *See* prime minister
PMQs (Prime Minister's Questions), 126, 217

political parties. *See also specific parties*
  appeals to Middle Britain, 112–113
  becoming a candidate, 273
  benefits of the party system, 127–128
  blogs, 173
  breakdown of system, 128
  coalition governments, 77, 87, 90–91
  collective responsibility in, 122
  conferences, 125–126
  core vote of, 74, 112
  defined, 117
  discipline in, 121–123
  election broadcasts by, 175
  extremism reduced by, 64
  falling membership in, 10
  formation of, 71
  heartlands of, 109–110
  history of, 71, 74–77
  ideologies of, 50
  independents, 272
  joining, 272–273
  leaders of, 119–121, 198
  leadership elections, 219
  manifestoes, 14, 118–119, 175
  marginalisation of minor parties, 88
  media bias regarding, 114–115
  minor parties, 135–137
  nationalist parties, 137–138
  natural supporters for, 118
  newspapers' support for, 18, 165,
      167, 168, 169
  Northern Irish, 139–140
  parliament seating according to, 207
  parliamentary sovereignty limited by, 188
  peers' independence from, 200–201
  policy formation by, 118–119
  powers of leaders, 14
  proportional representation systems, 90–93
  role of major parties, 118
  similarity of, 47, 76, 102
  single-issue parties, 117
  strategies for winning votes, 111–113
  as strength of British democracy, 45
  traditional allegiance to, 104
  US, 335, 340–343
political trends, 371–376
politicians. *See also* candidates for election;
      standing for election
  economic issues for, 27–29
  environmental issues for, 29–31
  global poverty issues for, 31–32
  international power issues for, 33
  local versus national, 8
  media manipulation by, 162–165
  responsibilities of, 21
  roles of, 24–27
  sound bites by, 162–163
  special media advisors of, 163–165
  terrorism issues for, 32–33
polls, opinion, 176–177
portfolio, minister without, 220
Portland, Duke of (PM), 354
postal voting, 12, 97, 103, 104
posthumous pardon, 248
poverty, 31–32, 159
president (US)
  assassinations of, 335, 336
  election of, 335
  great presidents, 336, 341
  impeaching, 336–337
  importance of, 328–329
  mystique of, 334
  not-so-great presidents, 339
  perks and perils of, 335–336
  powers of, 333–334
press barons, 165
pressure groups. *See also specific groups*
  backbench MPs influenced by, 148–149
  benefits of, 153
  big versus small, 142, 148
  business groups, 154
  cause-related, 142, 143–144
  charities, 154
  coherence needed for, 145
  corruption by, 151–152
  court challenges by, 147
  criticisms of, 152–153
  defined, 141
  direct action by, 150
  election sought by members of, 151
  environmental groups, 155
  European Union issues for, 156–157
  human rights groups, 155
  importance of, 23
  inside versus outside, 145–146
  liberal ideology of, 53
  long-standing, 142
  ministers influenced by, 147–148
  overview, 141–142
  party conferences influenced by, 150

pressure groups *(continued)*
professional groups, 155
professional lobbyists for, 147, 156
public opinion courted by, 149, 150–151
registration of gifts from, 151
sectional, 142–143, 144
tactics used by, 147–151
trade unions, 142, 146, 150, 156
ups and downs of, 146
prime minister (PM). *See also specific PMs*
as first among equals, 218
great PMs, 347–353
importance of, 215
limits on the power of, 218–219
media favouritism over MPs for, 15
minister appointment by, 281
monarch appointment of, 191, 192
not-so-great PMs, 354
origins of, 77–78
as party leader, 216, 218
path to becoming, 217
peers nominated by, 201
powers of, 14–15, 78, 216
Prime Minister's Questions (PMQs),
126, 217
residence of, 216
Prime Minister's Questions (PMQs), 126, 217
primus inter pares (first among equals), 218
principal authorities, 258, 259
private members' bills, 202, 203–205
Privy Council and councillors, 192
professional pressure groups, 155
Profumo affair, 355–356
proportional representation
breakdown between MPs and electors
with, 90
candidate list system, 91–92
coalition governments due to, 90–91
concept of, 90
D'Honte method, 92–93
Lib Dem support for, 135
mixed member system, 264
single transferable vote system, 91
prospective parliamentary candidates, 275
protest vote, 136, 137
public bills, 202–203
public services, as election issues, 105

qualities (newspapers)
defined, 165
left- versus right-wing, 167
overview, 166–167
readership of, 165
shrinking size of, 166
quangos (quasi non-governmental
organisations), 263
quantitative easing programme, 28–29
quasi-federalism, 183

radical feminists, 63
radio programmes (BBC), 170, 171
Reagan, Ronald (US president), 335, 341
recall law, 280
recession
defined, 29
financial crash of 2008, 369–370
quantitative easing programme, 28–29
red top tabloids, 165, 169
referendums, 38, 260
Reformation, 68–69
regional newspapers, 170
regional trading blocs, 304–305, 321
Register of Members' Interests, 151
religion
Church of England formation, 69
Northern Irish issues, 138–139
US religious right, 342
voting not influenced by, 111
remand, being held on, 247
representative democracy, 38
Republic of Ireland, 91
Republican party (US), 335, 340–341, 342–343
republicanism, 192–194
reserve currency, 374
reserved powers, 262, 264
revolutionary socialism, 56
revolutions, 34
Rhodes, Cecil (Victorian imperialist), 286
rights of British citizens. *See also* human
rights
constitution guaranteeing, 182
franchise (right to vote), 40–41, 43, 72–74
habeas corpus, 68, 182
legal precedents for, 182
overview, 43, 245–246
restrictions on civil liberties, 253–254
right-wing newspapers, 167
rigid constitutions, 183, 185–186
Robinson, Nick (blogger), 173
Rodgers, Bill (SDP co-founder), 124
Roe versus Wade (US case), 338

Roosevelt, Franklin D. (US president), 336, 341

rotten boroughs, 73, 96, 353

Rowntree, Joseph (social researcher), 159

royal assent for bills, 209

royal prerogative, 187

Royal Society for the Prevention of Cruelty to Animals (RSPCA), 146, 154

Russian relations with the EU, 317–318

• *S* •

safe seat, 86

Salmond, Alex (first minister of Scotland), 79

sanctions (UN), 296

scandals

  Aitken and Archer perjuries, 359–360

  Kelly affair, 358

  MP expenses (2009), 11, 164, 166, 213, 280, 356

  Profumo affair, 355–356

  selling honours, 358–359

  Thorpe affair, 360

  Watergate, 360

  Westland affair, 357

  Whitewater affair, 361

Scotland

  devolution of, 9, 79

  direct democracy in, 42

  independence movement, 94, 137, 264, 266

  judiciary, 16

  legal system of, 244, 250

  local government in, 259

Scottish National Party (SNP)

  first minister of Scotland from, 79

  independence sought by, 94, 137, 264, 266

  issues supported by, 138

  strength of, 79, 137

Scottish parliament

  additional member voting system, 94, 264

  bills process, 265

  central government right to abolish, 262

  coalition governments in, 96

  devolution max notion, 266

  direct democracy in, 42

  elections, 84, 264

  formation of, 9

  MSPs' responsibilities and powers, 280

  polls emailed to MSPs, 42

  responsibilities and powers of, 263–264

Second World War, 363–364

Secretariat (UN), 299

secretaries of state (cabinet ministers), 232, 281

Secretary of State for Wales, 267

secretary of the cabinet, 220, 235, 239–240, 281

sectarianism, 138

sectional pressure groups, 142–143, 144

Security Council (UN), 19, 293–294, 297–299

select committees, 209, 210–212

Senate (US), 332–333

Serjeant at Arms, 214

shadow cabinet, 229–230

shadow MPs, 229

sheriff principal, 250

silly season, 162

Single European Act of 1986, 156, 316

Single European Market, 316

single transferable vote system, 91, 120

single-issue political parties, 117

Sinn Féin party, 140

SNP. *See* Scottish National Party

Social Democratic and Labour Party (SDLP), 139

Social Democrats Party (SDP), 124

socialism

  communism, 56–57

  competition viewed in, 53–54

  defined, 50

  as Labour Party ideology, 50, 54–55

  Labour Party reform by Blair, 55

  Marxism, 56–57

  origins of, 52

  principles of, 53

  revolutionary, 56

  successes of, 54

  as working class ideology, 50

socialist feminists, 62

sofa government, 229

sound bites, 162–163

South Africa, 367–368

Soviet Union, end of, 365–366

Speaker of the House of Commons, 207, 212–213

Speaker of the House of Lords, 214

special interest groups, 141. *See also* pressure groups

special media advisors, 163–165, 229

spin doctors (special advisors), 163–165

spoiling a ballot paper, 104
Stalin, Joseph, 61
stalking horse, 219
standing committees, 209, 210
standing for election. *See also* candidates for
    election
  becoming a candidate, 273
  campaigning, 114, 174–176, 278
  joining a political party, 272–273
  to local office, 274
  to parliament seat, 274–275, 277–278
  preparing for election day, 277–278
  profile for, 273
  requirements for, 47, 137, 273, 276, 277
  targeting your constituency, 276–277
Standing Order No. 57 bills, 204
Star (tabloid), 169
Starr, Kenneth (US lawyer), 361
statute law. *See also* bills
  contradicting legal precedent, 252
  defined, 16, 197, 244
  local government structure set by, 256
  UK constitution supported by, 186
subjects, citizens versus, 43
suffragettes, 41, 73
summer holiday of parliament, 204
Sun newspaper, 115, 168, 169, 311
supplementary vote system, 90
Supreme Court
  UK, 248, 251
  US, 337–338
surgeries of MPs, 26, 279
swing voters, 113

• T •

tactical voting, 113
taxes
  council tax, 257
  growth regulated by, 28
Taylor, Richard (MP), 151
television programmes (BBC), 171
10 Downing Street, 216
ten-minute bills, 204
territories, 291–292
terrorism
  anti-terror laws, 253, 254
  issues for politicians, 32–33
  US war on, 331

Thatcher, Margaret (PM)
  business peer groups cultivated by, 146
  cabinet culture under, 219
  capitalist ideals promoted by, 55
  election of, 85
  as great PM, 348–349
  humble background of, 128
  as 'Iron Lady', 59
  Queen's dislike of, 192
  reform by, 59
  resignation of, 124
  war and re-election of, 105
Thatcherism, 50, 59
theocracy, 61
think tanks, 157–159
third way, the, 55, 58. *See also* Blairism
Thorpe, Jeremy (party leader), 360
three line whip, 123
The Times, 166, 167
Toraidhe (outlaw), 129
Tories, 71, 75, 129, 130. *See also* Conservative
    Party
totalitarian regimes, 60–61
trade unions
  direct action by, 150
  Labour Party ties to, 146, 156
  as pressure groups, 142, 156
traditions
  authority of, 22
  language rules for parliament, 208
  for parliament seating, 207
  parliamentary, 13
  party allegiance, 104
treasurer of parties, 121
treaties affecting the EU, 315, 321–322
Treaty of Lisbon, 315, 322
trends, political, 371–376
trial by jury, 247
Turkey, relations with the EU, 318–319
Twain, Mark (humorist), 165
24-hour TV, 172
Twitter, 174
two line whip, 123
two-ballot system, 89

• U •

UK Independence Party (UKIP), 136
Ulster Unionist Party (UUP), 139
union movement, 132

Unionists, Conservatives as, 129
unitary authorities, 258, 259
unitary constitutions, 183, 184–185
United Nations Scientific and Cultural
    Organisation (UNESCO), 300
United Nations (UN)
    agencies, 300–301
    Charter, 297
    climate change summits, 302
    Economic and Social Council, 299–300
    formation of, 295
    General Assembly, 297
    headquarters of, 296
    International Court of Justice, 296, 300
    official languages of, 296
    peacekeeping role of, 298–299
    resolutions of, 296, 298
    sanctions by, 296
    Secretariat, 299
    Security Council, 19, 293–294, 297–299
    UK membership in, 19, 293–294
United States of Europe, vision of, 309, 311
United States (US)
    bills process, 339–340
    China's rising power and, 306
    Congress, 332–333
    constitution of, 182, 183, 331, 333–334
    decline of the dollar, 373–374
    keys to dominance of, 328
    as only superpower, 327
    political parties, 340–343
    presidency, 333–337, 339
    president's importance, 328–329
    problems with UK relationship, 330–331
    religious right in, 342
    representative democracy in, 38, 39
    special relationship with UK, 288–289,
        329–331, 342–343
    Supreme Court, 337–338
    vice president, 336
    War of Independence, 332
unwritten constitutions, 183, 184. *See also*
    constitution (UK)
upper house, 196. *See also* House of Lords
UUP (Ulster Unionist Party), 139

• *V* •

vice president (US), 336
volunteering, 273
voting behaviour and trends. *See also* elections
    apathetic turnout, reasons for, 47–48
    core vote, 74, 112

declining local democracy, 102–103
declining voter turnout, 10, 101–102
hours for voting, 103
increasing turnout, 11–12, 48, 103–104
issues swaying voters, 104–111
media bias affecting, 114–115
of Middle Britain, 112–113
party strategies, 111–113
protest vote, 136, 137
registering to vote, 100, 101
spoiling a ballot paper, 104
swing voters, 113
tactical voting, 113
turnout by election type, 8
voter turnout, defined, 8, 100

• *W* •

Wales. *See also* Welsh Assembly
    civil cases in, 248–249
    criminal cases in, 244–245
    devolution of, 9, 79
    judiciary, 16
    legal system, 244
    local government in, 259
    Plaid Cymru party, 79
Walpole, Robert (PM), 78, 349
war
    as election issue, 105
    in Iraq, 224, 330, 339, 358, 369
    Second World War, 363–364
    on terror (US), 331
water shortages, 374–375
Watergate scandal, 360
weapons of mass destruction (WMD),
    298, 358
Weber, Max (sociologist), 22
Wellington, Duke of (PM), 354
Welsh Assembly
    additional member voting system, 94
    assembly measures, 267
    central government right to abolish, 262
    coalition governments in, 96
    elections, 84
    formation of, 9
    members' duties, 280
    responsibilities and powers of, 267–268
Westland affair, 357
Westminster Village, 45, 46
Whigs, 71, 78, 130
whips and whipping
    cabinet posts for whips, 223
    overview, 122, 123–124

whips and whipping *(continued)*
  power of, 15, 210, 279
  voting instructions, 123
  withdrawing the whip, 122, 124
White Papers, 203
Whitewater affair, 361
'will of the international community', 296
William, Duke of Normandy
    (the Conqueror), 67
William of Orange, 70, 71
Williams, Shirley (SDP co-founder), 124
Wilson, Harold (PM), 38, 219
witch-hunts, media, 164
withdrawing the whip, 122, 124
Wittingdon, Dick (London mayor), 261

women in parliament, 276
women-only candidate shortlists, 108, 276
women's suffrage
  elections influenced by, 108–109
  feminist movement for, 62
  history of, 41, 72, 73, 74
  seen as madness, 41, 52
Woodward, Bob (reporter), 360
Worcester woman, 108
work, British rights regarding, 246
World Bank (WB), 300
World Food Programme (WFP), 300
World Health Organisation (WHO), 300
World Trade Organisation (WTO), 305
written constitutions, 182, 183, 184

FOR DUMMIES®

Making Everything Easier!™

UK editions

BUSINESS

978-0-470-74490-1

978-0-470-74381-2

978-0-470-71382-2

FINANCE

978-0-470-99280-7

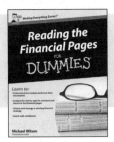

978-0-470-71432-4

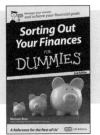

978-0-470-69515-9

HOBBIES

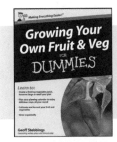

978-0-470-69960-7

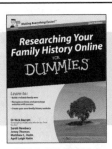

978-0-470-74535-9

978-0-470-68178-7

British Sign Language
For Dummies
978-0-470-69477-0

Business NLP For Dummies
978-0-470-69757-3

Cognitive Behavioural Therapy For
Dummies
978-0-470-01838-5

Competitive Strategy For Dummies
978-0-470-77930-9

Cricket For Dummies
978-0-470-03454-5

CVs For Dummies, 2nd Edition
978-0-470-74491-8

Divorce For Dummies, 2nd Edition
978-0-470-74128-3

eBay.co.uk Business All-in-One
For Dummies
978-0-470-72125-4

Emotional Freedom Technique For
Dummies
978-0-470-75876-2

English Grammar For Dummies
978-0-470-05752-0

Flirting For Dummies
978-0-470-74259-4

Golf For Dummies
978-0-470-01811-8

Green Living For Dummies
978-0-470-06038-4

Hypnotherapy For Dummies
978-0-470-01930-6

IBS For Dummies
978-0-470-51737-6

Lean Six Sigma For Dummies
978-0-470-75626-3

13061 p1

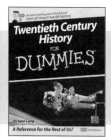
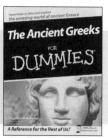

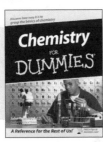

FOR DUMMIES®

Helping you expand your horizons and achieve your potential

COMPUTER BASICS

978-0-470-57829-2

978-0-470-46542-4

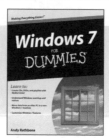

978-0-470-49743-2

DIGITAL PHOTOGRAPHY

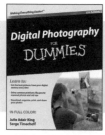

978-0-470-25074-7

978-0-470-46606-3

978-0-470-45772-6

MAC BASICS

978-0-470-27817-8

978-0-470-46661-2

978-0-470-43543-4

Access 2007 For Dummies
978-0-470-04612-8

Adobe Creative Suite 4 Design
Premium All-in-One Desk Reference
For Dummies
978-0-470-33186-6

AutoCAD 2010 For Dummies
978-0-470-43345-4

C++ For Dummies, 6th Edition
978-0-470-31726-6

Computers For Seniors For Dummies ,
2nd Edition
978-0-470-53483-0

Dreamweaver CS4 For Dummies
978-0-470-34502-3

Excel 2007 All-In-One Desk Reference
For Dummies
978-0-470-03738-6

Green IT For Dummies
978-0-470-38688-0

Networking All-in-One Desk Reference
For Dummies, 3rd Edition
978-0-470-17915-4

Office 2007 All-in-One Desk Reference
For Dummies
978-0-471-78279-7

Photoshop CS4 For Dummies
978-0-470-32725-8

Photoshop Elements 7 For Dummies
978-0-470-39700-8

Search Engine Optimization
For Dummies, 3rd Edition
978-0-470-26270-2

The Internet For Dummies,
12th Edition
978-0-470-56095-2

Visual Studio 2008 All-In-One Desk
Reference For Dummies
978-0-470-19108-8

Web Analytics For Dummies
978-0-470-09824-0

Windows Vista For Dummies
978-0-471-75421-3

**Available wherever books are sold. For more information or to order direct go to www.wiley.com
or call +44 (0) 1243 843291**

13061 p4